Wards of Court

To our parents

Wards of Court

By N V Lowe, LL B (Sheff)
of the Inner Temple, Barrister
Lecturer in Law, University of Bristol

and R A H White, LL B (Soton)
Solicitor of the Supreme Court,
Research Associate with the Association of
British Adoption and Fostering Agencies,
formerly Senior Assistant Solicitor to
the London Borough of Camden

London
Butterworths
1979

England Butterworth & Co (Publishers) Ltd
London 88 Kingsway, WC2B 6AB

Australia Butterworths Pty Ltd
Sydney 586 Pacific Highway, Chatswood, NSW 2067
Also at Melbourne, Brisbane, Adelaide and Perth

Canada Butterworth & Co (Canada) Ltd
Toronto 2265 Midland Avenue, Scarborough, M1P 4S1

New Zealand Butterworths of New Zealand Ltd
Wellington 77–85 Customhouse Quay

South Africa Butterworth & Co (South Africa) (Pty) Ltd
Durban 152–154 Gale Street

USA Butterworth (Publishers) Inc
Boston 10 Tower Office Park, Woburn, Mass. 01801

ISBN 0 406 27520 3

Printed by J. W. Arrowsmith Ltd, Winterstoke Road, Bristol BS3 2NT

Foreword

by Sir George Baker, PC, OBE,
President of the Family Division

The origins of wardship are shrouded in the mists of the Middle Ages and in the feudal system. There was a Court of Wards in 1540. There was an ancient process long extinct by writ of ravishment of wards—of the estate not the person. There was a Court of Orphans in the City of London. In 1827 Lord Chancellor Eldon in *Wellesley v The Duke of Beaufort* 2 Russell 1 referred to doubts about the origin of the jurisdiction but he had no doubt that the Court of Chancery ('His Majesty's Court') had acknowledged and enforced the duties of the father 'for centuries past'. It is consequently surprising that *Simpson on Infants*, of which the 3rd Edition was in 1908 and the 4th and last in 1926 was the only book of reference, although recently some standard text books have included a chapter on wardship. But now that the days have gone when the Chancery Judge could have all his wards to tea annually, and Family Division Judges in London alone are *hearing* 800–900 wardship summonses each year, many of which raise highly complex questions of law and fact and cover children and parents of every nationality and creed, a comprehensive book on wardship will be a blessing to everyone, be he or she judge, practitioner, academic lawyer, student, social worker or just interested in children.

It is a happy coincidence that Messrs Lowe and White's book, which I am sure will become a standard work, is being published in 1979, which the General Assembly of the United Nations has decreed as the International Year of the Child. Having watched it take shape from Mr Lowe's initial lecture in Toronto and having urged him to publish, I now commend it enthusiastically, not only for its wealth of information, but as a very readable book coming at the time when those concerned with family law ought to pause to ask where we are going, and to heed the warning bells in Chapter XIII. It has also the inestimable advantage that the authors have seen what actually happens in the courts, and have talked to the Official Solicitor, the Tipstaff and others about their work.

Finally I cannot resist quoting the accolade by a young man who had recently passed his Bar examinations when he read the proofs: 'If only I had seen all this before my papers in Family Law, how much time I would have saved, how much better I should have done and how much more exciting the subject would have been'.

George Baker
11 January 1979

Preface

In 1967 Mr Justice Cross (as he then was) wrote that wardship was a subject of 'general interest upon which there was little or nothing in print'. Although there have been articles since then there has been no comprehensive treatment of wardship. In 1976, therefore, we set out to remedy this omission.

The current popularity of wardship is an indication of the increasing awareness of the wide ranging benefits of the jurisdiction. It has been our aim to provide a work to which the practitioner may readily refer to assist him in attaining these benefits. At the same time we have also tried to place wardship in its context within the legal system relating to the welfare of children. Particular attention has therefore been paid to its relationship with other jurisdictions such as custody, custodianship and adoption and to local authorities' powers.

Recent trends indicate that the jurisdiction is being increasingly used to review decisions already made by other courts or bodies. We are concerned that continued expansion might not only overload the wardship jurisdiction itself but might also undermine the rest of the child welfare system. Although the exercise of the wardship power can be justified on the basis of the paramountcy of the ward's welfare the extent to which such a principle should be applied is questionable. It may be that the current increase in the conflict between wardship and other jurisdictions will be seen as detrimental to the interests of children generally. If so, some limitation of the principle that the welfare of the ward is paramount should be considered.

The book has been written on the basis that the Domestic Proceedings and Magistrates' Courts Act 1978 is in force but that the custodianship provisions in the Children Act 1975, as amended by the 1978 Act, are not in force. At the time of writing the 1978 Act is expected to be implemented late in 1979 and the custodianship provisions early in 1980. In general the law stated is that up to August 1978.

Since the completion of the text two points have arisen which are worthy of mention. First, there is a Legal Aid Bill which will empower the Lord Chancellor to prescribe maximum contributions payable by those receiving legal advice and assistance (including assistance by way of representation) and to prescribe different maxima for different cases or classes of cases. It is to be hoped that the discretion will be exercised in children cases.

Secondly in a case involving the London Borough of Lewisham the House of Lords has been considering the effects of section 1(3) of the Children Act 1948. The decision has now overruled *John v Jones* partly on the lines that we argued in our discussion of local authority powers under the 1948 Act and has obviated many of the difficulties referred to there.

We would like to take this opportunity to thank the many people who have answered our questions and helped us in various ways. We are particularly indebted to the Right Hon Sir George Baker OBE, Mr Norman Turner, the Official Solicitor, Mrs Registrar Butler-Sloss and to Mr R Tolson, the Senior Court Welfare Officer. We would also like to thank Mr Justice Stephen Brown, Mrs Justice Booth, Mr Registrar Turner, Mr Dorling, the Tipstaff, Mr Registrar Parmiter of Bristol, Messrs G Sullivan and J Rogers, Clerks to Bristol Magistrates, Sir John Donne, solicitor, Mrs Christine Betts, barrister with Berkshire County Council and Mr William Evans, solicitor with Avon County Council. We would also wish to record our thanks to our colleagues and in particular to Mrs Margaret Adcock, Assistant Director of the Association of British Adoption and Fostering Agencies and to Messrs Andrew Borkowski, David Clarke and David Feldman, Lecturers in the Faculty of Law, University of Bristol. We would further wish to acknowledge the invaluable typing services we received both in Bristol and London and to Mrs Jenny Dugdale who helped us in the later stages. Finally, but certainly not least we wish to thank Brenda and Alexandra who, during the preparation of the book, had become a "one parent family".

N V Lowe
R A H White
12 March 1979

Contents

Chapter 8
The Official Solicitor

Chapter 9
The Court Welfare Service

Chapter 10
The Role of Wardship and its Interaction with Related Jurisdictions

Chapter 11
Wardship and Local Authorities

Chapter 12
Kidnapping

Table of Statutes

References in this Table to '*Statutes*' are to Halsbury's Statutes of England (Third Edition) showing the volume and page at which the annotated text of the Act will be found.

(I)

... (I)

Table of Cases

In the following Table references are given to the English and Empire Digest where a digest of each case will be found.

PAGE

Chapter 1

Introduction

I The nature and origins of wardship

The law knows no greater form of protection for a child than wardship. Although the jurisdiction is now primarily concerned with the ward's welfare this has by no means always been so. Indeed it is ironic that a jurisdiction which began essentially by exploiting infants should now be preeminent as a jurisdiction for securing their welfare. How this transformation came about is a fascinating story in itself to which we shall now briefly refer.

Its early origins[1] date from feudal times when wardship was an incident of tenure arising when a tenant died leaving an infant heir. On such occasions the lord became guardian of both the infant heir's land and body. Although there was a protective element in the guardianship[2] in that the lord was supposed to look after the land for the ward and was obliged to maintain and educate him according to his station, it was essentially profitable since the lord was entitled to keep the profits of the land until the heir became of age[3]. Even the guardianship of the heir's body could be and was exploited for profit since the lord had the right to control and therefore to sell the heir's marriage.

1. For an account of the early history of wardship see generally Holdsworth: *A History of English Law* Vol. III, 61–6. See also Plucknett: *A Concise History of Common Law* (4th Edn., 1948, Butterworths) 504–5, 514–15. Milsom: *Historical Foundations of the Common Law* (1969 Butterworths) 94, 95. Baker: *An Introduction to English Legal History* (1971 Butterworths) 126–7. For a concise account see Cross: 'Wards of Court' (1967) 83 LQR 200–1.
2. Indeed this element was much more developed in wardship of socage tenants, see e.g. Holdsworth op. cit., Vol. III, 65–6, Milsom op. cit. 94 and Baker op. cit. at p. 126.
3. I.e. in the case of military tenure 21. But in socage tenure the Lord was made to account once the heir reached 14. See Baker op. cit. at p. 126.

The exploitation of wardship for profit was a particular trait of military tenure and no-one benefited more than the Crown whose prerogative rights arose on the death of a tenant-in-chief[4]. Indeed so profitable was the King's right of wardship that in 1540[5] under the presidency of the Master of Wards a special court, known as the Court of Wards, was set up charged with the enforcement of the Crown's rights and the execution of its duties in connection with wardship. The Crown's rights along with the Court of Wards remained until 1660 when they were abolished by the Military Tenures Abolition Act[6].

The wardship jurisdiction did not however die with the demise of the Court of Wards. On the contrary in the hands of the Court of Chancery it began to develop in its more modern form of a protective guardianship. There was of course a guardianship side to the feudal right of wardship even in military tenure, but essentially it remained an undeveloped embryo. Nevertheless it seems[7] that prior to the setting up of the Court of Wards the Lord Chancellor did have jurisdiction over all wardships, even those which were not lucrative to the Crown. Moreover this latter jurisdiction which was essentially guardianship in nature remained vested in him throughout the existence of the special court[8]. After the demise of the Court of Wards the Court of Chancery claimed jurisdiction over children on the basis that the jurisdiction, originally vested in the Lord Chancellor as the Crown's delegatee, now fully reverted to him and through him to the Court of Chancery. Indeed it claimed on the Crown's behalf that as parens patriae it had by virtue of the prerogative the ultimate right of supervision over all infants within its allegiance whether tenants-in-chief or not. Such an explanation can be found in the 1696 decision in *Falkland v Bertie*[9]

---

4. I.e. tenants who held land direct from the Crown. For an account of the structure of tenures, see e.g. Baker op. cit. 1234.
5. 32 Henry VIII c.46; 33 Henry VIII c.22. See Holdsworth Vol. I, 60 and Baker op. cit. 135.
6. 12 Car 11 c.24.
7. See e.g. Holdsworth Vol. VI, 648 and the reference to West C in Ireland East 11 Geo [1725] in the case of *Morgan v Dillon* (1724) 9 Mod Rep 155 in CAP CXVII WARDS 2 Eq Ca Abr 754.
8. See Holdsworth Vol. V, 315 and e.g. *Sweetman v Edge* (1577–1578) Cary 69–97; 21 ER 51 and *Burgh v Wentworth* (1576) Cary 54.
9. (1698) 2 Vern 333 at 342.

where it is said:

> 'In this court there were several things that belonged to the *King* as *Pater Patriae* and fell under the care and direction of this court, as [inter alia] infants ... and afterwards such of them as were of profit and advantage to the King were removed to the *Court of Wards* by the statute; but upon the dissolution of that court, came back again to the Chancery'.

By the nineteenth century it had become accepted[10] that the true origin of wardship lay in the concept that the Sovereign as parens patriae had a duty to protect his subjects, particularly those such as children who were unable to protect themselves and that this duty had been entrusted to the Lord Chancellor and through him to the Court of Chancery. In *Hope v Hope*[11], for example, Lord Cranworth LC described the basis of the jurisdiction in these terms:

> 'The jurisdiction of this Court [i.e. the Court of Chancery] which is entrusted to the holder of the Great Seal as the representative of the Crown, with regard to the custody of Infants rests upon this ground, that it is the interest of the State and the Sovereign that children should be properly brought up and educated; and according to the principle of our law, the Sovereign as parens patriae, is bound to look at the maintenance and education (so far as it has the means of judging) of all his subjects'.

In point of fact, as Holdsworth points out[12]:

> 'it would be difficult to maintain that any such jurisdiction was ever exercised extensively by the Chancery before the Court of Wards was created; nor is there any evidence that a specific grant of it to the Chancery was ever made'.

Nevertheless whatever the accuracy of its view it was upon this basis that wardship was developed. Indeed it was on the basis of the Crown's duty to protect his subjects that it became accepted that the wardship jurisdiction was not dependant upon the existence of property belonging to the

---

10. See e.g. Lord Campbell in *Johnstone v Beattie* (1843) 10 Cl & Fin 42 at 120; cf. Lord Eldon LC in *Wellesley v Duke of Beaufort* (1827) 2 Russ 1 at 20.
11. (1854) 4 De GM & G 328 at 344–5.
12. *A History of English Law* Vol. VI, 648.

infant. As Lord Cottenham LC said in *Re Spence*[13]:

> 'I have no doubt about the jurisdiction. The cases in which this Court [i.e. the Court of Chancery] interferes on behalf of infants are not confined to those in which there is property. Courts of law interfere by *habeas* for the protection of *any body* who is suggested to be improperly detained. This Court interferes for the protection of infants *qua* infants by virtue of the prerogative which belongs to the Crown as parens patriae and the exercise of which is delegated to the Great Seal'.

The existence of this jurisdiction at large to protect infants led Kay J to comment in *Brown v Collins*[14]:

> 'In one sense all British subjects who are infants are Wards of Court, because they are subject to that sort of parental jurisdiction which is entrusted to the court in this country, and which has been administered continually by the judges of the Chancery Division ... But then we use the words in a special sense. Certainly where an infant being a British subject is a party to an action for administration of his property such an infant cannot marry without the leave of the Court. Yet it would be absurd to say that the leave of the Court is requisite for the marriage of every infant who happens to be a British subject, whether the Court has property of that subject to administer or not—and in that sense certainly every British subject who is an infant is not a Ward of Court in the peculiar sense'.

In the twentieth century the general view seems to be taken that the inherent jurisdiction to protect children is not exclusively vested in the wardship jurisdiction but that that jurisdiction was a convenient machinery for administering it[15]. In other words there is still scope for invoking it outside the wardship jurisdiction[16].

Although wardship was no longer considered to depend

13. (1847) 2 Ph 247 at 251. See also *Johnstone v Beattie* (1843) 10 Cl & Fin 42, 145–6; 8 ER 657, 696 per Lord Langdale; *Barnardo v McHugh* [1891] AC 388, 395 per Lord Halsbury, *Re McGrath* (*infants*) [1893] 1 Ch 143 at 147 per Lindley LJ and *R v Gyngall* [1893] 2 QB 232 at 247 per Kay LJ. See also *Re D* (*an infant*) [1943] Ch 305 at 306, per Bennett J.

14. (1883) 24 Ch D 56 at 60–1.

15. See e.g. Lord Denning MR in *Re L* [1968] 1 All ER 20 at 24–5 cf. *S v McC*; *W v W* [1972] AC 24, per Lord MacDermott at 47–50.

16. See e.g. *Re N* (*infants*) [1967] Ch 512, [1967] 1 All ER 161.

upon the existence of property belonging to the infant, the jurisdiction remained essentially property based throughout the nineteenth century, and well into the twentieth. Nevertheless a further important change did develop throughout the last century, namely, regard for the ward's welfare. As the Latey Committee[17] have commented, to understand wardship:

> 'it is essential to realise that its original function was to protect property of a minor whose parents were either dead or unavailable. Inevitably it was originally called in only where the property was substantial, and had to handle only a small number of cases. *With this small number, however, it dealt exhaustively and tried to offer all the protection of a parent'*. [emphasis added]

By the end of the nineteenth century this concern as a parent had reached the stage where decisions were based on what was best for the child. This is apparent from the leading case of *R v Gyngall*[18] particularly that part of Kay LJ's judgment where he comments that wardship:

> 'is essentially a parental jurisdiction and that description of it involves that the main consideration to be acted upon in its exercise is the benefit or welfare of the child. Again, the term 'welfare' in this connection must be read in its largest possible sense, that is to say, as meaning that every circumstance must be taken into consideration, and the Court must do what under the circumstances a wise parent acting for the true interests of the child would or ought to do. It is impossible to give a closer definition of the duty of the Court in the exercise of this jurisdiction'.

Eventually, this concern for the child's welfare at least in respect of his custody, upbringing and the administration of his property found legislative expression in the Guardianship of Infants Act 1925, section 1 and now in section 1 of the Guardianship of Minors Act 1971 so that his welfare in these matters has become the first and paramount consideration.

By the turn of the century wardship had acquired all the

---

17. Report of the Committee on the Age of Majority (1967) Cmnd. 3342 para. 193.
18. [1893] 2 QB 232 at 248. See also Lord Esher MR at 239. See also Lindley LJ's comments in *Re McGrath (infants)* [1893] 1 Ch 143 at 147–50. For a review of the development of the concern for the child's welfare see *J v C* [1970] AC 668, [1969] 1 All ER 788.

characteristics that it now has save that because of the procedural constraints it was still only invoked in practice in
connection with wealthy wards. However, when in 1949
these procedural shackles were removed[19] the way was open
for the current and much broader based use to which we shall
refer shortly.

II Characteristics of the jurisdiction

A fundamental characteristic of wardship is that both the
ward's person and property are subject to the court's control
and that the parents' rights in this respect are superseded. In
effect the court becomes the ward's parent. The courts have
expressed this notion in different ways[20]. In the past it was
said that the court became the ward's guardian[1] but the
modern approach[2] is to say that custody (in the widest sense)[3]
of the ward vests in the court.

The court exercises the supervisory parental function
throughout the wardship from the moment the application is
made until the wardship is terminated. A ring of care is
thrown immediately around the ward *even before any order is
made* so that as soon as the child is warded, as Cross J said[4]:

'No important step in the child's life can be taken
without the court's consent'.

Even after the court has granted care and control[5] to individuals the rights thereby vested remain subject to the court's

19. By s.9 of the Law Reform (Miscellaneous Provisions) Act 1949 see post p.
    45.
20. See the excellent review by Eekelaar: 'What are Parental Rights?' (1973) 89
    LQR 210, 229–31.
 1. See e.g. Lord Esher MR in *R v Gyngall* [1893] 2 QB 232 at 239 '[Wardship]
    was a parental jurisdiction, a judicially administrative jurisdiction, in
    virtue of which the Chancery Court was put to act on behalf of the Crown,
    as being the guardian of all infants, in the place of the parent, and as if it
    were the parent of the child thus superseding the natural guardianship of the
    child.' See also *Re Newton (infants)* [1896] 1 Ch 740 at 745, per Kay LJ
    arguendo cited by Roxburgh J in *Re E (an infant)* [1956] Ch 23 at 26. All
    referred to by Eekelaar op. cit.
 2. See e.g. Ormerod LJ in *Re W (an infant)* [1964] Ch 202 at 210.
 3. I.e. akin to what would be classified as 'legal' custody under the Children
    Act 1975. See s.86.
 4. In *Re S (an infants)* [1967] 1 All ER 202 at 209.
 5. This expression is used to denote the day-to-day upbringing of the ward. In
    this sense it means little more than 'actual' custody as defined under s.87 of
    the Children Act 1975.

directions and supervision. In other words the court never completely divests itself of control over a ward but only delegates certain parts of its duties[6].

The second major aspect of wardship arising from its parental role is that the court is primarily concerned with the welfare of the child. As the House of Lords emphasised in *J v C*[7], no-one can be said to have rights in respect of a child in wardship. Where the issue concerns the legal custody or upbringing of the child or the administration of his property, the statutory principle[8] is that the welfare of the child is the first and paramount consideration. This of course applies equally in all courts where the issue arises. The extent to which this principle applies generally in wardship is uncertain and will be examined in detail later in the book[9]. It is clear, however, that the ward's welfare will normally be the first and paramount consideration from the issue of the application until the child is dewarded. This has led Cross J to describe the jurisdiction in these terms[10]:

> 'Wardship proceedings are not like ordinary civil proceedings. There is no "lis" between the parties. The plaintiffs are not asserting any rights; they are committing their child to the protection of the court and asking the court to make such order as it thinks is for [the ward's] benefit'.

In such cases the disposal of controverted questions is only an incident and not the main issue in the proceedings[11]. It is

---

6. See Ormerod LJ's comments in *Re W (an infant)* [1964] Ch 202 at 210 'in a wardship case the court retains custody of the infant and only makes such orders in relation to that custody as may amount to delegation of certain parts of its duties'. Although in the past the court used to appoint a guardian to act on its behalf it is submitted that this only amounted to a different way of expressing what would now be referred to as granting 'care and control'. It has at all times been central to the concept of wardship that control of the ward vests in the court. For this reason we disagree with the comment by Bevan and Parry: *Children Act 1975* (1978 Butterworths), p. 102 that the wardship practice was a post-war imitation of the 'split order' made by the Divorce Court in custody matters.

7. [1970] AC 668, [1969] 1 All ER 788.

8. Under s.1 of the Guardianship of Minors Act 1971 as amended by the Domestic Proceedings and Magistrates' Court Act 1978.

9. See Chap. 4.

10. *Re B (JA) (an infant)* [1965] Ch 1112 at 1117. See also Cross's extra judicial comment in the same vein in (1967) 83 LQR 200, 207.

11. Cf. Lord Haldane LC in *Scott v Scott* [1913] AC 417 at 437: '[The Court's] jurisdiction is in this respect parental and administrative and the disposal of controverted questions is an incident only in the jurisdiction.'

secondary to the continuing supervision of the welfare of the child, both in the trial of the issue of the proceedings and during the currency of the wardship.

In so far as the hearing itself and preparation for it are concerned, the distinctions should not be exaggerated, since the approach is common to welfare issues in other jurisdictions concerned with children. Even though the parties ask the court to make the order it thinks best for the child, they will inevitably argue in their own favour in making proposals about what is in the interests of the child. Furthermore it should be noted that a child is now frequently made a ward for the purposes of deciding a particular issue, and the parties would expect the child to be dewarded[12] when that issue is settled. They should however be reminded that the pervasive powers of wardship will not lightly be terminated.

Another notable feature of wardship is that it is not a creature of statute. This has enabled it to develop and adapt to changing social conditions and values. At the present time the wardship jurisdiction has managed to combine a high degree of flexibility with relative lack of formality and ease of access to the court. The court is able to exercise wide powers without being hampered by technical problems which frequently arise from statutory provisions. Such a high degree of flexibility has, however, both its virtues and its dangers so that, for example, while the court has the power to ensure that technicalities do not obstruct the welfare of its wards, at the same time lack of certainty thereby produced could prejudice their welfare.

A further feature of wardship worth mentioning at this introductory stage is the frequency with which the child himself is separately represented. Although separate representation has recently been introduced in other jurisdictions it has long been a feature of wardship. Wherever there is a danger that the interests of the child may take second place to the evidence and arguments of the adult adversaries, the court is likely to require separate representation for the ward[13]. For this purpose the child will be made a party to the proceedings and a guardian ad litem appointed to act on his behalf usually in the person of the Official Solicitor. In this way the judge

12. Or at least not be made subject to the court's general control.
13. See Heilbron J in *Re D* (*a minor*) (*wardship: sterilisation*) [1976] Fam 185 at 197.

will be able to hear a balanced argument and obtain adequate information on which to base his decision.

III Modern development

Wardship has become significantly more important in recent years. This is demonstrated by the growth in the number of applications. The statistics[14] show clearly the steady increase since 1951.

No. of originating summons

1951	74
1961	258
1971	622
1974	959
1975	1203
1976	1369
1977	1491

The recent increase in references to the Official Solicitor is also indicative of continued growth.

	New references	Total number of references
1974	106	437
1975	161	521
1976	218	688
1977	203[15]	779

There are numerous factors contributing to this increase, but they have all combined to create conditions in which the scope of the jurisdiction has developed almost beyond recognition from its feudal roots and even since 1949.

The year 1949 was important because the Law Reform (Miscellaneous Provisions) Act was passed which enabled a child to be made a ward solely for the purpose of protecting him[16]. The Legal Aid and Advice Act 1949 which made legal aid available opened the jurisdiction to a wider category of

14. For the statistics prior to 1974 we have relied on Cretney: *Principles of Family Law* (First Edn., 1974 Sweet & Maxwell) 289. The figures for 1974 onwards can be found in the Judicial Statistics for each year.
15. The drop of referrals in 1977 went unexpectedly against the trend but a further increase is expected in 1978.
16. By s.9.

people. Although by 1961 the figures had increased slightly these developments only really cleared the way for more substantial growth later on. Thus further procedural changes in 1971 transferring wardship from the Chancery Division to the Family Division[17] led to the use of district registries and increasing familiarity with wardship in the provinces[18].

Without these procedural changes it is doubtful whether the expansion would ever have begun, but since then four major factors may be seen as contributing to further growth. First, and probably most important, is the change in social attitudes during the 1970's. It has been more widely recognised that the future well-being of society lies in the welfare of our children. The achievement of this requires that children are regarded as separate beings whose welfare is not always best served by having their interests treated, as in the past, as one with their parents. There has been a growing realisation that wardship provides probably the best method by which the child's interests can be given more prominence. It also provides third parties with an opportunity of being heard by the court. Secondly, and related to this, local authorities, who have defined statutory responsibilities for children, have begun to appreciate that the restrictions and difficulties presented by legislative provisions can be avoided by the use of the wide jurisdiction in wardship. Thirdly, the most recent development, but again related to the greater concern for the interests of the child, is that the courts have been far more prepared to act in a supervisory capacity and review the decisions of other courts or local authorities. Fourthly, over a number of years there has been greater mobility in the population, especially in Europe, both as a result of economic developments and improved travel facilities. This has led to an increase in the so-called 'kidnapping' cases, that is, where a child is taken from one jurisdiction to another by one parent without the consent of the other. The wardship jurisdiction is the best for dealing with the inevitable international problems.

It must be added that concurrent with the increase in actual

17. By the Administration of Justice Act 1970, s.1(2) and Sch. 1 with effect from 2 August 1971.
18. See the summary by Ormrod LJ in *Re H (a minor) (wardship: jurisdiction)* [1978] Fam 65 at 67, [1978] 2 All ER 903 at 906 though it is to be noted that it was the Administration of Justice Act 1970 and not the Courts Act 1971 which transferred wardship to the Family Division.

applications, it may be anticipated that in all these areas there is a similar expansion in the number of cases in which advice on wardship is appropriate. Numerous well-publicised cases have occurred recently, and it is inevitable that the public will at times relate them to their own circumstances and wish to know whether they could or should make a child a ward.

The expansion has brought with it problems. When the jurisdiction was small it dealt with each case exhaustively and tried to offer all the protection of a parent. There is now a danger of overloading the system. Although there have always been delays in the High Court, part of the advance in knowledge of child welfare has been the realisation that decisions about children need to be taken as quickly as possible. Unless the system responds to the modern demands wardship will be doing a positive disservice to its wards.

The broadening scope of the jurisdiction has also brought problems in defining the area of its application. Until relatively recently the boundaries were reasonably clear, but now conflicts are developing particularly in connection with the power to review in wardship decisions taken by other courts or bodies. In addition to increasing the numbers of cases, there is the risk that the authority of the bodies whose decisions are reviewed will be undermined. While the opportunity for review is important, it would be beneficial if the circumstances in which this could happen were clarified. At the heart of this problem lies the application of the welfare principle under section 1 of the Guardianship of Minors Act 1971. On a wide application wardship could be expanded further but as will be made clear throughout this book it is our belief that the section should be limited. In any event it is our submission that the ambit of the section should be carefully scrutinised before the wardship jurisdiction is further developed.

Chapter 2

Who Can be Made a Ward of Court

I Application must be made in respect of minors

Wardship applications can only be made in respect of minors, that is, persons under the age of 18[1]. Whether a married minor can be made a ward has yet to be resolved for unlike New Zealand, for example, where statute[2] expressly provides that the child must be unmarried there appears to be no authority directly upon the point in English law. In *Re Elwes*[3], however, the court expressly stated that the wardship order should continue despite the ward's marriage and this would provide some authority for saying that a married minor can be made a ward. Taking a pragmatic view of the matter it is submitted that married minors can be made wards since their need for protection (on which principle the jurisdiction is based) does not diminish merely by reason of the change in status.

No doubt the court would normally be loath to exercise its jurisdiction[4] but there may be occasions when such a power

---

1. Under s.1 of the Family Law Reform Act 1969.
2. Guardianship Act 1968, s.9(1). See Bromley: *Family Law* (First New Zealand Edn., 1974 by P R H Webb) p. 513.
3. (1958) Times, July 30; [1958] CLY 1620, cf. Sachs LJ in *Hewer v Bryant* [1970] 1 QB 357 at 373 B, who stated that the 'bundle of powers' enjoyed by a parent or guardian over a child which includes the power to *apply* to the courts to exercise the powers of the Crown as parens patriae end when the female infant marries. Some support for the view that a married *female* minor cannot be made a ward might also be derived from cases which suggest that a guardianship order comes to an end upon the female's marriage. See *Mendes v Mendes* (1747) 1 Ves Sen 89, 91. However, the distinction is by no means certain—see the discussion in Bevan: *The Law Relating to Children* (1973 Butterworths) 409–410 and in any event guardianship may not be truly analogous to wardship.
4. One could hardly imagine the court would entertain an application to restrain a seventeen year old wife from meeting friends to whom her husband objects.

may be justified and useful. Take, for example, the situation which arose in *Mohamed v Knott*[5] where it was sought to take into care a thirteen year old Nigerian girl who by Nigerian law, and therefore English law[6], was validly married to a twenty six year old man. The case fell to be decided upon the difficult point as to whether the child could be said to be in need of care and protection because she was exposed to moral danger[7]. Had she been made a ward of court instead, a decision as to whether she should have been taken into care could have been made on what was thought to be in her best interests[8] there being no other statutory constraints upon the jurisdiction.

Another area of doubt is whether an unborn child can be made a ward. Until recently there was no authority on the point at all but in *Paton v Trustees of British Pregnancy Advisory Service*[9] a husband sought an injunction to prevent his wife from having an abortion. In the course of dismissing the application, Sir George Baker P commented that in his view 'a foetus cannot in English law have any right of its own at least until it was born and has a separate existence from the mother'. On this basis there would appear to be no jurisdiction to ward an unborn child. The court may, however, agree to make a child a ward of court the moment it is born. In that sense an application may be possible in respect of an unborn child.

II Jurisdiction

Jurisdiction to entertain wardship applications is based on the minor's allegiance. Any minor who can be said to owe allegiance to the sovereign enjoys the corresponding right to protection from the Crown and may be made a ward of court.

Some attempts[10] have been made to argue that jurisdiction

5. [1969] 1 QB 1; [1968] 2 All ER 563.
6. Capacity to marry in this instance being governed by the parties' ante nuptial domicile.
7. Under what is now the Children and Young Persons Act 1969, s.1(2)(c). It is to be noted that if the child is 16 and is or has been married then no care order can be made at all under the 1969 Act—s.1(5)(c).
8. I.e. pursuant to s.1 of the Guardianship of Minors Act 1971.
9. [1978] 2 All ER 987, [1978] 3 WLR 687.
10. See, for example, Dicey and Morris: *Conflicts of Laws* (7th Edn.) 390. Domicile is the basis of jurisdiction in Scotland, see post. p. 27 et seq.

should be based on the child's domicile but this was decisively rejected in favour of the allegiance test by the Court of Appeal in *Re P(GE) (infant)*[11]. As Pearson LJ said[12]:

'It is clear from the authorities that the English court has, by delegation from the Sovereign, jurisdiction to make a wardship order wherever the Sovereign, as parens patriae has a quasi parental relationship towards the infant. The infant owes a duty of allegiance and has a corresponding right to protection and therefore may be made a ward of court.'

It is on this basis that it has been held that any minor who is a British subject can be made a ward whether or not the child is born in or out of allegiance and irrespective of where he is domiciled, resident or physically located at the date of the application. As Sachs J said in *Harben v Harben*[13] the High Court has been held to have an inherent jurisdiction to deal with:

'any child who is a British subject whether by parentage or even (as is exemplified by *Re Willoughby*[14]) by virtue of having a British grandfather. This inherent jurisdiction exists even if the child is born out of allegiance and it exists irrespective of where the child may be physically located at the relevant times. It has been exercised irrespective of the fact that one parent was also resident out of the jurisdiction and that there was no property of the child within the jurisdiction. It has been exercised even where the father was dead and the mother and child were both domiciled in a foreign country.'

Despite these decisions it is to be noted that the court has not yet had to deal with the complications arising as a result of the British Nationality Act 1948 by which the concept of citizenship of the United Kingdom and Colonies and of Commonwealth countries has replaced British nationality (on which the cases referred to above are based) as the primary test of allegiance. In *Re P(GE) (infant)* Russell LJ[15], in particular, adverted to possible problems arising as a result of

11. [1965] Ch 568 at 583, 4 (per Lord Denning MR) at 589 (per Pearson LJ) and at 592, 3 (per Russell LJ).
12. In *Re P(GE) (infant)* ibid., at 587.
13. [1957] 1 All ER 379 at 381.
14. (1885) 30 Ch D 324.
15. [1965] Ch 568 at 592.

the 1948 Act but refrained from discussing them. It may be, therefore, that should the need arise the earlier decisions as to the meaning of a 'British Subject' will have to be reappraised in the light of the 1948 Act. As one leading text book writer has pointed out[16]: 'It seems unlikely that the court would exercise jurisdiction on the basis of nationality over, e.g., an Australian or Canadian minor or a minor resident in a distant colony like Hong Kong, even though they are all British subjects and even though the Hong Kong minor is a citizen of the United Kingdom and Colonies'. It might, for instance, be thought more appropriate to confine the meaning of British subjects for these purposes to those minors born in or whose parents or grandparents were born in the United Kingdom.

A. ALIEN MINORS

i) *Physical presence*

As jurisdiction is based on allegiance British subjects are not the only minors that may be made wards of court. The court has jurisdiction to entertain applications in respect of alien minors who are physically present in the jurisdiction quite irrespective of their nationality or domicile. This is because even aliens owe temporary allegiance whilst present in the jurisdiction[17]. An extreme example is *Re C (an infant)*[18] where the court held that it had jurisdiction to hear an application in respect of a child who was en route from the USA to the USSR but who was physically present in England at the date of the application. Wynn Parry J held not only that the court had jurisdiction but in the circumstances he should exercise it. He rejected the argument that the court should decline to exercise its jurisdiction since the ward was only in transit holding that it would have been a dereliction of the court's duty not to investigate the merits of the case at such a crucial stage

16. Dicey and Morris: *Conflicts of Laws* (9th Edn. 1973) 401.
17. Per Lord Cranworth LC in *Hope v Hope* (1854) 4 De GM & G 328 at 346; 43 ER 534, 54. See also S A de Smith: *Constitutional and Administrative Law* (2nd Edn. 1973 Penguin) 419, and 438. Hood Phillips: *Constitutional and Administrative Law* (6th Edn. Hood Phillips and Jackson 1978 Sweet & Maxwell) 415, 457–60.
18. (1956) Times, December 14. Referred to by the Court of Appeal in *Re P(GE) (an infant)* ibid., at 852. See also *Johnstone v Beattie* (1843) 10 Cl & Fin 42 and *Re D (an infant)* [1943] Ch 305.

of the child's life, that is, whether he should become a USA or a USSR citizen.

Physical presence is usually taken to mean being present at the date that application is made but Russell LJ has commented[19], obiter, that the child's subsequent presence at the time of the order might be sufficient to remedy the defect provided the proceedings have not already been struck out.

ii) *Ordinary residence*

In *Re P(GE)(infant)* it was held that the court had jurisdiction in respect of a stateless alien minor, who though not physically present in the jurisdiction could be said to be 'ordinarily resident' in England. The test of ordinary residence was justified on the basis of justice and convenience in that it would be, in the words of Pearson LJ[20]:

> 'unjust if the wronged parents or parent were prevented from obtaining relief in the English court by the accident of the child being on holiday at a particular date, or by the wrongful act of kidnapping.'

Some authority[1] was found in the law of treason for saying that an alien resident in England could still owe allegiance even though he was outside the jurisdiction but in any event Lord Denning MR characteristically commented[2]:

> 'We are not deterred by the absence of authority in the books. Our forefathers always held that the law was locked in the breasts of the judges ready to be unlocked whenever the need arose.'

To be ordinarily resident the court held that the child must be said to have had his home or base in the jurisdiction at the date of the application. The court acknowledged that this test

---

19. In *Re P(GE)* *(infant)* [1965] Ch 568 at 592. On the same basis presumably lack of jurisdiction can be cured if the minor subsequently becomes a British subject or ordinarily resident in England.
20. *Re P(GE)* *(infant)* ibid., at 588.
 1. Foster's Crown Cases 1792 (3rd Edn.) and *Joyce v Director of Public Prosecutions* [1946] AC 347.
 2. Ibid., at 583. Lord Denning MR also endorsed (at 586) the test of 'ordinary residence' proposed by the Hodson Committee (Conflicts of Jurisdiction Affecting Children (1959) Cmnd. 842) as a pre-eminent jurisdiction and not as an exclusive jurisdiction. For a discussion of the Hodson Committee's proposals and more recent proposals see post p. 31 et seq.

was not without its difficulties[3] especially in the case of a young child whose parents were living apart. Prima facie it was thought a child has his ordinary residence with the parent with whom he is living, but problems arose where one parent unilaterally withdrew the child from the other parent. The facts of *Re P(GE) (infant)* itself illustrate this difficulty. The child lived with his mother but at weekends visited his father. It was during one of these weekend visits that the father, without the mother's knowledge or consent, took the child to Israel. The mother applied to make the child a ward of court within two months of the removal. The Court of Appeal unanimously held that the English court had jurisdiction because the child's ordinary residence was still in England. Pearson and Russell LJJ[4] were content to say that on the facts the father had not yet abandoned his ordinary residence in England and therefore could not be said to have deprived his son of a similar residence. Lord Denning MR thought that the son's ordinary residence remained that of his mother. As he said[5]:

> 'Quite generally, I do not think a child's ordinary residence can be changed by one parent without the consent of the other. It will not be changed until the parent who is left at home, childless, acquiesces in the change, or delays so long in bringing proceedings that he or she must be taken to acquiesce. Six months' delay would, I should have thought, go far to show acquiescence. Even three months might in some circumstances. But not less.'

iii) *Commentary*

Although the decision in *Re P(GE) (infant)* is an extension of the previous authorities it is a logical and justifiable development. There is considerable force in Lord Denning MR's argument that[6]:

> 'The Crown protects every child who has his home here

3. See the dissenting note of Michael Albery QC to the Report by the Hodson Committee who foresaw many such difficulties—see also post p. 31–2.
4. Ibid., at 590 and 595.
5. Ibid., at 586.
6. Ibid., at 584. Lord Denning MR did acknowledge that there may be some difficulties of enforcement in such circumstances.

and will protect him in respect of his home. It will not permit anyone to kidnap the child and spirit it out of the realm. Not even its father or mother can be allowed to do so without the consent of the other. The kidnapper cannot escape the jurisdiction of the court by such a stratagem. If, as in this case, it is the father who flies away with the child, the mother is not bound to follow him to a foreign clime. She can bring her proceedings against him in England.'

Elsewhere[7] the decision has been described as 'unassailable' upon the basis that 'it would be a monstrous thing if a wronged parent or parents could obtain no relief from an English court because their child, ordinarily resident in England, had been spirited out of the realm in circumstances involving some element of force, deception or secrecy.' The decision has since been followed in Ontario[8], New Zealand[9] though not in Scotland[10]. Moreover the notion that jurisdiction should be generally based on 'residence' rather than allegiance has again been proposed by the Law Commission[11].

Despite the widespread acceptance of the decision there is perhaps some doubt as to its application. The complication arises by the fact that in *Re P(GE) (infant)* the parties in question were stateless and it is possible therefore that the strict ratio of the case is that jurisdiction based on ordinary residence only applies if the minor is stateless[12]. It is submitted that the decision is wider than that and extends to any alien minor who can be said to be ordinarily resident in England. It is true that the court referred to the fact that both father and son held travel documents entitling them to return to England, issued pursuant to the Final Act and Convention relating to the Status of Stateless Persons 1954[13] but this plus

---

7. By P R H Webb (1965) 14 ICLQ 663 at 674.
8. *Nielsen v Nielsen* (1970) 16 DLR (3d) 33. *Re Kemp and Dawson* (1974) 46 DLR (3d) 321; *Re Chester* (1975) 62 DLR (3d) 367.
9. *Scheffer v Scheffer* [1967] NZLR 466.
10. *Oludimu v Oludimu* 1967 SLT 105 at 107, Cf. *Kelly v Marks* 1974 SLT 118.
11. Law. Com. Working Paper No. 68 and Scottish Law Com. memorandum No. 23: Custody of Children—Jurisdiction and Enforcement within the United Kingdom (1976). The proposal is that jurisdiction should be based on 'habitual' rather than 'ordinary' residence.
12. See e.g. the statement in *Rayden on Divorce* (13th Edn., 1979, Butterworths) 1108.
13. Cmnd. No. 9509 of 1954 Art. 28.

the fact that the parties had only obtained a temporary tourist visa to visit Israel pointed to their being resident in England so that the decision would appear not to be confined to stateless minors[14].

B. EXCEPTIONS

There are two alleged exceptions to the generally wide jurisdiction to make minors wards of court. The first relates to diplomatic immunity and the second concerns a refusal by immigration officers to allow alien minors to enter the country.

i) *Diplomatic immunity*

It is stated in one leading text book[15] that the court has no jurisdiction in respect of a minor whose parent claims diplomatic immunity. However, this statement needs to be treated with caution, as the authority relied upon, *Re C (an infant)*[16], is cited elsewhere[17] for the more limited proposition that the court cannot exercise its wardship jurisdiction in the case of a child whose parent, *while retaining parental rights*, claims diplomatic immunity. In view of this apparent conflict the decision in *Re C* merits close scrutiny.

An English stepmother initiated wardship proceedings against a Greek father to resolve a dispute as to where the child should complete his education. The father, having entered a conditional appearance, applied to have the wardship proceedings stayed on the grounds that he was entitled to diplomatic immunity. Harman J had no doubt that the father was entitled to succeed since he had been named as respondent and diplomatic immunity entitled him to reject the paternal jurisdiction of the court. However, the learned judge thought it necessary to consider whether the son himself was entitled to immunity since the proceedings could

---

14. See e.g. Bromley: *Family Law* (1976 5th Edn. Butterworths) 398. The Supreme Court Practice 1979 Vol. 1, 1343.
15. *Rayden on Divorce* (13th Edn. 1979) 1108. See also Polak (1977) 7 Fam Law 87, 88.
16. [1959] Ch 363, [1958] 2 All ER 656.
17. E.g. Halsbury: *Laws of England* (3rd Edn. 1977) Cumulative Supp. Vol. 21 para. 478. See also F G R Jordan: *Wards of Court* (1962, 2nd Edn. Oyez Practice Notes No. 21) 7.

have been continued simply by adding the child as a party. It was held that the immunity would extend to the son because as a matter of law[18] immunity extended to the personal family of the ambassador's staff provided he was ordinarily resident with or under his father's control. The question remained whether on the facts the son could be regarded as a member of his father's family for this purpose. It was held that he could even though at the time of the proceedings both the son and his stepmother were living apart from the father, the son attending boarding school and spending his holidays with his stepmother's parents. It was accepted that to a large extent the father had surrendered control to the stepmother but he had not surrendered his control over the boy's education and this was regarded as sufficient reason for saying that the son remained a member of his father's family.

Although it was perhaps arguable at the time whether Harman J was right to hold that immunity extended to members of the personal family[19] the provisions of the Diplomatic Privileges Act 1964[20] now seem clearly to provide for such an extension provided the members of the family form part of the household and are not nationals of or permanently resident in the receiving State.

The Diplomatic Privileges Act 1964 and *Re C* would seem to be authority for the following propositions. (1) Diplomatic immunity includes immunity against wardship proceedings and if proceedings are brought against a parent who is entitled to immunity, those proceedings will be set aside. (2) If, however, proceedings name the child as a defendant[1] they will only be stayed if that child himself is entitled to immunity by reason of being a member of the household of the parent entitled to immunity and is not an English national or a permanent resident in England.

The question remains as to what meaning should be given to the term 'household'. Authority apart it might be thought to imply the notion of 'home'[2]. However, *Re C* would seem

---

18. Following Lord Phillimore in *Engelke v Musmann* [1928] AC 433 at 450.
19. See Lyons (1959) 36 BYBIL 260, cf. Wilson (1965) 14 ICLQ 1265.
20. S.2(1)(a) and Sch. I Article 37(1). The relevant Act before Harman J was the Diplomatic Privileges Act 1708.
 1. To do this an ex parte application pursuant to RSC Ord. 90, r.3(2) (see post p. 39) must be made.
 2. This would seem to be in line with current trend as, for example, in adoption under the Children Act 1975, s.9.

to be authority for attributing a much wider meaning so that a child will be considered to remain in the 'household' of a parent who retains *any* parental rights. If this is correct then it will be difficult to show that a child is not a member of his parent's household. It may be, however, that *Re C* should not be regarded as authority for defining 'household' by reference to the concept of parental control or parental rights. Harman J regarded the issue of whether a child is entitled to immunity as one of fact[3] in which case the decision cannot be taken as authority for anything more than that on the facts the son was regarded as part of his father's household. Certainly the decision can be justified on its own facts[4] since the applicant, being the stepmother, was a person who could not be considered to have any parental rights over the child[5] and in any event the dispute specifically concerned the boy's education which was the very aspect of control not surrendered by the father. It remains to be seen whether the court will adopt a similar approach in other situations or treat *Re C* as turning on its own facts.

Re C specifically concerned wardship proceedings being brought against a parent claiming diplomatic immunity but there remains the question of whether there would have been jurisdiction had the father consented or alternatively whether the father himself could have made the child a ward of court. It would seem that in neither case is there any jurisdiction since a child who is entitled to diplomatic immunity is not likely to be considered as owing allegiance to the Crown[7].

It should be further added that the diplomatic immunity referred to above only extends to diplomatic agents and not, for example, to the administrative and technical staff nor to the service staff of the mission even if they are not English

3. Ibid., at 365. Criticised it is submitted, correctly, on this point by Lyons (1965) 35 BYBIL at 262.
4. Stone at (1959) 22 MLR 193 thought that as a matter of policy the decision was correct.
5. See *Re N (minors) (parental rights)* [1974] Fam 40, [1974] 1 All ER 126.
6. As, for example, where the dispute is between the parents there is the difficulty not present in *Re C* that each parent must be considered to have equal and separately exercisable rights. S.1(1) Guardianship Act 1973.
7. There is no authority directly on this point, though, for example, Hood Phillips: *Constitutional and Administrative Law* (6th Edn. 1978) at 457 states that diplomatic agents do not owe allegiance and it seems likely that this would be true of members of his household.

nationals[8], nor does it extend to consular officials[9].

ii) *Refusal to allow an alien minor to enter the country*

It is debatable whether it is possible to ward an alien minor who has been refused entry to the country by immigration officials[10]. The uncertainty arises from the decisions in *Re Mohamed Arif (an infant)* and *Re Nirbhai Singh (an infant)*[11]. In each of these cases following the refusal by immigration officials[12] to allow the child to enter the country, wardship proceedings were instituted by the alleged father as a means of challenging the decision. Two questions were raised in the proceedings: (1) Did the issue of the summons make the children wards of court? (2) Assuming that it did, ought the court to allow the wardship to continue? In fact the court preferred to approach the matter on the second issue of whether it should exercise its jurisdiction and held that it should not[13]. However, at first instance, Cross J thought it was at least arguable that an alien child who had been refused entry and ordered to return to his country of origin could not be said to owe allegiance to the Crown and hence there was no jurisdiction to make the child a ward of court. In the event he left the point open but nevertheless ordered the summons to be struck out. On appeal the decision to strike out the summons was upheld but again the jurisdiction point was not finally decided. Lord Denning MR did say[14], however, that 'there may be exceptional cases where such a jurisdiction may be desirable' while Russell LJ thought[15] that if the two parents were already in England and were in dispute as to the child's future, then should the removal order subsequently be cancelled a summons issued before that cancellation might be held to have effect at least between the parties.

8. See Diplomatic Privileges Act 1964 Sch. I Article 37(2), (3).
9. Consuls and members of their staff are not within the terms of the Vienna Convention on Diplomatic Relations, and have no immunity in respect of their private acts; see *Engelke v Musmann* [1928] AC 433 at 437/8 and the Consular Relations Act 1968. Discussed e.g. by Morris: *Conflicts of Law* (1971 Stevens & Sons) 55.
10. Cf. *Rayden on Divorce* (13th Edn.) at 1108.
11. [1968] Ch 643. The appeals were heard together.
12. The officials were acting under the Commonwealth Immigrants Act 1962. See now the Immigration Act 1971.
13. For a discussion on this aspect of the decision see post p. 230.
14. Ibid., at 660.
15. Ibid., at 664.

It is therefore still undecided whether a minor in these circumstances can be made a ward though the dicta of Lord Denning MR and Russell LJ would support the view that the jurisdiction does exist.

While it must remain a moot point as to whether an alien minor does owe allegiance in such circumstances it might be thought justified on policy grounds to hold that jurisdiction exists to make such minors wards of court. The policy so far adopted has been to claim jurisdiction on a wide basis and since the child is physically present in the jurisdiction that might be thought sufficient to justify being able to make him a ward[16]. Moreover, there is a further reason for advocating jurisdiction in these circumstances. The question might arise as to whether an alien minor, who has been allowed into the country for only a limited time, can be made a ward. It may well be that the purpose of the application is exactly the same as in *Re Mohamed Arif*, that is to challenge the Home Office's decision[17] but it might be hard to deny jurisdiction particularly where the application is made in respect of a minor who is in England prior to the expiry of permission. The sensible policy would seem to be to accept jurisdiction in all cases but leaving a discretion to the judge as to whether he should exercise it in the particular circumstances.

No doubt in the vast majority of cases the court would decline to exercise the jurisdiction on the grounds that it is not for the court to usurp the function of the Immigration Officers, but in the rare case where it can be shown that there is some impropriety[18] then the exercise of the wardship jurisdiction would seem desirable[19].

16. In *Re P(GE)* (*infant*) Pearson LJ said (at 588) 'An infant of a foreign nationality owes a duty of allegiance to the Sovereign and is entitled to protection and so may be made a ward of court, if he is in some sense in this country.' A minor who is physically present in the jurisdiction even though under an order to return might still be thought to be 'in some sense in this country' within Pearson LJ's definition.
17. In which case the application will almost certainly fail. In *Re Mohamed Arif* Russell LJ (at 662) thought that a deportation order would overrule the normal position that a ward must not leave the jurisdiction without permission of the judge and presumably a wardship order cannot bind the immigration authorities.
18. In *Re Mohamed Arif* no attempt was made to challenge the propriety of the officer's action.
19. An analogy might be drawn in this respect with the principles upon which the court will interfere with a local authority decision concerning a child. Discussed post p. 294 et seq.

C. THE DISCRETION TO EXERCISE THE JURISDICTION

Although the wardship jurisdiction is potentially extremely wide it is important to bear in mind that in each case the court retains a discretion whether to exercise that jurisdiction. This discretion provides an important practical limitation on the width of the jurisdiction. For example, the court will be reluctant to exercise its jurisdiction in respect of a minor who is not present in the country even if he is of British nationality since there will be difficulties of enforcement and a risk of conflict between the English court and the foreign court[20]. Much will depend upon the circumstances of each case but a relevant consideration will always be whether, if made, an order can be enforced, and to this end it will be important if the parent or ward owns property in this country[1]. Another consideration, as we have seen, is whether the child's absence is temporary or is in consequence of the unilateral act of one of the parents. In both cases it will be reasonable to expect that the court will exercise its jurisdiction[2].

The physical presence of the child in England does not guarantee that the court will exercise its jurisdiction. It is unlikely to do so, for instance, where the child's presence is merely transient unless it can be shown that the court's intervention is needed in an emergency or to support a foreign order[3]. Another situation where the court might not exercise its jurisdiction at least in the sense of investigating

---

20. See Pearson LJ in *Re P(GE)* ibid., at 587. See also Goff J in *Re S(M) (an infant)* [1971] Ch 621 at 625; Sachs J in *Harben v Harben* [1957] 1 All ER 379 at 381; Cotton LJ in *Re Willoughby (an infant)* (1885) 30 Ch D 324 at 331; Lord Cranworth LC in *Hope v Hope* (1854) 4 De GM & G 328 at 345. See also *Harris v Harris* (1949) 2 All ER 318 at 322 per Lord Merriman P and *R v Sandbach JJ, ex parte Smith* [1951] 1 KB 62, [1950] 2 All ER 781.

1. See e.g. *Re Willoughby (an infant)* (1885) 30 Ch D 324, 331. It should be stressed that absence of the ability to enforce the order does not mean that there is no jurisdiction to make it. See Lord Cranworth LC in *Hope v Hope* (1954) 4 De GM & G at 346. In *Re Chrysanthou* [1957] CLY 1748 the court acceded to a wife's application to make her child a ward but declined to make an order against the husband who was in Cyprus with the child to return to England with the ward on the grounds that there was no evidence that the order, if made, would be obeyed. Cf. *Re O (infants)* [1962] 2 All ER 10 at 13. See also *T v T* (1976) 6 Fam Law 78.

2. For example see *Re P(GE) (infant)* [1965] Ch 568, [1964] 3 All ER 977; *Harben v Harben* [1957] 1 All ER 379, [1957] 1 WLR 261, and *Re N (infants)* [1967] Ch 512; [1967] 1 All ER 161.

3. See Pearson LJ in *Re P(GE) (infant)* ibid., at 588. Cf. *Re C (an infant)* (1956) Times, December 14. See also *Nugent v Vetzera* (1866) LR 2 Eq 704 at 712.

the merits of the case is in the so-called 'kidnapping' case, that is, where the child has been taken from a foreign jurisdiction where he has had his home and brought to England by the unilateral act of one of the parents either in defiance of a court order or simply without the consent of the other parent. We shall discuss these kidnapping cases in a separate chapter[4] but suffice to say at this stage that though not bound by a foreign order the court may make a summary order for the child's return to the jurisdiction whence he was taken rather than investigating the full merits of the case.

If proceedings are pending in another jurisdiction there is authority to support the view that the court will decline to exercise its jurisdiction if it feels that the forum conveniens lies in that other court[5]. In deciding where the forum conveniens lies the court will take into account such factors as the physical convenience of the parties and witnesses and importantly the system of law to be applied by the other tribunal and the appropriateness of that tribunal to apply that law. If the foreign tribunal would in any event apply English law it is likely that the English court will be treated as the convenient forum[6]. It should be stressed, however, that the forum conveniens is by no means conclusive in deciding which court should hear the case since in all circumstances the court is statutorily enjoined to regard the child's welfare as the first and paramount consideration and that, as recent cases have emphasised, is a principle which applies to the choice of forum. One commentator has sought to argue that:

> 'the general principle of forum non conveniens will operate only where the choice of forum will not be affected by consideration of the child.'[7]

It is submitted, however, that the convenience of the forum should now be regarded as but one of the factors in deciding which tribunal would best serve the child's interests.

---

4. In Chap. 12.
5. See e.g. *Re Kernot (an infant)* [1965] Ch 217, [1964] 3 All ER 339; *Re G (an infant)* [1969] 2 All ER 1135, [1969] 1 WLR 1001 (permission granted to take a ward to Scotland, where divorce proceedings were pending), *Re S(M) (an infant)* [1971] Ch 621, [1971] 1 All ER 459 (wardship proceedings stayed).
6. See Buckley J in *Re Kernot (an infant)* ibid., at 222E.
7. David C Jackson: *The 'Conflicts' Process* (Oceana Publications 1975) 240.

In practice the child's physical presence in the jurisdiction, at least where such presence is not fleeting, weighs very heavily with the court. As Buckley J said in *Re Kernot (an infant)*[8] wardship is a jurisdiction:

> 'which invokes, to a very high degree the discretion and intimate judgment of the court; and it is a jurisdiction which one would think, apart from authority the court ought to be slow to leave to be exercised by any other tribunal.'

III Criticisms and proposals for reform

Before leaving the topic of jurisdiction mention should be made of criticisms levelled at the existing rules and of the proposals for reform. Although the breadth of the wardship jurisdiction is tempered by the discretion not to exercise it in any particular case, many feel that even with the twofold test the jurisdiction remains too wide and too uncertain. This is certainly the view of the English and Scottish Law Commissions. In their working paper on *Custody of Children—Jurisdiction and Enforcement within the United Kingdom*[9], they comment that of the two criteria that require to be satisfied one is a preliminary factual test which is easy to apply but is itself too wide; the second is a discretionary power based on the child's welfare, uncertain in its effects and much more difficult to apply, but with the advantage of flexibility[10].

Undoubtedly one of the Commissions' major objections to the current wardship jurisdiction is that because it is so wide it is an encouragement to kidnappers to forum shop in the English court. They point out that even with the discretion the current rules can produce unfairness between the parties both in the sense of the putting of the 'innocent' party to the trouble and expense of litigation in this country even

---

8. Ibid., at 222F. Indeed it is this reluctance to decline jurisdiction when the child is physically present in England that has led to the most acute form of conflict of jurisdiction with Scotland. See particularly *Babington v Babington* 1955 SC 115, discussed post p. 28.

9. Law Commission Working Paper No. 68, Scottish Law Commission Memorandum No. 23 (1976). See also the earlier report of the Hodson Committee on *Conflicts of Jurisdiction Affecting Children* (1959) (Cmnd. 842).

10. Para. 3.17.

to obtain a summary order for the child's return to his 'home' jurisdiction and by affording the kidnapper the chance of 'getting away with it'. As they comment, despite judicial strictures against kidnapping, by removing the child to England the kidnapper stands a good chance of having his case decided on the merits. We shall consider the development and application of the discretionary test in detail when discussing kidnapping cases generally but it is worth pointing out as the Law Commissions have done[11] that the:

> 'discretionary power to refuse to exercise jurisdiction is necessary solely or primarily because the rules for the assumption of jurisdiction based on nationality, allegiance or mere presence[12] are too wide. If more appropriate rules are selected, such a discretionary power would become both unnecessary and inappropriate.'

A. CONFLICTS OF JURISDICTION WITHIN THE UNITED KINGDOM

Another problem and one which the Law Commission are specifically concerned to resolve and which is consequent in part to what one commentator[13] has described as the 'undiscriminating character' of the English jurisdictional rules is the conflicts of jurisdiction arising within the United Kingdom. The conflict is most acute between the English High Court and the Scottish Court of Session[14]. Indeed conflict between the two is almost inevitable since each apply different jurisdictional rules, both are reluctant to disclaim jurisdiction when once according to its rules it has been entrusted and neither considers itself bound by the other's decision. Since the Scottish court recognises that the court of the child's domicile has pre-eminent jurisdiction[15] the most likely area of conflict with the High Court is where the child is physically present in England but domiciled in Scotland.

11. Para. 3.21(*d*).
12. As far as wardship is concerned jurisdiction is based squarely on the concept of allegiance, and nationality of presence are merely different factors in finding whether the particular child owes allegiance.
13. Dicey and Morris: *Conflicts of Law* (9th Edn.) 403.
14. Conflicts can and do also occur between England and Northern Ireland but they are rarer than those between England and Scotland.
15. See e.g. *Barkworth v Barkworth* 1913 SC 759; *Radoyevitch v Radoyevitch* 1930 SC 619; *Ponder v Ponder* 1932 SC 233 and *Kitson v Kitson* 1945 SC 434.

Perhaps the outstanding example of this conflict is the notorious case of *Babington v Babington*[16]. In that case the wife, a Scottish domiciliary, left the matrimonial home in Scotland and went to live in England. The child in question, a girl of eleven, was at a boarding school in England but prior to the parental separation spent her holidays with her parents in Scotland. The wife applied to have her daughter made a ward from which moment, of course, the child was forbidden to go to Scotland, without the court's consent. Meanwhile the husband, also a Scottish domiciliary, petitioned the Court of Session for custody and applied for interim access to the child in Scotland during the Christmas holidays. Dismissing the wife's application to sist[17] the proceedings on the plea of 'forum non conveniens' the Court of Session held not only that it did have jurisdiction but being the court of domicile it was the pre-eminent jurisdiction and it granted the husband's motion for access. The husband then applied to the English court for leave to take the child out of the jurisdiction for the period of access. The wife opposed the application and herself sought an order for leave to take the child to Switzerland for a holiday. Notwithstanding the Court of Session's order the English court refused the husband's application but granted the wife's. The English order prevailed because it could be enforced and so the husband had to forgo the period of access granted by the Scottish court and had to stand aside while the child was taken to Switzerland. As the Law Commissions commented[18]:

> 'The English court disregarded the order of the Scottish court and the Scottish court disregarded the fact that the child was an English ward of court. The English court's order prevailed merely because it could be enforced, although the child had stronger connections with Scotland where she was domiciled, had her home, and normally spent her holidays.'

Cases like *Babington* are sometimes referred to in Scotland as examples of 'legal kidnapping' by which is meant that orders of the Scottish court concerning children are frus-

---

16. 1955 SC 115. See also para. 39 of the Report on Conflicts of Jurisdiction Affecting Children (1959) Cmnd. 842 and para. 3.12 of the Law Com. Working Paper No. 68 and Scottish Law Com. Memorandum No. 23.
17. I.e. to suspend the proceedings.
18. Ibid., at para. 3.12.

trated by a contrary order of the English court simply by the removal of the child across the border into England. It should be said, however, that it is by no means unknown for an English court order to be frustrated by the Scottish Court of Session. Indeed at one time it was not uncommon for wards to seek to evade an order restraining their marriage by crossing what was sometimes referred to as the 'tartan curtain'[19]. Illustrative of the Scottish Court of Session's lack of co-operation is *Hoy v Hoy*[20]. In that case a mother obtained an order in wardship proceedings restraining her 16 year old daughter, who was domiciled in England but resident in Scotland, from marrying a domiciled Scotsman then resident in Scotland. The mother sought to have this order enforced by the Court of Session but the court refused. It was held that while it looked upon a High Court order with respect it was nevertheless not bound by its decision and in this particular case since neither the child nor the man in question were present in England the English order was 'clearly one which the Court of Chancery had no jurisdiction to pronounce.' This decision, which in many ways is the reverse of *Babington*, is all the more surprising since not only has the Court of Session repeatedly declared that it recognises that the court of the child's domicile has pre-eminent jurisdiction: it has also condemned the High Court's readiness to assume jurisdiction on the basis of physical presence.

Although conflict between the two jurisdictions will continue to arise so long as each rigidly adheres to its own rules two decisions lend support for the view that the High Court at least is prepared on occasion to decline jurisdiction in favour of the Scottish Court of Session. In *Re G (an infant)*[1] after obtaining interim custody of his $3\frac{1}{2}$ year old son in divorce proceedings instituted in Scotland the father, who was domiciled and resident in Scotland, was allowed in subsequent wardship proceedings instituted in England to enforce the Scots order, by being permitted to take the child back to Scotland. It was held by Buckley J that this was the right course because as between two courts of co-ordinate jurisdiction, one in England and the other in Scotland, prima facie the more convenient forum for investigating the merits

19. See e.g. (1958) 108 LJ 17.
20. 1968 SLT 413.
1. [1969] 2 All ER 1135, [1969] 1 WLR 1001.

of the case lay in the court in which the substantive divorce proceedings had been heard and in which the original order giving custody to the father had been made. In the second case, *Re S(M)* (*an infant*)[2] the Scottish court was again held to be the more convenient forum for hearing the case. A father had taken his son to his parents' home in Scotland with the knowledge and consent of the mother on the understanding that he should be returned to the mother in England at the end of the holiday. As the child was not returned, the mother instituted wardship proceedings but subsequently the father, a Scots domiciliary, obtained first an interim custody order from the Court of Session and then instituted divorce proceedings in Scotland. It was held as a preliminary point that although the wardship proceedings were first in point of time the more convenient forum for hearing the case was Scotland since not only was the child already in Scotland but that was also where the divorce proceedings were pending.

It is to be noted that in both these cases, divorce proceedings were pending in Scotland and indeed it has been said[3] that the two decisions suggest that the courts have usually allowed the question of custody to be settled in the divorce proceedings. Certainly support for this view can be derived from the two judgments since both judges drew on the analogy of the then current practice[4] of the Chancery Division to leave the issue of custody to the Divorce Division if the divorce proceedings were already pending. However, it it submitted that it would be unwise to assume that the decisions will necessarily be followed even if divorce proceedings are pending in Scotland. The reason for this caution is twofold. First, in both cases the applicant had been granted interim custody and in *Re S(M)* (*an infant*) the fact that the child was not physically present in England but in Scotland was held to be a material factor while in *Re G* (*an infant*) although the child was present, neither party sought an immediate investigation into the full merits. It may be, therefore, that the cases establish nothing more than on the particular facts it was thought preferable to have the Scottish court investigate the merits. Second, and perhaps more importantly, the Court of Appeal has since repeatedly stated

2. [1971] Ch 621, [1971] 1 All ER 459.
3. By the English and Scottish Law Commissions ibid., at para. 3.13.
4. Discussed in Chap. 10.

that the question of jurisdiction, that is, whether to hear the case on its merits or even summarily to order the child's return to another jurisdiction, must in each and every case be decided upon the interests of the child[5]. In other words the convenience of the forum, on which both Goff J and Buckley J to some extent relied, can only be relevant in so far as it relates to the interests of the child. Where divorce proceedings are pending in Scotland it may well be in the child's interests that the custody issue should be heard there since, as Goff J convincingly said, in *Re S(M) (an infant)*[6]:

> 'I cannot feel that it is for the welfare of the infant that there should be proceedings concerning him in both countries, with the risk of possibly conflicting orders.'

The point should be made, however, that in the light of the Court of Appeal decisions it cannot be *guaranteed* that the English court will defer the custody issue to the Scottish court even if there are divorce proceedings since it will depend upon its views of where the child's interests lie. A fortiori it cannot be assumed that the High Court will decline to investigate the merits where there are no Scottish proceedings pending nor even if the child has been brought to England in defiance of the Scottish court order. In other words, the risk of conflict between the two jurisdictions is just as great as it ever was.

B. THE PROPOSED JURISDICTIONAL RULES

There have been two reports concerned to reform the present jurisdictional rules. The first was that of the Committee under the chairmanship of Lord Justice Hodson (as he then was) which reported in 1959[7]. The Committee's exclusive concern was to reform the jurisdictional rules within the United Kingdom. The main proposal was that there should be a pre-eminent jurisdiction based on the ordinary residence of the child at the date of application. There was,

---

5. *Re L (minors) (wardship: jurisdiction)* [1974] 1 All ER 913, [1974] 1 WLR 250 and *Re C (minors) (wardship: jurisdiction)* [1978] Fam 105, [1978] 2 All ER 230.
6. [1971] Ch at 626.
7. Report of the Committee on Conflicts of Jurisdiction Affecting Children 1959. Cmnd. 842.

however, a strong dissenting note to the Committee's proposals[8] and they were never implemented.

More recently the English and Scottish Law Commissions
have published a joint working paper[9] which again is aimed
exclusively at resolving conflicts of law problems arising
within the United Kingdom. Their proposals are, therefore,
confined to cases where the child is habitually resident in
some part of the United Kingdom[10].

One of the major proposals is that there should be unified
jurisdictional rules throughout the United Kingdom[11]. To
this end, the Commissions make the following proposals:

(1) Where a United Kingdom court has jurisdiction in
proceedings for divorce, nullity or separation, it should have
jurisdiction, as at present, to make custody orders in the
course of those proceedings. Accordingly, save in emergencies, matrimonial proceedings should have primacy over
other proceedings so that while such proceedings are
continuing or within six months of the proceedings, any
other United Kingdom court should decline jurisdiction to
entertain custody or wardship proceedings[12].

(2) In independent custody or wardship proceedings (i.e.
where no other proceedings are involved) the Commission
propose that jurisdiction should be founded as follows[13]:

(a) Generally a United Kingdom court should have
jurisdiction if *the child*[14] is 'habitually resident' in
the country at the date of the commencement of the
proceedings.

(b) Unless it is established that the child is habitually
resident in some other country it should be presumed that his habitual residence is in the country

8. By Michael Albery QC. See also the criticisms of O Kahn-Freund (1960) 23
   MLR 64 and Gareth Jones (1960) 14 ICLQ 15.
9. Custody of Children—Jurisdiction and Enforcement within the United
   Kingdom 1976. Law Com. Working Paper No. 68. Scottish Law Com.
   Memorandum No. 23.
10. Para. 3.2. A second paper will be published to cover 'international' conflicts
    problems.
11. Other proposals include making formal provision for staying
    proceedings, having a scheme of recognition and enforcement of a U.K.
    custody or wardship order and improving the various administrative
    procedures for preventing the removal of children from the jurisdiction.
    For further discussions of some of these proposals see Ch. 12.
12. See paras. 3.25–3.31.
13. Para. 3.78.
14. See para. 3.62.

where he has resided cumulatively for the longest period in the year immediately preceding the commencement of the proceedings.

(c) But where the child's residence has been changed without lawful authority during the year immediately preceding the commencement of the proceedings, no account should be taken of the period of that changed residence in reckoning the periods of the child's residence for the purpose of (b) above.

(d) In cases of emergency[15], jurisdiction should be based on the child's physical presence at the date of the commencement of the proceedings. An emergency order would, however, be liable to be superseded by an order of the court of the child's habitual residence or the court of the matrimonial proceedings.

(e) Views were invited as to whether courts should be able to assume jurisdiction where the parties consent[16].

In choosing 'habitual residence' as the basic test, the Commission had in mind[17] the following objectives which it was thought jurisdictional rules should attempt to attain: (1) the rules should point to a forum with which the child and preferably the other persons concerned have the closest long-term connections; (2) the forum should be convenient for the persons concerned; (3) the jurisdictional rules should be clear and easy to apply; (4) the rules should point to a forum whose jurisdiction will be recognised abroad and (5) be of a kind which a United Kingdom court would itself recognise; (6) the basis of the jurisdiction should not be so wide as to encourage forum shopping or create the likelihood of conflicts of jurisdiction; (7) the jurisdictional rules should not preclude the court of the place where the child is physically present from taking measures to secure the protection of that child in cases of emergency or urgency.

Bearing these criteria in mind the Commissions rejected[18] (a) the present test of jurisdiction in wardship cases, namely, allegiance and (b) nationality because neither necessarily point to a forum which is fair or convenient to the parties or

15. Para. 3.95.
16. See paras. 3.79–3.84.
17. Para. 3.36.
18. Paras. 3.41–3.49.

with which the child has subsisting practical connections nor could either be adopted without creating a risk of conflicts of jurisdiction within the United Kingdom. Domicile was also rejected, inter alia, because it does not necessarily point to the court with which the child has any real connections, since the child's domicile depends on the intentions of his parents. Mere physical presence was rejected as a general test since it would encourage kidnapping, though it was retained as a test in emergencies.

The criteria did, however, point to some type of residence as being the correct test. 'Ordinary' residence which had been proposed by the Hodson Committee was thought to lead to too many difficulties, unless it was further qualified[19]. It was felt that these difficulties would be reduced if the test of 'habitual' residence were adopted. The test in any event has the advantage of already being internationally recognised. According to the Law Commission[20].

> 'Habitual residence denotes a kind of connnection, distinguishable from domicile in that no stress is laid on future intention, and differing from ordinary residence in that greater weight is given to the quality of the residence, its duration and continuity and factors pointing to durable ties between a person and his residence.'

C. COMMENTS ON THE PROPOSALS

There seems little doubt that the proposed jurisdictional rules would largely avoid conflicts arising within the United Kingdom, thus eliminating the unedifying spectacle highlighted by *Babington v Babington*[1] of the English and Scottish courts ignoring each other's jurisdiction and making contradictory orders. Such a clash could, however, be avoided by the simple expedient of making provision for the staying of proceedings in the jurisdiction where another is seized of the matter, and by providing for the recognition and enforcement of custody orders within the United King-

19. Paras. 3.67–3.69. The comments of Michael Albery QC in his dissenting vote were endorsed though it was conceded that some of the problems would be reduced if Lord Denning MR's approach in *Re P(GE) (infant)* [1965] Ch 568, [1964] 3 All ER 977 (see ante p. 16–17) were adopted.
20. At para. 3.70.
1. 1955 SC 115.

dom. On the other hand, it seems right that the opportunity should be taken to harmonise and unify the jurisdictional rules themselves.

The carefully argued case in favour of having a residence-based test for assuming jurisdiction seems right. However, the Commissions are perhaps a little sanguine about the clarity of 'habitual' residence as a test. An earlier Commission[2] conceded that it is not a 'sharp definition' and the concept has yet to be fully tested in the courts[3]. It may be, however, that coupled with the proposed presumption of fact that a child is habitually resident in the jurisdiction in which he has resided cumulatively for the longest period within the year immediately preceding the commencement of proceedings, the basic test would provide a reasonably certain and workable concept. Since, however, the presumption of fact would be rebuttable one may envisage problems arising where, for example, the child is old enough to acquire a residence of his own. For this reason it may be helpful to augment the Commission's proposal by saying that:

> 'A child should be presumed to be habitually resident in the same country as the person or persons who have actual custody of him unless he has shown an intention of acquiring an independent habitual residence of his own and has carried out his intention.'[4]

Further comments on the Commissions' proposals will be deferred until Chapter 12 which deals with 'kidnapping' cases generally.

---

2. Report on Jurisdiction in Matrimonial Causes 1973 Law Com. No. 48 para. 42.
3. *Cruse v Chittum* [1974] 2 All ER 940 is the only English decision on the meaning of 'habitual residence' but the decision merely stated that 'habitual' indicated quality rather than the period of residence.
4. We wish to acknowledge that such an amendment was proposed by Prof. P M Bromley in his submission to the Law Commission.

Chapter 3

Parties to the Proceedings

Although it may be thought that wardship proceedings are unlike other civil proceedings, in that there is no 'lis' between the parties and they are not asserting rights[1], the parties will be concerned to argue their own interests and make their own proposals since they will usually consider that they are acting most in the interests of the child's welfare. Even though the court will have continuous custody of the child while he remains a ward, the judge must still decide matters brought before him on the basis of the evidence produced. One of the advantages of wardship is that in appropriate circumstances many different prople can commence the proceedings or become party to them. This can include the child so that his interests can be independently represented.

I The plaintiff

The person who makes the initial application to the court will be the plaintiff in the proceedings. Where there is a clear dispute between parties, say two parents or parents and a third party, the plaintiff will make the other party the defendant.

It is less clear who may apply to the court. There is no specific provision in the rules of court and on the face of it therefore any person could ward a child for any purpose. This gap was exposed in *Re Dunhill*[2] when a night club owner

---

1. See Cross J in *Re B(JA)* (*an infant*) [1965] Ch 1112 at 1117 and extra judicial comment in (1967) 83 LQR at 202.
2. (1967) 111 Sol Jo 113. The report is brief, but one must assume that the applicant was prepared to risk the penalty he might incur for his contempt in giving publicity to proceedings concerning a ward. See Chap. 7.

applied to make one of his models a ward purely for publicity purposes. The summons was struck out as an abuse of process and the applicant was held liable for costs.

By a *Practice Direction*[3] it is now provided that the applicant must state his relationship to the ward when producing the originating summons to the recording officer. If the recording officer is in any doubt as to the propriety of the application he will immediately refer the matter to the registrar of the day. He may dismiss the summons forthwith if he considers the application to be an abuse of process, or he may refer the matter to a judge. It is possible that the abuse of process could amount to contempt[4].

It is not clear precisely what relationship the applicant must have, and definition must be in terms of what has been permitted since the introduction of the direction. Certainly anyone with a personal interest in the child can apply, so that a blood tie as of parent, grandparent, aunt or uncle or putative father must be considered to give a right of application. Persons with whom the child has had his home appear also to have established a relationship which satisfies the court, and again this can be recognised on the basis of personal interest. This could include foster parents or the spouse of a deceased parent.

Applications are now frequently made by local authorities and may even be made as in *Re D (a minor)*[5] by an individual officer attached to a local authority. The *Practice Direction* cannot therefore be interpreted to mean that the applicant must have a relationship to the ward, and perhaps the best explanation is that it provides a device whereby the court can be satisfied even before the child becomes a ward, that the application is made in the interests of the child[6]. Equally this is not an invariable requirement since those with a personal interest would not have to show that they were acting in the interests of the child.

3. [1967] 1 All ER 828, [1967] 1 WLR 623.
4. See Borrie and Lowe: *The Law of Contempt* (1973) 258 *et seq.*
5. *Re D (a minor) (wardship: sterilisation)* [1976] Fam 185, [1976] 1 All ER 326. The case also established that the Official Solicitor does not have power to institute proceedings.
6. This can be particularly important since the child becomes a ward automatically for 21 days on issue of the originating summons. See Chap. 4 on Procedure.

In summary one may say that the procedure may act as a screen to prevent any gross abuse, but the court is likely to take a lenient view of applications since the question of what is in the interests of the child is the substantive issue to be tried.

There seems to be no reason why a child should not apply to have himself made a ward of court and it is unfortunately the case that many older children could benefit from seeking protection of wardship and directions of the court as to their upbringing. With young children the statutory powers of local authorities are usually sufficient to protect them against uncaring parents but with older children the authorities are often reluctant to try to use their powers.

In the past wardship has often been used by parents to control their erring offspring. The jurisdiction may, however, provide a method whereby children could assert their own rights. This aspect of wardship has yet to be fully explored though some possible uses are discussed in Chapter 10. In the meantime, however, the following points should be noted.

First, under RSC Order 80, rule 2 the application can only be made through a next friend and in the nature of the likely circumstances of such applications this requirement might cause difficulties. Normally the child's parents act as his next friend but this will be inappropriate if the parents are the defendants. In such cases it would seem that the child's only recourse is to find some relative or friend who is prepared to act for him. To what extent the court would be prepared to act if no-one was prepared to represent the child has yet to be decided.

Secondly, one of the main aims of the application would be to obtain an order for maintenance for living separately or for further education. There are technical difficulties caused by the form of section 6 of the Family Law Reform Act 1969 which are discussed in Chapter 5[7].

Thirdly, the child may wish to be in the care of the local authority so that someone is legally responsible for him. The authority will then have a duty to give first consideration to promoting and safeguarding his welfare throughout his childhood[8]. If the authority has been unwilling to help him

7. See p. 97 et seq.
8. S.12(1) of the Children Act 1948.

without coercion it remains to be seen whether the court would view a child's application favourably and whether the authority would respond positively.

II The defendant

If the application concerns a dispute between parties the defendant should be the person against whom an order is sought. The proceedings may be about the child, but he is not normally the defendant. If there is no person other than the child who is a suitable defendant then application may be made for leave to make him the defendant. RSC Order 90, rule 3(2) provides:

'An application may be made ex parte to a registrar for leave to issue either an ex parte originating summons or an originating summons or an originating summons with the minor as defendant thereto; and except where such leave is granted the minor shall not be made a defendant to an originating summons under this rule in the first instance'.

If the minor is old enough to understand the consequences of the proceedings it would seem advisable to apply ex parte for leave to issue an originating summons with him as defendant. Such a situation could arise where the parents are in agreement in opposing a child maintaining an undesirable situation. The proper course is to apply ex parte for leave to make the child a defendant. The person considered to be undesirable should not be made a defendant[9]. This has considerable advantages since there will then be no need to serve him with all the evidence filed in the proceedings, and he has no access to the papers. He will only be served with a copy of the court order.

If a local authority has statutory powers in respect of the child they should be made a party to the proceedings, and it may be wise to join them if the child has very recently been removed from care. In such cases the proper defendant is the authority as a body and not an individual officer[10]. It is questionable whether the voluntary nature of these provisions operates in the best interests of the ward. Although

9. See *Practice Note* [1962] 1 All ER 156, [1962] 1 WLR 61.
10. *Re L (an infant) Practice Note* [1963] 1 All ER 176.

the evidence would often disclose the true position, and could scarcely fail to do so in the case of an application by foster parents, it should surely be a requirement to join the authority as a party if the child is in care, and to disclose any periods in care say within the six months prior to the application. The court could then decide whether it wishes to seek information from the authority. Alternatively or additionally if a party was required to give notice to the authority where a child was or has recently been in care, the authority could take the initiative if they felt they were in possession of information which it would be in the child's interest for the court to know.

It is obviously advisable for the plaintiff to make defendants to the proceedings all persons against whom he seeks an order[10a]. The plaintiff should also consider joining other people who have a close interest, since it will inevitably cause unwelcome delay if they have to be joined at a late stage. The danger of an order of costs means that such a step will not be taken lightly, but it is better to have thought about this when proceedings are instituted. Where, for example, proceedings are taken against a parent by a stranger careful consideration must be given to the question whether a separated spouse, cohabitee, mother or putative father should be joined[11].

There is no procedure for interveners as such but any person who does wish to become a party to the proceedings can make an ex parte application to the registrar for leave to be joined. An affidavit should be filed in support setting out why he wishes to be joined. If he thinks fit the registrar may then order that the applicant be joined as a further defendant.

It is important to remember that at any stage of the proceedings where it is thought that the interests of the ward should be independently represented, the summons may be amended and the ward joined as a defendant. A guardian ad litem will of course be required, and unless another suitable person is available, the Official Solicitor should be contacted as subject to his consent he may be appointed to fulfil this role[12].

10a. Except where it is desirable not to serve a person with the papers.
11. In such a case the problems of delay by having to serve an absentee defendant must also be considered.
12. For the role of the Official Solicitor see Chap. 8.

III The Crown

It has not yet been decided whether a Minister of the Crown can be made a party in wardship proceedings. The issue did arise in *Re Mohamed Arif (an infant)*[13], where following the refusal by immigration officers to allow a child to enter the country the alleged father issued an originating summons naming the Secretary of State for Home Affairs as defendant. As a matter of convenience the Crown entered an unconditional appearance, but reserved the point that a Minister of the Crown should not be made a party to wardship proceedings. Counsel for the Crown pointed out that the Crown cannot be impleaded in its own courts unless an express statutory provision permits it, and that there is nothing in the Crown Proceedings Act 1947 to cover wardship proceedings[14]. Counsel suggested that if there is any interest of the Crown which may be affected, the correct procedure is for the Attorney-General to be invited by the court to represent the Crown. This argument would appear to be well-founded, but in view of the lack of authority, it may be wise to seek directions as to how to deal with the Crown's interest.

IV The court's role in initiating proceedings

Normally it is left to the individual parties to institute wardship proceedings. It is however possible for the court, at least on occasion, to take the initiative. Under section 42 of the Matrimonial Causes Act 1973 the court can in proceedings under that Act 'direct that proper proceedings be taken for making the child a ward of court'. It would seem that the Court of Protection could similarly direct that wardship proceedings be brought when acting under its general powers conferred by section 103(1)(*h*) of the Mental Health Act 1959.

The power under section 42 is not often exercised but could be useful where the court wishes to retain some control over the child. It may also be advantageous in cases such as where the child's whereabouts are being concealed or where a mandatory order requiring a party to deliver physical

13. [1968] Ch 643.
14. Ibid., at 652. The point was not mentioned in any of the judgments.

custody of the child to another is necessary, since the court will have wider powers under wardship[15]. If the court does exercise its power it will normally direct the Official Solicitor to bring proceedings.

To what extent the court can act outside its statutory powers is uncertain. In *Re C(MA) (an infant)*[16], however, a High Court judge apparently directed wardship proceedings to be brought at the conclusion of an adoption hearing so as to preserve the status quo pending the appeal. More recently in *Re H (a minor)*[17] Ormrod LJ commented that a judge of the Family Division hearing an appeal against a juvenile court order under the Children Act 1948 'could assume the powers of the wardship procedure by simply giving one party leave to issue a formal summons under the Law Reform (Miscellaneous Provisions) Act 1949'. It will be noted that Ormrod LJ did not go so far as to say that the court could *direct* a party to bring wardship proceedings though of course it will usually be in the interests of the party to accept the court's invitation.

Whether the court is empowered to act upon its own motion where there are no other proceedings has yet to be decided though such a power would be useful as, for example, where a child wishes to institute proceedings but has no-one to act on his behalf. Some support for such a power might be derived from *Re N (infants)*[18] where Stamp J held that he had power inter alia under the inherent jurisdiction of the High Court to grant an injunction restraining the removal of children from one jurisdiction to another even though no other proceedings had been instituted. He granted the injunction on terms that an originating summons would be issued at the earliest opportunity. The decision therefore provides authority for saying that the court can, when acting under its inherent jurisdiction, direct that wardship proceedings be brought. However, the initiative for invoking

---

15. In the former case the court can summarily order any person who might know of the ward's whereabouts to attend the court and give evidence. See Chaps. 5 and 7. In the latter case the court can direct the Tipstaff to obtain custody of the child and deliver him to the person named in the order. See Chap. 5.

16. [1966] 1 All ER 838. See the reference at 849 by Willmer LJ.

17. *Re H (a minor) (wardship: jurisdiction)* [1978] Fam 65 at 76, [1978] 2 All ER 903 at 909–10.

18. [1967] Ch 512, [1967] 1 All ER 161.

the inherent jurisdiction had already been taken by the applicant. *Re N* cannot therefore be relied upon as authority for saying that the High Court has an inherent jurisdiction to act upon its own motion. Whether the court would be prepared to go that far remains to be seen. It might, however, be thought that unless some proceedings are before the court, the judge himself has no locus standi to act.

Chapter 4

Procedure

I Introduction

Wardship is a matter which can only be dealt with in the High Court and by the Administration of Justice Act 1970[1], all such business is assigned to the Family Division. It was formerly dealt with by the Chancery Division[2].

Before 1949 there was no uniform or direct procedure for making a child a ward of court, instead wardship automatically arose in a number of ways[3]. For example, the child became a ward if an action was commenced in his name whether with respect to his person, or his property, or where an order was made on a petition for the appointment of a guardian[4], or possibly where an order was made for maintenance on a petition or summons without suit, or if funds belonging to him were paid into court under the Trustee Act 1925.[5]

This had obvious disadvantages. No child even if in need of protection, could be made a ward by a simple application to that effect. Instead, resort had to be made to the clumsy device of making a nominal settlement on the child and then commencing an action to administer the trusts of the settle-

1. S.1(2) and Sch. 1.
2. Under the Supreme Court of Judicature (Consolidation) Act 1925, s.56(1)(*b*). For the possible continued role of the Chancery Division see Bromley, *Family Law* (5th Edn. 1976), p. 390. It is also possible that the Chancery Division will retain jurisdiction over a child made a ward before the transference of the jurisdiction to the Family Division.
3. For a general account of the pre-1949 position see e.g. Simpson: *The Law of Infants* (94th Edn.) 1925) and *A Century of Family Law*, edited by R H Graveson and F R Crane 91957 Sweet and Maxwell), 82, 83 by P H Pettit.
4. *Stuart v Marquis of Bute* (1861) 9 HL Cas 440; *Re McCullock* (1844) 6 Ir Eq R393.
5. *Re D (an infant)* [1943] Ch 305, [1943] 2 All ER 411.

ment[6]. On the other hand the same device meant that a child could become a ward quite unintentionally when not only was there no need for the exercise of the court's special jurisdiction but also where that very protection was undesirable. As Stamp J observed in *Re N* (*infants*)[7]:

> 'Awkward questions sometimes arose whether a child was or was not a ward. He might have become so almost by accident, as when proceedings were taken for the administration of property in which he was interested, such proceedings not being designed in the least to make an infant a ward of court. This was very awkward because the effect of the infant becoming a ward of court was that he or she could not be taken out of the jurisdiction without leave of the court and could not marry without leave of the court, and I have no doubt whatsoever that many infants were married and taken out of the jurisdiction of the court without their parents being aware that a contempt of court was being committed'.

II The current position

Section 9(1) of the Law Reform (Miscellaneous Provisions) Act 1949 now states:

> 'Subject to the provisions of this section, no infant shall be made a ward of court except by virtue of an order to that effect made by the court'.

> 'Where application is made for such an order in respect of an infant, the infant shall become a ward of court on the making of the application, but shall cease to be a ward of court at the expiration of such period, as may be prescribed by rules of court, unless within that period an order has been made in accordance with the application'.

The prescribed period is 21 days, or until the determination of the application made by the summons, if an application for an appointment for the hearing of the summons is made within 21 days[8]. The scheme is therefore, that no child can become a ward unless the court makes an order to that effect, save that the child becomes a ward immediately on

6. See *Re D* ibid., at 306 and *Re X's Settlement* [1945] Ch 44 at 45.
7. [1967] Ch 512 at 529, 530.
8. RSC Ord. 90, r. 4(1).

application for a limited period. Hence a minor cannot be made a ward of court unintentionally.

The provisions of the 1949 Act are augmented by RSC Order 90 but as the title of the Order, namely 'Miscellaneous Provisions in the Family Division', suggests the provisions are not exclusively concerned with wardship nor indeed are they comprehensive. It might be suggested that the position could be made more clear if there were separate and more comprehensive rules relating exclusively to wardship.

A. THE APPLICATION

Application is by originating summons[9] in the High Court in accordance with RSC Order 90, rule 3 and must issue out of the principal registry or a district registry as defined by the Matrimonial Causes Rules 1977. If issued out of the district registry the registrar must send particulars of the summons to the principal registry for recording in the Register of Wards[10]. This means that there may be a choice of venues. In many cases convenience of the parties and witnesses will dictate the venue, though occasionally choice of counsel might determine where the case is heard. It is also possible that the registrar will transfer proceedings to another venue, to enable, for example, the case to be heard more quickly.

Such applications under the 1949 Act are commonly coupled with an application under the Guardianship Acts 1971 and 1973.[12] The latter application may be useful if the court wishes to discharge an order or dismiss the wardship appli-

9. See Appendix for full form. Application should be made in the matter of the Law Reform (Miscellaneous Provisions) Act 1949. If there is an application for custody, see post p. 217, it should also be made, in the matter of the Guardianship Acts 1971 and 1973—see RSC Ord. 90, r. 5. When the custodianship provisions are brought into force (under the Children Act 1975 Part II) it may in certain circumstances be appropriate to couple the wardship application with an application for custodianship (see post p. 244) and presumably applications should be made 'in the matter of Part II of the Children Act 1975'.

10. Ord. 90, r. 3(3).

11. Though it is to be pointed out that a Deputy High Court Judge appointed for the day, would have power to hear the case. It is not unknown for registrars to transfer the case to London in cases of difficulty but this should rarely be necessary since the powers of both registrar and judge are the same wherever the venue is.

12. Ord. 90, r. 5.

cation and grant custody or possibly guardianship of the child[13]. Joint applications of this sort have become almost indiscriminate, but it is to be noted that they may not always be appropriate. Local authorities cannot apply under the Guardianship Acts, whether for custody or guardianship[14]. It is not open to third parties to apply for custody and for an application for guardianship by them, at least one of the parents must be dead[15]. In the latter case, however, when the provisions relating to custodianship contained in Part II of the Children Act 1975 come into force, it may be appropriate to couple the wardship application with an application for custodianship.

B. CONTENT OF SUMMONS

RSC Order 90 should be read with Order 7, with regard to the content of the original summons. The form issued for the purposes comprises the following:

(1) The names of the minor or minors
(2) The parties
(3) Statement of claim
(4) Date of birth of the minor
(5) Present whereabouts of the minor

i) *The minor*

Any person under the age of 18 may be made a ward of court[16]. The full names of the minor should be recited where possible. If the ward is an unnamed baby, it may be referred to as 'Baby . . . ', and if a parent changes his mind about the name to be given to the baby before the birth is registered, but after proceedings have been issued in a specific name, leave may be sought for the name to be changed in the proceedings.

---

13. Without such application it would appear that there would be no power to discharge wardship and grant instead custody or guardianship. See post p. 86–87.
14. Applications under the 1971 and 1973 Acts can only be made by the child's biological parents.
15. See the Guardianship of Minors Act 1971 ss. 3 and 5 discussed in Chapter 10.
16. See Chapter 2.

ii) *The parties*

Parties to the originating summons have been discussed in Chapter 3.

iii) *Statement of claim*

RSC Order 90 does not specify what the statement of claim should comprise, but by Order 7, rule 3(1) (which applies to originating summons generally) it should:

> 'include a statement of the questions on which the plaintiff seeks the determination or direction of the High Court or as the case may be a concise statement of the relief or remedy claimed in the proceedings begun by the originating summons with sufficient particulars to identify the course or courses of action in respect of which the plaintiff claims that relief or remedy'.

Under this rule therefore the statement of claim should contain the specific order or orders sought by the plaintiff. In all cases this will be that the child should be made a ward of the court. In most cases[17] the plaintiff will be seeking care and control of the child and this too should be specified. In the case of a 'kidnapped' child where the claim may be for a peremptory order, the plaintiff should specify in the statement that the child should be returned forthwith to him with leave to take the child out of the jurisdiction. If the object of the application is to obtain an injunction, then this too should be specified in the statement but it would seem prudent to specify injunctions sought even if they are ancillary to the main purpose of the application.

iv) *Date of birth*

The originating summons must state the date of birth of the minor unless otherwise directed.[18]

The plaintiffs shall

(a) on issuing the summons or before or at the first hearing thereof lodge in the registry out of which the summons is

---

17. But not in all: see e.g. *Re D (a minor) (wardship; sterilisation)* [1976] Fam 185, [1976] 1 All ER 326, where the application sought only to prevent the ward from being sterilised.
18. Ord. 90, r.3(3A) and *Practice Direction* [1972] 1 All ER 797.

issued a certified copy of the entry in the Registry of Births or as the case may be in the Adopted Children Register relating to the minor, or

(b) at the first hearing of the summons apply for directions as to proof of birth of the minor in some other manner.

Clearly it will normally be most convenient to lodge the birth certificate in the registry when the originating summons is issued. If this is not possible, for example, because the birth of the baby has not been registered, evidence as to the date of birth can be filed on affidavit by a person having that knowledge[19].

v) *Whereabouts*

Unless the court otherwise directs the originating summons shall state the whereabouts of the minor or as the case may be that the plaintiff is unaware of his whereabouts[20]. After being served with the summons every defendant other than the minor shall forthwith[1],

(a) lodge in the registry a notice stating the address of the defendant and the whereabouts of the minor or as the case may be, that the defendant is unaware of his whereabouts, and

(b) unless the court otherwise directs serve a copy of the notice on the plaintiff.

Further where any party other than the minor changes his address or becomes aware of any change in the whereabouts of the minor, after the issue or, as the case may be, service of the summons, he shall unless the court otherwise directs, forthwith lodge notice of the change in the registry and serve a copy of the notice to defendants in the summons[2]. These requirements must be set out in a notice to every other party[3].

These requirements are of course, of particular importance in the case of a missing ward, but local authorities must also

---

19. Proof of Birth can in some cases be difficult and may delay proceedings e.g. when the child is born in a country which has no system of registering births.
20. Ord. 90, r.3(4).
 1. Ord. 90, r.3(5).
 2. Ord. 90, r.3(6).
 3. Ord. 90, r.3(7).

be aware of their effect. If the whereabouts of a child in care is being withheld from the parent he can quickly ascertain this information by making the child a ward, unless the authority applies to the registrar for a direction that a copy of the notice filed shall not be served on the plaintiff. The rules are designed to ensure that the court is properly informed about the minor, and concealing the whereabouts of a ward, is a grave contempt[4]. The court may order any person who is in a position to give information as to the child's whereabouts, to attend before a judge. Even a solicitor is obliged to divulge to the court, any information which may lead to the discovery of a ward's whereabouts[5]. It would appear that no privilege may be claimed when the court requires this information.

The originating summons shall now also contain the following endorsement[6]:

> 'IMPORTANT NOTICE. It is a contempt of court which may be punishable by imprisonment, to take any child named in the summons out of England and Wales, even to Scotland, Northern Ireland, the Republic of Ireland, the Channel Islands or the Isle of Man, without the leave of the court.'

C. ISSUING PROCEEDINGS

When completed the originating summons should be taken first to the cashiers' office for the fee to be paid[7] and noted and then with a duplicate to the Wardship and Adoption office for recording in the register of wards. If the matter is proceeding in the principal registry this will be at Somerset House. When issued in the district registry the registrar will send particulars of the summons to the principal registry for recording in the register of wards.

One copy of the summons duly stamped will be returned together with a notice of wardship[8] and a file number slip[8] stating that the summons has been lodged and recording the number of the matter. The notice instructs the applicant to serve a copy of the notice on the defendant (or, where the

4. *Mustafa v Mustafa* (1967) Times, September 11 and 13.
5. *Hockly v Lukin* (1762) 1 Dick 353; 21 ER 305; *Rosenberg v Lindo* (1883) 48 LT 478 and *Ramsbotham v Senior* (1869) LR 8 Eq 575.
6. Pursuant to a *Practice Direction* [1977] 3 All ER 122 [1977] 1 WLR 1067.
7. £20 at the time of going to press.
8. For a copy of the forms see Appendix.

defendant is a minor, on the person on whom the originating summons is served) with the originating summons, the original being produced at the time of service. A copy may also be served on any other person[9] who should be made aware that the minor is a ward of court. A copy should be served on the minor if he is of such age and situation that he may be in need of advice and assistance. The notice specifies that the minor became a ward of court on a particular day and states:

'The ward may not marry or go outside England and Wales without the leave of the court, but is under no further restraint until the court's directions are given'.

It advises the ward that he may consult the Official Solicitor pending the appointment of a formal guardian if he is in doubt what to do.

The plaintiff will also have to file a certificate as to other pleadings, certifying whether there are in existence matrimonial proceedings in which the minor is a child of a family, and if so, describing them, and whether there are any other proceedings in which the minor is involved, if so, describing them[10].

D. AFTER ISSUE OF THE ORIGINATING SUMMONS

The effect of the issue of the originating summons is that the minor immediately becomes a ward of court[11]. The summons may not be served later than 12 months after the date of issue, unless renewed by order of the court and it will require the defendant to enter an appearance within 14 days of the date of service. The summons should be served on all defendants in accordance with normal High Court procedure, but if this does not prove possible, it should not be allowed to cause undue delay in proceeding with the application.

If the matter is not one in which there is an emergency, the next step is to take out an appointment. The application for this appointment must be made within 21 days of the issue of the summons, since failure to apply will cause the wardship to lapse[12]. It is not necessary that the hearing should take place

9. E.g. a relative or even a headmaster of the school at which the child attends.
10. See Appendix for the Certificate as to other pleadings.
11. S.9(2) of the Law Reform (Miscellaneous Provisions) Act 1949.
12. RSC Ord. 90, r.4(1)(*a*).

within 21 days, but only that the appointment should be made within that time.

The High Court Rules are not precise about what to do after the issue of the summons, but this has the advantage of providing considerable flexibility. RSC Order 28, rule 2(1) would seem to apply and that states that the plaintiff may obtain an appointment for the attendance of the parties before the court for the hearing of the summons, where an appearance has been entered or has not been entered within the time limit. A day and time for attendance shall be fixed by notice sealed with the seal of the principal registry of the Family Division or the appropriate district registry. Since the time limit for filing an appearance is 14 days after service of the originating summons, it can be seen that this direction should not be interpreted too strictly, since any delay in service of the summons might mean that an appointment could not be fixed before the wardship lapsed. At this stage the most important concern is to take out the appointment. Any difficulties as to service of the originating summons or the notice of appointment can be sorted out, if necessary, at the hearing of the appointment. If the defendant is known to have solicitors, it is wise if possible, to fix the appointment in consultation with them. If not and he cannot immediately be traced, it may still be helpful to proceed with the appointment and get some directions.

III The registrar

The first appointment will normally be a hearing before the registrar. He is a most important person in wardship. It is a significant feature that in London once a case has been assigned to a registrar it remains on his file until the wardship order ends, so that he is a constant figure throughout. He is generally reluctant to make orders in a case which is assigned to another registrar. He exercises considerable influence on the course of the proceedings because of his continuing knowledge of and responsibility for the case. Parties may readily consult him on any matters arising in the wardship. Moreover, this ready accessibility is achieved without undue formality. Outside London the situation is not necessarily the same. In view of the numbers it may not always be possible for the same registrar to hear the case. Since the accessibility of a judicial figure familiar with the case, is one of the advantages of the jurisdiction it is submitted that every effort should be made to provide the same continuity in the provinces.

As a matter of practice when a case is assigned to him in which the ward is also involved in divorce proceedings[13], the registrar will inform the divorce registry of the wardship proceedings, and the divorce proceedings will then be transferred to the High Court[14].

The first appointment will be heard by the registrar unless there has been an emergency application to the judge on which directions have been given. At that appointment he can give directions for the filing of evidence, the addition of other parties, the appointment of the Official Solicitor or a court welfare officer, and, he may adjourn the application to another hearing before himself for further directions especially if substantial matters remain outstanding. To speed up the case he has the power to limit affidavit evidence and to direct that oral evidence should be adduced instead[15]. He may also adjourn the matter generally with liberty to the parties to re-apply, so that the child can remain a ward without any final order having been made. He may refer to a judge any matter which he thinks should properly be decided by a judge, and this will normally include any final order[16]. Where there is to be a full hearing, he will certify the case as fit to be adjourned to the judge and may do so at the first appointment if the case will be prepared by the time it comes for hearing. His course of action will be determined by the nature of the case, the state of the evidence and the wishes of the parties, but clearly the decision is of crucial importance to the progress of the case.

The parties' solicitors will have to consider how they wish the case to proceed. If the child has been warded as a tactical device and the appointment taken out to preserve the status of the child as a ward, it may be considered sufficient for the

13. It will be recalled that the existence of other proceedings will be established because the plaintiff has to file a certificate inter alia certifying whether are in existence other proceedings in which the minor is involved. See Appendix for the Certificate as to other pleadings.
14. See r.97(2) of the Matrimonial Causes Rules 1977.
15. See *Re W (infants)* [1965] 3 All ER 231 at 248–9 and *Practice Direction* [1966] 3 All ER 84, [1966] 1 WLR 1368.
16. For the respective powers of judge and registrar see Chap. 5.

application to be adjourned generally. This can also arise where it has been impossible to trace the defendant to serve notice of the proceedings. The registrar can then make such orders as are immediately necessary in the interest of the ward, and if necessary give directions for substituted service. For the avoidance of doubt it is wise to ask the registrar to confirm the wardship pending further order.

After the registrar has certified the case, a party can apply to the Clerk of the Rules for a hearing before a judge. If a direction has been given for a report by the court welfare officer[17], practitioners are advised not to delay their application for an hearing until the report is completed. The proper course is to contact the court welfare officer to obtain an estimate as to when the report will be ready, and seek a date shortly after[18].

In considering his directions for a hearing before a judge, the registrar may wish to have regard to the most appropriate venue. Although, obviously, both registrars and judges have the same power in London and in the provinces, there may be advantages in transferring a case for its hearing. This will depend to a certain extent on the availability of a judge and on the convenience of the parties and their witnesses.

There is no doubt that the registrar is an influential figure, especially if he takes the initiative in ensuring that the best interests of the ward are protected. He offers significant advantages to the parties and maintains a suitable degree of informality. There is also a registrar of the day available in London who will assist with practical problems.

IV The judge

The judge will of course have a function similar to that in other High Court proceedings, though it must again be emphasised that he is only deciding an action between the parties, in so far as his decision is consistent with the interests of the child. This has been described[19] as a parental and

---

17. For the role of Court Welfare Officers see Chap. 9.
18. *Practice Direction* [1972] 2 All ER 352, [1972] 1 WLR 598. The same procedure should surely also apply if a report is required from the Official Solicitor or a local authority.
19. See e.g. Lord Devlin in *Official Solicitor v K* [1965] AC 201 at 242 and Lord Atkinson in *Scott v Scott* [1913] AC 417 at 462.

administrative function, but it is quite clear that as à matter of practice the judge must conduct the case in a judicial fashion. Thus he has no personal right to call witnesses, and must reach his decision on the information available to him[20]. The appointment of the Official Solicitor will enable him to ensure that he gets evidence which he feels he needs but the parties have failed to call. It is likely, however, that he will, if he considers it necessary, act in an inquisitorial manner and question parties more than in an ordinary case, to ensure that he does act in the interests of the child, especially if the Official Solicitor is not appointed to act on behalf of the child.

Although wardship proceedings are heard in the Family Division, it must be noted that a judge could be appointed to sit with little previous experience of child care cases. He could also be a deputy sitting for a brief period, and in the district registries it may well be the same judge who sits in the Crown Court. He will have the same powers, so that it is important that he is fully aware of the welfare principles of the jurisdiction, and what contributes to that welfare.

For urgent applications the judge is as accessible as the registrar. A duty judge is available every day and for emergencies even at night and weekends. It is also important to remember that wardship applications are heard in chambers[1], so that a solicitor has a right of audience before the judge. The judge may adjourn the matter into court 'if he considers that by reason of its importance or for any other reason it should be so heard'[2]. This may happen where the judge wishes to give publicity to a case or considers that a judgment should be reported. In such circumstances a solicitor advocate should seek the waiver of the court on his restriction to appear.

V Emergency proceedings

The act of making a child a ward of court means that he must not marry or go outside England or Wales without the leave

---

20. He can, however, act on information given to him in private. See post p. 59 et seq. for a discussion on evidence.
1. RSC Ord. 32, r.11. This differs from the former procedure followed in the Chancery Division where such cases were heard in camera. See *Rayden on Divorce* (13th Edn.) 1122 n.(a).
2. RSC Ord. 32, r.13.

of the court. Since he is under no further restraint until the court's directions are given, it must follow that other parties can continue to exercise their legal rights in the matter[2a]. Accordingly, if it is necessary to prevent some action being taken in respect of the child, immediate steps may need to be taken by way of injunction. For example, if there is a dangerous threat to remove a child from his parent, it may be necessary to obtain an injunction to prevent this. Similarly if a child is in care under section 1 of the Children Act 1948 and is threatened with removal from care by a wholly unsuitable parent an injunction may be required.

Where an injunction is sought, the provisions of RSC Order 29, rule 1 apply. They state as follows:

'(1) An application for the grant of an injunction may be made by any party to a cause or matter before or after the trial of the cause or matter whether or not a claim for the injunction was included in that party's writ, originating summons, counter claim or third party notice as the case may be.

(2) Where the applicant is the plaintiff and the case is one of urgency such application may be made ex parte on affidavit but except as aforesaid such application must be made by motion or summons.

(3) The Plaintiff may not make such an application before the issue of the writ or originating summons by which the cause or matter is to be begun except where the case is one of urgency, and in that case the injunction applied for may be granted, on terms providing for the issue of the writ or summons and such other terms if any as the court thinks fit.'

An application ex parte can be made at very short notice and in urgent cases the applicant should not hesitate to act quickly to protect the child's welfare. The most convenient method of getting an application before the court is to contact the Clerk of the Rules, if in London or the district registry, to explain the situation and obtain an expedited hearing. He will provide information as to the judge, the court and the time of hearing. There is also a duty judge available out of hours for emergencies, and he can be contacted through the High Court at any time.

2a. For the various restraints on other parties upon warding a child see Chap. 5.

The application must normally be supported by affidavit evidence which should be sworn after issue of the summons, although it can subsequently be re-sworn. It is also advisable to have the deponent present at the application if possible in case any difficulties arise, and also possibly to give evidence on any matters which have arisen since swearing. In dire emergencies the need for an affidavit may be dispensed with, and the evidence can be filed later.

It is very important in a case of emergency to obtain a copy of the order immediately after the hearing, and the judge's clerk should be advised that it will be so required. It can be served on the relevant parties so that they cannot deny knowledge of it if there is any subsequent contempt of court by breach of the order. It will be of assistance in this respect for the order that is sought, to have been drafted, so that subject to the approval of the judge, it can be sealed and issued without delay.

In *Re N* (*infants*)[3] Stamp J held that he had power to grant an injunction to protect the person of the infant even before the summons was issued. Although there should normally be sufficient time to issue an originating summons, it is clear from *Re N* that the injunction may be sought before proceedings are commenced, outside office hours and even on a Sunday. The injunction should be granted on terms providing for the issue of the originating summons, and the intended summons should be left with the judge so that it may be issued. Its form should be 'in the matter of an intended action between A and B', and it should be drawn so that if it had been issued, the injunction could have been granted.

Where an emergency application is made either before or after the issue of the originating summons, it will almost certainly be ex parte. When the defendant is known to be represented as he may be when an application is made some time after the issue of proceedings, it is considered courteous at least to inform his solicitors of the intended application. Very often an injunction will only be granted as an interim

3. [1967] Ch 512, [1967] 1 All ER 161, both on the basis of RSC Ord. 29 and upon his inherent jurisdiction disapproving on this latter point *Re E* (*an infant*) [1956] Ch 23, [1955] 3 All ER 174. See also *L v L* [1969] P 25, [1969] 1 All ER 852.

measure, until such time as the defendant can appear to present his case. Good grounds must be shown why the application is not made on notice, but where removal of the child from a safe place is seriously threatened, evidence should be available to support the urgency.

It has been held that a summary or peremptory order, where the child is to be sent from the jurisdiction, should not normally be made ex parte [3a]. Where an injunction is granted in the absence of the defendant he should apply to have it set aside, and if that application is refused, request a stay of execution and leave to appeal to the Court of Appeal.

Where there is no such emergency but there is still an important need for an early order relating to something beyond the powers of the registrar, it may be advisable to issue an immediate summons for a hearing before the judge. This can happen for example, where care and control has effectively passed into the hands of one parent, and he wishes to ensure that it is not lost through sudden removal. Consent to the order cannot be guaranteed and therefore an application to the registrar may be inadequate, but an application to the judge by summons supported by evidence on affidavit can produce the desired order. The defendant, having had notice[4], will have had an opportunity to file some evidence, and the judge will be able to reach some decision as to what is best for the children pending a full hearing. During vacation the summons will only be issued with leave of the registrar, so that it will be necessary to persuade him that he cannot deal with the matter, and that it is sufficiently urgent and important to get an early hearing before the judge.

An early application of this kind can in suitable cases, provide for a much quicker hearing than might otherwise be obtained. A judge can make all the directions that a registrar can, and has been known simultaneously, to arrange for representation by the Official Solicitor and to obtain a hearing date from the Clerk of the Rules. It is probably right to add that this required considerable co-operation from all the parties, since any delay will cause the hearing date to be missed.

3a. See *Re C (a minor)* (1976) 6 Fam. Law 211.
4. Two clear days notice must be given RSC Ord. 32, r.3.

Another example where consideration should be given to an application for an early hearing before the judge may occur where a party seeks for the child to be dewarded soon after the originating summons is issued. Since it is an automatic effect of warding the child, that he may not leave the jurisdiction, wardship is sometimes used as a device to frustrate the intention to remove. This may happen even though carefully planned arrangements have been made, either to go on holiday for a short period or to settle in another country. In such a case leave should be sought to take the ward out of the jurisdiction, coupled with an application for him to be dewarded if appropriate.

Local authorities may also wish to apply without delay for a child in their care to be dewarded, if they oppose a wardship application on the grounds that the court should not interfere with the exercise of their statutory powers under the Children Acts[5]. A local authority should settle this aspect of the case as soon as possible for two reasons. First they will not wish their actions, decisions or plans for the child to be fettered any longer than is essential. Secondly they must take the point at the earliest possible opportunity or they may be estopped from raising it. In particular in view of the decision in *Re D (a minor)*[6] they will have to apply before the Official Solicitor is appointed, since if he subsequently disagrees with the local authority the court will consider the case on its merits.

VI Evidence

Evidence in wardship cases will be on affidavit which may be supported by oral evidence at the hearing. Affidavits should be filed at the registry in which the matter is proceeding[7], and should be endorsed with a note showing on whose behalf

---

5. Following decisions like *Re M (an infant)* [1961] Ch 328, [1961] 1 All ER 788, and *Re T (AJJ) (an infant)* [1970] Ch 688 [1970] 2 All ER 865. Discussed in detail in Chap. 11.
6. (1978) 122 Sol Jo 193, Times 14 February. Discussed in detail in Chap. 2.
7. I.e. the district registry or, if the principal registry, Room 30, Somerset House.

they are filed[8] and the dates of swearing and filing. Failing these technicalities the affidavits may only be used with the leave of the court, and although the practice of the Family Division is not so strict as to exclude evidence which may be beneficial to the ward, the proper form should be followed, if for no other reason than it can assist the smooth running of the proceedings.

If it is desired to proceed with reasonable speed, evidence should be filed before the first appointment, sufficient at least to support the application. It is questionable how helpful it is to set down in detail on affidavit at the commencement of the proceedings all the evidence that a party might wish to use at a full hearing. It may transpire that much of the evidence is not needed, and the effect of it merely to waste time and lead to polarisation of the parties. Further evidence can be filed at a later stage with the leave of the court and in reply to any evidence filed on behalf of other parties. Although there is a danger that matters left out of affidavits and raised at the hearing will cause adjournments to be sought, this should not be necessary provided the general area of dispute is raised. Matters will inevitably be dealt with in far more detail at the hearing and considerable time is spent on oral evidence, no matter what the content of the affidavits.

Subject to any limitations imposed by the registrar all parties may file evidence and this will include the Official Solicitor as guardian ad litem of the child. Thus while the proceedings still concern an issue between the parties which must be decided on judical principles, because of the emphasis given to the welfare of the ward and the parental role of the court, the case is more likely to be conducted in an investigative manner. This may have various effects. In civil cases a judge normally has no right to call a witness but in wardship he can through appointment of the Official Solicitor ensure that he has all the evidence he considers desirable. It is also long-established practice that the judge may interview the child and even his parents privately, and receive reports not revealed to the parties, though these powers should be used most sparingly. This latter point was recently

8. RSC Ord. 41, r.9(5).

affirmed by the House of Lords in *Re K* (*infants*)[9] in relation to the submission of the Official Solicitor's report.

To the objection that it is contrary to natural justice for a judge to act on information not disclosed to the parties, it was held in *Re K* that as wardship was sui generis not all the rules of a judicial inquiry are necessarily relevant to wardship. In wardship the judge is not sitting as an arbiter but is charged with the paramount duty of protecting the ward's interests, hence rules designed to ensure fairness between the parties have less relevance. In particular a judge is not bound to choose a course of action which is harmful to the ward merely because it is fair to the parties. That does not mean that the parties' interests can be ignored but merely that ultimately even in procedural matters, it is the welfare of the minor which must prevail[10]. A judge therefore has the power to act on evidence confidentially submitted to him by the Official Solicitor or on information gained as a result of a private interview with the ward or the parents[11]. It was emphasised, however, that even in wardship the court is bound to act in a judicial manner and that the discretion to withhold evidence from the parties is to be exercised with caution having proper regard both to the interests of the ward and of the parties.

Another effect which is thought to follow from the nature of the proceedings is the general admissibility of hearsay evidence. In the High Court this is regulated by the Civil Evidence Act 1968. Section 1 provides that 'a statement other than one made by a person while giving oral evidence in those proceedings shall be admissible as evidence of any fact stated therein to the extent that it is so admissible by virtue of any provision of this Part of this Act or by virtue of any other statutory provision or by agreement of the parties, but not otherwise.' By section 2 'a statement made whether oral or in a document or otherwise may be admitted as evidence of any fact of which direct oral evidence would be admissible

---

9. [1965] AC 201 [1963] 3 All ER 191.
10. See e.g. Lord Hodson ibid., at 234 et seq. and Lord Devlin at 238 et seq.
11. Lord Hodson ibid., at 235 thought that it was undesirable for the judge to see the parents privately, but Lord Evershed at 222 made no such comments and added that the judge had the power to interview in private other interested parties.

whether or not the person making the statement is called as a witness.'

Thus first hand hearsay is admissible evidence. This is extended to second hand hearsay by section 4 which says: 'a statement contained in a document shall be admissible evidence of any fact stated therein of which direct oral evidence would be admissible, if the document is or forms part of a record compiled by a person acting under a duty from information which was supplied by a person (whether under a duty or not) who had or may reasonably be supposed to have had personal knowledge of the matters dealt with in that information, and which if not supplied by that person to the compiler of the record direct, was supplied by him to the compiler of the record indirectly through one or more intermediaries each under a duty'.

Duty includes trade, profession or business or what is done as an employer or employee. Medical or school records, for example, do not therefore necessarily require the attendance of the doctor or teacher who made the observation. Similarly evidence of an oral allegation may now be given to prove the facts alleged.

In wardship proceedings the practice has developed that the judge is not bound by the rules of evidence, apparently, on the basis expressed by Lord Devlin in *Re K* when he said[12]:

> 'A judge in chambers is quite capable of giving hearsay no more than its proper weight. An inflexible rule against hearsay is quite unsuited to the exercise of a parental and administrative jurisdiction.'

He continued that he could not imagine that a judge would allow a grave allegation against a parent to be proved solely by hearsay, at any rate in a case in which direct evidence could be produced. This rather begs the question since it is in just such cases where hearsay is most likely to be used[13].

The other judgments in *Re K* are less certain about the admissibility of hearsay evidence. Lord Hodson said[14]:

12. [1965] AC 201 at pp. 242–3. See also Cross's comment in (1967) 83 LQR at 208: 'After the decision of the House of Lords in *Re K* (*infants*) one may, I think, say with some confidence that in exercising the wardship jurisdiction the judge is not bound by the rules of evidence'. But see the comments below.
13. E.g. a local authority may use wardship instead of care proceedings under the Children and Young Persons Act 1969 specifically because hearsay evidence is more readily admitted.
14. Ibid., at 235. Lord Evershed at 223 (with whom Lord Reid agreed) left the point open.

'When there is a contest as to fact and the judge receives conflicting reports he will gain no assistance and he must rely upon proof. This will normally be given upon affidavit subject to cross-examination and the ordinary rules of procedure will be followed, involving the exclusion of inadmissible evidence. See *Rossage* v *Rossage*[15] where the Court of Appeal held that the provisions of Order 38[16] are applicable to affidavits sworn in such proceedings.'

Lord Devlin considered that the order contemplated proceedings where written evidence was not admissible unless on affidavit. He distinguished wardship, where evidence might not be on affidavit as with a statement of facts from a guardian ad litem. He went on to say[17]:

'If however the parties in wardship proceedings wish to use affidavit evidence, they must in my opinion, comply with the rules. I think therefore, that *Rossage v Rossage* and in *Re J (an infant)*[18] were rightly decided, but they need not be taken to mean that the judge must disregard altogether hearsay in affidavit evidence unless the proceedings are interlocutory. It would be pedantic for him to tell the party that the offending material must be written out all over again in an unsworn document before it can be received. But he should not attach to the material the superior value of sworn evidence unless it complies with the rules'.

In *Re K (infants)* was of course decided before the Civil Evidence Act, and so it must be a matter for debate how much weight can be placed on the dicta above. Most matters should come within the provisions of sections 2 and 4, but if not *Re K (infants)* seems to provide the only guidance. If section 1 of the 1968 Act is interpreted strictly, this would prevent a judge receiving hearsay evidence and require statements in affidavits not within the rules to be struck out. As a matter of policy Lord Devlin is surely right, that in wardship proceedings, where no other evidence is available, the ward's interests require that regard must be had to the information that is available. His argument is based on a view of wardship as parental and administrative rather than a judicial inquiry

15. [1960] 1 All ER 600, [1960] 1 WLR 249.
16. Now RSC Ord. 41.
17. [1965] AC 201 at 243.
18. [1960] 1 All ER 603, [1960] 1 WLR 253.

which is preferred by other judges. It means also that precise and sometimes prejudicial evidence may be adduced without adequate means of rebuttal, but ultimately it should be a matter for the judge to reach his decision having seen the witnesses and weighed the evidence.

The relevance of psychiatric evidence is another issue which raises problems in wardship. The accepted view established in *Re S (an infant)*[19] is that the court has a discretion whether or not to allow such evidence. There is a reluctance to accept any need for it, unless the child is already receiving psychiatric treatment or is thought to be suffering from mental illness. One view is that psychiatric evidence about the effects of different events on the child can be as well judged by the courts as by psychiatrists[20]. Thus the mere fact that a child comes from a broken home may not justify examination of the child or expert psychiatric evidence as to where the child would be best placed. This can be understood in so far as it may be unwise to submit an otherwise entirely normal child to psychiatric or psychological testing which may produce few positive results. However, most children will have been damaged in some way by the battles which lead them to become the subject of wardship proceedings, and there is an increasing area of cases where their interests may be better served by expert opinion as to their needs. This may involve examination or expert opinion about the effects of early life experience on children or a combination of both. There is an increasing involvement of research in children's matters and the knowledge being collected should be available to the courts. The same may be said of evidence of experienced social workers, who have worked closely with children, read widely and seen the results of their work.

It is clear that no examination of the child, psychiatric or otherwise, should be undertaken without the consent of the court[1]. Such consent would be given where both parties agreed on the need for an examination and on who should conduct it, but where they disagreed, the matter should be referred to the Official Solicitor (if appointed as guardian ad litem), who would advise the court whether he considered an

19. [1967] 1 All ER 202, per Cross J.
20. See e.g. Lord Upjohn's comments in *J v C* [1970] AC at 726.
 1. Per Cross J in *Re S (infants)* ibid., at 209.

examination necessary. The object of this procedure is to try and ensure that a psychiatric examination is carried out on the basis of unbiased instructions. The Court of Appeal has since confirmed this procedure[2] and the profession has recently been reminded to follow it[3].

While it is desirable to ensure that a child is not exposed to repeated interviews with strangers, it does mean that a party will have some difficulty in challenging the psychiatric evidence. While it may be possible to get another opinion, it is subject to the consent of the court which is unlikely to be granted save in very exceptional circumstances. One of the consequences of this is that parties may be encouraged to obtain any expert opinion before making the child a ward. Although the court may take a poor view of this, it may be justified on the basis that it is important to know in advance if expert evidence would support an application.

VII Termination or lapse of wardship

One of the drawbacks of the position prior to 1949 was that short of attaining majority at 21 there was no way in which a child could cease to be a ward. This age has now been reduced to 18 and the child does then automatically cease to be a ward[4].

There are two other ways in which a child may cease to be a ward. Section 9(3) of the Law Reform (Miscellaneous Provisions) Act 1949 states:

> 'The court may, either upon an application in that behalf or without such application, order that any infant who is for the time being a ward of court shall cease to be a ward of court.'

Thus there may be an application by a party for termination of wardship or the court may deward on its own motion. Although the court will not hesitate to order a child to cease to be a ward where the continuation of the order would serve no useful purpose, it has also been said that as long as there is a

2. *B(M) v B(R)* [1968] 3 All ER 170, [1968] 1 WLR 1182.
3. By Dunn J in *Re A-W (minors)* (1975) 5 Fam Law 95. Failure to obtain the court's consent might constitute contempt of court. See Chap. 7.
4. By s.1 and Sch. 3 para. 3 of the Family Law Reform Act 1969.

need for control by the court it is a mistake to discontinue the wardship[5].

A child may also cease to be a ward if the order lapses. As stated previously section 9 of the 1949 Act provides that a child automatically becomes a ward of court immediately the originating summons is issued, but ceases to be a ward on the expiration of such period as may be prescribed by the rules of the court, unless within that period an order has been made in accordance with the application.

This period is specified[6] as 21 days after the issue of the summons or until the determination of the applications in the summons where an application for an appointment for the hearing of the Summons is made within 21 days. What is required under this rule is not that the appointment should be heard but simply that an application for one has been made.

The hearing of the appointment which takes place before a registrar may therefore be some time after the original summons has been issued. If no application is made within 21 days then a notice must be left in the registry stating whether the applicant intends to proceed with the summons[7]. This provision does have some difficulties. There are numerous cases, especially where an injunction or mandatory order is sought before a judge at an early stage, when no appointment before a registrar is sought. The court is empowered to order that the wardship should continue notwithstanding the fact that no appointment has been taken.[8] Without such an order the wardship will normally lapse, unless the application before the judge can be said to be 'an appointment for the hearing of the summons'.[9] If the application is for an injunction and nothing more, then that application cannot be said to be for the hearing of the summons and the wardship is in danger of lapsing. It is clearly, therefore, good practice in such circumstances to seek an order from the judge that specifies that the wardship does continue.

5. Per Buckley LJ in *Baldrian v Baldrian* (1974) 4 Fam Law 12. For further discussion on dewarding see Ch. V.
6. By RSC Ord. 90, r.4(1)(*a*).
7. RSC Ord. 90, r.4(3).
8. RSC Ord. 90, r.4(1)(*b*). Such an order is usually expressed to be temporary pending the full hearing of the summons. See the Supreme Court Practice 1979 p. 1347.
9. Within the meaning of RSC Ord 90, r.4(1)(*a*).

Not all cases, however, are as clear as that and it is sometimes left to the registrar to determine whether the wardship has lapsed. The view generally taken is that if the court order necessarily implies the continuation of the wardship as for example, giving care and control to one of the parties pending a full hearing, then the wardship will not be treated as lapsing. Should the registrar decide that the wardship has lapsed, he will if necessary, send out a notice to that effect to the parties.

Although the lapse of the wardship may not be a serious matter, since it can always be revived by an ordinary summons issued subsequent to the originating summons or by the issue of a further originating summons[10], and furthermore, the orders of the court remain in force[11], it may nevertheless cause delay and inconvenience. If the wardship lapses and no other orders have been made, powers may again be vested in other parties, for example, the power to remove the child from the country.

As stated above the best practice is always to ensure that an order is sought, if no registrar's appointment is taken within 21 days. However, the rather inexact way in determining whether wardship has lapsed could easily be avoided if there was a simple amendment to the current rule so that once any order in respect of the ward is made, the wardship shall continue unless the order specifies to the contrary.

VIII Appeals

If a party is dissatisfied with a decision of a registrar he may appeal to a judge in chambers where the matter will be reheard[12].

An appeal from an order of a judge lies in the Court of Appeal[13].

---

10. See *Rayden on Divorce* (13th Edn.), p. 1117.
11. See the Supreme Court Practice p. 1347. For this reason it is not always thought necessary to have the wardship proceedings reconstituted.
12. RSC Ord. 58, r.1.
13. RSC Ord 59. For the powers of the Court of Appeal see e.g. *Re O (infants)* [1971] Ch 748, [1971] 2 All ER 744 and *Re F (a minor) (wardship: appeal)* [1976] Fam 238, [1976] 1 All ER 417.

IX Legal aid

By section 7 and Schedule 1 of the Legal Aid Act 1974 legal aid is generally available for proceedings in the High Court, and persons who are parties to wardship proceedings may therefore be eligible for legal aid. There are some restrictions which can create problems.

Section 7(5) provides:

> 'A person shall not be given legal aid in connection with any proceedings unless he shows that he has reasonable grounds for taking, defending or being a party thereto, and may also be refused legal aid if it appears unreasonable that he should receive it in the particular circumstances of the case.'

This leaves a wide discretion to the legal aid committee of the Law Society. In particular it is open to the interpretation that legal aid will only be granted for wardship proceedings as a last resort and after all other remedies have proved ineffective or inappropriate. It is submitted that the decision should be based on what provides the best remedy for the particular circumstances of the case. This may entail granting legal aid for wardship proceedings rather than insisting on appeals against magistrates' decisions in custody or care proceedings[14], or permitting an initial application to be made in wardship in preference perhaps to a custody application. In this context the legal aid application will have to be completed in sufficient detail and with careful argument to show why wardship is to be preferred.

A major restriction is the financial conditions which have to be satisfied to enable legal aid to be granted. With current standards of income a person does not have to be an especially high wage earner to be outside the legal aid limits[15]. Yet the costs of wardship proceedings can be prohibitively high and uncertain at the outset. It is also possible that with the delay in proceedings a party could start proceedings within the legal aid limits, but subsequently increase income, requir-

---

14. As in Re H (a minor) (wardship: jurisdiction) [1978] Fam 65.
15. At the time of going to press the figures are likely to be as follows. The maximum disposable income is £3600 and disposable capital £2500. A contribution may be required in respect of income not greater than one third of the amount by which disposable income exceeds £1500 and in respect of capital not greater than the amount by which disposable capital exceeds 600.

ing a change in assessment. This may be a significant deterrent to a person near the edge of the legal aid limits.

Another problem frequently associated with legal aid is the position of successful unassisted parties. Injustice can be done in ordinary litigation because of the advantage held by a party receiving legal aid and to whom expense is therefore no problem, over the party who has to be conscious that he is paying all his own costs and running the risk of being ordered to pay the other side's costs if he loses.

In wardship the problem seems to be exacerbated by the provisions of section 13 of the Legal Aid Act 1974. Section 13(1) states:

'Where a party receives legal aid in connection with any proceedings between him and a party not receiving legal aid (referred to as the "unassisted party") and those proceedings are finally decided in favour of the unassisted party, the court by which the proceedings are so decided may, subject to the provisions of this section, make an order for the payment to the unassisted party out of the legal aid fund of the whole or any part of the costs incurred by him in those proceedings.'

Wardship proceedings are not like other litigation and the aim of taking or defending the proceedings may not necessarily be to win or lose but may be to protect the child. Yet it would seem that unless a clear decision in favour of the party is made he cannot hope to recover any costs.

Section 13(2) then provides that an order may only be made if it is just and equitable in all the circumstances. There is then a further restriction in that by section 13(3) no order can be made unless:

'(a) the proceedings in the court of first instance were instituted by the party receiving legal aid; and

(b) the court is satisfied that the unassisted party will suffer severe financial hardship unless the order is made.'

This is treating the proceedings far too much like a property transaction rather than an attempt to ensure that the best arrangements are made for a child. It also means that a party who is obliged to be cost-conscious may be deterred from taking pre-emptive proceedings. It is clear that under the present legislation a party without legal aid must if he wishes to consider wardship reckon to run the risk of a considerable financial outlay without much prospect of recovering it. This position is quite wrong where the welfare of a child is concerned, and it is submitted that consideration must be given to providing a less strict assessment, so that costs could be recovered from public funds unless the unassisted party's case was lacking in merit.

Chapter 5

The Powers of the Court

I Forms of protection not requiring a court order

A. INTRODUCTION

Wardship is unique among child jurisdictions because not only is the court empowered to make a wide range of orders concerning its wards but there are also certain forms of protection which arise automatically by reason of the wardship. Moreover this protection lasts so long as the child remains a ward.

The theory behind this instant and continuing protection is that throughout the time that the child is a ward the court is his legal protector and guardian and is thereby vested with special control over both the ward's person and property. It will be recalled[1] that the child becomes a ward immediately the application is made under the Law Reform (Miscellaneous Provisions) Act 1949, section 9 and continues until either the wardship lapses[2] or is discharged[3].

There are a number of consequences of this automatic protection. First, to a certain extent, it puts the ward himself under restraint but the protection goes beyond this and affects other persons too[4]. Indeed, as will be seen, the restraining effects of wardship are more extensive on other persons than on the ward. A second consequence is that it may enable a party to obtain instant protection over the ward without

---

1. See ante, Chap. 4 on Procedure.
2. I.e. because no appointment is made within 21 days of issuing the originating summons under the Law Reform (Miscellaneous Provisions) Act 1949, s.9(2) and RSC Ord. 90, r.4(1)(a).
3. Either by a court order (see post p. 81) or by the ward attaining his majority.
4. This latter consequence is not made clear on the Notice of Wardship (Form F.D. 590) see post p. 73.

having to take the matter to court[5]. A third consequence is that since the ward remains subject to the court's control throughout the wardship it will be necessary at least to inform the court and on occasion to seek its prior consent before any important step can be taken in the ward's life.

B. MARRIAGE AND REMOVAL FROM THE JURISDICTION

The two classic and long-established examples of the protection are that no-one may marry a ward nor remove him from the jurisdiction without the court's prior consent[6]. Indeed the latter consequence has been emphasised by a recent *Practice Direction*[7] which reminds persons that it is a contempt to take a ward out of England and Wales even to Scotland, Northern Ireland, the Republic of Ireland, the Channel Islands or the Isle of Man without prior leave of the court.

In each of these cases and throughout the wardship, failure to obtain the court's permission will render the offender guilty of contempt of court[8]. It is to be emphasised that the restraint not to marry and not to remove the ward from the jurisdiction lies against anyone, including the ward, and not merely those who are parties to or even those who have notice of the proceedings[9]. Nevertheless, although no order is strictly necessary, the protection will clearly be more effective if the relevant person has knowledge of it. Hence, where it is sought to restrain a person who is not a party to the proceedings, it is sensible to seek a specific order which can then be served on him. In any event if it is sought to restrain the ward's association with a third party and not merely to prevent their marriage a specific order will have to be obtained[10].

5. Though it will be important to make the necessary appointment before a registrar to prevent the wardship from lapsing.
6. These restrictions are both referred to in the notice of wardship (Form F.D. 590—see Appendix).
7. [1977] 3 All ER 122, [1977] 1 WLR 1067.
8. The contempt is criminal. See Ch. 7.
9. Discussed in Ch. 7.
10. Discussed post p. 107.

C. OTHER FORMS OF PROTECTION

i) *Restraint on the ward*

The Notice of Wardship[11] states that:

> 'A Ward of Court may not marry or go outside England and Wales without the leave of the Court *but is under no further restraint until the Court's directions are given.*' [Emphasis added.]

In so far as this comment refers to the personal restraint on the ward it is in accordance with the established cases. It has been suggested by one commentator[12], however, that since a ward cannot leave the jurisdiction without the court's leave, that child cannot become a member of the armed forces without the court's approval. Further the court ought to be notified about any choice of career in which the ward becomes liable to be sent overseas. The point is certainly arguable, though whether the court would in fact interfere is another matter. Russell LJ has commented[13] that 'the judge would have no right to complain of or countermand a lawful posting overseas of a ward who was in the armed forces. The law refers the military control of the ward to the military authorities'. This comment would seem to indicate that a minor who is already in the forces could not be warded to prevent him from being posted abroad, but it does not counter the initial point about having to seek the court's approval to *join* the services. It does perhaps indicate that consent would be readily given.

ii) *Restraint on other persons*

a) No important step in the ward's life to be taken without the court's consent

So far as persons other than the ward are concerned the court's control certainly extends beyond marrying a ward or removing him from the jurisdiction.

11. Form F.D. 590. See Appendix.
12. B D Inglis: *Family Law* (2nd Edn. 1970, New Zealand) Vol. 2, p. 476. This is supported by *Harrison v Goodhall* (1852) Kay 310; 69 ER 131 where a ward had joined the army and was due to be posted overseas. Parker LC thought removal from the jurisdiction in those circumstances would still be a contempt. In the event permission was granted.
13. In *Re Mohamed Arif (an infant), Re Nirbhai Singh (an infant)* [1968] Ch 643 at 662. Cf. *Harrison v Goodhall* ibid.

Discussion of the scope of protection may be usefully started by reference to Cross J's statement in *Re S (an infant)*[14] that once a child has been made a ward:

> 'No important step in the child's life can be taken without the court's consent'.

Although it is dangerous to take the words of a judgment out of context and to treat them as if they were in a statute, nevertheless the statement has since been adopted in other cases and should now be regarded, it is submitted, as laying down the general principle. The question remains, of course, as to what constitutes an 'important' step.

i) Adopting a ward. One step which is quite clearly important is adoption of the ward. It was held in *F v S*[15], for example, that leave of the court is necessary before proceedings for adopting a ward can be commenced. Although the case specifically concerned an applicant who had previously been granted care and control of the ward it is submitted that leave is always required even if the prospective adopter was not a party to the wardship proceedings since clearly adoption is an important step so far as the child is concerned.

ii) Psychiatric examination. In *Re S* itself, Cross J considered that the examination of the ward by a psychiatrist with a view to the report being put in evidence in the case constituted an important step. Hence it is essential to obtain the court's consent before such examinations are undertaken. Although obiter this statement has since been approved by the Court of Appeal[16] and should be regarded as being authoritative. Indeed in *Re R(PM) (infant)*[17] Goff J held that such an examination without the court's consent was improper and counsel's advice in this respect was a 'serious error of judgment'. Similar warnings were also sounded by Dunn J in *Re A-W (minors)*[18]. The significance of these warnings is that advisers who do not ensure that the correct procedure is followed could find themselves guilty of contempt[19].

14. [1967] 1 All ER 202 at 209.
15. *F v S (adoption: ward)* [1973] Fam 203, [1973] 1 All ER 722. Discussed also in Ch. 10.
16. *B(M) v B(R)* [1968] 3 All ER 170 at 174 per Willmer LJ.
17. [1968] 1 All ER 691n, [1968] 1 WLR 385.
18. (1975) 5 Fam Law 95.
19. See Chap. 7 for a more detailed discussion.

Quite apart from contempt proceedings, were a proposed improper examination to come to the notice of the other side, it is open to them to apply to the court to prevent the examination taking place.

Although an action for contempt is a possibility, there is perhaps a more potent deterrent against failing to obtain the court's permission, namely, disregarding or attaching little weight to the evidence adduced. No court has gone to the extreme of holding the evidence inadmissible but since the evidence adduced is one-sided it is likely to carry little weight[20].

The cases referred to above were all specifically concerned with psychiatric examinations but there seems no reason to suppose that they should be confined to such reports. For example, the same arguments can be levied against psychological reports and perhaps less appropriately to any medical report. It is to be stressed, however, that in each case what is objected to is the obtaining of a report purely for the purposes of evidence. There is no objection to referring a ward who is physically ill to a medical practitioner[1].

iii) Blood tests. Perhaps on a slightly different footing but clearly analogous to the above cases is the question of blood tests for the purpose of establishing paternity. Although there is no case directly in point it is submitted that such tests do constitute an important step and therefore require the court's prior sanction[2]. As will be seen, however, the court will only refuse to sanction such a test if satisfied that it is against the ward's interests to be so tested[3].

iv) Medical treatment. It might be argued that because custody of a ward vests in the court so does the power to give or withhold consent to his medical treatment. Such a

---

20. See e.g. Goff J's comments in *Re R(PM)* [1968] 1 All ER at 693 B–C.
1. Indeed quite the opposite. See Dunn J's comments in *Re A - W* (1975) 5 Fam Law 95. See also Lord Upjohn's comments in *J v C* [1970] AC 688 at 726.
2. It is true that under s.21(3) of the Family Law Reform Act 1969 the power to order a blood test on a child under the age of 16 is dependent upon the person having *care and control* consenting. It is submitted nevertheless that wardship overrides this provision in much the same way as it overrode contrary to the implication of s.8 of the 1969 Act, the consent of the mother to her daughter's sterilisation in *Re D (a minor) (wardship: sterilisation)* [1976] Fam 185, [1976] 1 All ER 326, see below.
3. *S v McC, W v W* [1972] AC 24. Discussed post at p. 124 et seq.

conclusion, however, would overburden the courts and would hardly be conducive to the interests of wards generally. It would clearly be impracticable every time a ward needed medical treatment to have to refer the matter to court, and potentially disastrous in cases of emergency. It is therefore submitted that the need for medical treatment, though important to the ward, does not in general have to be referred to the court, still less is its prior consent required. The theoretical justification for not having to refer the matter is that though the court remains the ward's guardian, the day-to-day decisions concerning the child, including the power to consent to medical treatment, must be taken to reside in the person having de facto care and control.

Despite the above submission a distinction might be drawn between treatment for therapeutic purposes and for non-therapeutic purposes. That the latter might fall under the court's automatic control is supported by *Re D (a minor)*[4]. In that case an application was successfully made via wardship to prevent an 11 year old girl from being sterilised. The proposed operation, which had parental consent, was not to relieve the ward of any condition but to prevent the possibility of giving birth to an abnormal child. In other words the operation was for non-therapeutic purposes. In granting the injunction Heilbron J commented[5]:

> 'It is quite clear that once a child is a ward of court, no important step in the life of that child can be taken without the consent of the court, and I cannot conceive of a more important step than that which was proposed in this case'.

The clear implication of this statement is that though an injunction was granted, no order was necessary, it being the automatic effect of warding the child that the court's sanction for the operation was required. In view of this decision parties not obtaining the court's consent run the grave risk of being held guilty of contempt, at least provided that they know that the child is a ward[6]. It would still be wise, however, for a party wishing to invoke wardship to prevent such an operation, to seek a specific order so as to ensure that the effect of that order is made absolutely clear to the relevant persons.

4. *Re D (a minor) (wardship: sterilisation)* [1976] Fam 185.
5. Ibid. at p. 196 D.
6. I.e. it is submitted that mens rea is required. See Ch. 7.

To what extent *Re D (a minor)* can be relied upon for saying that the automatic control of a ward extends to all cases of non-therapeutic treatment is a matter of debate. Non-therapeutic treatment could arguably[7] include such matters as the removal of tonsils, whooping cough vaccinations, circumcisions, prescription of the contraceptive pill, abortion, donating organs to others or even the removal of a life-support system for a child who has no hope of recovery. That all such matters should become subject to the court's consent immediately a child is warded would surely be impracticable. It is therefore submitted that in so far as *Re D (a minor)* can be regarded as establishing that non-therapeutic treatment requires the court's prior sanction, it should be confined to sterilisation or analogous treatment[8].

Such a submission would not, however prevent applications being made to prevent such treatment[9], but it would mean that the burden of obtaining an injunction is thrown on the applicant, while until such an order is granted the medical profession could rely on parental consent.

Pending clarification on this point, where the child is already a ward it might be wise at least to inform the court of any proposed major non-therapeutic treatment and in cases of uncertainty to seek court directions. Of course, wherever there is a dispute resort must always be had to the court.

b) Publicity

Another area of doubt is whether wardship automatically precludes all press reports about the ward. It is commonly assumed that warding a child instantly removes him from the glare of publicity but it is difficult to find authority for the point[10]. What undoubtedly is prohibited according to the Administration of Justice Act 1960, section 12 is publishing information relating to wardship proceedings. What is meant by 'information relating to the proceedings' was

7. See e.g. A Bissett-Johnson and A R Everton: 'Preserving the Status Quo: Re D (a minor) (1976) 126 NLJ 104 and M D A Freeman: 'Custodianship and Wardship' (1977) 7 Fam Law 116 n.32.
8. E.g. a vasectomy.
9. Discussed post p.108.
10. Interestingly in *Re Elwes* (1958) Times, July 30 Roxburgh J required both parties to undertake to avoid publicity. Breach of the undertaking or aiding and abetting the breach would then be a contempt. See Ch. 7.

considered in *Re F (otherwise A) (a minor)*[11]. At first instance Tudor Evans J held that it referred to a 'continuing state of affairs for as long as the wardship exists'[12]. This was tantamount to saying that there was an absolute ban on publishing anything about the ward from the moment application is made under the 1949 Act until the wardship ceases. The Court of Appeal considered this to be far too wide a meaning. As Scarman LJ said[13] the definition would have included information about the ward irrespective of whether the information related to the hearing or not. Hence as Lord Denning MR said[14] it would have meant that a newspaper could be guilty of contempt merely for saying of a ward that he has won a scholarship to Oxford or that she has got into bad company and is taking drugs.

According to Scarman LJ[15]:

> 'What is protected from publication is the proceedings of the court; in all other respect the ward enjoys no greater protection against unwelcome publicity than other children. If the information published relates to the ward, but not to the proceedings, there is no contempt.'

The difficulty with Scarman LJ's definition is that it leaves undefined 'proceedings of the court'. It is clear that it means more than the actual hearing. As Geoffrey Lane LJ said[16]:

> ' "Proceedings" must include such matters as statements of evidence, reports, accounts of interviews and such like, which are prepared to use in court once the wardship proceedings have been properly set on foot.'

Hence, publication of details of the Official Solicitor's or a Court Welfare Officer's report is prohibited. The question remains, however, as for whether it is permissible to publish anything about the background facts of a wardship case prior to the hearing. In all events it must be 'sailing close to the wind' to refer to the facts of a case once a wardship appli-

---

11. *Re F (otherwise A) (a minor) (publication of information)* [1977] Fam 58, [1977] 1 All ER 114, noted by Lowe: 'Wardship Contempt and Freedom of Speech' (1977) 93 LQR 180. See also post Chap. 7 for a discussion on the requisite mens rea.
12. Ibid. at p. 72E.
13. Ibid. at p. 99A.
14. Ibid. at p. 86C.
15. Ibid. at p. 99D.
16. Ibid. at p. 105E–F.

cation has been made since that could be regarded as publishing evidence, and newspapers would be well advised to avoid all such references. Nevertheless a distinction may be made between a case in which the facts have been the subject of extensive publicity prior to the wardship application and one where there has been no such publicity. In the former case it surely cannot be a contempt to publish the fact that the child has been made a ward, and it may also be permissible to refer back to the previous published facts. In the latter case it would seem wrong to reveal the ward's identity by publishing that a particular child has been made a ward and certainly wrong to use the wardship application as an excuse for publishing the facts of the case.

The embargo against publishing information relating to wardship proceedings clearly applies after the hearing but the restraint is not necessarily perpetual. Lord Shaw said in *Scott v Scott*[17] 'when respect has thus been paid to the object of the suit, the rule of publicity may be resumed. I know of no principle which would entitle the Court to compel a ward to remain silent for life in regard to judicial proceedings which occurred during his tutelage.' It would seem to follow that the embargo is lifted once the ward attains his majority[18]. The restraint may, however come to an end before this for as Geoffrey Lane LJ said[19]: 'where all necessity for preserving the confidentiality of information about an infant has with the passage of time disappeared, publication will not be a contempt.'

The embargo against publishing information relating to wardship proceedings may not be the only restraint on the press. In *Re T(AJJ) (an infant)*[20] Russell LJ issued the following warning:

> 'We decided to hear this appeal in camera with a view to protecting the infant from harm, and we now give our judgment in open court taking every care that we can to avoid identification of the persons concerned. No doubt

17. [1913] AC 417 at 483.
18. Query if there is freedom to publish whenever the wardship ends.
19. Ibid. at p. 107D, cf. *Re C (an infant)* (1969) Times June 18 where the BBC were allowed to televise a programme discussing the implications of the House of Lords' decision in *J v C* [1970] AC 668, [1969] 1 All ER 788.
20. [1970] Ch 688 at 689. Cf. Lord Denning MR's extra judicial comments reported in *Gazette News* (November 1970) p. 14. Criticised by Borrie and Lowe: *The Law of Contempt* at 125.

diligent investigations would enable anyone interested
to tear aside the veil. But it must be borne in mind that
the infant is a ward of court under the judge's order and
if anyone is minded to question or interview the infant
they may well be at risk of being in contempt.'

It is not clear exactly what Russell LJ had in mind when he
issued the warning. He may have considered that the
contempt would be committed by revealing the ward's identity. It may be that he thought that the information gained
and subsequently published contravened section 12 of the
1960 Act. But he may have considered that the interview
alone constituted a contempt. Being hounded by the press
could certainly be held to interfere with the ward's welfare
and on this basis constitute a contempt. At all events parties
would be well advised not to interview a ward whether or not
the interview is published.

iii) *Local authorities*

Before leaving the topic of automatic protection in wardship
mention should be made about the position of local authorities in whose care a ward has been placed by the court. Since it
is clear that the ward remains subject to the court's directions
it may appear that the initiative for making decisions about
the child rests with the court'. It is submitted that this is not
so. Section 7(2) of the Family Law Reform Act 1969 expressly
states that once the court has committed the ward to the care
of a local authority, Part II of the Children Act 1948 which
relates to the treatment of children in care applies as if the
child had been received into care under section 1 of the 1948
Act. In other words the local authority should treat the ward
in exactly the same way as any other child in their care
remembering that as section 12 states in reaching any decision relating to the child:

'a local authority shall give first consideration to the
need to safeguard and promote the welfare of the child
throughout his childhood.'

On this basis it would seem that, subject to express directions
from the court, the local authority can make arrangements

---

1. See e.g. *Re Y* (*a minor*) (*child in care: access*) [1976] Fam 125, [1975] 3 All ER
348, discussed post at p. 309. They ought to inform the court of any major
decisions and must notify a change of address.

for the boarding out of the ward to foster parents or even to return the ward to the parents. On the basis of FvS^2, however, it would seem that placing a ward with a view to adoption would require the court's leave.

II Orders that can be made

A. CONTINUING OR ENDING THE WARDSHIP

Barring lapse or termination upon the ward attaining his majority, a child only ceases to be a ward by a court order and by section 9(3) of the Law Reform (Miscellaneous Provisions) Act 1949 such orders can be made either upon application or by the court acting upon its own motion. Although applications to deward can be made at any time, a distinction should be made between applications made at the initial hearing and those made subsequently. It will be appreciated that in all cases, barring emergencies[3], the child will already be a ward at the time of the hearing simply by virtue of the application having been made under the 1949 Act. The task of the court, therefore, even at the initial hearing is to decide whether the wardship should be continued, but whereas at the initial hearing arguments as to the court's jurisdiction to make the order may be raised, once the wardship has been confirmed applications to deward will be judged solely according to the ward's interests.

i) *At the initial hearing*

There are a number of reasons why at the first hearing the court may decide not to make the wardship order but broadly speaking the cases can be divided between those which are dismissed as a matter of law and those where on the facts the continued control by the court is thought to be inappropriate. In the former category the wardship application may be dismissed in limine without a full investigation into the merits of the case, whereas in the latter the issue being one of fact, the application will only be dismissed in the light of the interests of the child after a full investigation into the merits.

2. [1973] Fam 203, [1973] 1 All ER 722.
3. See e.g. *Re N (infants)* [1967] Ch 512, [1967] 1 All ER 161. Discussed ante at p. 57.

Examples of applications being dismissed as a matter of law are as follows:

(a) where it has been held that the court has no jurisdiction to hear the case at all as, for example, where the child belongs to the household of a parent entitled to diplomatic immunity[4] or where an alien child has been refused entry into the country by immigration officials[5]. In these cases the application will be dismissed or even struck out[6] with no regard to the child's interests or to the merits of the case.

(b) where though the court might have had jurisdiction it has been held on the facts that other interests outweigh the child's. The best example is *Re X (a minor)*[7] where the court dismissed an application to make the child a ward in order to restrain the publication of a book on the grounds that its contents were harmful to the child because it was held that the interests of freedom of speech outweighed those of the child.

(c) where the court has undoubtedly the power to exercise its jurisdiction but declines to exercise its discretion to do so. A number of cases fall into this category but generally it arises where the wardship application has been made to challenge a decision already taken by another court or body as, for example, in the so-called 'kidnapping cases' where a foreign court is already seized of the jurisdiction[8], or where under statute a care order has been made or parental rights are vested in a local authority[9], or where a custody order or an adoption order has already been made by another court.

Once it has been decided that as a matter of law the wardship jurisdiction can be exercised, the issue of whether to continue the wardship becomes one of fact in which the court will be guided by the child's welfare. In such cases there will normally be a full investigation into the merits of the

4. *Re C (an infant)* [1959] Ch 363, [1958] 2 All ER 656. Discussed in Ch. 2.
5. *Re Mohamed Arif (an infant)*, *Re Nirbhai Singh (an infant)* [1968] Ch 643. Discussed in Ch. 2.
6. The summons was struck out in *Re Mohamed Arif*.
7. [1975] Fam 47 [1975] 1 All ER 697. Discussed post p. 110 et seq.
8. Discussed in Ch. 12.
9. Discussed in Ch. 10.

case. The exception to this is the rare case of an application being held frivolous as in *Re Dunhill*[10] in which event, there being no merits to investigate, the application will be dismissed in limine.

Although the court will not hesitate to order a child to cease to be a ward where the continuation of the wardship would serve no useful purpose, it has also been said[11] that so long as there is a need for control by the court it is a mistake to discontinue the wardship. Thus in *Baldrian v Baldrian*[12] it was held to be wrong to deward the two children and grant instead custody to the mother with a supervision order. It was held that the proper order was to continue the wardship and grant the mother care and control.

An example of where it might be thought to be inappropriate to continue the wardship is where an application has been made to prevent one parent taking the child out of the jurisdiction but at the time of the hearing the court is satisfied, perhaps upon the strength of an undertaking, that there is no longer a serious threat of removal. Alternatively the court might think it right that the child should leave the jurisdiction in which case a common order is to grant care and control to the defendant with liberty to take the child out of the country and ordering that upon removal from England or arrival at a designated country the child should cease to be a ward[13]. Another example is where an applicant seeks via wardship a mandatory order for the child's return to him. If the application for care and control is dismissed, the court might think it appropriate to end the wardship and grant custody to the defendant.

There is no compulsion on the court to end the wardship even in the foregoing examples[14] and indeed it is unlikely to do so where there remains a serious possibility of further dispute. Although the court can end the wardship of its own volition, the normal course where the child remains in the jurisdiction is to continue the wardship. A party wishing the child to be freed from court control is therefore well advised specifically to seek the termination of the wardship.

10. *Re Dunhill (an infant)* (1967) 111 Sol Jo 113. Discussed ante p. 36.
11. Per Buckley LJ in *Baldrian v Baldrian* (1974) 4 Fam Law 12 at 13.
12. (1974) 4 Fam Law 95.
13. See e.g. *Re H (infants)* [1966] 1 All ER 886 [1966] 1 WLR 381 and *Re L (minors)* [1974] 1 All ER 913, [1974] 1 WLR 250.
14. See e.g. *Re D* Court of Appeal (Civil Division) Transcript No. 12 of 1977.

ii) *Subsequent hearings*

Applications to deward can still be made after the initial confirmation of the wardship. In deciding whether to discharge the order the court will have regard to the ward's welfare in the light of the circumstances prevailing at the subsequent hearing. Clearly applications should only be made where circumstances have changed. The court, however, is unlikely to oppose the discharge where both parties have applied for it pursuant to an agreement between them. In *Re an infant*[15] for instance, the parents of a three year old ward had come to an arrangement and both desired that the child be dewarded so that each could separately take the child abroad for holidays. The court could see no reason to oppose the application. In such cases the court will have regard to the parties' undertakings and another and highly relevant factor will be the prospects of future co-operation between the parties in respect of the child.

B. DECIDING WHO SHOULD BRING UP THE WARD AND RELATED ORDERS

The decision to continue the wardship will mean that the child remains subject to the court's control with all the consequences that have been previously described, but in addition the court can make a whole range of orders. Of these clearly the most important relates to who should look after the child. In theory since custody of the ward vests in the court, the issue of who should bring him up should always be disposed of by the court. In practice, however unless special circumstances are brought to its notice, the court is only likely to make an express order where one is specifically sought[16]. Hence in the so-called 'teenage wardships' where the parents act in unison in making their child a ward in order to restrain an alleged undesirable relationship, the court will not interfere in other matters. Again in *Re D (a minor)*[17] where application was made to prevent the ward

---

15. (1962) Times, May 26. See also *Re S (infants)* (1964) Times, August 6.
16. If no order is made the wardship application does not affect the position as to care and control.
17. *Re D (a minor) (wardship: sterilisation)* [1976] Fam 185, [1976] 1 All ER 326. The issue of care and control was originally raised but not pursued. See p. 192 F–G.

being sterilised, the court was solely concerned with whether the operation should be restrained. On the other hand, once the issue of who should look after the ward has been raised, then it is submitted that the court must make an order dealing with the matter.

In resolving the issue of who should bring up the ward the court must treat the ward's welfare as the first and paramount consideration pursuant to section 1 of the Guardianship of Minors Act 1971. The ward's welfare will also dictate the type of order that the court will make. There are a number of options; for example, the court can grant care and control with or without a supervision order, it can commit the ward to the care of a local authority or alternatively it can deward the child and grant custody. Apart from the power to commit the ward to the care of a local authority[18], the court is free to make any of the above orders in respect of a ward up to the age of 18. There is for instance, no comparable restriction to that, say, of New Zealand where statute[19] provides that:

> 'the court shall not direct any child of or over the age of sixteen years to live with any other person unless the circumstances are exceptional.'

i) *Care and control*

The normal order is to grant care and control to one of the parties and to continue the wardship. By this order the court maintains some control over its ward, since he remains subject to the court's directions, while the person granted care and control has the de facto care and possession of the ward.

If the court decides to make the more usual form of order it has the power to direct that care and control simpliciter be granted or it can make a more detailed order. It can, for example, give specific directions as to where the ward should reside and where he should be educated[20].

ii) *Joint orders*

To what extent there can be a variation of the above order is debatable. It may be, for instance, that both parties will accept

18. When the ward must be under the age of 17. See post p. 87, n.8.
19. Guardianship Act 1968, s.9(3).
20. See e.g. *Re H(GJ)* (*an infant*) [1966] 1 All ER 952, [1966] 1 WLR 706.

a compromise under which both will have a say in the child's future. Alternatively, the court might feel that some kind of joint order would be appropriate. Is there a form of joint care and control order comparable to the 'split orders' under the matrimonial jurisdiction?[1]

Clearly a joint care and control order is inappropriate because both parties cannot have de facto control at the same time if they are living apart. A possible alternative is to make no order at all but this seems to be an abdication of the court's function[2]. A further solution is to grant extensive rights of access. The solution adopted by Bagnall J in *Re D (minors)*[3] was to make a joint *custody* order directing that the proceedings be amended by entitling them in the matter of the Guardianship of Minors Act 1971. Presumably, though the report is silent on this, such an order meant that the children were dewarded since a custody order is inconsistent with the continuation of wardship. It is submitted that a possible form of joint order which *is* consistent with the continuation of wardship, is to grant care and control to one party but to specify exactly what rights the other should retain. This type of order is now provided for by the Domestic Proceedings and Magistrates' Courts Act 1978[4], but it remains to be seen whether it will be adopted in wardship cases, though it would seem to be clearly within the court's powers to do so.

iii) *Custody and custodianship*

Since control of a ward always resides in the court, it is inconsistent with the continuation of wardship to grant custody of the child. Accordingly, custody can only be granted if the child is dewarded, but even then the view

---

1. In proceedings under the Matrimonial Causes Act 1973 the form of the 'split' order now is to grant joint custody with care and control to one party. See e.g. *Rayden on Divorce* (13th Edn.), p. 1043 and Bromley: *Family Law* (5th Edn.) 315 and 321, and Lowe: 'Joint Custody and Maintenance Order' (1977) 127 NLJ 184. Cf. the new type of 'split' order introduced by the Domestic Proceedings and Magistrates' Courts Act 1978 referred to below.
2. Cf. *Re M (infants)* [1967] 3 All ER 1071 [1967] 1 WLR 1479 where no order as to custody was made at all but where the mother was granted care and control.
3. [1973] Fam 179 at 197 per Bagnall J.
4. Ss. 8(4) and 37.

generally taken seems to be that a custody order can only be made provided an application has been made under the Guardianship of Minors Acts 1971 and 1973. Indeed it is common practice to couple an application under the 1949 Act with one under the 1971 and 1973 Acts. The basis of this practice is presumably that once the court dewards the child, it has no further jurisdiction in the matter at least under the 1949 Act. The validity of this view has never seriously been challenged, but while it is a perfectly tenable one, it is arguable that the court still retains its inherent jurisdiction[5] over the child despite the dewarding and does therefore retain some powers including, possibly, that of granting custody.

Custodianship, it is submitted, will be similarly inconsistent with the continuation of wardship and like custody could only be granted if the child has been dewarded first. It is submitted that it will be imperative for an application to have been made under Part II of the Children Act 1975[6] as well as the 1949 Act before the order could be granted, there being no scope for arguing that it lies within the court's inherent jurisdiction to grant custodianship, since it is clearly a statutory creation.

iv) *Committal to the care of a local authority*[7]

a) Power
The power to commit a ward under the age of 17[8] to the care of a local authority is conferred by section 7(2) of the Family Law Reform Act 1969 which inter alia provides:

'Where it appears to the court that there are exceptional circumstances making it impracticable or undesirable for a ward of court to be, or to continue to be, under the care of either of his parents or of any other individual the court may, if it thinks fit, make an order committing the care of the ward to a local authority.'[9]

5. Following *Re N (infants)* [1967] Ch 512, [1967] 1 All ER 161 cf. *Re E (an infant)* [1956] Ch 23, [1955] 3 All ER 174. Discussed in Ch. 1.
6. At least so far as non parents are concerned.
7. For the use of this power see Chap. 11.
8. Matrimonial Causes Act 1973, s.43(4) which applies to orders made under the 1969 Act by reason of s.7(2) as amended by the Matrimonial Causes Act 1973, Sch. 2 para. 8(a).
9. The local authority means one of the authorities referred to by s.43(1) of the Matrimonial Causes Act 1973.

It seems clear from this provision (which is phrased in similar terms to a number of other statutes[10]) that the power to make a care order is one which should be exercised only as a last resort when all other options have been exhausted. There is, however, no statutory guidance as to precisely when such an order should be made and in particular there is no definition of what is meant by 'exceptional circumstances'. In the absence of such guidance Professor Bevan has suggested[11] in relation to the similar power exercisable in custody proceedings following a divorce etc. that the court 'ought to be guided, though not bound' by the same considerations as would lead a local authority to act under section 1 of the Children Act 1948. While this suggestion might be useful as a possible starting point, it cannot be regarded as being more than that. It is clear that the court is not bound in any way by the restrictions of the 1948 Act so that the words 'exceptional circumstances' cannot be defined by reference to that Act. In any event it may be pointed out that even if circumstances exist which satisfy section 1 of the 1948 Act, it may not necessarily mean that the requirements of section 7(2) of the 1969 Act are satisfied. Section 1 is exclusively concerned with the ability of the parents or guardians to look after their children, whereas section 7(2) requires the court to be satisfied that 'it is impracticable or undesirable for the ward to be or to continue to be under the care of either of his parents or *of any other individual*'. In other words the court is required to consider whether persons other than the ward's parents or guardians should have his care and control[12].

At the end of the day it must be accepted that Parliament has conferred on the court a wide discretion which cannot be closely defined other than to say that it must be exercised within the confines of treating the ward's welfare as the first and paramount consideration pursuant to section 1 of the Guardianship of Minors Act 1971. The words 'exceptional circumstances' should, it is submitted, be taken as indicating

10. See e.g. Matrimonial Causes Act 1973, s.43(1); Domestic Proceedings and Magistrates' Court Act 1978, s.10; Guardianship Act 1973, s.2(2)(b); Children Act 1975, ss. 17 and 34(4). Presumably each provision is intended to have the same effect.
11. *The Law Relating to Children* (1973 Butterworths) p. 155.
12. Although admittedly, if no suggestion is made that any other person should look after the child, the requirement is likely to be held satisfied. See *F v F* [1959] 3 All ER 180 at 181D.

nothing more than that the power to commit a ward into care should be exercised sparingly. As Scarman J said in *G v G*[13]: 'It was the intention of the statute that children were to remain with their parents if it was at all possible'. Though as the same judge so poignantly said 'what had to be looked at was not what was ideal but what was best in the circumstances'.

To determine what is best in the circumstances, the court is required, as *G v G* makes clear, to look at the 'totality of the circumstances'. In making this examination the court will have regard both to the personal fitness of each party to look after the ward and to the parties' ability in all the circumstances to have care and control of the ward. In *F v F*[14] for instance, a care order was made because, while the father was not a fit and proper person to have custody, the mother though perfectly fit to have custody, was living in circumstances which made it impossible for the child to live with her.

b) Effect of an order

Once a ward is committed to care section 7(2) provides that:

> 'Part II of the Children Act 1948 (which relates to the treatment of children in the care of the local authority) shall, subject to the next following subsection apply as if the child had been received by the local authority into their care under section 1 of that Act.'

By section 7(3)[15] it is provided that the provisions of section 43(2)–(6) of the Matrimonial Causes Act 1973 shall apply to the making of an order under section 7(2). The effect of the provisions is as follows.

By section 43(3), provided the order remains in force, the ward continues in the local authority's care 'notwithstanding any claim by a parent or other person'. In other words if a parent wishes to have the care order terminated he should apply in wardship proceedings to have the order discharged[16].

---

13. (1962) 106 Sol Jo 858—a case under s.2(1)(e) of the 1960 Matrimonial Proceedings (Magistrates' Courts) Act 1960.
14. [1959] 3 All ER 180—a case concerned with custody following a divorce. See also *Re Y (a minor) (child in care: access)* [1976] Fam 125, [1975] 3 All ER 348. The mother had abandoned the child and the father was unable to provide the child with a home.
15. As amended by the Matrimonial Causes Act 1973, Sch. 2 para. 8(a).
16. Under s.7(5) of the Family Law Reform Act 1969.

Although an order made under section 7(2)[17] has a similar effect to a section 2 resolution under the 1948 Act in so far as the parent cannot require the child to be returned, the order cannot be regarded as its equivalent in that the local authority will not be vested with 'parental rights and duties' with respect to the ward[18]. By section 43(6) any parent or guardian of the ward committed to care is under a duty to ensure that the local authority are informed of his address for the time being. If such a person knowingly fails to do so he is liable on summary conviction to a fine not exceeding ten pounds.

With regard to the treatment of the child whilst in care, although section 7(2) of the 1969 Act states that Part II of the Children Act 1948 shall apply, it does so subject to the proviso under section 43(5) of the 1973 Act which states:

'(a) the exercise by the local authority of their powers under sections 12[19] to 14 of that Act (which among other things relate to the accommodation and welfare of a child in the care of a local authority) shall be subject to any directions given by the court;
and
(b) section 17 of that Act (which relates to arrangements for the emigration of such a child) shall not apply.'

An issue, which has now been resolved, was whether section 43(5)(a) empowered a judge to make specific directions as to access when committing a ward to the care of a local authority. It was held in *Re Y (a minor)*[20] that it did. At first instance, Arnold J held that local authorities do not have the power to control access under sections 12–14 of the 1948 Act, and hence a judge in wardship proceedings was entitled to 'fill the gap'. On appeal Ormrod LJ rejected this reasoning holding that the local authorities did have power by virtue of sections 12–14 to control access even in respect of a child in care under section 1, but that where a child had been committed to care by the court, such powers were subject to the court's control. Although this reasoning has not escaped criticisms[1], it seems difficult to argue with Ormrod LJ's

---

17. I.e. committing a ward to care under s.7(2) is different to a child in care under the Children Act 1948 s.1, because a parent has no right to require child's return. See post p. 276.
18. See Bevan op. cit. at p. 115.
19. As substituted by the Children Act 1975 s.59.
20. [1976] Fam 125, [1975] 3 All ER 348.
 1. See Freeman (1976) 6 Fam Law 136.

conclusion that local authorities' powers under section 13(2) of the 1948 Act[2] include the power to grant access and there seems little doubt that when the High Court commits a child to an authority's care it has power to give specific directions about access[3].

Although section 43(5)(a) reserves the court's right to make specific directions, it must be remembered that as the child will remain a ward of court he will still be under the overall control of the court. This will mean that at the very least the court will need to be informed of any important decisions relating to the child[4] and in certain cases the court's *prior* consent will be required[5]. In cases of doubt an authority should always seek directions from the court[6].

Any order made under section 7(2) can upon application of any interested party including the local authority[6], subsequently be discharged or varied by a judge in wardship proceedings[7], but in any event the order will cease to have effect once the ward becomes 18[8].

c) Procedure
An application for an order to commit a ward to the care of a local authority must normally be made to a judge[9].

An application may be made by any party to the wardship proceedings including a local authority. In any event before an order is made committing the ward to care the registrar will fix a date, time and place for the hearing of any

2. S.13(2) provides that: 'a local authority may allow a child in their care either for a fixed period or until the local authority otherwise determine to be under the charge and control of a parent, guardian, relative or friend'.
3. S.43(5)(a) seems conclusive.
4. Discussed ante p. 73 et seq.
5. For example to institute adoption proceedings; see *F v S (adoption: ward)* [1973] Fam 203, [1973] 1 All ER 722. Arguably this includes placing the child for adoption. See ante p. 81. It is because of the court's continued control that local authorities should be wary of warding a child, already in their care. See Chap. 11.
6. In cases of urgency, or where the application is likely to be unopposed, directions may be sought by letter addressed to the court, though where practical, notice should also be served on any interested party. RSC Ord. 90, r.11, MCR 1977, r.93(4).
7. Family Law Reform Act 1969, s.7(5).
8. Matrimonial Causes Act 1973, s.43(4).
9. RSC Ord. 90, r.11(1); MCR 1977, r.92(1). However a registrar may in practice make an order at the behest of a local authority where the ward is already in care at least where the order is agreed between the parties and possibly where it is unopposed—see post p. 117.

representations by the local authority and will send a notice in form 18[10] to the authority not less than 14 days before the date so fixed[11]. If the local authority wish to represent that, in the event of an order being made the court should make financial provision for the child, the authority must within seven days after the receipt of the notice file an affidavit setting out such facts as are known to the authority relevant to the property and income of the person against whom the order is sought[12]. At the same time the authority must serve a copy of the affidavit on that person[12], who in turn may within four days after service, file an affidavit in answer a copy of which must be served on the local authority[13].

In such cases they may be represented by their director of social services or other officer employed by them for the purposes of their social services functions under the Local Authority Social Services Act 1970[14]. In difficult cases or where the local authority is a party they should be legally represented.

v) *Supervision orders*

a) **Power**

The power to place a ward under the supervision of an independent person is conferred on the court by section 7(4) of the Family Law Reform Act 1969, which provides inter alia as follows:

> 'Where it appears to the court that there are exceptional circumstances making it desirable that a ward of court (not being a ward who in pursuance of an order under subsection 2 of this section is in the care of a local authority) should be under the supervision of an independent person, the court may, as respects such period as the court thinks fit order that the ward be under the supervision of a welfare officer or of a local authority; . . .'

It will be noted that no order can be made if the ward has been committed to care under section 7(2).

---

10. See Appendix.
11. RSC Ord. 90, r.11(2); MCR 1977 r.93(1).
12. MCR 1977, r.93(2).
13. MCR 1977, r.93(3).
14. MCR 1977, r.93(5).

Section 7(4) is worded in a similar way to section 7(2) in that there must be 'exceptional circumstances' before the order can be made, but it will be noticed that under this section all the court must be satisfied about is that a supervision order is desirable for the ward[15]. The effect of this provision would appear to be that while the court will not lightly make a supervision order, the circumstances do not have to be so extreme as to justify committing a child to care. One example illustrating this point is the order made in *Re C (minors)*[16]. In that case, following their mother's death, the children who had been living in California together with their stepfather were brought to England by their father in defiance of a Californian court order. It was held in all the circumstances that the father should be granted care and control but under the supervision of Hampshire County Council for two years. Although the order was possibly influenced by the fact that the father and his young wife had become Jehovah's Witnesses[17], Ormrod LJ said it was made[18]:

> 'not because the court has any desire (as it were) to look over the shoulders of the father and stepmother, but rather that there should be some experienced person readily available to whom they can turn for advice if and when they need it.'

Another case widely reported in the press[19] concerned a child born as a result of artificial insemination. The extraordinary feature of the case was that a couple paid the mother to have the baby in this way, the plan being that they should bring him up as their own. In the event the mother reneged on the agreement. The court granted her care and control but made a supervision order because of her personal circumstances.

If the court decides to make a supervision order it has a discretion to place the ward under the supervision of a

15. Whereas before a child can be committed to care under s.7(2) the court must be satisfied that it is either *impracticable* or *undesirable* for either parent or any other individual to have or continue to have care of the ward.
16. *Re C (minors) (wardship: jurisdiction)* [1978] Fam 105, [1978] 2 All ER 230. Discussed in more detail in Chap. 12.
17. It will be noted that the father was required to give an undertaking that he would not permit the wards to take part in house-to-house visiting in connection with his work as a Jehovah's Witness.
18. Ibid. at p. 120.
19. See *Re C (a minor)* [1978] LS Gaz R 711 and reports in e.g. the *Daily Mail* and the *Daily Telegraph* 21 June 1978.

welfare officer or a local authority. In the former case, in practice more appropriate for older children, the person appointed will be a probation officer appointed for, or assigned to, the petty sessional division in which the ward for the time resides. He will be selected in the same manner as a probation officer who is to be responsible for the supervision of a probationer. A particular officer will then be allocated to the case by local arrangements[20]. In the latter case the appropriate officer is the director of social services[1].

The court has a discretion to determine the duration of the supervision order[2], but in any event application may have to be made to have the order varied or discharged[3]. The supervising officer can apply in the same way as any other interested party both for a variation or for directions, though as in the case of committals to care, in matters of urgency or where the application is likely to be unopposed, application may be made by letter to the court[4].

Where a supervision order is made, any person or persons having care and control of the ward must inform the supervising officer of any change of address. If the child is moved into an area of another local authority, the supervising authority might consider that a transfer of supervision is desirable, in which case they will send written particulars of the new address and reasons why a variation is sought both to the new authority and to the registrar. The court will then consider whether to vary the order[5].

b) The use of a supervision order in wardship
While not seeking to deny the general usefulness of a supervision order, it may be questioned why it should be resorted to in wardship cases, since it is one of the features of the jurisdiction that the court maintains control over its wards even after the hearing. A case in point is *Baldrian v Baldrian*[6]. Following the parties' separation the mother made her two children wards of court to prevent her Austrian husband

---

20. S.7(4) as amended by the Matrimonial Causes Act 1973 Sch. 2, para. 8(*b*) and s.44(2) of the 1973 Act, and see *Rayden on Divorce* (13th Edn. 1979) p. 1046.
 1. MCR 1977 r.93(5). Local Authority Social Services Act 1970, s.6.
 2. S.7(4).
 3. S.7(5).
 4. MCR 1977 r.93(4). In which case the officer should where practicable notify any interested party of the intention to make the application.
 5. See *Rayden* op. cit. at p. 1046.
 6. (1974) 4 Fam Law 12.

from taking them out of the jurisdiction. At first instance the judge gave custody of both children to the mother, made a supervision order and ordered that the two children be dewarded. On appeal it was held that technically the form of the order was wrong. As Davies LJ said:

'The proper form would have been to continue the wardship, give care and control to the mother and not make a supervision order, as wards of court would be supervised.'

It may further be pointed out that it is within the court's inherent power to direct that some specified person, such as a court welfare officer, assist in the arrangements of say an access order[7] and/or to make a further report on the child's situation at some specified later date[8].

The foregoing situations are illustrative of a need for continued active control by the court, but where there is no need to resort to a supervision order. The common feature of the examples is that supervision was not required on a day-to-day basis. Were this to be the case then it is submitted a supervision order should be made so that advantage can be taken of the existing procedure common to all child jurisdictions and of the experience and expertise of supervising officers.

vi) *Access*

Like any other jurisdiction dealing with children there is power in wardship proceedings to make access orders. The court also has the power to grant access to a child living abroad[9]. The court can grant access not only to parents but

7. As was done in *Re K (infants)*. Court of Appeal (Civil Division) Transcript No. 84 of 1976.
8. As was done in *Re L (minor)*. Court of Appeal (Civil Division) Transcript No. 425B of 1976.
9. This was done e.g. in *Smiths' (formerly Bulmer) v Bulmer*. Court of Appeal (Civil Division) Transcript No. 234 of 1977. In *Re S (infants)* (1964) Times, August 6, the court accepted an undertaking by the mother to give the father access in the United States of America. The court has a similar power to grant access abroad under the Guardianship of Minors Act 1971; see *Re F (a minor) (access out of jurisdiction)* [1973] Fam 198, [1973] 2 All ER, not following *Re E (an infant)* [1956] Ch 23, [1955] 3 All ER 174. Cf. *Re D* Court of Appeal (Civil Division) Transcript No. 12 of 1977 where despite ordering that the mother should have care and control of the children and be allowed to take them to the USA, it was held that the wardship should be kept in being so that 'the safeguard of the English court would be available, if access could be organised for this family in England in the future'.

also to any other party to the proceedings. In *Re K*[10], for example, access was arranged both for the father and the paternal grandparents.

In deciding whether and to whom access should be granted, the court should be guided by the child's welfare[11]. Since it is usually regarded as being for the child's welfare to maintain contact with both parents, access will normally be granted at least to a parent, unless it can be shown to be harmful to the child[12]. To assist the court in its decision, regard will be had to the report and recommendations of the Official Solicitor[13] if appointed, or to the report of a welfare officer[14]. Indeed either officer may be called upon to help in making the necessary arrangements for access[15].

In absence of dispute the amount of access should be left to the parties to work out. Initially, therefore access is left open ended, the normal order being that 'reasonable access' be granted to the relevant party. Where the parties cannot agree the court has ample powers to make more detailed orders. The court can stipulate the exact time and place and duration of the access[16]. Access can also be supervised[17], though this will not normally be undertaken by the Official Solicitor[18]. In *Re*

10. Court of Appeal (Civil Division) Transcript No. 84 of 1976. Applications for access can now be made by grandparents under the Domestic Proceedings and Magistrates' Court Act 1978, ss. 14 40 and 64. Discussed in Ch. 10.

11. I.e. s.1 of the Guardianship of Minors Act 1971 applies. See also *M v M (child:access)* [1973] 2 All ER 81 per Wrangham J at p. 85F: per Latey J at p. 88A. Discussed in Ch. 11.

12. For a case where access was refused see *Re D A (infants)*, Court of Appeal (Civil Division) Transcript No. 171 of 1976. Access was also refused in *Re B*, Court of Appeal (Civil Division) Transcript No. 237 of 1976 but the original order that no further application could be made by the father without the court's leave was varied so that no application could be made for 12 months. Cf *Re R(PM) (an infant)* [1968] 1 All ER 691n.

13. See post Ch. 8.

14. See post Ch. 9. The welfare officer may be appointed specifically to report on the access problem.

15. See e.g. *Re R(PM) (an infant)* [1968] 1 All ER 691n and *Re K* Court of Appeal (Civil Division) Transcript No. 84 of 1976.

16. See e.g. *Smith (formerly Bulmer) v Bulmer*, Court of Appeal (Civil Division) Transcript No. 234 of 1977 where staying access in Canada was granted over every other Christmas with seven days' access in England in the alternate year and for three weeks in the summer in Canada every other year.

17. See e.g. the original order made in *Re B*, Court of Appeal (Civil Division) Transcript No. 237 of 1976 where access took place on neutral ground in the presence of both parents and the supervising officer.

18. See N Turner (1977) 2 *Adoption and Fostering* at p. 34. Discussed further in Chap. 8.

R(PM) (*an infant*)[19], however, it was provided inter alia during interim proceedings that if the parties could not agree, access would be at such times as the Official Solicitor directed. *Re R(PM)* also illustrates the point that the court can regulate communication with the ward. Hence in that case it was ordered that each parent could write to the ward one letter a week in addition to birthday cards and presents, and that there should be no communication either by letter or telephone between the parents and the couple who had been granted care and control of the ward.

It should be added that like an access order made under any other jurisdiction, it is never final and applications can be made to vary it[20].

vii) *Maintenance*

a) **General power**

Prior to the Family Law Reform Act 1969 it was thought[1] doubtful whether in wardship proceedings the Chancery Court enjoyed the power of the Divorce Court to make maintenance orders in favour of children. To overcome this doubt the practice had grown up of coupling with the wardship application, an application under the Guardianship of Infants Acts which practice involved some extra expense and work. The Latey Committee endorsed the suggestion that to obviate needless expense and work it should be statutorily declared that the court does have the power to make maintenance orders in favour of wards. This power is now conferred on the court by section 6 of the Family Law Reform Act 1969.

By section 6(2) the court may make an order requiring either parent of a ward to pay to the other parent[2] or requiring either or both parents of a ward to pay to any other person having care and control of the ward[3] such weekly or other periodical sums towards the maintenance and education of

19. [1968] 1 All ER 691n. Discussed further in Chap. 8.
20. The court will not vary the order so as to terminate access without hearing from both parties. See *Re W G* Court of Appeal (Civil Division) Transcript No. 951 of 1976 reported in 1978 LAG Bulletin at p. 162.
  1. See the comments of the Latey Committee: The Report of the Committee on the Age of Majority 1967. Cmnd. 3342, para. 250.
  2. S.6(2)(*a*).
  3. S.6(2)(*b*).

the ward as the court thinks reasonable having regard to the means of the person or persons on whom the requirement is imposed. It is to be noted that under this provision the sum is not payable to the ward personally. Where care and control is vested in one of the parents[4] then it is provided by section 6(5) that no order can be made nor liability under any order accrue where the parents reside together[5] and where after such an order has been made they reside together for a period of three months[6] that order ceases to have effect.

b) Former wards who have not attained the age of 21

Although a child ceases to be a ward once he attains the age of 18, section 6(3) makes it clear that the court may make any sum payable until the person attains the age of 21. Further once the child reaches 18 the order may be made payable to the former ward personally. In addition to this power section 6(4) provides:

> 'Subject to the provisions of this section, where a person who has ceased to be a minor but has not attained the age of twenty-one has at any time been the subject of an order making him a ward of court, the court may, on the application of either parent of that person or of that person himself, make an order requiring either parent to pay to the other parent, to anyone else for the benefit of that person or to that person himself, in respect of any period not extending beyond the date when he attains the said age, such weekly or other periodical sums towards his maintenance or education as the court thinks reasonable having regard to the means of the person on whom the requirement is imposed.'

---

4. I.e. s.6(5) does not apply where the child is in the care and control of a third person to whom the maintenance order is made payable.
5. There is no definition of 'residing together' but presumably it will be taken to mean 'living together in the same household' following *Naylor v Naylor* [1962] P 253, [1961] 2 All ER 129. Query whether 'residing together for a period of three months' refers to a continuous period of three months or a number of periods amounting to three months in all.
6. It is worth noting that by s.25 of the Domestic Proceedings and Magistrates' Courts Act 1978 magistrates are empowered to make a maintenance order where the parties are living together. The order only ceases to have effect where they have lived together for a continuous period exceeding *six* months. It might be thought that the provisions of s.6(5) of the 1969 Act should be brought into line with these provisions.

The object of this provision is to allow an application to be made for a maintenance order in respect of a former ward who has not yet attained the age of 21. Section 6(4) cannot, however, be said to be a model of draughtsmanship and the following points call for comment:

(1) For the section to apply the person in whose favour the maintenance order is sought must be over 18 but under 21 and must have at some time have been the subject of an order making him a ward. Presumably the latter requirement refers to an order either by a judge or a registrar continuing the wardship. It would surely be insufficient that the child had at some point become a ward by reason of the issuing of an originating summons[7], since in such cases it cannot be said that the child has been the subject of any *order* making him a ward.

(2) It will be noted that the applicants may be either parent or the former ward himself but not any third party. Hence, for example, the person who formerly had care and control and with whom the former ward may still be living cannot apply.

(3) It is provided that 'either parent' can be required to pay maintenance, so that it would seem that an order cannot be made against both parents[8] in favour of a third party or the former ward.

(4) Payment can be ordered to be made either to the other parent, to the former ward himself or to anyone else for the benefit of the former ward. It will be noted that where payment is ordered to be paid to a third party for the benefit of a former ward, it is not expressed to be limited to the person formerly having care and control[9].

(5) It would appear that section 6(4) is subject to section 6(5), so that if the former ward's parents are residing together, no order can be made, and if any order has been made it will cease to have effect once the parents have resided

7. It will be recalled that a child immediately becomes a ward upon the issuing of the summons pursuant to s.9(2) of the Law Reform (Miscellaneous Provisions) Act 1949. See ante p. 45.
8. Cf. s.6(2)(*b*) Presumably this result was unintentional.
9. Cf. s.6(2)(*b*). Of course as the former ward is no longer a minor no one can be said to have care and control of that person.

together for more than three months. It is surely an unnecessary and irrelevant embargo on an order being made to enable the former ward to continue his education, say at a university, that his parents reside together[10].

c) Illegitimate wards

It is provided by section 6(6) that:

> 'No order shall be made under this section requiring any person to pay any sum towards the maintenance or education of an illegitimate child *of that person.*' [Emphasis added.]

It is sometimes stated[11] that under this provision no order can be made if the ward is illegitimate. In fact section 6(6) is not so restrictive in that it only prohibits an order being made against either parent of an illegitimate child, but it does not prevent an order being made against a non-parent since the ward would not be the child of *that person*. Where, for example, a mother of an illegitimate child marries a man who is not the father, then in any subsequent wardship proceedings the court would have the power to order the husband to pay towards the maintenance of the ward.

Although the embargo on ordering a parent to pay maintenance in respect of his illegitimate child is in line with a similar prohibition in the Guardianship of Minors Act 1971[12] it does seem a major and unjustifiable gap in the court's powers. Perhaps an example will serve to highlight this defect. Suppose a man and woman live together and have a child, but subsequently the mother is killed. The father then marries and the wife treats the child as one of the family. Later the father deserts his wife and threatens to take the child out of the jurisdiction as a result of which the wife brings wardship proceedings. Even if care and control is granted to the wife she would be unable to obtain a maintenance order by reason of section 6(6). Yet if the facts were reversed, so that it was the mother who married a man who was not the father, she could obtain an order. The prohibition in the former example is even more startling since the wife could obtain a

---

10. This restriction is all the more serious since unless the parents are divorced (see *Downing v Downing (Downing intervening)* [1976] Fam 288 [1976] 3 All ER 474) there would appear to be no other means for the former ward to obtain an order.
11. See Bromley: *Family Law* (5th Edn. 1976) p. 592.
12. Under s.1 4(2).

maintenance order from a magistrates' court under the Domestic Proceedings and Magistrates' Courts Act 1978[13].

d) Variation discharge and enforcement

By reason of section 6(8) the court has the power to vary or discharge any previous order it has made under section 6 and presumably, though the section does not expressly say so, applications may be made by any of the interested parties.

Under section 6(7) any order under section 6 or any other corresponding enactment of the Parliament of Northern Ireland shall be included among the orders to which section 16 of the Maintenance Orders Act 1950 applies[14]. They are also included among the orders mentioned in the Reserve and Auxiliary Forces (Protection of Civil Interests) Act 1951.

viii) *Residence: removal from the jurisdiction*

It is possible for the court to circumscribe a care and control order by making specific directions as to the ward's residence. The court will normally only be concerned to do this where there is a danger of the ward being unlawfully removed from the jurisdiction[15].

As we have seen[16], one of the automatic consequences of warding a child is that he cannot lawfully be removed from the jurisdiction[17] without the court's prior consent[18]. Hence, whenever it is sought to take a ward out of the jurisdiction, even temporarily, the court's leave must first be obtained. At first[19] the court jealously guarded its power to keep its wards within the jurisdiction but this attitude has now been relaxed, the guiding principle now being the ward's welfare.

---

13. The child would by reason of s.88(1) be a 'child of the family'.
14. I.e. it can be enforced in any part of the United Kingdom.
15. See e.g. *Re H(GJ)* (*an infant*) [1966] 1 All ER 952, [1966] 1 WLR 706.
16. See ante p. 72.
17. I.e. out of England or Wales.
18. For the administrative procedure to prevent removal see Chap. 12. For a discussion of the contempt in removing the ward see Chap. 7. Where the ward has been unlawfully removed the court can make an order for the child's return. See e.g. *Re O* (*a minor*) (*wardship: adopted child*) [1978] 2 All ER 27, [1977] 3 WLR 732 and *Re O* (*infants*) [1962] 2 All ER 10, [1962] 1 WLR 724.
19. In *Mountstuart v Mountstuart* (1801) 6 Ves 363 Lord Eldon LC commented that the court should never allow a ward to leave the jurisdiction. See also *De Manneville v De Manneville* (1804) 10 Ves 52.

A distinction should be made between seeking permission for the ward's permanent removal and his temporary removal.

a) Permanent removal

Special leave is always required to remove a ward permanently from the jurisdiction. In deciding whether to give leave the principle applied is what is in the best interests of the ward. In *Re O* (*infants*)[20], for example, a wealthy Sudanese father sought permission to take his two children (a boy and a girl) who had been warded by his English wife, back to the Sudan. It was held that it was in the long term interests of the boy to be brought up in the Sudan where he might eventually succeed to his father's business, and accordingly care and control was granted to the father with permission to take him to the Sudan[1]. On the other hand it was thought to be in the long term interests of the daughter to remain in England with her mother and leave to take her to the Sudan was therefore refused.

Normally, in deciding whether to give leave the court will investigate the full merits of the case, but this is not inevitably so. It is established that provided it is in the child's interests to go, the decision to allow a person to take him out of the jurisdiction can be made on a summary basis[2]. Such a peremptory order is most likely to be made in the so-called 'kidnapping' cases[3], where following the unilateral removal of the child from the jurisdiction in which they had their home and the subsequent residence of the parties in England, the so-called innocent party asks the court for an order to be allowed to take the child back forthwith.

Where leave is granted to remove the child permanently,

20. [1962] 2 All ER 10, [1962] 1 WLR 724. See also *Re R* (*a minor*) (1974) 4 Fam Law 153.
 1. Whether the court correctly applied the welfare test in the boy's case is open to doubt. It seemed to dismiss lightly the so-called short term effects of the boy's removal and indeed the references to having regard to the wishes of the unimpeachable parent must now be regarded as dubious. See *S*(*BD*) *v S*(*DJ*) (*children: care and control*) [1977] Fam 109, [1977] 1 All ER 656 especially per Ormrod LJ at pp. 115–16. See also *Re K* (*minors*) (*children: care and control*) [1977] Fam 179, [1977] 1 All ER 647.
 2. Established by *Re L* (*minors*) (*wardship:jurisdiction*) [1974] 1 All ER 913, [1974] 1 WLR 250. Discussed at length in Chap. 12.
 3. Such orders are not exclusive to kidnapping cases. See *Re M-R* (*a minor*) (1975) 5 Fam Law 55. Discussed in Chap. 12.

the common form of order[4] is to deward the child after his removal from the jurisdiction, but this is not invariable. In *Re O (infants)*[5], for instance, the wardship was continued and the father was required to give an undertaking that he would bring him back to England should any further order require him to do so.

b) Temporary removal

Although in one sense leave will more readily be given to remove a ward temporarily, the court will obviously be concerned about the dangers of permanent removal. Hence in all cases the court must be satisfied that the applicant genuinely intends to return the child and will require a written undertaking to that effect[6]. Nevertheless, despite the obvious dangers of permanent removal, special leave does not now always have to be obtained. It is provided by a *Practice Direction*[7] that where the court is satisfied that the ward should be able to leave England and Wales for temporary visits abroad without the necessity for special leave, an order may be made giving general leave for such visits, subject to compliance with the condition that the party obtaining the order (who will normally be the party having care and control of the ward) must lodge at the Registry at which the matter is proceeding at least seven days before each proposed departure:

(a) a written consent in unqualified terms by the other party or parties to the ward's leaving England and Wales for the period proposed;

(b) a statement in writing giving the date on which it is proposed that the ward shall leave England and Wales the period of absence and the whereabouts of the minor during such absence;

4. See e.g. *Re H (infants)* [1966] 1 All ER 886, [1966] 1 WLR 381 and *Re L (minors)* [1974] 1 All ER 913, [1974] 1 WLR 250.
5. [1962] 2 All ER at 13.
6. In this respect Roxburgh J's statement in *Re E (an infant)* [1956] Ch 23, 25 26, [1955] 3 All ER 174, that 'it is well known that the court practically never allows any English infant to leave the jurisdiction without undertakings by some person that the child shall be returned within the jurisdiction' is still true. See also *Re A B (a minor)* Court of Appeal (Civil Division) Transcript No. 150 of 1977.
7. [1973] 2 All ER 512, [1973] 1 WLR 690.

(c) unless otherwise directed, a written undertaking by the applicant to return the ward to England and Wales at the end of the proposed period of absence.

On compliance with these requirements a certificate for production to the immigration authorities, stating that the conditions of the order have been complied with, may be obtained from the Registry.

Special leave, however, must be obtained where the parties are in dispute about the removal. In deciding whether to grant leave the court will bear in mind the child's welfare at least in the sense that the visit must not be harmful either to the child's health or to other aspects of his welfare. If the proposed visit would unduly interrupt his education for instance, then permission will be refused. Apart from factors relating to the child the chief concern will be about the genuineness of the party's intention to return the child. The court will require an undertaking to that effect, and in one case[8] the undertaking was buttressed by requiring the mother's solicitor to produce to the father's solicitor a return ticket. There is some authority for saying that permission will be more difficult to obtain where the other parent cannot afford to travel to the country in question in the event of a refusal to return[9].

ix) *Education*

Clearly the education of a child is an important aspect of his welfare, and evidence of the ward's schooling or proposed schooling can be extremely important in deciding who should have care and control.

The court does have power to make separate and specific directions about the ward's education, but this power has been held to be limited by the terms of the Education Act

8. *Re A B (a minor)* Court of Appeal (Civil Division) Transcript No. 150 of 1977.
9. *Re A B (a minor)* ibid. In practice this attitude will work against fathers. In *Re A B* the first instance judge was quoted as saying: 'As a rule one is a little apprehensive in these cases because it is so often the father who is anxious to take the child to visit grandparents or relatives . . . and if he gets the children there, there is virtually nothing which the court here can do to ensure the return of the children. But when it is the mother who is taking the children . . . providing the father can afford to pay for the journey, there is little difficulty if the mother breaks her undertaking to the court for the father to go out there and bring the children back . . .'.

1944. Hence in *Re B (infants)*[10] it was held that the court would not give directions about education at the behest of the local authority in a case where a mother was not causing her children to receive full time education, and repeatedly refused to comply with school attendance orders, at least[11] until the powers under that 1944 Act had been fully pursued[12].

x) *Religious upbringing*

Another facet of the ward's welfare is his religious upbringing and like education it can be a factor in deciding care and control.

The court is empowered to make specific directions about the ward's religious upbringing and will do so upon the basis of the ward's welfare. Hence a parent has no right to insist on the religious upbringing of a child in a particular way though such wishes will be taken into account. In *Re E (an infant)*[13], for example, having failed in their adoption application a non practising Jewish couple sought via wardship care and control of an illegitimate child whose mother was English Roman Catholic and whose father, who had disappeared, was of mixed Cuban and Chinese blood. The mother who sought to have the wardship discharged, opposed the couple on the grounds of religion. She did not want the child herself, but proposed that the child be eventually placed with a Catholic family with a view to adoption. It was held on the facts that the child, whom it was thought would be difficult to place, should remain with the applicants, but to accommodate the mother's wishes on religion, care and control was granted subject to an undertaking that the child would be brought up in the Catholic faith.

---

10. [1962] Ch 201 sub nom. *Re Baker (infants)* [1961] 3 All ER 276. The case is also discussed in Chap. 11.
11. Per Upjohn LJ ibid. at 218, 219.
12. Whether this decision can stand with subsequent cases (e.g. *Re B (a minor) (wardship: child in care)* [1975] Fam 36 per Case J at 44 and *Re Y (a minor) (child in care: access)* [1976] Fam 125 per Ormrod LJ at 138) which have held that the court can assist an authority in respect of their duties under the various Children and Children and Young Persons Acts (discussed fully in Chap. 11) is perhaps questionable.
13. [1963] 3 All ER 874, [1964] 1 WLR 51. See also *Re A (an infant)* [1955] 2 All ER 202. For other cases see *Rayden on Divorce* (13th Edn. 1979) p. 1132.

xi) *Property*

Historically, wardship was very much concerned with administering property on the ward's behalf. Indeed at one time it was thought that wardship was dependent on the existence of property belonging to the child[14]. The property aspects of wardship have now declined in importance[15], but it remains a useful jurisdiction both for administering the child's property or for resolving any disputes over it.

In so exercising its powers the court is expressly enjoined to treat the child's welfare as the first and paramount consideration[16].

xii) *Miscellaneous powers*

Apart from the orders already mentioned the court has wide powers to deal with any aspect of the ward's welfare. Hence it can supplement main orders by making directions on a whole range of matters. It can, for example, back up a care and control order by specifically restraining any party from molesting or communicating with the ward or custodian[17] or even from discovering the ward's whereabouts[18]. More unusually the court has been known to restrain a father from inserting an advertisement in a newspaper asking people to write complaining about a school to which he did not want his daughter to be sent[19]. And in a recent case a court stipulated that a ward should be told nothing about the bizarre circumstances of his birth[20]. The court is also competent to make directions concerning the ward's surname or his medical treatment.

---

14. See Ch. 1.
15. Partly because of the growth of trustees' powers under the 1925 property legislation.
16. S.1 of the Guardianship of Minors Act 1971 specifically includes the administration of the minor's property as an issue in which the minor's welfare is the first and paramount consideration.
17. See e.g. *Re R(PM) (an infant)* [1968] 1 All ER 691, [1968] 1 WLR 385.
18. See *Re B (a minor) (wardship: child in care)* [1975] Fam 36, [1974] 3 All ER 915.
19. See the unreported decision referred to in *Re X (a minor)* [1975] Fam 47 at 55.
20. *Re C (a minor)* [1978] LS Gaz R 711. The case went on appeal on the question of access. Query whether the direction could be enforced.

C. ORDERS NOT RELATED TO WHO SHOULD BRING UP THE WARD

i) *Restraining the ward's marriage, personal relationships or other activities*

Not all wardship applicants are concerned to obtain care and control of the ward. For example, the jurisdiction may be invoked by united parents who wish to restrain their child's continued association or marriage to a third party. Formerly, particularly in the eighteenth and nineteenth centuries, wardship was frequently invoked for this purpose, the jurisdiction being used as a means of protecting wealthy wards' (particularly females) property, rank and fortune[1]. With changes both in the law and social values this use of wardship has inevitably declined and particularly since the reduction of the age of majority to 18[2] is not now frequently resorted to as a means of preventing a child's marriage even for moral reasons. Nevertheless the court is empowered to make restraining orders preventing a third party's continued association with the ward and such orders can be buttressed by orders not to communicate with or harbour the ward[3]. In practice the orders are made against the third party in question rather than against the ward so as to avoid the possibility of having to imprison the ward in the event of disobedience[4].

Applications, if they are made at all, are usually directed against an individual, but orders can be brought against a group or a sect. In *Iredell v Iredell*[5], for example, an injunction was granted restraining a group of persons who had attempted to induce the ward to become, against her father's wishes, a member of the Roman Catholic Church, from having any further communication with her.

Iredell shows that the court's powers are not limited to

---

1. See e.g. Eversley on *Domestic Relations* (6th Edn. 1951 Sweet & Maxwell) p. 601 et seq. See also the plethora of cases referred to in *Rayden on Divorce* (13th Edn.) p. 1129 et seq.
2. Following s.1 of the Family Law Reform Act 1969.
3. See e.g. *Re B(JA) (an infant)* [1965] Ch 1112, [1965] 2 All ER 168 and *Re F (otherwise A) (a minor) (publication of information)* [1977] Fam 58, [1976] 3 All ER 274, (First instance) [1977] 1 All ER 114 CA.
4. Though the ward could still be guilty of contempt by aiding and abetting a breach of the order. See Ch. 7.
5. (1885) 1 TLR 260 per Kay J. Injunctions might be appropriate today in connection with drugs or the more bizarre or fanatical quasi religious sects.

restraining the ward's personal relationships and theoretically wardship can be invoked to control any activity of the ward[6]. The limiting factor in all of these cases is that the court will be concerned to promote the child's welfare. Hence it will not simply rubber stamp the parents' views. Furthermore it is worth remembering that as with all court actions wardship has only a limited value, so that while it may prove useful where a ward is amenable to persuasion, it is unlikely to produce fruitful results if the child remains unrepentant.

ii) *Restraining or sanctioning the ward's medical treatment*

In so far as a parent or guardian is entitled to give or withhold consent to a minor's medical treatment it is clear that the court can in wardship overrule that decision[7]. In *Re D (a minor)*[8], for instance, the court refused to allow sterilisation of a ward although her mother had consented to it. On the other hand, wardship has been used to overcome parental refusal to consent to an operation as, for example when Jehovah's Witnesses refuse to allow their child to have a blood transfusion.

Whether the court can overrule the child's consent has yet to be decided. The Family Law Reform Act 1969 section 8(1) provides:

> 'The consent of a minor who has attained the age of sixteen years to any surgical, medical or dental treatment which, in the absence of consent, would constitute a trespass to his person, shall be as effective as it would be if he were of full age; *and where a minor has by virtue of this section given an effective consent to any treatment it shall not be necessary to obtain any consent for it from his parent or guardian'.*
> [Emphasis added.]

It might be argued that the effect of the section is to vest the power of consent to treatment *exclusively* in the minor and that since the court is in no better position than a parent it has no powers to intervene. It is submitted, however, that the section is better interpreted to mean that while it is not

6. Cf. controlling the activities of others. See post p. 109.
7. The law relating to the consent to medical treatment on a minor is far from certain. See e.g. P D G Skegg: 'Consent to Medical Procedures on Minors' (1973) 36 MLR 370 and 'A Justification for Medical Procedures Performed Without Consent' (1974) 90 LQR 512 and Bromley: *Family Law* (5th Edn.) p. 336–8.
8. *Re D (a minor) (wardship: sterilisation)* [1976] Fam 185.

essential to obtain parental consent in addition to the minor's, that does not exclude the power of the parent either to consent or withhold consent. On this basis it is submitted that the court can intervene even where the ward has given an otherwise effective consent.

In theory the court could intervene in respect of any treatment of the ward, but in practice it will rarely interfere with any medical decision. *Re D (a minor)*[9] establishes, however, that where the treatment is for non-therapeutic purposes the decision does not lie entirely within the doctor's clinical judgment. In other words in such cases the court might be prepared to intervene. Exactly what would be regarded as 'non-therapeutic' is a moot point, but as we have said before[10] it could arguably cover such diverse treatment as whooping cough vaccinations, circumcision, prescription of the contraceptive pill, donating organs to others or even the removal of a life-support system for a child who has no hope of recovery. It remains to be seen whether the court would interfere with medical decisions in relation to such treatment.

According to *Re D (a minor)*, in deciding whether or not to sanction treatment the court will act upon the principle that the welfare of the ward is of first and paramount importance[11]. Hence even if the treatment is for non-therapeutic purposes, the court might sanction it if it thinks that it is in the child's best interests. While the application of the welfare principle might be thought appropriate to such cases, it could lead to difficult problems. For example, if application was made to ward a child to prevent him donating a kidney to his sibling could the court ever say that it was in his best interests to do so where there is an obvious danger to his health in the donation?[12]

iii) *Restraining the activities of persons unconnected with the ward*

Wardship orders can certainly bind persons other than those who are concerned to bring up the child. Indeed orders can be

9. *Re D (a minor)* [1976] Fam 185 at 196D.
10. Ante at p. 77.
11. Ibid., at 194E. For a discussion of exactly when the paramountcy principle applies see Ch. 6.
12. It might be accepted that it is in his best interests to preserve the life of his sibling at the expense of possible harm to himself.

made against complete strangers. In *Re Harris* (*an infant*)[13], for example, an order was made restraining certain airlines from carrying or facilitating the carriage of a ward in any of their aircraft. The extent to which wardship can be used to restrict the activities of those unconnected with the ward must now be considered in the light of the leading decision in *Re X* (*a minor*)[14].

a) Re X (a minor)

The stepfather of a girl aged 14 applied for an order that she be made a ward of court and that an injunction be granted restraining the publication of a certain book. The book in question contained in its first chapter details about the ward's dead father's alleged sexual predilections and behaviour. The applicant contended that as his daughter was psychologically fragile and highly strung were she to read the book or hear from others about the passages detailing her father's behaviour (variously described as being utterly depraved, bizarre and salacious and scandalous) it would be psychologically grossly damaging to her.

At first instance Latey J had no doubt that he did have the power to grant the injunction since the court's powers being derived from the Crown as parens patriae were not limited by statute and existed 'to protect the young against injury of whatever kind or from whatever source'[15]. The more difficult question was whether in the circumstances he should exercise his jurisdiction. In deciding this Latey J thought that the following requirements had to be satisfied, namely that: (1) the object of the application is genuinely to protect the child[16]; (2) there is no overriding public interest the other way; (3) there is a likelihood of substantial injury to the child if the publication or its contents came to the child's notice and (4) there is a real danger of the contents coming to the child's notice. It was held that all four requirements in this case were satisfied and, accordingly, the injunction was granted.

13. (1960) Times 21 May.
14. [1975] Fam 47, [1975] 1 All ER 697.
15. Ibid. at 52. Reliance for this assertion was placed inter alia on *Wellesley v Wellesley* (1828) 2 Bli N S 124 per Lord Redesdale at 136 and per Lord Manners at 142. Reference was also made to Chambers on *Infancy* (1842), p. 28.
16. I.e. it would be insufficient if the application was to achieve an ulterior motive e.g. a commercial one. *Re X* (*a minor*) [1975] Fam 47 at p. 52E.

With regard to the second requirement Latey J acknowledged that freedom of publication was an important and in some cases an overriding consideration. If, for example a man who has children was charged with some particularly serious and unpleasant offence he thought that it was unlikely 'save perhaps in a very exceptional case' that the court would make the children wards of court to restrain the publication of the court proceedings, since there was an overriding public interest in having justice openly administered. In the case before him, however, he held that there were no overriding interests and after weighing all the considerations including the implication for freedom of publication the balance in this case came down in favour of protecting the ward.

The Court of Appeal unanimously overruled Latey J's decision on the narrow basis that the interests of the ward at least in the case before them should not be allowed to prevail over the interests of freedom of publication. Both Lord Denning MR and Roskill LJ stressed the importance of preserving freedom to publish, pointing out that but for the proceedings before them there was no doubt that the publishers were entitled to publish the book. Lord Denning MR did not think that the court was called upon simply to balance the interests of freedom of the press with those of protecting young children from harm, holding in effect that the interests of freedom of publication overrode any child's interests. As he said[17]:

> 'It would be a mistake . . . to give the judges a power to stop publication of true matter whenever the judge—or any particular judge—thought that it was in the interests of the child to do so'.

Roskill LJ[18] commented that what some might regard as deficiencies in the law of defamation or the law of privacy could not be made good by resort to the wardship procedure. He could not accept the argument that the interests of the child should be allowed to prevail over the wider interests of freedom of publication. Sir John Pennycuick agreed[19] that on the facts there was no justification for interfering with the freedom of publication but added that he was not prepared to

17. *Re X (a minor)* [1975] Fam 47 at p. 58G. It is noticeable that his Lordship specifically referred to publications of *true* statements. The position might then be different if statements are false.
18. Ibid. at p. 60E.
19. Ibid. at p. 61F.

say that the court should never interfere with the publication of matter concerning a ward and that in exceptional circumstances the court should do so.

b) Commentary

Re X is the first authority for saying that there are limits to the protection which the court can afford its ward. That there are limits comes as no surprise for as Sir John Pennycuick said[20], it is impossible to protect a ward against everything that might do her harm. Few would disagree with Roskill LJ's stricture[1] on Latey J's comment that wardship would protect the young 'from whatever harm from whatever source', since, as he said, that was tantamount to saying that in every case where a minor's interests are involved, those interests are always paramount and must prevail. Again, few[2] would quibble with the actual decision in *Re X* for it would surely be placing too much weight on a ward's interests and too little on the interests of freedom of publication, if an article or book could be restrained upon the basis of possible harm that might indirectly be caused to a child. The difficulty of the decision lies in deciding what limitations it has placed upon the future applications of wardship.

Although the application in *Re X* went beyond the conventional limits of wardship in that it was seeking to interfere with the otherwise lawful activities of persons unconnected with the ward it seems clear that the application failed on the grounds that in the circumstances it was inappropriate to grant the injunction rather than that the court had no power at all to make the order. It has been argued[3], however, that in effect the whole application was misconceived since there has never been a power in wardship to restrain the activities of those unconnected with the ward. This is because, it is said, in wardship proceedings, the court is exercising a purely 'domestic function' and is concerned only with those who have an intimate or family connection with the ward. Even in the case of restraining undesirable associations between the ward and a third party it is said that

20. *Re X (a minor)* [1975] Fam 47 at p. 61D.
 1. Ibid. at p. 61B.
 2. But see A Lawrence Polak: 'The Law of Wardship' (1977) 7 Fam Law 87 91–2.
 3. Ann R Everton: 'High Tide in Wardship' (1975) 125 NLJ 930.

the court's 'sole capacity for external encroachment is upon merely the personal sensibility of the object of the ward's affections' and in no way impinges upon that party's proprietary or commercial rights.

The argument has the undoubted merit of providing readily ascertainable limits to the jurisdiction and some support for it can be found in the only judgment to deal with the wider issues in this regard, namely, that of Sir John Pennycuick. He commented that it was obvious that 'far-reaching limitations in principle on the exercise of this jurisdiction must exist'. He thought[4] that the jurisdiction had to be exercised with due regard to the rights of outside parties who he specifically defined as those not in a family or personal relationship with a ward.

It is submitted that despite the statements of Sir John Pennycuick, it would be premature to seek to limit the exercise of the jurisdiction upon the principle that there should be no interference with the activities of outsiders. Indeed Roskill LJ specifically stated that no limits to the jurisdiction had yet been drawn nor was there a need to consider what, if any, limits there are to the jurisdiction. Significantly he added[5]: 'the mere fact that the courts have never stretched out their arms so far . . . is in itself no reason for not stretching out those arms further than before when necessary in a suitable case'. Even Sir John Pennycuick said[6]: 'it would be impossible and not I think desirable to draw any rigid line beyond which the protection of a ward should not be extended'. It is submitted that far from closing the categories of interference *Re X* leaves open the possibility of further development. There may yet be circumstances where wardship can be invoked to restrain the activities of those completely unconnected with the ward. It is submitted that the key factor in deciding whether to exercise the jurisdiction will be the weight to be accorded to the ward's welfare. Hitherto it has been assumed that once a child has been made a ward his welfare becomes the 'first and paramount' consideration pursuant to section 1 of the Guardianship of Minors Act 1971. Indeed it was upon this assumption that Latey J made his decision in *Re X*. The appeal judgments

4. *Re X (a minor)* [1975] Fam 47 at p. 61D.
5. Ibid. at p. 60C.
6. Ibid. at p. 61E.

show, however, that the ward's welfare may not always be the first and paramount consideration. Perhaps the best explanation of this was given by Sir John Pennycuick. As he pointed out[7] section 1 applies, inter alia, whenever 'the custody or upbringing of a minor' is in question and in his judgment restraining the publication of a book to protect the ward fell into neither category and so the section was inapplicable.

Although the point has yet to be developed[8] it is submitted that the limited application of section 1 offers the most satisfactory way of limiting the extent of the court's powers to protect its ward.

It is submitted that if the section applies then because the ward's welfare must be regarded as the first and paramount consideration the court must exercise its jurisdiction so as to serve the ward's best interests. If on the other hand, the section is inapplicable then while that does not necessarily mean that the court will not exercise its powers it does mean that in weighing the various considerations the welfare of the ward would be accorded no special significance. It may be that the countervailing interests are so important that they should be preserved at the expense of possible harm to a ward. Freedom of speech is a case in point.

The countervailing interests may not always be so compelling so that it is possible that the court will act to protect its ward despite holding section 1 inapplicable. Indeed it is submitted that it does not follow from *Re X* that the interests of free speech must *necessarily* prevail over a ward's welfare. Sir John Pennycuick commented[9] that he was not prepared to say that the court should never interfere with publication of matter concerning a ward, adding that in 'exceptional circumstances' the court should do so. In the absence of further explanation it is a matter of conjecture what circumstances Sir John had in mind. It may be that he was thinking of the restrictions on publishing information about a child who has already been made a ward. These restrictions are largely statutory and will be discussed in Chapter 7. There remains the question of whether recourse may be had to wardship specifically to restrain publications. It is submitted that *Re X* does not necessarily close the door

7. *Re X* (*a minor*) [1975] Fam 47 at p. 62.
8. See the discussion in Chap. 6.
9. Ibid. at p. 61F.

even to this possibility. Two features of *Re X* may help to limit the decision, namely, that the purported harm was indirect and that there was no other legal remedy in respect of the publication. It may be, therefore, that the court will act in respect of a publication which directly concerns the child and is, for example, prima facie defamatory[10].

III Enforcement

Like any other High Court jurisdiction the court may enforce a wardship order or undertaking by the sanctions available for contempt. These sanctions will be discussed in Chapter 7 where consideration is given to contempt matters generally. In addition the court can call upon the services of the Tipstaff to enforce its orders in wardship.

Before considering the Tipstaff's role in wardship proceedings a little may be said about the nature of his office. The Tipstaff is an officer attached to the Supreme Court of Justice and his main function today is to arrest contemnors and take them to prison. Indeed he and his deputies are the only persons entitled to arrest anybody within the precincts of the Royal Courts of Justice.

The Tipstaff's role in wardship proceedings is not, however, confined to arresting contemnors since pursuant to RSC Order 90, rule 3A the court can direct him to enforce any of its directions[11]. Hence the court can direct the Tipstaff to take the ward into his custody and deliver him to the person named in the order[12]. The court commonly directs the Tipstaff to take steps to trace missing wards[13]. The Tipstaff

10. Query for example whether the court would restrain *repetition* of the libel. Such intervention would not represent a vast inroad into freedom to publish and might well prevent possibly unnecessary harm. As the law now stands no such injunctions are normally granted provided the publisher swears that he will plead justification. See *Bonnard v Perryman* [1891] 2 Ch 269; *Fraser v Evans* [1969] 1 QB 349, [1969] 1 All ER 8; *Wallersteiner v Moir* [1974] 3 All ER 217 at 230, and *J Trevor & Sons (a firm) v P R Solomon* (1977) Times, December 16.

11. Formerly the proper person to enforce wardship orders was the Serjeant-at-Arms but in 1946 the Lord Chancellor directed that the court or a judge might for this purpose nominate a Senior Clerk of the Official Solicitor's department. Following objections to this by the Official Solicitor the 1946 order was withdrawn and the new order RSC Ord. 90, r.3A replaced it.

12. *G- v L-* [1891] 3 Ch 126; see also Atkin's Court Forms (1975 Supplement) Form 120A at 429.

13. See Chap. 12 for further details.

may also be used to ensure compliance with an order directing a party to return his child to another jurisdiction on a
particular plane. It is even known for the court to direct the
Tipstaff to collect and take a truanting ward to his boarding
school.

The availability of the Tipstaff's services certainly
enhances the efficacy of orders particularly mandatory orders
made in wardship proceedings. The Tipstaff's services are
unavailable in the lower courts. It is uncertain[14] whether his
extended services are available to the High Court acting
under other jurisdictions, and in practice they are not so used.

IV The respective powers of judge and registrar

Before considering the respective powers of judge and registrar in wardship proceedings two preliminary points should
be made. First, the respective powers are the same throughout
the registries. In other words a district registrar has exactly
the same powers as a principal registrar and the judge (even if
appointed for the day) has the same powers wherever he is
sitting. Secondly, although, as will be seen shortly, the rules
themselves give little guidance as to the respective roles of
judge and registrar the cardinal principle is that registrars
should not, as it were, step into the shoes of the judge. Hence
it is not so much the type of order that is important but the
role in making it. In principle a registrar should consider
whether in granting an order he is making a judicial decision
which is really the province of a judge. Within this general
principle there is, as will be appreciated, a vast area of
discretion. Some registrars are bound to be more cautious
than others. However, the vagueness of the rules preserves the
all important flexibility which is the hallmark of a wardship
jurisdiction and which allows registrars within broad limits
to deal with problems as they arise. From the practitioner's
point of view initial recourse should normally be had to the
registrar if only to seek a hearing before the judge. It should
also be remembered that in cases of dispute a registrar's
decision can always be taken to a judge.

14. See Law Com. Working Paper No. 68 (Scots Law Com. Memorandum No.
    23) para. 6.23.

A. COMMITTAL TO CARE AND SUPERVISION
ORDERS

Although in general the rules do not specify the respective powers of judge and registrar, they do with regard to committing a ward to the care of a local authority or making a supervision order. RSC Order 90, rule 11(1) states that the Matrimonial Causes Rules relating to sections 43, 44 of the Matrimonial Causes Act 1973 apply with the necessary modifications inter alia to proceedings under section 7 of the Family Law Reform Act 1969. The relevant rule is Rule 92 of the Matrimonial Causes Rules 1977, the whole of which provides:

'Subject to paragraph (2) an application for an order relating to the custody or education of a child, or for an order committing him to the care of a local authority under section 43 of the Act of 1973 or providing for supervision under section 44 of that Act shall be made to a judge.'

Quite clearly a registrar cannot under this rule make an order committing a ward to care nor make a supervision order. There are, however, problems as to the scope of the rule. One such problem relates to a consent order. At first sight this is covered by rule 92(2) which states:

'An application by the petitioner or the respondent[15] for—

(a) an order in terms agreed between the parties relating to the custody or education of a child, or

(b) access to a child where the other party consents to give access and the only question for determination is the extent to which access is to be given,

may be made to the registrar who may make such order on the application as he thinks fit or may refer the application or any question arising thereon to a judge for his decision.'

The general object of rule 92(2) is to give the registrar the power to make an order where the parties are agreed. Does this, however, apply to care orders or supervision orders? Paragraph 2 does not expressly say that it does, and there are arguments both for and against its application. In favour is

---

15. The references to 'petitioner' and 'respondent' should be taken to refer to 'plaintiff' and 'defendant' when applied to wardship proceedings.

that paragraph 1 seems to be generally subject to paragraph 2 and while the latter paragraph does not in terms mention committal to care or supervision orders such orders may be said to relate to custody or education or access. Against its application it can be argued that since paragraph 1 expressly distinguishes 'custody or education' from 'care or supervision orders' the reference in paragraph 2(*a*) must be limited to the custody or education. On this interpretation paragraph 1 should be read as being subject to paragraph 2 only in so far as it relates to custody or education. Given the ambiguity in the rules it seems valid to point out that allowing the registrar to have the power may help to relieve the enormous pressure on judges' time and in any event the wider interpretation is both in line with the general power of registrars to make consent orders and the trend in the Family Division to avoid undue technicality. On this pragmatic basis it is submitted that registrars technically do have the power to make a consent order committing a ward to care or placing him under supervision. Whether in practice a registrar could ever be persuaded to make such an order is another matter. Certainly he should be cautious to do so but as with his powers generally his decision must always be a matter of discretion. As rule 92(2) expressly states: 'the registrar may make such order on the application as he thinks fit or may refer the application or any question thereon to a judge for his decision'.

Whether one can go further and say that registrars have the power to make *unopposed* orders for care or supervision is even more doubtful as rule 92(2) expressly refers to orders agreed between the parties. Nevertheless the policy arguments referred to above could be relied upon to justify the existence of the technical power. In practice, however, it is unlikely that a registrar would be prepared to make such an order.

Another problem relating to the scope of rule 92 is whether it applies where the ward is already in care. It could be argued that an order 'that the ward *remains* in the care of the local authority' does not amount to *committing* the child into care and therefore falls outside the ambit of rule 92. Whether this is always technically correct is a moot point, for while it is no doubt true that the child remains in care, the legal consequences of the wardship order for a child already in care under section 1 of the Children Act 1948, can be different in that the ward cannot be removed without the court's consent. Whether or not rule 92 is applicable the view can, however, be legitimately taken that it is within the powers of the registrar to order that the ward remains in the (interim) care of the local authority where the parties are agreed thereby in effect preserving the status quo. Certainly this is a view known to be taken by some registrars and indeed some are even prepared to make unopposed orders.

B. CARE AND CONTROL ORDERS

Apart from Order 90, rule 11 the only other provision specifically dealing with registrars' power in wardship is Order 90, rule 12. Rule 12(1) states:

> 'In proceedings to which this Part of this Order applies a registrar may transact all such business and exercise all such authority and jurisdiction as may be transacted and exercised by a judge in chambers.'

Although, as various commentaries made clear[16], in practice registrars' powers were narrower than rule 12(1) suggested, on the face of it the rule placed registrars in a similar position to a judge and seemed to justify a registrar making, for example, a care and control order. This is exactly what a deputy district registrar did in *Re L (a minor)*[17]. It was held, however, by the Court of Appeal that the order was contrary to the usual practice. It was accordingly set aside and the case was remitted forthwith to the district registry to be dealt with by the appropriate judge.

Ormrod LJ drew the attention of the Rules Committee to the wording of rule 12 which as he pointed out is totally inconsistent with the Matrimonial Causes Rules 1977 rule 92, commenting[18]:

> 'We have this apparently absurd anomaly that in custody cases arising after divorce, registrars have no jurisdiction to make orders relating to custody or education.

16. See e.g. the commentary in the Supreme Court Practice 1976 at 1312 and *Rayden on Divorce* (12th Edn.), p. 1036. Presumably r.12(2) which states 'Paragraph (1) is without prejudice ... to the power of the judges to reserve to themselves the transaction of any such business or the exercise of any such authority or jurisdiction' is intended to limit the ambit of r.12(1), but its terms are too vague to be satisfactory (see now the Supreme Court Practice 1979, p. 1350).
17. *Re L (a minor) (wardship proceedings)* [1978] 2 All ER 318.
18. Ibid. at 320.

Indeed, they have only a jurisdiction except by consent, to make orders relating to the quantum of access. They have no jurisdiction to make an order as to access where one party is maintaining that there should be no access at all.

So that under the Matrimonial Causes Rules in, I suppose 95 per cent of cases involving children, the registrar's jurisdiction has been expressly limited by the Matrimonial Causes Rules. Then by some extraordinary oversight RSC Order 90, rule 12 purports to give a registrar jurisdiction to make an order for care and control in wardship proceedings. That is something of which I have never heard in the whole of my experience.'

His Lordship concluded:

'There is a footnote in *The Supreme Court Practice* (1976), p. 1312 which says that this generally will be a matter for a judge save where the parties consent to the order. This ambiguity ought to be cleared up as soon as convenient by the Rules Committee.'

In view of Ormrod LJ's justifiable strictures on and suggested reforms of rule 12 it may be better to regard the care and control order made in *Re L* as not being merely contrary to practice but ultra vires the powers of the registrar[19].

Although the rejection of the care and control order was reasonably predictable the clear implication in *Re L* that such an order could have been made had the parties consented may have surprised some. It was formerly thought, at least in some quarters, that care and control orders fall outside registrars' powers altogether[20]. That such a power exists, however, is clearly consistent with registrars' powers under rule 92(2) and does not impinge on the idea that a registrar must not act as if he were a judge. It is to be stressed, however, that such an order lies at the registrar's discretion, so that in practice he may be reluctant to make even a consent order preferring instead to refer the matter to the judge. He might, however be more amenable to granting an agreed interim care and control order.

19. In fact the rule has not been amended apparently to maintain flexibility to allow registrars to act, for example in an emergency.
20. This is the impression given by the comment in *Rayden* (12th Edn.) at 1036 that 'in general care and control is a matter for the Judge while most other matters will be decided by the Registrar'.

Whether a registrar technically has the power to make an unopposed care and control order remains uncertain. No reference was made to this point in *Re L* (though it is not clear from the report whether the original order was actually opposed or not) nor is the matter mentioned in any of the Rules. In the absence of guidance it is suggested that registrars do have the power but that they should be most cautious in exercising it and no doubt in most cases would decline to do so.

C. ACCESS AND OTHER ORDERS

Apart from the orders so far discussed there is little guidance on the respective powers in relation to other types of orders. Rayden comments that[1]:

> Care and control is a matter for the Judge while most matters will be decided by the Registrar.'

This comment should, however, be treated with care. In principle the registrar is not empowered to make *any* order that is opposed by one of the parties. This even applies to access though by analogy with rule 92(2) if the parties are agreed that there should be access the registrar does have power to determine the extent. Whether a registrar can make unopposed access orders is unclear but it is submitted that he is empowered to do so.

If the parties are agreed upon an order then in general it is safe to assume that the registrar is empowered to make the order. He would, for example be able to accept voluntary undertakings and probably can grant an injunction in terms agreed by the parties. Whether he is empowered to discharge a wardship order made by a judge is more doubtful. It is established that the court must be satisfied that discharge is for the ward's benefit and it may be that such an order even if agreed should normally be left to the judge[2].

D. CRITIQUE

It will have become clear that for the most part the respective powers of judge and registrar are a matter of practice rather than the subject of detailed rules. Undoubtedly this has the

---

1. (13th Edn.), at 1118.
2. The Registrar has certainly been known to discharge the order.

advantage of flexibility which is an important asset. However, the vagueness of provisions can lead both to uncertainty and to regional variations of practice. It may also lead to differences between wardship and other child jurisdictions. All these points are highlighted by *Re L*. It is to be noted that Ormrod LJ pointed to what he described as an 'anomaly' between RSC Order 90, rule 12 and the Matrimonial Causes Rules 1977, rule 92. Such references are to be welcomed for it is surely right that High Court registrars should have broadly the same powers whatever jurisdiction they are exercising. It is submitted that consideration should be given as to whether more specific guidance along the lines of rule 92 should be given to wardship matters. If so it may be appropriate to consider what powers registrars should have where the orders are unopposed.

Chapter 6

The Principles Upon Which the Court Acts

I Introduction

It has become almost axiomatic that the welfare of the ward is the first and paramount consideration[1]. There is no doubt, however, that this cannot be true in all cases for, if it were, the jurisdiction would be unacceptably wide. It would mean, for instance, that the jurisdiction could be used to interfere in any circumstances in which the ward may be harmed and could even be used to defeat the application of criminal, military or immigration law[2].

It is to be remembered that the requirement to make the child's welfare first and paramount is based on statute, now section 1 of the Guardianship of Minors Act 1971[3]. Section 1, however, only applies where '(a) legal[4] custody or upbringing of a minor; or (b) the administration of any property belonging to or held on trust for a minor or the application of the income thereof is in question'. This provision has been spoken of as declaratory of the pre-statutory position[5] but no reference is made either at common law or by statute to a

---

1. See, for example, Ormrod LJ's comments in *Rennick v Rennick* [1978] 1 All ER 817 at 819. 'If this matter [i.e. an application to exclude the husband under the Domestic Violence and Matrimonial Proceedings Act 1976] had come before the court in the wardship jurisdiction—*where the welfare of children is the paramount consideration*, there could be no doubt but that the court would order the father to leave.' [Emphasis added.] See the excellent note to this case in (1978) 8 Fam. Law 55.
2. For a statement that the court would not interfere in any of these circumstances see the judgment of Russell LJ in *Re Mohamed Arif (an infant), Re Nirbhai Singh (an infant)* [1968] Ch 643 at 662 et seq. See also *Re D* [1978] L S Gaz. 857.
3. The provision is a re-enactment of s. 1 of the Guardianship of Infants Act 1925.
4. The insertion of the word 'legal' is consequent upon an amendment under the Domestic Proceedings and Magistrates' Courts Act 1978, s.36(1)(a).
5. See *J v C* [1970] AC 668, [1969] 1 All ER 788. Discussed post p. 131.

requirement to treat the ward's welfare as the first and paramount consideration if custody or upbringing or property matters are not in question. It is submitted that there is no such requirement. That does not mean that the court has no jurisdiction to act in cases falling outside the scope of section 1. On the contrary, it is submitted that the court is entitled to act on behalf of its wards under its inherent *protective* jurisdiction. Under this jurisdiction, however, the ward's interests will not be first and paramount and instead will have to be weighed in the balance with any other countervailing interests.

II The Custodial and Protective Jurisdictions Distinguished

The distinction between what might loosely be termed the 'custodial jurisdiction' and the protective jurisdiction does not merely lie in the different weight to be accorded to the ward's welfare but goes to the very function of the court. Under the custodial jurisdiction the court must act in the ward's best interests and because the ward's welfare is the first and paramount consideration, other interests can only be considered incidentally and only in so far as they reflect on the ward's welfare. Under the protective jurisdiction, on the other hand, the court's concern is to protect the child from harm, but because the child's welfare is not accorded overriding significance, other interests assume a much greater importance. In such cases the court will be forced to make a policy decision as to which interest to protect.

The distinction between the two jurisdictions and the court's functions in each was recognised by the House of Lords in *S v McC; W v W*[6]. That case was concerned with the principles upon which the court should order a blood test of a child. It had been submitted on the child's behalf by the Official Solicitor that no blood test of any child ought ever to be ordered unless it could be shown to be in the interests of the child that there should be a test. In other words the court had to follow the criterion laid down by what is now section 1 of the 1971 Act[7]. That submission was, however, rejected, it

6. [1972] AC 24.
7. The relevant provision before the court was s.1 of Guardianship of Infants Act 1925.

being held that Section 1 was inapplicable and instead the court was being called upon to exercise its protective function[8]. Accordingly, it was held that the correct test was that the court should order a blood test unless it was shown to be against the child's interests to do so. As Lord Hodson said[9]:

> 'The court in ordering a blood test in the case of an infant has, of course, a discretion and may make or refuse an order for a test in the exercise of its discretion, but the interests of other persons than the infant are involved in ordinary litigation. *The infant needs protection but that is no justification for making his rights superior to those of others*'. [Emphasis Added.]

Admittedly *S v McC* was not a wardship case but it is submitted that it provides authority for the approach to be adopted in cases where section 1 is inapplicable. There is also authority that the court may be called upon to weigh the various interests in wardship. In *Re R (MJ) (a minor)*[10] permission was sought by a trustee in bankruptcy to obtain a copy of the transcript of wardship proceedings for use in a subsequent bankruptcy hearing. In deciding whether to grant the application Rees J commented as follows[11]:

> 'A judge dealing with such an application has an unfettered discretion to grant or to refuse it. He will place the interest of the minor in the forefront of his considerations. He will also give considerable weight to the public interest in ensuring that frankness shall prevail in [wardship] proceedings by preserving confidentiality. The public interest in upholding the law of the land by providing relevant evidence for use in other legitimate proceedings must also be considered together with all the other circumstances of the case.'

In the event Rees J held that as no legitimate interest of the ward would be harmed permission to release the transcript should be granted.

It does not follow, however, that because some harm to the ward may be contemplated that the court will necessarily exercise its protective function. It may be that the countervailing interests are so important that they outweigh the

---

8. See particularly Lord MacDermott's analysis ibid. at pp. 47–51 and that of Lord Hodson at 58, 59. Cf. Lord Reid's approach at pp. 44, 45.
9. Ibid. at p. 58G.
10. *Re R (MJ) (a minor) (publication of transcript)* [1975] Fam 89.
11. Ibid. at 98.

interests of the ward even at the expense of possible harm to him. This was established by *Re X* (*a minor*)[12] in which, as we have seen, the court refused to restrain publication of a book on the grounds that its contents might have been harmful to the ward.

Clearly the weight to be accorded to the ward's interests must depend on the strength of the countervailing interests. It may be that such interests will be particularly strong as in the case of freedom of speech. Alternatively they may be comparatively weak in which case the court may decide to act in the ward's interests even though section 1 is inapplicable.

For the most part the distinction between the custodial and the protective jurisdictions has not been significant in wardship cases, no doubt for the very good reason that in the vast majority of cases it has been clear that it is the custodial jurisdiction which is being invoked. It is submitted, however, that the distinction between the two jurisdictions should not be overlooked and indeed may prove of key importance to the future development of wardship. For instance, the application of section 1 will be extremely relevant to determining the limitation of the court's powers over its wards and lies at the heart of the currently important issue of the extent to which wardship can be used to interfere with the decisions of other courts or bodies.

III The scope of section 1 of the Guardianship of Minors Act 1971

The Guardianship of Minors Act 1971 Section 1 (as amended) provides:

'Where in any proceedings before any court ...
(a) the legal[13] custody or upbringing of a minor, or
(b) the administration of any property belonging to or held on trust for a minor, or the application of income thereof, is in question,

the court in deciding that question shall regard the welfare of the minor as the first and paramount con-

---

12. *Re X* (*a minor*) (*wardship: jurisdiction*) [1975] Fam 47 Discussed in detail ante at p. 110 et seq.
13. Inserted by s.36(1)(a) of the Domestic Proceedings and Magistrates' Courts Act 1978.

sideration, and shall not take into consideration whether from any other point of view the claim of the father, or any right at common law possessed by the father, in respect of such custody, upbringing, administration or application is superior to that of the mother, or the claim of the mother is superior to that of the father'.

The first issue is when does the section apply. This will depend upon the meaning of sections 1(*a*) and 1(*b*)[14]. No case has directly considered the meaning of the provisions beyond holding that a particular issue fell outside the scope of section 1. Accordingly, the following discussion is necessarily tentative and it is to be stressed that the court has, in the absence of detailed authority, a discretion to construe the section widely or narrowly.

The provision under section 1(*b*) seems straightforward but difficulty may be encountered in determining what is meant by 'legal custody or upbringing' under section 1(*a*). To a certain extent the insertion of the word 'legal' before 'custody' by section 36(1)(*a*) of the Domestic Proceedings and Magistrates' Courts Act 1978 has made the meaning more clear. The 1978 Act amendment is to further the policy of having uniformity in statutory provisions relating to custody of children[15]. Accordingly 'legal custody' is by the new section 20(2)(*a*) of the 1971 Act[16] to be construed in accordance with Part IV of the Children Act 1975. By section 86 of the Children Act 1975:

'unless the context requires, "legal custody" means, as respects a child, so much of the parental rights and duties as relate to the person of the child (including the place and manner in which his time is spent);"

By section 85

'unless the context otherwise requires "the parental rights and duties" means as respects a particular child (whether legitimate or not), all the rights and duties which by law the mother and father have in relation to a legitimate child . . .; and references to a parental right or

14. It is to be noted that provided the issue comes within the terms of s.1(*a*) or (*b*) the section applies 'in *any* proceedings before *any* court'. For the meaning of 'court' see s. 15.
15. See the comments of Law Commission Report No. 77, para. 5.04–5.12.
16. Substituted by s.36(1)(*c*) of the Domestic Proceedings and Magistrates' Courts Act 1978.

duty shall be construed accordingly and shall include a
right of access and any other element included in a right
or duty.'

As has been pointed out elsewhere[17] the use of the phrase
'parental *rights*' is singularly inappropriate in the area of
child law. Nevertheless the court is likely to treat the phrase as
referring to the 'bundle of powers'[18] which a parent has over a
child. These include the power to control the child's education or religion, to veto the issue of the child's passport, to
withhold consent to marriage, physically to control the child
and the right to consent to the child's medical treatment[19].
The phrase 'legal custody' will also include the right to
physical possession of and access to the child.

Given the width of the meaning of 'legal custody' it is
difficult to see what the word 'upbringing'[20] adds. Taken
together, however, section 1(*a*) would seem to cover cases
whenever the right or any aspect of that right to bring up a
child or the manner in which he is to be brought up is in issue.
Such an interpretation, however, might be thought too wide
and it might be better to confine the application of the section
to cases where legal custody or upbringing of the child is
directly in issue. The need to add this qualification might be
thought to be illustrated by a case like *Re Bailey*[1] where a wife
sought against the trustee in bankruptcy to have the sale of the
matrimonial home postponed until the son had completed

17. See e.g. Bromley: *Family Law* (5th Edn.), p. 302; Eekelaar: 'What are
Parental Rights?' (1973) 89 LQR 210 and Hall: 'The Waning of Parental
Rights' [1972 B] CLJ 248.
18. Per Sachs LJ in *Hewer v Bryant* [1970] 1 QB 357 at 373.
19. Whether a parent has a right to consent to his child's medical treatment is
uncertain particularly where that consent relates to non essential treatment
see e.g.: Bromley op. cit. 336-8; Eekelaar op. cit. at pp. 224, 225; Coode:
The Law of the Individual (1968, Sweet and Maxwell), p. 62; PDG Skegg:
'Consent to Medical Procedures on Minors' (1973) 36 MLR 370 and 'A
Justification For Medical Procedures Performed Without Consent' (1974) 90
LQR 512, 519-23, and D. Foulkes: 'Consent to Medical Treatment' (1970)
120 NLJ 194. Given this uncertainty, however, it would seem fair comment
to say that non essential treatment does come within the definition of 'legal
custody' and hence Heilbron J was justified in invoking the principle that
the ward's welfare was the paramount consideration in *Re D (a minor)*
(*wardship: sterilisation*) [1976] Fam 185 at 194.
20. Defined as 'The action of bringing up; the fact of being brought up or the
manner of this; early training or rearing.' by the Shorter Oxford
Dictionary.
1. [1977] 2 All ER 26, [1972] 1 WLR 278, where the child's interests were held
to be incidental. S. 1 of the 1971 Act was not cited Sed quaere?

his school education. While it is perhaps debatable whether the sale of the home in this context[2] would come within the meaning of 'legal custody or upbringing' (so making the welfare of the child first and paramount) it could be argued that as the issue was only indirectly raised, the section should be inapplicable. To use another example while a child's legal custody or upbringing will be affected by his parents' divorce, his interests can hardly be said to be central to the issue of whether a divorce should be granted. In other words it is submitted that section 1 should be inapplicable.

The submission that 'legal custody or upbringing' has to be directly in issue for section 1 to apply is supported by *S v McC, W v W*[3] where, it will be recalled, it was held that the issue of whether to test a child's blood for the purposes of obtaining evidence of paternity fell outside the scope of section 1. As Lord MacDermott said[4]:

'The question raised by a blood test application is quite distinct from the question of custody and other questions mentioned in section 1 of the Guardianship of Infants Act. It is true that in deciding as to the custody of a child its welfare may depend on the weighing and assessment of various factors, including the rights and wishes of the parents and that the question of paternity may therefore not only arise but be very relevant. But that is not to make the question of paternity a question of custody. It is only part of the process in deciding the ultimate and paramount question, namely, what is best for the welfare of the child'.

Clearly this is a fine distinction but it does mean that blood test evidence is more likely to be admitted. This is perhaps ironic since it could certainly be argued that it is in the best interests of the child to know the truth so that the evidence could have been admitted under the paramountcy test.

S v McC, W v W is to be contrasted with the earlier House of Lords' decision in *Official Solicitor v K*[5] where in deciding that a judge was entitled to act on confidential information

2. It might be thought to be covered by the closing words in s.86 of the Children's Act 1975, namely, '(including *the place* and manner in which his time is spent)' [Emphasis Added]. Cf. *Rennick v Rennick*, [1978] 1 All ER 817, [1977] 1 WLR 1455 noted ante at p. 123n. 1.
3. [1972] AC 24.
4. Per Lord MacDermott ibid., at 50H.
5. [1965] AC 201, [1963] 3 All ER 191.

submitted by the Official Solicitor, which was not available to the parties, express reliance was placed on what is now[6] section 1 of the 1971 Act. At first sight the two cases seem to conflict because both appear to be dealing with matters of evidence. However, they can be reconciled on the basis that, whereas *S v McC, W v W* was concerned with the issue of paternity, *Official Solicitor v K* was solely concerned with the question of the minors' custody or upbringing and that disclosure of the evidence might have been harmful to their future upbringing.

S v McC, W v W might also be contrasted with *Re D (a minor)*[7] in which it was held that in determining whether to allow a sterilisation operation for non therapeutic purposes the court had to treat the ward's welfare as its first and paramount consideration, i.e. section 1 applied. Although at first sight blood tests and sterilisation seem analagous the purpose of the former was directed to the question of paternity and as such did not directly concern the legal custody or upbringing of the child, whereas the performance of the latter very much affected the child's future and must have surely been within the terms of section 1.

Further support for the view that 'legal custody or upbringing' should be directly in issue for section 1 to apply is supported by Sir John Pennycuick in *Re X (a minor)*[8]. He held that the question of whether a book containing details of the ward's dead father's sexual habits should be restrained on the grounds that it might harm the ward, fell outside the scope of section 1. It is submitted that such an interpretation is perfectly tenable, as the publication of a book surely concerns neither 'legal custody' nor 'upbringing' of a child, or if it does, it only raises the issue indirectly.

That the question should be directly in issue might also support the view that the decision of whether the court should exercise its wardship jurisdiction in cases where another court or body has already made a decision, also falls outside section 1[9]. This is because like evidence as to paternity the issue of jurisdiction could be regarded as a distinct and

6. Then s.1 of the Guardianship of Infants Act 1925.
7. [1976] Fam. 185, (1976) 1 All ER 326.
8. [1975] Fam. 47 at 62. Discussed ante p. 110.
9. Discussed post p. 360 cf 'kidnapping' cases which have been held to be within s.1. See Buckley LJ in *Re L (minors)* [1974] 1 All ER 913 at 924— Discussed post p. 344.

preliminary point in deciding whether to hear argument concerning 'legal custody or upbringing' of the minor. The advantage of this approach, as will be argued in later chapters, is that it enables the court to decide as a matter of policy whether to uphold the interests of the particular child or to respect the decision of other tribunals.

IV J v C[10]: The application of s.1 to disputes between parents and third parties

To complete the discussion of the meaning and application of section 1, reference must be made to the House of Lords' decision in *J v C*[10]. The case concerned a ten year old boy of Spanish parents but born in England. Following his birth in 1958 he spent much time with foster parents and indeed spent only 17 months with his parents in Madrid between then and 1965, when the case was first heard. The trial judge found that the child lived in happy surroundings in a united and well-integrated family. He also found that the surroundings and circumstances to which the child could go in Spain were suitable, which they had not previously been.

It was submitted on behalf of the appellants that united parents are *prima facie* entitled to the custody of their infant children and that the court will only deprive them of care and control if they are unfitted by character, conduct or position in life to have this control, and that in the case of an unimpeachable parent the court must, save in very exceptional cases, give the care and control to the parent. It was also argued that section 1 applied only to disputes between parents and not between parents and strangers. The House of Lords was unanimous in finding against these submissions. Lords Guest, MacDermott and Upjohn all reviewed the law at some length, both before and after 1925. Lords Guest[11] and Upjohn[12] referred with approval to *Re O'Hara*[13], an Irish case. Lord Guest quoted Holmes LJ who said:

'The Court of Chancery, from time immemorial has exercised another and distinguishable jurisdiction—a jurisdiction resting on the paternal authority of the

10. [1970] AC 668.
11. Ibid., at 695, 696.
12. Ibid., at 722.
13. [1900] 2IR 232.

Crown, by virtue of which it can supersede the natural guardianship of a parent and can place a child in such custody as seems most calculated to promote its welfare.'

Both quoted the passage:

'No doubt the period during which a child has been in the care of the stranger is always an important element in considering what is best for the child's welfare. If a boy has been brought up from infancy by a person who has won his love and confidence, who is training him to earn his livelihood, and separation from whom would break up all the associations of his life, no court ought to sanction in his case a change of custody.'

This statement is particularly interesting as it represents an early understanding of modern thought on the importance of a 'psychological' parent[14].

They also quoted with approval from the same case a passage in the judgment of Fitzgibbon LJ:

'In exercising the jurisdiction to control or ignore the parental right the Court must act cautiously, not as if it were a private person acting with regard to her own child, and acting in opposition to the parent only when judicially satisfied that the welfare of the child requires that the parental right should be superseded or suspended.'

Thus it was established that even before 1925 the court could act in the way which most promoted the welfare of the child. As a result of the 1925 Act the position is put more clearly in terms of the duty imposed on the court. Having emphasised that section 1 referred to any court in any proceedings, Lord MacDermott said[15]:

'The section would apply to cases, such as the present, between parents and strangers. This construction finds further support in the following considerations. In the first place since (as the Act and authorities already mentioned by way of background show) welfare was being regarded increasingly as a general criterion which was not limited to custody disputes between parents, it would be more than strange if the earlier part of section 1 were meant to apply only to that single type of dispute.

14. See *Beyond the Best Interests of the Child* (1973, The Free Press), Goldstein, Freud and Solnit.
15. *J v C* [1970] AC 668 at 710.

Secondly, the questions for decision which are expressly mentioned—custody, upbringing, administration of property belonging to or held in trust for the infant, and the application of income thereof—are of a kind to suggest the involvement not only of parents but of others such as guardians or trustees. And thirdly there is nothing in the rest of the Act to require a limited construction of section 1.'

V The meaning of 'first and paramount'

Lord MacDermott proceeded to consider the other critical question of the case, namely, the scope and meaning of the words 'shall regard the welfare of the infant as the first and paramount consideration'. He said[16]:

'Reading these words in their ordinary significance, and relating them to the various classes of proceedings which the section has already mentioned, it seems to me that they must mean more than that the child's welfare is to be treated as the top item in a list of items relevant to the matter in question. I think they connote a process whereby, when all the relevant facts, relationships, claims and wishes of parents, risks, choices and other circumstances are taken into account and weighed, the course to be followed will be that which is most in the interests of the child's welfare as that term has now to be understood. That is the first consideration because it is of first importance and the paramount consideration because it rules on or determines the course to be followed.'

He also referred favourably to the judgment of Danckwerts LJ in *Re Adoption Application 41/61*[17] who said:

'I would respectfully point out that there can only be one "first and paramount consideration", and other considerations must be subordinate. The mere desire of a parent to have his child must be subordinate to the consideration of the welfare of the child, and can be effective only if it coincides with the welfare of the child. Consequently it cannot be correct to talk of the

16. *J v C* [1970] AC 668 at 710, 711.
17. [1963] Ch 315 [1962] 3 All ER 553.

preeminent position of parents, or their exclusive right to the custody of their children, when the future welfare of those children is being considered by the court.'

It is right to emphasise that having specified welfare as the first and paramount consideration, it follows that there are other considerations which cannot be excluded. Their Lordships placed different weight on this aspect of the case. Lord Upjohn considered that Danckwerts LJ in *Re Adoption Application No. 41/61* did little justice to the position of the natural parents. He said[18]:

'The natural parents have a strong claim to have their wishes considered; first and principally no doubt because normally it is part of the paramount consideration of the welfare of the infant that he should be with them, but also because as the natural parents they have themselves a strong claim to have their wishes considered as normally the proper persons to have the upbringing of the child they have brought into the world.'

He referred for support to the judgment of Eve J in *Re Thain, Thain v Taylor*[19] when he expressed his belief that among other considerations the wishes of an unimpeachable parent undoubtedly stood first. Lord MacDermott also mentioned this case and quoted Eve J as follows[20]:

'I am satisfied that the child will be as happy and well cared for in the one home as the other, and inasmuch as the rule laid down for my guidance in the exercise of this responsible jurisdiction does not say that the welfare of the child is the sole consideration but the paramount consideration, it necessarily contemplates the existence of other conditions, and amongst these the wishes of an unimpeachable parent undoubtedly stand first.'

Lord MacDermott explained this in terms that the judge, 'having found that the child would be as happy and well-cared for in one home as the other must have been satisfied that her welfare would be best provided for by respecting the wishes of the unimpeachable father.'

These are clearly issues where the discretion of the judge

18. [1970] AC at 724.
19. [1926] Ch 676.
20. [1970] AC 668 at 711.

is going to play a large part and it is difficult to balance the various considerations. The danger inherent in Lord Upjohn's approach, which accepts the paramountcy of the welfare consideration but reemphasises the claim of the natural parent, is the risk that too much weight is placed on the rights of the parents rather than the rights of the child.

Lord MacDermott perhaps expresses the position in the most balanced and accurate way, when he sums up as follows[1]:

> 'In applying section 1, the rights and wishes of parents whether unimpeachable or otherwise, must be assessed and weighed in their bearing on the welfare of the child in conjunction with all other factors relevant to that issue. . . . While there is now no rule of law that the rights and wishes of unimpeachable parents must prevail over other considerations, such rights and wishes, recognised as they are by nature and society, can be capable of ministering to the total welfare of the child in a special way, and must therefore preponderate in many cases. The parental rights, however, remain qualified and not absolute for the purposes of the investigation, the broad nature of which is still as described in the fourth of the principles enunciated by Fitzgibbon LJ in *Re O'Hara*'[2].

While Lord MacDermott accepts the concept of parental rights, he emphasises them not as separate and distinct, but as they weigh in relation to the welfare of the child. It is submitted that this is the correct approach, because, as he says, this being the paramount consideration, it rules on or determines the course to be followed.

J v C poignantly illustrates the significance of according the child's welfare the first and paramount consideration, establishing in effect that even unimpeachable parents may lose custody or care and control of their own child if his welfare so demands. The case concerned a dispute between parents and third parties but of course the child's welfare is just as important where the dispute is between the parents over their child or between the parents and their child. In other words the approach in *J v C* is to be regarded as the locus classicus on all disputes relating to children. The reference, however, to 'unimpeachable' parents must now be treated

---

1. [1970] AC 668 at 715.
2. [1900] 2 IR at 240. Quoted ante, p. 132.

with caution, for it has since been held[3] that at least in relation to an inter-parental dispute it is nothing more than a misleading and outmoded advocate's phrase. In other words a party's conduct is relevant only in so far as it provides evidence of a person's standing as a parent.

3. Per Ormrod LJ in *S(BD)* v *S(DJ)* (*children: care and control*) [1977] Fam 109 at 115 and per Stamp LJ in *Re K* (*minors*) (*children: care and control*) [1977] Fam 179 at 183. The phrase may still have a place in a parent-non parent dispute. See Ormrod LJ in *S(BD)* v *S(DJ)* ibid., at 116.

Chapter 7

Wardship and Contempt

I The ways in which contempt may be committed[1]

Broadly speaking contempts committed in relation to wardship proceedings fall into one or more[2] of the following categories, namely (a) interfering with the court's special protection over its wards, (b) publishing information relating to wardship proceedings contrary to section 12 of the Administration of Justice Act 1960 and (c) disobeying court orders.

A. INTERFERING WITH THE COURT'S SPECIAL PROTECTION OVER ITS WARDS

It is sometimes said[3] that it is a contempt to interfere with the welfare of a ward, but while this may be a convenient short-hand statement of the position, it is apt to be misleading. Though rooted in the need to protect the ward's welfare the essence of the contempt lies in interfering with the special protective jurisdiction which the court has over its wards. As Cross J once said[4]:

'Any action which tends to hamper the court in carrying out its duty [to protect its wards] is an interference with the administration of justice and a criminal contempt'.

Not all acts which may be harmful to a ward are necessarily

---

1. For contempt generally see Borrie and Lowe: *The Law of Contempt* (1973 Butterworth), especially pp. 124–8, 243–7 for its effect on wardship. See also Miller: *Contempt of Court* (1976 EleK) especially pp. 209, 222–4.
2. See below at p. 154.
3. See e.g. Halsbury's *Laws of England* 4th Edn. para. 36. Bromley: *Family Law* (5th Edn.), p. 395 and Borrie and Lowe op. cit. 243–7.
4. *Re B (JA) (an infant)* [1965] Ch 1112 at 1117.

contempts. For example, it was held in *Re X (a minor)*[5] that publication of a book could not be restrained because of the possible indirect harm that it might have caused the ward. A fortiori it could not have been a contempt to have published the book. Even acts which directly harm a ward do not automatically constitute a contempt. For example, assaulting a ward may no doubt be harmful to him yet even if the offender knows that the child is a ward such an act will not normally constitute a contempt[6]. As Lord Denning MR once said[7]: 'The existence of wardship does not give the ward a privilege over and above other young people who are not wards'. His Lordship was specifically referring to publications concerning children who happen to be wards, but his statement applies equally to other acts. Were the position otherwise the protection afforded a ward would be too wide to be practicable.

On the other hand it is by no means always necessary when establishing a contempt to show that the act complained of has actually harmed the ward or that it is even potentially harmful to him. For example, removing a ward from the jurisdiction without the court's leave is a contempt irrespective of whether the move is good, bad or indifferent for the ward's interests. All that has to be proved is that the act complained of has interfered with the court's special protective jurisdiction.

For the most part the contempt powers in this respect are best seen as another aspect of the automatic protection which arises by reason of the wardship and which was discussed in Chapter 5. In other words the contempt powers are not dependent upon there being a court order.

It should be added that as the protective jurisdiction is peculiar to wardship the contempt powers are in this respect considerably wider than in relation to other jurisdictions concerned with children.

(1) *Marriage and removal from the jurisdiction*

The two classic and long-established examples of contempt

5. [1975] Fam 47, [1975] 1 All ER 697. Discussed ante in Chap. 5.
6. Aliter if his intention is to influence court proceedings. See *Re B(JA) (an infant)* [1965] Ch 1112, [1965] 2 All ER 168. Discussed below at p.142.
7. *Re F (otherwise A) (a minor) (publication of information)* [1977] Fam 58 at 86. Discussed further below.

are marrying the ward and removing him from the jurisdiction without, in each case, the court's prior leave. In each case the embargo arises as soon as the child becomes a ward and is not dependent on any specific restraining order[8].

Historically control of the ward's marriage was an important aspect of wardship[9]. Indeed in feudal times the lord's control over his ward's marriage was a profitable one[10]. In later times the major concern of the court was to protect the property interests of its wards. Permission to marry would only be granted where the marriage was thought to be fitting and suitable in terms of the relative ages of the parties and, perhaps more importantly, where there was a fair equality of rank and fortune between them and a suitable settlement had been agreed upon[11]. Not surprisingly marriage of a ward without the court's permission was regarded as a very serious contempt and indeed the law in this regard was well developed[12]. Today the embargo against marrying a ward is not nearly as important particularly since the age of majority has been reduced to 18[13].

Despite the decline in importance of the ward's marriage there remains a considerable body of case law. It is established that all persons actively involved in the marriage, be they the marriage partners themselves, including the ward[14], or the celebrant[15] or witnesses or any other person responsible for encouraging the marriage may be held guilty of contempt[16]. Moreover it is no defence that the marriage is invalid[17], that

8. Though in practice such orders may be made, particularly to restrain the ward's marriage.
9. In the chapter on Wards of Court in Eversley's *Law of Domestic Relations* (6th Edn. 1951 Sweet and Maxwell) more than half is devoted to marriage. See also Seton's *Judgment and Orders* Vol. II (7th Edn. 1912, Sweet and Maxwell) 1004–19.
10. See Chap. 1.
11. See e.g. Eversley op. cit. at p. 602. See also Chap. 5.
12. Particularly in relation to consequential settlements of property. See e.g. Eversley op. cit. pp. 609–10; Seton op. cit. 1013 et seqi. See also Rayden on *Divorce* (13th Edn. 1979), at pp. 1130–31.
13. By s.1 of the Family Law Reform Act 1969.
14. *Re Leigh, Leigh v Leigh* (1888) 40 Ch D 290, *Re H's Settlement, H v H* [1909] 2 Ch 260. See also *Re Crump (an infant)* (1963) 107 Sol Jo 682.
15. At least, according to *Nicholson v Squire* (1809) 16 Ves 259, he was liable to censure.
16. *Eyre v Countess of Shaftesbury* (1722) 2 P Wms 103. See also *Long v Elways* (1729) Mos. 249.
17. See e.g. *Warter v Yorke* (1815) 19 Ves 451.

the ward, father or guardian consented[18], nor, more controversially, is it a defence to plead ignorance of the fact that the
child is a ward[19]. Once the child has attained 18 he ceases to be
a ward and it cannot then be a contempt to marry him[20].

Like marrying a ward it has long been established that it is a
contempt to remove him from the jurisdiction. The reason
for this is that such a removal would effectively deprive the
court of its power to supervise the ward's upbringing. Unlike
marriage, this aspect of contempt has become more
important. A recent *Practice Direction*[1] now provides that on
every originating summons by which application is made to
make the child a ward of court there should be the following
indorsement:

> 'IMPORTANT NOTICE: It is a contempt of Court
> which may be punished by imprisonment, to take any
> child named in this summons out of England and Wales,
> even to Scotland, Northern Ireland, the Republic of
> Ireland, the Channel Islands or the Isle of Man, without
> the leave of the Court'.

By analogy with marrying a ward it is probably a contempt
to attempt to remove the ward from the jurisdiction[2]. If the
child has already been lawfully removed from the jurisdiction the court does have the power in wardship to order the
child's return and failure to comply with the order will also
amount to contempt[3]. The embargo lies against anyone be
they the parents or strangers and again the cases as they stand
establish that it is no defence to plead ignorance of the fact

---

18. *Wellesley v Duke of Beaufort* (1829) 2 Russ 1. See also s.3(6) of the Marriage
Act 1949.
19. *Herbert's Case* (1731) 3 P Wms 116; 24 ER 992 affirmed in *Re H's Settlement H
v H* [1909] 2 Ch 260. Cf *Re F (otherwise A) (a minor) (Publication of
Information)* [1977] Fam 58 at 88 per Lord Denning MR discussed below.
20. *Bolton v Bolton* [1891] 3 Ch 270.
 1. [1977] 3 All ER 122, [1977] 1 WLR 1067.
 2. Cf. *Warter v Yorke* (1815) 19 Ves 451. It is not yet established whether there
is an offence known as attempting to commit contempt but on the basis of
Balogh v St. Albans Crown Court [1975] QB 73, [1974] 3 All ER 283, mere
preparation to take the child out of the jurisdiction may not be enough to
constitute contempt. Query whether buying an airline ticket in the ward's
name would be a contempt.
 3. See e.g. *Re O (a minor) (wardship: adopted child)* [1978] 2 All ER 27. See also
Re O (infants) [1962] 2 All ER 10, [1962] 1 WLR 724. Query whether in such
cases a specific restraining order is necessary before a contempt can be
established.

that the child is a ward[4] or that the act was done on the solicitation of the ward[5].

The fact that in each of these cases it seems well established that contempts may be committed in ignorance of the fact that the child is a ward has not escaped censure. In Lord Denning MR's view[6] neither should be a strict offence and it is difficult not to agree with him. As one learned author has commented[7]:

'There is no sense in holding an offence to have been committed by a person who lacks knowledge of the status of the person with whom he is dealing and whose interference with the protective jurisdiction of the court was no more than a matter of bad luck'.

To this may be added the comment that since the wardshp numbers have increased the strict law approach has become impracticable. Clearly Lord Denning MR's comments though obiter have put a query against the established cases and it may be hoped that should the matter arise the court will be disposed to follow his views. At all events it is unlikely that the cases would be extended to other circumstances.

ii) *Concealing the ward's whereabouts*

It is clearly important to the proper exercise of its jurisdiction that the court should know the whereabouts of its wards[8]. Concealing the ward's whereabouts is therefore a serious contempt[9]. Furthermore all parties who either know or are supposed to know of the ward's residence can be summarily ordered to attend the court and give such information as is within their knowledge[10]. Refusal to answer such questions constitutes a contempt. Even a solicitor is obliged to give the court any information which may lead to the discovery of the ward's whereabouts, nor can he withhold such information

---

4. *Re J (an infant)* (1913) 108 LT 554. See also *Re Witten* (1887) 4 TLR 36.
5. *Re J (an infant)* ibid.
6. Expressed in *Re F (otherwise A) (publication of information)* [1977] Fam 58 at 88.
7. Miller: *Contempt of Court* op. cit. at p. 224. See also Munro (1977) 40 MLR 343.
8. By RSC Order 90, rules 3(4) (5) parties are obliged to *state* in the summons the ward's whereabouts. See Ch. 4.
9. *Mustafa v Mustafa* (1967) Times. September 11 and 13.
10. See e.g. *Rosenberg v Lindo* (1883) 48 LT 478 where a RC bishop and a lady superior were ordered to attend.

on the basis that it has been imparted to him during the course of his professional employment[11].

iii) *Interfering with the evidence relevant to wardship proceedings*

It is also important to the proper exercise of its jurisdiction that the court should have before it all the available evidence. Any act which tends to interfere with the availability of the evidence will constitute a contempt. The most blatant example of this occurred in *Re B (JA) (an infant)*[12]. The parents had warded their daughter to restrain her association with a much older man, one W. Pending the hearing of the motion, they applied and obtained an order restraining W from communicating with their daughter. Notice of that motion was served inter alia both on the girl and W. Subsequently W attempted to prejudice the course of justice by making threats to another girl in order to induce her to refrain from giving further evidence and to withdraw the evidence already given. Far from being successful his threats had no effect for the girl in question told the ward's father who immediately launched a motion for committal.

It was held that W had committed a grave contempt. As Cross J said[13]:

'the mere fact that no harm has been done in this particular case is neither here nor there. It would be unfortunate if the idea got abroad that if people threaten witnesses in this way, the worst that is likely to happen to them will be that they will have to pay some costs and make an apology. That is certainly not a course which I can adopt in this case. Nor do I think that the case is appropriate for a fine. This is a case in which I think it is my duty to make a committal order'.

Re B (JA) was specifically concerned with an improper approach to a witness but it would be equally a contempt to approach a party or even the ward with a view to improperly influencing them in their evidence[14]. It would also be a grave contempt to punish any person for having given evidence[15].

11. *Ramsbotham v Senior* (1869) LR 8 Eq. 575.
12. [1965] Ch 1112.
13. Ibid. at 1123.
14. See Borrie and Lowe op. cit. at p. 223 et seq.
15. *A-G's Application, A-G v Butterworth* [1963] 1 QB 696. Discussed in Borrie and Lowe at p. 213 et seq.

As for the mens rea required it seems clear that it must be shown that the offender was aware of the wardship and that he knew that the person he approached was a potential witness or party as the case may be[16].

iv) *Obtaining psychiatric reports without the court's leave*

The court has on several occasions warned the profession that the examination of a ward by a psychiatrist with a view to putting a report in evidence constitutes an 'important step in the child's life' and as such should not be undertaken without the court's leave[17]. Practitioners[18] who ignore these warnings do so at their peril for although no contempt proceedings have yet been brought the clear implication is that they could be[19]. Counsel's advice to have the ward so examined was held in *Re R (PM) (an infant)*[20] to be a 'serious error of judgment' and in the light of this if contempt proceedings were to be brought it would be difficult to argue, as counsel successfully did in *Re R (PM) (an infant)* that he was acting in good faith in what he considered to be his duty to the court.

Whether the embargo extends to other kinds of examinations or the obtaining of blood tests from a ward with a view to establishing paternity is uncertain[1]. In each case, however, it is at least arguable that they would be regarded as important steps and failure to obtain the court's leave might be regarded as a contempt.

The precise nature of the contempt with regard to improperly obtaining reports is a moot point. It may be seen as interfering with the evidence before the court in which case the contempt would not be confined to wardship cases.

16. Following *Re B(JA)*. See Cross J's comments at pp. 1122, 1123.
17. See *Re S (an infant)* [1967] 1 All ER 202 at 209 per Cross J; *B(M) v B(R)* [1968] 3 All ER 170 at 174 per Willmer LJ; *Re R(PM) (an infant)* [1968] 1 All ER 691n, [1968] 1 WLR 385 and *Re A-W (minors)* (1975) 5 Fam Law 95.
18. I.e. Counsel or solicitors. Medical Practitioners may also be liable though to be guilty they would have to know the child is a ward (or subject to pending custody proceedings). Following *Re F (otherwise A) (a minor)* [1977] Fam 58, [1976] 3 All ER 274 they might also have to be aware of the legal significance of such a status. See below.
19. Such proceedings may be brought, if as in *Re R(PM)* the examination jeopardises any future plans for the child. For other sanctions see ante Chap. 5.
20. [1968] 1 All ER at 692 per Goff J.
1. See ante Chap. 5.

On the other hand the contempt may be viewed as interfering with the court's duty to protect its ward. Either view is tenable. Certainly warnings have been given in other proceedings than wardship[2] which suggests that the contempt in this respect does not exclusively arise from the special nature of wardship. On the other hand, the notion that no important step should be taken in a child's life without the court's permission seems confined to wardship cases.

v) *Other possible contempts*

It seems clear that the ambit of contempt goes beyond the cases already mentioned but its precise scope is uncertain. In principle it would seem that the contempt sanction is available whenever the automatic protection of a ward is impaired. However the precise scope of the court's automatic control is also uncertain. In Chapter 5 it was submitted[3] that following *Re D (a minor)*[4] it is now part of the automatic control of a ward that he should not be sterilised, nor possibly receive other non therapeutic treatment without the court's leave. If this is correct it would therefore be a contempt so to act without the court's prior consent, at least provided the offenders knew that the child was a ward of court[5].

Apart from impairing the court's automatic control it might also be a contempt to jeopardise[6] a court order made for the ward's benefit. It is on this basis that Russell LJ's warning[7] to the press that to interview a ward might be a contempt could be justified. On a similar basis it may be a contempt to change the child's surname without the court's leave or to act in any way which will seriously affect an order made by the court[8].

---

2. As in *B(M) v B(R)* [1968] 3 All ER, 170, [1968] 1 WLR 1182.
3. Ante at p. 76.
4. *Re D (a minor) (wardship: sterlisation)* [1976] Fam 185 [1976] 1 All ER 326.
5. Following *Re F (otherwise A) (a minor)* [1977] Fam 58. According to Lord Denning MR it might even be necessary to be aware of the significance of the status—see below.
6. I.e. as opposed to breaking an order which will clearly be a contempt. See below.
7. In *Re T(AJJ) (an infant)* [1970] Ch 688 at 689. Discussed in Chap. 5.
8. See Chap. 5 for discussion of these points.

B. PUBLICATIONS CONTRARY TO SECTION 12 OF THE ADMINISTRATION OF JUSTICE ACT 1960

i) *Scope of the restriction*

Like other proceedings heard in private the publication of information relating to wardship proceedings is restricted by section 12 of the Administration of Justice Act 1960. Section 12(1) provides inter alia:

> 'The publication of information relating to proceedings before any court sitting in private shall not of itself be contempt of court except in the following cases that is to say: (a) where the proceedings relate to the wardship . . . of the infant.'

It will be noted that a prerequisite to the operation of section 12 is that the court must be sitting in private. In wardship this will usually be the case but the judge does have a discretion to deliver judgment in open court, and will do so where he feels that there is a matter of some importance. In such cases the judgment can be reported and provided it is fair and accurate it cannot be a contempt.

A second condition is that the offending material must be *published*. Hence the mere receipt of such information will not constitute a contempt. By 'publication' is meant the communication of the information[9] in any form, be it printed, or broadcast or simply passed on by word of mouth.

A third condition of liability is that the information must relate to the wardship proceedings. The Court of Appeal in *Re F (otherwise A) (a minor)*[10] has held that this provision refers to the court proceedings and not to the state of wardship. In other words not all references to the ward are prohibited under this section. Nevertheless the restriction encompasses the publication of reports (including speculative reports[11]) of both the actual hearing and the evidence filed for the hearing such as the Official Solicitor's report, affidavits and pleadings.

---

9. Nevertheless it would still have to be shown that the offender intended to publish the material. Hence the person, such as a newspaper boy, who is both ignorant of the contents of the publication and has no responsibility for it will not be guilty of contempt. See Borrie and Lowe op. cit. at pp. 178–80 and *McLeod v St Aubyn* [1899] AC 549.
10. *Re F (otherwise A) (a minor) (publication of information)* [1977] Fam 58, [1976] 3 All ER 274. Discussed in more detail on this point in Chap. 5.
11. See the warning given in another context by Lord Widgery CJ reported (1971) 121 NLJ 548 and (1971) Times 17 June p. 4.

The restriction, therefore arises before the hearing and continues after it though in the latter respect it may not be permanent[12]. It should be added that the restriction applies both to proceedings before the registrar and the judge[13].

Even if a publication satisfies the above conditions it may still not be a contempt despite the apparent absolute prohibition under section 12(1)[14]. Whether it was intended to be absolute has been obscured by section 12(4) which states:

> 'Nothing in this section shall be construed as implying that any publication is punishable as contempt of court which would not be so punishable apart from this section'.

This provision had given rise to two conflicting interpretations[15]:

(1) that apart from cases expressly governed by section 12(1) no publication can be a contempt unless it is by common law. In other words in the instances covered by section 12(1), including therefore wardship, the common law has been entirely replaced.

(2) that section 12 as a whole is not intended to create any new instances of contempt and that therefore even in the cases expressly mentioned by section 12(1) a publication will only amount to contempt if it does so according to the common law. In other words the common law is relevant in every case.

This conflict has now been resolved by the Court of Appeal in *Re F (otherwise A) (a minor)*[16] in favour of the latter interpretation. Accordingly, section 12(1) is to be interpreted as meaning that publications of information relating inter alia to wardship proceedings heard in private *may*[17] be a contempt, it being left to the court's discretion to determine when, 'remembering', as Lord Denning MR said[18], 'that the

---

12. See Chap. 5 at p. 79 for further discussion.
13. See s.12(3).
14. The phrase that 'a publication shall not of itself be a contempt except in the following circumstances' could fairly be interpreted to mean that in those instances publications would automatically be a contempt.
15. See Borrie and Lowe op. cit. p. 119.
16. [1977] Fam 58, [1977] 1 All ER 114. Noted by Lowe: 'Wardship Contempt and Freedom of Speech' (1977) 93 LQR 180.
17. I.e. the section should not be read as implying that the specified exceptions should automatically amount to contempt.
18. [1977] Fam 58 at p. 87A.

courts are not to make punishable anything which would not previously be punishable'.

Under this interpretation not all publications of information relating to wardship proceedings heard in private will necessarily be contempt. In the first place the alleged offender will only be guilty of contempt if he has the requisite mens rea. Secondly publications are permissible provided the court has sanctioned them.

ii) *Mens rea*

That a *mens rea* is required was established by the Court of Appeal in *Re F (otherwise A) (a minor)*. Contempt proceedings had been brought against the *Daily Telegraph* and the Slough *Evening Mail* for publishing articles which referred to the contents of the confidential reports of the Official Solicitor and a social worker and which specifically stated that the girl in question had been made a 'temporary ward of court'. Both newspapers pleaded in their defence that at the time of publication they did not know that the child was still a ward. They mistakenly believed that the wardship order had ended.

It was held relying on the supposed common law position[19] that the newspapers' ignorance of the wardship was a defence. However, while agreeing on its need their lordships were not in entire agreement as to exactly what mens rea is required. Scarman LJ described[20] the defence in terms of 'no notice' so that no offence can be committed unless the publisher is aware that he is publishing information relating to proceedings heard in private. Lord Denning MR was more explicit[1]:

> 'a person is only to be found guilty ... if he has published information relating to wardship proceedings in circumstances in which he knows that publication is prohibited by law, or recklessly in circumstances in which he knows that the publication may be prohibited by law, but nevertheless goes on and publishes it, not caring whether it is prohibited or not'.

19. Relying on *Re Martindale* [1894] 3 Ch 193 and *Re De Beaujeu's Application* [1949] Ch 230 and drawing an analogy with civil contempts. For a criticism of this approach see Lowe at pp. 182, 183.
20. [1977] Fam at p. 96. Geoffrey Lane LJ saw the defence in similar terms ibid. at p. 107.
 1. This quotation is taken from [1976] 3 WLR at 825 as there appears to be a series of misprints at [1977] Fam p. 90.

In other words the publisher must not only know of the existence of wardship proceedings but also that publication of those proceedings is prohibited by law. This latter requirement would, it was thought, give adequate protection to 'ordinary folk' while not giving too much freedom to newspapers since they would be taken to know that such publications are prohibited.

While sympathising with Lord Denning MR's desire to cut down the scope of the offence as far as the parties to the proceedings are concerned, his views are not without difficulties. It could mean, for example, that unless warned against publishing details of the proceedings, parties (provided they are ignorant of the law) would be free not only to talk to their friends about the case but also to give details to the press including the contents of the Official Solicitor's report with the consequent possibility of these details being published by the press in ignorance of the existence of the wardship. Indeed this is more or less what actually happened in *Re F (otherwise A)* itself.

In consequence of this decision the practice now is to attach to the Official Solicitor's report a warning stating: 'Confidential—Not To Be Published'. A similar practice is undertaken with regard to reports of a court welfare officer. Whether this is enough to bring notice of possible contempt is debatable[2]. Certainly the warning could be clearer as for example, by stating 'Confidential—you are warned that it is a contempt of court, which may be punished by imprisonment, to divulge the contents of this report'. Even with an appropriate warning attached to the report the parties may still be free to reveal details of the case. Accordingly, it would be good practice if the judge specifically warned those attending the hearing not to do so.

Although it is clear that once it is known that the information relates to wardship proceedings the news media will be taken to know that such proceedings are normally heard in private it is uncertain what obligation, if any, there is to check whether there are wardship proceedings. None of their Lordships expressly referred to this point, though Lord Denning MR's reference to recklessness must be taken to mean that there is some obligation to check the existence of

2. It might be thought to be 'reckless' to ignore such a warning.

such proceedings. On the face of it the obligation to make such checks does not seem to be that great. The *Daily Telegraph*[3] had enough information at its disposal to learn of the current existence of a wardship order for had the Official Solicitor's report been read properly the reporter would have known the facts. It is to be hoped that the position will be clarified. It is submitted that the fairest position both for the protection of the ward and from the newspaper's point of view, is to make the defence of 'no notice' conditional on having taken all reasonable care[4].

iii) *Publications with consent*

Despite the apparent embargo on publishing information relating to wardship proceedings, it is stated in a *Practice Direction*[5] that:

'Although it is provided by section 12 of the Administration of Justice Act 1960 that no information regarding wardship and other proceedings in private relating to children may be published, it is considered by the President of the Family Division that the parties to such proceedings may obtain transcripts of the proceedings without the leave of the court.

Those who are not parties to the proceedings may obtain a transcript only in special circumstances and by leave of the judge'.

The validity of this direction was considered in *Re R (MJ) (a minor)*[6]. It was argued that as section 12 did not expressly enable a judge to permit publication the direction was ultra vires. Rees J rejected this argument holding instead that section 12 had to be read subject to the common law under which[7] the judge had a complete discretion whether or not to permit publication. Accordingly, the direction was held to be intra vires.

3. The *Evening Mail* on the other hand had not only checked with the director of social services of the local authority but also with the Official Solicitor whose reply did not directly indicate that the child was a ward, sed quaere?
4. This would have been the position had the defence's argument that s.11(1) of the 1960 Act which in certain circumstances provides a defence to prejudicing the administration of justice applied to s.12 contempts. For an argument that it could have applied see Lowe at pp. 183, 184.
5. [1972] 1 All ER 1056.
6. [1975] Fam 89, [1975] 2 All ER 749.
7. Relying on Wynn-Parry J in *Re De Beaujeu's Application* [1949] Ch 230 at 235.

The interpretation that section 12 should be read as being subject to the common law has, as we have seen, been subsequently upheld in *Re F*. The common law position as to publication of proceedings was perhaps not beyond doubt,[8] but *Re R (MJ) (a minor)* is likely to have settled the issue particularly as there is no doubt that it has been the long standing practice of the courts to invoke the co-operation of the press and authorise publication of details of the case in order to trace missing wards[9].

The current position is as follows. Under the *Practice Direction* parties can obtain a transcript without the court's leave but non parties can only do so in special circumstances and with the court's consent. The court can on its own initiative allow publication of proceedings and commonly does so in cases of missing wards.

In deciding whether to authorise publication in the latter case the court will clearly act according to the ward's best interests but this is not the invariable guiding principle as *Re R (MJ)* shows. In that case a trustee in bankruptcy sought leave to obtain a transcript of the evidence given in wardship and adoption proceedings with a view to using it in a subsequent bankruptcy hearing[10]. Rees J rejected[11] the Official Solicitor's argument that leave should only be given in cases where disclosure could be shown to be for the ward's benefit or for the benefit of minors generally in future cases. While accepting[12] that a judge should place the interests of the minor in the forefront of his considerations and that considerable weight had to be given to the public interest in ensuring that frankness should prevail in such proceedings by preserving confidentiality Rees J pointed out that there were other interests to be considered. Of these a most

---

8. See Tudor Evans J in *Re F (otherwise A)* [1977] Fam at 72.
9. In *Re F (otherwise A) ibid.* at 73 Tudor Evans J recognised this practice and sought to explain it on the basis that the court had as part of its protective power over its ward, the power to confer an immunity on an act which would otherwise be a contempt.
10. In fact the trustee in bankruptcy had already obtained a copy of the transcript which was used in the bankruptcy hearing. A motion of contempt was brought against the trustee and although it was dismissed the trustee was ordered to pay half the applicant's costs on his summons and all her costs on the motion. See [1975] Fam at 99.
11. [1975] Fam 89 at 97 C.
12. Ibid. at 98.

important one was the public interest in upholding the law of the land by providing relevant evidence for use in other legitimate proceedings. In the instant case it was conceded that no legitimate interests of the ward would be harmed by the disclosure and accordingly leave was granted. In other words in the circumstances of the case the interests of justice in the bankruptcy hearing outweighed the interests of minors generally in the confidentiality of wardship proceedings[13]. Such a decision, as we have argued elsewhere[14] is in line with our submission that unless the ward's custody or upbringing is directly in issue, the ward's interests have to be weighed against other competing interests. Although Rees J made it clear that leave would not often be granted, unless it can be shown that the interests of the ward will be harmed, leave is likely to be granted in connection with other legal proceedings notably criminal[15].

C. DISOBEYING COURT ORDERS OR BREAKING UNDERTAKINGS

As was described in Chapter V the court has a wide power to make orders in wardship proceedings and it is incumbent upon the parties to obey them. Even if the order is ultra vires it may still be a contempt to disobey it.[16] In such cases the advisable course of action is to appeal against the order[17].

Court orders are essentially of two types prohibitory or mandatory. Prohibitory orders restrain particular acts, for example, restraining further communication with a ward[18], enjoining a party not to continue associating[19] with or

13. For an interesting contrast see *Re Poulson a bankrupt, ex parte Granada Television Ltd v Maudling* [1976] 2 All ER 1020, [1976] 1 WLR 1023 where the court refused leave to use evidence given in a bankruptcy hearing heard in private for use in subsequent libel proceedings.
14. See Ch. 6.
15. Though query whether a transcript would be released to the police. The more appropriate procedure might be thought to refer the matter to the Director of Public Prosecutions.
16. See Miller op. cit. at pp. 253–4 and the cases there cited.
17. As was done in *Re X (a minor) (wardship: jurisdiction)* [1975] Fam 47 [1975] 1 All ER 697.
18. See e.g. *Re R(PM)(an infant)* [1968] 1 All ER 691n [1968] 1 WLR 385; *Re B(JA) (an infant)* [1965] Ch 1112, [1965] 2 All ER 168 and *Re Elwes* (1958) Times 30 July.
19. See e.g. *Re PC (an infant)* [1961] Ch 312, [1961] 2 All ER 308.

harbouring[20] a ward; restraining marriage[1] of a ward or his removal from the jurisdiction[2]. Mandatory orders on the other hand, enjoin a particular act to be done as, for example, delivering custody of the child[3] to the other party or returning the child to the jurisdiction[4]. Disobedience to either type of order is a contempt.

Undertakings entered into with or given to the court by a party or his counsel or solicitor have exactly the same force as a court order. Accordingly, breaking an undertaking amounts to a contempt[5] in exactly the same way as disobeying a court order. The conditions for enforcement by the contempt process are the same as for a court order and are set out below.

Three conditions must be satisfied before any one can be held to have committed a contempt by disobeying a court order. First, the order itself must be clear and unambiguous[6]. Secondly, the alleged contemnor must have had adequate notice of the order. Thirdly, the breach must be proved beyond all reasonable doubt[7].

With regard to the requirement of notice the general rule under RSC Order 45 rule 7 is that no order can be enforced unless:

(a) a copy of the order has been served personally on the person required to do or abstain from doing the act in question[8], *and*

(b) in the case of an order requiring a person to do an act, the copy has been so served before the expiration of the time

---

20. See e.g. *Re F (otherwise A) (a minor)* [1977] Fam 58 [1977] 1 All ER 114.
 1. See e.g. *Re PC (an infant)* ibid.; *Re Crump (an infant)* (1963) 107 Sol Jo 682 and *Re Elwes* ibid.
 2. See e.g. *Re H(GJ)(an infant)* [1966] 1 All ER 952, [1966] 1 WLR 706. Other examples include restraining the discovery of the ward's whereabouts see e.g. *Re B (a minor) (wardship: child in care)* [1975] Fam 127, [1975] 2 All ER 449.
 3. See e.g. *G- v L-* [1891] 3 Ch 126. Failure to allow the other party to have access can also amount to contempt. Cf *Re K (a minor) (access order: breach)* [1977] 2 All ER 737, [1977] 1 WLR 533.
 4. See e.g. *Re Liddell's Settlement Trusts, Liddell v Liddell* [1936] Ch 365, [1936] 1 All ER 239.
 5. See generally Borrie and Lowe op. cit. at 325–8 and Miller op. cit. at 235 et seq.
 6. See Borrie and Lowe op. cit. at 316.
 7. See *Re Bramblevale Ltd* [1970] Ch 128, [1969] 3 All ER 1062 and Borrie and Lowe op. cit. at 319 et seq.
 8. RSC Ord. 45, r.7(2)(a).

within which he was required to do the act[9], *and* most importantly

(c) there is indorsed on the copy served a notice, commonly referred to as a 'penal notice', informing the person so served that if he neglects to obey the order within the time specified therein, or, if the order is to abstain from doing an act, that if he disobeys the order, he is liable to process of execution to compel him to obey it[10].

In the case of *prohibitory* orders *only* RSC Order 45 rule 7(6) specifically provides that an order can be enforced:

> 'notwithstanding that service of a copy of the order has not been effected in accordance with this rule if the Court is satisfied that, pending such service, the person against whom or against whose property it is sought to enforce the order has had notice thereof either—
> (a) by being present when the order was made, or
> (b) by being notified of the terms of the order, whether by telephone, telegram or otherwise'.

Although as one author[11] has put it 'personal service is little more than a convenient way of establishing notice where the order is couched in negative or prohibitive terms', the procedure of serving personal notice should normally be observed[12]. Moreover, it is to be borne in mind that it is a defence for the alleged offender to show that he had a bona fide and reasonable belief that no injunction has been granted[13].

It is to be noted that rule 7(6) does not apply to mandatory orders but by rule 7(7) *the court* has the power to dispense with the service of a copy of *any* order where it thinks it just to do so. In the case of mandatory orders notice will only be dispensed with where it can be shown that the defendant having notice of the term of the order is deliberately evading service[14].

9. RSC Ord. 45, r.7(2)(*b*). For the procedure for enforcing an order against a body corporate see RSC Ord. 45, rr. 7(3), 7(4)(6).
10. RSC Ord. 45, r.7(4).
11. Miller op. cit. at 243.
12. As the Supreme Court Practice 1979 at 733 puts it, the Rule is most useful where negative orders are sought ex parte in circumstances of great urgency.
13. *Re Bishop, ex parte Langley, ex parte Smith* (1879) 13 Ch D 110.
14. See *Re Tuck, Murch v Loosemore* [1906] 1 Ch 692 and *Turner v Turner* (1978) 122 Sol Jo 696. RSC Ord 45 r.7(7) also preserves the court's right to order substituted service under Ord. 65, r.4.

Clearly the parties expressly enjoined to do or refrain from doing the act in question are under a duty to comply with the order, but anybody, provided he has notice of the order can be held guilty of contempt if he aids and abets the breach[15]. It would seem that a person can be held guilty of contempt for aiding and abetting a breach of either a prohibitory or a mandatory order and a breach of an undetaking[16].

II Classification of contempts

Traditionally contempts are classified as being either criminal or civil[17], yet this division is far from clear when applied to the 'wardship contempts'. While contempts committed by interfering with the court's duty to protect its wards are generally regarded as criminal[18], disobeying a court order is usually categorised as a civil contempt. The two types, however, overlap in the wardship context. For example, removing a ward from the jurisdiction amounts to a criminal contempt or at least one which is accompanied by criminal incidents, whether or not there is a court order[19]. If however the removal is contrary to a specific court order it may also be regarded as civil contempt. The same difficulty of classification also attends publication of wardship proceedings. Publications of court proceedings heard in private contrary to section 12 of the Administration of Justice Act 1960 may be regarded as civil contempts[1], but a strong case could be made for arguing that publication of wardship proceedings is a criminal contempt, since it could be said to hamper the court's duty to protect its ward.

The issue of classification is by no means otiose because

---

15. The leading case is *Seaward v Paterson* [1897] 1 Ch 545. See Borrie and Lowe op. cit. at 323 et seq. and Miller op. cit. at 247 et seq.
16. See Borrie and Lowe op. cit at 324 and the cases there cited.
17. See Borrie and Lowe op. cit. at 369 et seq.
18. See e.g. *Wellesley v Duke of Beaufort* (1831) 2 Russ & M 639, 39 ER 538; *Re B (JA) (an infant)* [1965] Ch 1112, 1117. It is so classified by Halsbury: Laws of England (4th Edn.) Vol. 9 para. 36 and by the Supreme Court Practice 1979 p. 811.
19. See *Wellesley v Duke of Beaufort* ibid.
 1. See *Scott v Scott* [1913] AC 417; Borrie and Lowe op. cit. at 121 and 370–1 and Miller op. cit. at p. 214.

although most of the distinctions have been swept away[2] those remaining are of relevance to wardship. Of particular consequence is the availability of sequestration by which the contemnor's property is placed in the hands of persons known as sequestrators who manage the property and who receive the rents and profits[3]. The contemnor's assets are in effect frozen. Though a process of contempt[4] sequestration is a coercive remedy and a form of civil execution. As such it is only available in cases of civil contempts. The remedy is likely to be most useful against an individual contemnor where he is abroad but leaves property in England or Wales[5]. Ironically, the situation where this is most likely to arise namely, where the contemnor has removed the child from the jurisdiction without the court's leave, may only be classified as a criminal contempt[6]. Although it could be argued that the Family Division should not be unduly concerned with technicalities when protecting its wards the same cannot be said of its regard for the contemnor's rights. Nevertheless it is submitted that sequestration should be available if that is the appropriate remedy, and in order to satisfy the technicalities the contempt could be classified as partaking both of a criminal and civil nature, at least where the act done is contrary to a court order[7]. Such a dual classification would also allow the court to commit the offender to prison for an unspecified period[8] which is another remedy peculiar to civil contempt and not irrelevant in the wardship context.

2. E.g. there is now right of appeal in all cases and the court can fine an offender in all cases. See Borrie and Lowe op. cit. at 371 The Phillimore Committee 1974 Cmnd. 5794 recommend the distinction to be abolished.
3. For further details see e.g. Borrie and Lowe op. cit. at 344 et seq.
4. See *Pratt v Inman* (1889) 43 Ch D 175.
5. See *Re Liddell's Settlement Trusts Liddell v Liddell* [1936] Ch 365, [1936] 1 All ER 239 and *Romilly v Romilly* [1964] P 22, [1963] 3 All ER 607.
   Sequestration is also useful as a remedy against a corporate body. It was applied for in *Re F (otherwise A) (a minor) (publication of information)* [1977] Fam. 58.
6. Particularly where no court order has been made, but even where there is an order according to *Wellesley v Duke of Beaufort* ibid.
7. In *Re Liddell's Settlement Trust Liddell v Liddell* ibid. for example sequestration was applied for following the disobedience to a court order. Where the removal took place before any court order it is suggested that an order seeking the child's return should be obtained prior to applying for a writ of sequestration.
8. Imprisonment for criminal contempts should be for a fixed period. See e.g. *A-G v James* [1962] 2 QB 637 at 641 per Lord Parker CJ, cf civil contempts see post p.162.

III Initiating proceedings

The initiative for setting contempt proceedings in motion principally rests on the party prejudiced by the alleged contumacious conduct. This will be particularly so where the contempt partakes of a 'private nature'; such as the failure to produce the ward for access, but is generally true in all cases of alleged contempt. Occasionally, however others may take the initiative. In *Re F (otherwise A) (a minor)*[9] for example upon becoming aware of the publication of a newspaper article containing inter alia details of his confidential report, the Official Solicitor (who was acting as guardian ad litem to the ward in question) applied for an order restricting further publication of information relating to the proceedings. Subsequently the court directed him to institute contempt proceedings against the newspaper concerned. In *Re Crump (an infant)*[10] following the blatant flouting of a court order restraining the ward's marriage the Attorney-General brought a motion for committal.

Neither the Official Solicitor nor the Attorney-General will readily institute proceedings. The Official Solicitor for example takes the view that it is normally better for the adult party prejudiced by the conduct to institute proceedings. Moreover if the contempt proceedings are successful the Official Solicitor may find himself involved in a conflict of duties, namely, acting as the ward's guardian ad litem while at the same time being concerned to represent the imprisoned contemnor's interests[11]. Although in practice this conflict can be resolved by the Official Solicitor instructing private solicitor's to represent the contemnor[12], his reluctance to be involved in initiating proceedings is understandable. For this reason, if proceedings are instituted at all it will be more usually by the Attorney-General. Such intervention is only likely in the case of criminal contempts such as the unlawful removal of the ward from the jurisdiction[13] or where the

---

9. [1977] Fam 58. See e.g. p. 65. Apparently the Attorney-General was aware of the proceedings but was content to allow them to be conducted by the Official Solicitor—see p. 63. The Official Solicitor has instituted contempt proceedings where the ward has been unlawfully removed from the country.
10. (1963) 107 Sol Jo 682. This was apparently the first reported instance of his intervention. He was widely criticised for doing so. See (1963) 113 LJ 585.
11. For his duties in this regard see e.g. Miller op. cit. at 258-9.
12. His powers are apparently wide enough to allow this and to pay their fees.
13. It is sometimes advantageous to have a respected official involved in a case which has an international context.

contempt is committed by strangers to the proceedings as for example, by those who are responsible for unlawful publication of proceedings[1] .

The court also has the power to act upon its own motion[15]. It will do so where the contempt is committed in the face of the court as, for example where a party or witness refuses to answer a question. Alternatively it may act where a person has refused to obey a summons and attend the court[16]. The court may also act once a contempt issue has been brought to its notice. In *Re F (otherwise A)*, for example the court directed contempt proceedings to be brought.

It will be seen, therefore that although the burden for setting contempt proceedings in motion principally rests on the individual party he does have a number of options. He can, for example, inform the Attorney-General or the Official Solicitor (if acting as the ward's guardian ad litem) in the hope that one or the other will bring proceedings. This approach could reasonably be taken in cases of criminal contempt although even then there is no guarantee that any further steps will be taken. Secondly, he could seek directions from the court in the hope that it will either act on its own motion or direct that proceedings be brought. Thirdly, he can take steps to bring proceedings himself. He can do this in all cases of alleged contempt[17] and would certainly be advised to do so where the contempt partakes of a private nature.

As a rider to the above it is important to remember that contempt is a remedy of the last resort. Motion for commital should not be launched without good cause. Indeed litigants would do well to heed Ormrod LJ's words[18]:

'Breach of . . . an order is perhaps unfortunately called contempt of court the conventional remedy for which is a summons for committal. But the real purpose of bringing the matter back to the court, in most cases is not so much to punish the disobedience as to secure compliance with the order in the future. It will often be wiser to bring the matter before the courts again for

14. Or by those who have sought to prevent the course of justice.
15. This is expressly reserved by RSC Ord. 52, r.5.
16. These latter instances are likely to arise in cases where the ward's whereabouts are being concealed.
17. Moreover he does not have to seek the Attorney-General's permission even if the contempt is criminal. Cf. the Phillimore Committee's proposals at para. 187. Query whether the Committee considered the effect in wardship.
18. In *Ansah v Ansah* [1977] 2 All ER 638 at 643.

further direction before applying for a committal order. Committal orders are remedies of the last resort; in family cases they should be the very last resort'.

IV Procedure

A. APPLYING FOR A COMMITTAL ORDER

The normal procedure in cases of alleged contempt is to seek a committal order and by RSC Order 52, rule 1(3) such orders can only[19] be made by a judge of the Family Division where it relates to wardship proceedings. It is clear that the Family Division remains the only venue even if the alleged contempt does not directly concern the ward. This is one of the consequences of *Re B(JA)* *(infant)*[20] where it will be recalled, an approach had been made not to the ward but to another young girl to induce her to refrain from giving evidence in the wardship proceedings. It was held that the motion in regard to that contempt was properly brought in the wardship proceedings.

The precise means by which a committal order should be sought is not beyond doubt. By RSC Order 52, rule 4(1) the application should be by motion. However the normal practice in the Family Division is to proceed by summons as provided for by rule 90(1) of the Matrimonial Causes Rules 1977. Strictly speaking rule 90(1) does not apply to wardship[1]. Nevertheless it seems that in practice the Family Division in wardship will accept committal applications by summons.

The essential difference between procedure on motion and procedure by summons is that a motion is heard in court and a summons in chambers. This distinction is blurred by the fact that by Order 52, rule 6 motions for committal in wardship proceedings can be heard in private while summonses are in practice listed for hearing in open court, though again the hearing can take place in private. However because of this technical difference, it is thought that pro-

19. I.e. it is mandatory to go to the Family Division. See Miller op. cit. at 30.
20. [1965] Ch 1112, [1965] 2 All ER 168.
 1. The MCR only apply to wardship in so far as RSC. Ord 90, r.11 provides. In this respect the statement in *Rayden on Divorce* (13th Edn) at p. 1134 that a summons should be used should be treated with caution.

cedure by motion is more applicable in cases of contempt by strangers as in the case of unlawful publication of proceedings by newspapers[2], since such matters are essentially outside the domestic context, and it is therefore difficult to see any justification for proceeding in chambers.

Although no doubt the court would in practice override any objection to the precise procedure adopted provided the defendant had properly been served with notice, the uncertainty is another example of the lack of precision in the rules concerning wardship matters. It would surely be possible for a rule to deal specifically with this point.

Procedurally there is little difference[3] between applying by motion and applying by summons. If application is made by motion it is clear that even if the contempt does not directly concern the ward, the proper practice is to bring a motion within the wardship proceedings and not to proceed by an originating motion[4]. By RSC Order 52, rule 4 an application by motion must be supported by an affidavit[5], and the notice of motion, stating the grounds of the application and accompanied by a copy of the supporting affidavit[6] must be served personally on the person sought to be committed. The court can[7] dispense with personal service but will in practice do so only in exceptional cases as, for example, where the defendant deliberately evades service[8]. Application by summons[9] must similarly be supported by affidavit which should be filed before the summons is served and again save in exceptional cases a copy of the affidavit together with the summons must be served personally on the person sought to be committed[10].

Although the court might be prepared to waive minor defects in process it will not do so where the safeguards are laid down in the contemnor's interests. In this regard it is of

---

2. Application was by motion in *Re F (otherwise A)* [1977] Fam 58, [1977] 1 All ER 114. See also *Re R (MJ) (a minor)* [1975] Fam at 99.
3. It might, however, be quicker to proceed by motion.
4. See *Re B(JA) (an infant)* [1965] Ch 1112, [1965] 2 All ER 168.
5. RSC Order 52, r. 4(1).
6. Ord. 52, r.4(2).
7. Ord. 52, r.4(3).
8. See e.g. the Supreme Court Practice 1979 at 814.
9. See Halsbury: *Laws of England* (4th Edn.) Vol. 13 para. 1206.
10. In serious cases involving a matter of urgency a committal order may be made on an ex parte application. See *Ansah v Ansah* [1977] Fam 138, [1977] 2 All ER 638.

cardinal importance that the grounds are set out in the notice of motion[11] or summons as the case may be and that the affidavits are served at the same time as the notice of motion or summons.[12]

B. APPLYING FOR SEQUESTRATION

Obedience to court orders can be enforced by a writ of sequestration by which sequestrators are authorised to hold the contemnor's property until such time as he complies. Writs of sequestration can only be issued with the court's leave and application for leave must be to a judge by motion[13]. The motion should set out the grounds for application and should be accompanied by an affidavit in support[13]. The notice of motion, stating the grounds of the application and accompanied by a copy of the supporting affidavit, should be served personally on the person against whose property it is sought to issue the writ[14]. The court may exceptionally dispense with personal service[15].

The remedy of sequestration is perhaps most applicable against a body corporate but it can be used against the individual particularly when he is abroad but leaves property in this country.

C. HEARING OF THE APPLICATION

Formerly applications for committal could only be made by a litigant in person save in the Divisional Court of the Queen's Bench Division. It has recently been held[16], however, that litigants in person are at liberty to move for a committal order in the Chancery Division. It seems likely

---

11. See *Re B (JA) (an infant)* [1965] Ch 1112, at 1117–8 per Cross J. A number of committal orders made in the County Court have been held defective on this ground see e.g. *Wellington v Wellington* (1978) 122 Sol Jo 296; *Cinderby v Cinderby* (1978) 122 Sol Jo 436 and *Pekesin v Pekesin* (1978) 8 Fam Law 130. Cf. *Kavanagh v Kavanagh* [1978] LS Gaz R 825 where Eveleigh LJ suggested that the same particularity was not required in a High Court order. Sed quaere?
12. Per Cross J in *Re B (JA)* ibid. at 1118.
13. RSC Ord. 46 r.5(1).
14. Ord. 46, r.5(2).
15. Ord. 46, r.5(3).
16. Per Goulding J in *Bevan v Hastings Jones* [1978] 1 All ER 479, [1978] 1 WLR 294.

that a similar practice will be adopted in the Family Division[17].

Unless the court otherwise gives leave the only grounds that can be relied upon for the committal are those stated in the motion[18]. The person sought to be committed is entitled to give oral evidence on his own behalf[19].

When hearing an application for committal for a matter arising out of wardship proceedings the judge has a discretion, which is usually exercised, to sit in private[20]. If he does so sit he must[1] nevertheless state in open court, the name of the person sought to be committed, the general nature of the alleged contempt and if he is being committed the length of that period.

V Powers of the court

The court must first decide whether the alleged contempt has been proved. In all cases the appropriate standard of proof is the criminal standard, namely being satisfied beyond all reasonable doubt[2].

Once the contempt is made out the court has at its disposal wide powers to deal with it. It is not bound to make the order sought be it committal or sequestration. In either case it can fine the offender instead or even dismiss the application making the offender pay the costs[3]. At all events the drastic remedy of committal or sequestration will be used sparingly and generally only where the contempt is serious or the breach deliberate.

Even if the court does decide that the case merits committal it may choose to suspend the order[4]. The threat of committal can of course be most effective but it has been said[5] that suspended orders should be made with care and that in

17. Though this should not be taken to encourage litigants to apply in person. See Goulding J at 481.
18. RSC Ord. 52, r.6(3).
19. Ord. 52, r.6(4).
20. By Ord. 52, r.6(1)(a).
1. By Ord. 52, r.6(2).
2. See *Re Bramblevale Ltd* [1970] Ch 128, [1969] 3 All ER 1062 and *Kent County Council v Batchelor* (1976) 75 LGR 151.
3. See e.g. *Re R(MJ)* (*a minor*) [1977] Fam at 99.
4. Pursuant to RSC Ord 52, r.7.
5. Per Ormrod LJ in *Ansah v Ansah* [1977] 2 All ER 638 at 643.

particular the conditions of suspension should be such that control remains in the court. Even if the conditions of suspension are broken the court is still not bound to commit the offender but has a discretion to do what is just in all the circumstances[6].

The court can and has imprisoned a ward for contempt[7] but such an order is extremely rare especially as the remedy seems to defeat the purpose of the protective jurisdiction.

The court has a complete discretion as to how long the period of imprisonment should be. However in the case of criminal contempts committal should be for a fixed period[8] and though it can be for an unspecified time for civil contempts, it has been said[9] that even then the period should be fixed for *past* breaches. Despite the unlimited powers, in practice contemnors are rarely committed for longer than one month[10] in the case of criminal contempts though it may be longer where it is sought to persuade an offender to obey an order.

If the court does make a committal order it will authorise the tipstaff to seize the body's person and convey him to prison[11].

In all cases there is a right of appeal against an order[12]. The appeal lies to the Court of Appeal (Civil Division)[13].

6. See *Re W(B)* (*an infant*) [1969] 2 Ch 50, [1969] 1 All ER 594.
7. One of the more recent examples was *Re Crump* (*an infant*) (1963) 107 Sol Jo 682 where the ward was two months' pregnant. In practice orders are not now made against the ward when restraining marriage. However the ward could still be guilty of contempt for aiding and abetting the breach.
8. See *A-G v James* [1962] 2 QB 637 at 641 per Lord Parker LJ.
9. Per Lord Denning MR in *Danchevsky v Danchevsky* [1975] Fam 17 at 21.
10. Committal was for four weeks in *Re B* (*JA*) (*infant*) [1965] Ch 1112 [1968] 2 All ER 168 and for 28 days in *Re Crump* (*an infant*) (1963) 107 Sol Jo 682.
11. See RSC Ord. 90, r.3A.
12. Under s.13 of the Administration of Justice Act 1960, which applies both to criminal and civil contempts and to the prosecution as well as the defence.
13. S.13(2)(b).

Chapter 8

The Official Solicitor[1]

I Introduction

Although by no means unique to wardship[2] the services of the Official Solicitor are an important feature of the jurisdiction. The title, 'Official' Solicitor may give the misleading impression that he is, to quote the words of a former holder of the position[3], 'some dreadful pompous chap who sits up in London and whose job is to throw spanners in the works and make [the] business more difficult'. In fact nothing could be further from the truth. His role in wardship proceedings, if called upon to act, is to represent the ward's interests, which though often difficult and delicate, is a task which the Official Solicitor and his staff execute with humanity and expertise. Indeed the value of the Official Solicitor's services is that it gives the court 'the assistance of an experienced and impartial person whose only interest is the child's welfare'.[4]

That the Official Solicitor became involved in wardship cases at all was the happy consequence of ad hoc development which is so characteristic of English legal history. Initially the office was an essentially administrative one created in

1. For a general account of the nature and role of the office see J M L Evans, CBE (a former Official Solicitor): 'The Office of the Official Solicitor to the Supreme Court' (1966) 63 *Law Society Gazette* 270–2, 335–7. For an account of the office's role in wardship see N Turner, CBE (the present Official Solicitor) 'Wardship: the Official Solicitor's role'. (1977) 2 *Adoption and Fostering* 30 (published by the Association of British Adoption and Fostering Agencies) from which parts of the following account are extensively drawn.
2. The Official Solicitor appears as guardian ad litem in adoption cases and can be so appointed in matrimonial proceedings under the Matrimonial Causes Act 1973 pursuant to MCR 1977, r.115.
3. J M L Evans, CBE (1966) 63 *Law Society Gazette* at 270.
4. Per Heilbron J in *Re D (a minor) (wardship: sterilisation)* [1976] Fam 185 at 197.

163

1739[5] to provide for centralised control by an independent office of suitors' money paid into the old Court of Chancery. The holder of this office was originally known as 'the Solicitor to the Suitors of the High Court of Chancery' which was later changed to 'the Solicitor to the Suitors' Fund'. Its transformation into an essentially representative office dates from the mid-nineteenth century following the reforms of the Court of Chancery. In the course of those reforms one of the many offices to be abolished was the Office of the Six Clerks which unlike other offices had not become a mere sinecure but had some duties of substance. The Office was responsible for the provision of assistance to parties to Chancery Suits proceeding in forma pauperis and for the representation of infants and lunatics who might be necessary parties to such suits but who would otherwise be unrepresented. These and other duties concerning the visitation of contempt prisoners derived from the old style Chancery Masters fell to the lot of the well regarded but reluctant Solicitor of the Suitors' Fund initially as a temporary expedient because no one else was available but which in time became permanent. Indeed these representative duties became so well established and of such importance that when in 1869 the Suitors' Fund was abolished thereby removing the original reason for its existence, the office nevertheless survived. In 1871 the name was changed to the 'Official Solicitor to the High Court of Chancery'.

The modern office of 'the Official Solicitor to the Supreme Court of Judicature' was created by Lord Cairns LC under a General Order dated 6 November 1875. This was followed by a second Order dated 7 February 1876 by which the former 'Official Solicitor to the Court of Chancery' was appointed to the new office and by which his former duties were also assigned thereby becoming available to all the High Court Divisions and to the Court of Appeal. Apart from these two Orders, which in any case only refer to the Official Solicitor's duties in the broadest possible terms[6], the working constitution of the office is unwritten. The advantage of this has been

5. 12 Geo 2 c 24.
6. The 1875 Order, for instance, concludes with the words that the Official Solicitor 'shall perform all such duties in relation to the said Supreme Court as the Lord Chancellor shall, from time to time, direct'. See J M L Evans' comments: (1966) 63 *Law Society Gazette* at 271.

to allow considerable flexibility in the day-to-day working of the office.

Until 1919 the office was a part-time appointment but under the Official Solicitor Act 1919 (now replaced by the Supreme Court of Judicature (Consolidation) Act 1925) the post became a full time public appointment and the office was given a quasi corporate status by which the duties cast upon the Official Solicitor fall to be carried out by the holder of the office for the time being and the property vested in him passes automatically to his successor on death or retirement[7]. The Official Solicitor himself must be a solicitor of ten years standing[8]. His tenure is similar to that of a High Court Master or Registrar[9] so that he enjoys a measure of independence from the executive. His appointment lies in the hands of the Lord Chancellor.

Administratively the office is a sub-department of the Lord Chancellor's Office, the staff being civil servants of the Court Service administered by the South Eastern Circuit Office pursuant to the Courts Act 1971. The main office is in Chancery Lane, London with off-shoots in the Royal Courts of Justice. There are no offices outside London[10].

Although there is only one Official Solicitor he has a staff (excluding typists, messengers, etc.) of 190 of whom 10 are professionally qualified[11]. Wardship cases are dealt with by a sub-division of the Litigation Division which has a staff of 16. The appointment of the Official Solicitor does not necessarily mean that he will personally conduct the enquiries, indeed it is more likely that that task will be delegated to a more junior officer. The report, however, must be regarded as that of the Official Solicitor in his quasi corporate capacity since it will always be sent either to him personally, or, if he is unavailable, to his Deputy for final consideration and signature[12].

---

7. See now the Supreme Court of Judicature (Consolidation) Act 1925, s. 129.
8. Fourth Schedule of the 1925 Act.
9. I.e. he remains in office during good behaviour with a retiring age of 72—s.115 of the 1925 Act.
10. Whether there should be offices outside London is discussed post at p. 190–1.
11. The 1978 staffing figures were kindly supplied by Mr N Turner. In 1977 the figures were 180 with 10 lawyers, while in 1966 there was a staff of 147 of which 8 were professionally qualified. See N Turner (1977) 2 *Adoption and Fostering* at p. 31. See Evans (1966) 63 *Law Society Gazette* at p. 271.
12. Discussed in more detail post p. 183.

II Involvement in wardship proceedings

The Official Solicitor may become involved in wardship proceedings in different ways. Normally he will be appointed to act as guardian ad litem to the ward in which case, unlike welfare officers, he will be called upon to represent the ward's interests. He may occasionally be called upon to act as guardian of the ward's estate. Such appointments, which are made under the High Court's inherent jurisdiction are not frequent but may still be appropriate where, for example, the ward has inherited or otherwise becomes entitled to property from abroad[13]. Formerly it was not unknown for the Official Solicitor to be appointed as guardian of the person but this has now fallen into desuetude as a result of the development of the statutory responsibilities of local authorities in relation to children.

The Official Solicitor may sometimes be called upon to represent in wardship proceedings, not the ward but his parent. This may occur where the parent is himself under a disability as for example where he is a minor himself or where he is under a mental disorder.

The Official Solicitor may be directed by the court to bring wardship proceedings on behalf of a minor in which case he will be acting as the minor's next friend. The court[14] has statutory power to do this under the Matrimonial Causes Act 1973, section 42, that is, in the course of matrimonial proceedings brought under that Act. Though only occasionally used the power under section 42 is useful where it is thought desirable to bring the wide powers of wardship to bear in aid of the statutory jurisdiction or where there are circumstances rendering it desirable that the court itself should retain legal custody of the child rather than granting it to any of the parties to the matrimonial proceedings.

The Court of Protection exercising its jurisdiction under the Mental Health Act 1959, section 103(1)(*h*) can also direct the Official Solicitor to bring wardship proceedings as next friend of a parent under its jurisdiction. Whether the court has the power to direct the Official Solicitor to bring wardship proceedings other than by these two statutory provisions is perhaps a moot point. The indications such as they are,

13. N Turner (1977) 2 *Adoption and Fostering* at 31.
14. I.e. the High Court or Divorce County Court.

however, would seem to suggest that the High Court does have such a power under its inherent jurisdiction. In *Re C (MA) (an infant)*[15] Willmer LJ referred, without further comment[16], to the fact that at the end of an adoption hearing the High Court judge directed that the child be made a ward principally to preserve the status quo pending the appeal. Presumably if the judge had the power to make such a direction he could have directed the Official Solicitor to act as the child's next friend. More recently in *Re H (a minor)*[17] Ormrod LJ commented that a judge of the Family Division hearing an appeal against a Juvenile Court order under the Children Act 1948 'could assume the powers of the wardship procedure by simply giving one party leave to issue a formal summons under the Law Reform (Miscellaneous Provisions) Act 1949'. While this statement does not go as far as *Re C (MA)* it would seem but a small step to say that the court could in such proceedings direct that wardship proceedings be brought and again in appropriate cases there seems no reason why the Official Solicitor should not be asked to act as the next friend.

Quite apart from these examples it seems clear that during the course of wardship proceedings the court can ask the Official Solicitor to act as next friend. This may occur, for example, where during the course of a wardship it becomes expedient to reconstitute the proceedings as for instance where for good cause the plaintiff wishes to withdraw as a party and it becomes necessary for the court to substitute the ward as plaintiff with the Official Solicitor as next friend[18].

It is important to note that the foregoing instances or suggested instances of the court directing the Official Solicitor to bring wardship proceedings are confined to cases where the High Court[19] is already exercising jurisdiction in relation to the welfare of the child. Whether the High Court has the power upon its motion to direct that wardship proceedings be brought in cases where there are no prior

15. [1966] 1 All ER 838.
16. Ibid., at 849.
17. [1978] Fam 65 at 76, [1978] 2 All ER 903 at 909–10.
18. Referred to by Turner (1977) 2 *Adoption and Fostering* at 31. It is not unknown for the Official Solicitor to appear as amicus curiae—see *Re N (infants)* [1967] Ch 512 at 522 G.
19. Including the Divorce County Court if acting under the Matrimonial Causes Act 1973, s.42.

proceedings has yet to be decided[20]. it is, however, clear that the Official Solicitor cannot without a direction of the court initiate wardship proceedings even at the request of an interested party.

Heilbron J concluded in *Re D (a minor)*[1]:

'The Official Solicitor ... though a solicitor, does not seek clients. He only acts on behalf of minors who are the subject of existing procedures.'

The requirement for the formal institution of proceedings should not be confused with informal approaches made to the Official Solicitor. He takes the view that he should not like to discourage practitioners from seeking informal advice and guidance as to what attitude he is likely to take on any application they might contemplate leading to his involvement on behalf of a party to wardship proceedings whether as next friend or guardian ad litem and whether for the ward or some other party under a legal disability.

There is one situation in which the Official Solicitor may be required to give advice and assistance to a ward for whom he has not been constituted guardian ad litem. This arises by virtue of the Notice of Wardship on Form FD 590[2] which states:

'Wherever the age and situation of the minor are such that he or she may be in need of advice and assistance a copy of this notice should also be served on him or her, whether or not he or she is the defendant.'

The notice served explains that 'where necessary a guardian (probably the Official Solicitor) will be appointed to present the Ward's views to the Court and give any assistance. If the Ward is in doubt about what to do he or she may approach the Official Solicitor ... who will give advice pending the formal appointment of a guardian'.

III Appointment as guardian ad litem

There is no mandatory requirement[3] that a ward be represented by a guardian ad litem. Instead, the question of separate

---

20. Discussed ante in Chap. 3.
 1. *Re D (a minor) (wardship: sterilisation)* [1976] Fam 185 at 197.
 2. For a copy of this form see Appendix.
 3. Cf. adoption.

representation is a matter which lies at the court's discretion. Indeed the court has a discretion not only whether to appoint but also as to who it should appoint as guardian ad litem. Normally the court will invite the Official Solicitor so to act but it is at liberty either upon its own motion or by application to appoint someone else. The rules themselves do not stipulate who other than the Official Solicitor can be considered a 'suitable person' for these purposes but since the object of the appointment is to give the ward a 'separate voice' in the proceedings it would seem that at the very least the appointee should be independent of the parties and preferably with some professional qualification either in law or social work. Possible candidates could be a court welfare officer or a Director of Social Services.

The need to appoint some other person will not arise very often but could occur where, for example, the Official Solicitor declines to accept the appointment[4]. Although it is open to a party to seek appointment of their own nominee as guardian ad litem even though the Official Solicitor is willing to act, it would seem that in practice it would be extremely difficult to persuade the court to accept the nomination[5]. For this reason it is suggested that the commentary[6] to RSC Order 90, rule 3(2), that, 'if no other suitable guardian ad litem is available for the infant defendant, the Official Solicitor may be authorised to act in that capacity' is misleading in as much as it suggests that the court will *normally* appoint some other person if suitable rather than the Official Solicitor.

A. PROCEDURE FOR APPOINTMENT

Before a ward can be separately represented he must first be made a party to the proceedings. RSC Order 90, rule 3(2) states that if no person other than the minor is a suitable defendant leave may be obtained ex parte from a registrar to issue an originating summons with the minor as defendant thereto in the first instance. Since by virtue of RSC Order 80, rule 2(1) a minor cannot defend proceedings in his own right

4. For circumstances when the Official Solicitor may decline appointment see post p. 171.
5. See by way of analogy *Re A B (an infant)* [1948] 2 All ER 727.
6. The Supreme Court Practice 1979 Vol. 1 at 1343.

wherever Order 90, rule 3(2) is applied the ward must be represented by a guardian ad litem.

Rule 3(2) is intended to apply where the parents or other guardians are themselves in agreement but are in dispute with their child, the classical example being, where application is made to restrain a ward's allegedly 'undesirable' association with a third party. In other cases where it is thought desirable to have the ward separately represented the procedure is governed by RSC Order 15, rules 6(1) and 6(2)(b)(i). Rule 6 enables the court either on its own motion or upon application to join as a party to any proceedings any person whose presence before the Court is necessary to ensure that all matters in dispute may be effectively and completely determined and adjudicated upon. This rather general provision includes a person who is a minor but again by reason of Order 80, rule 2(1) he must be represented by a guardian ad litem.

The need to have the ward formally joined as a party before he can be separately represented seems questionable. There is, for example, no comparable requirement in matrimonial proceedings under the Matrimonial Causes Act 1973 pursuant to Rule 115 of the Matrimonial Causes Rules 1977 which according to the present Official Solicitor[7] does not seem to cause any practical difficulties and results in some saving in administrative expense both in the Official Solicitor's office and in the Registries.

B. CONSENT OF THE OFFICIAL SOLICITOR IS REQUIRED

The appointment of any person as guardian ad litem is subject to the appointee's consent. This is no less true of the Official Solicitor as was emphasised by Heilbron J in *Re D (a minor)*[8] where she said that his consent is a 'prerequisite to his acting for the ward'. Where the court has acted of its own motion then such consent is normally given as a matter of course but where the order is on the application of a party the Official Solicitor can require a costs undertaking before consenting to act though in practice such an undertaking is

7. N Turner (1977) 2 *Adoption and Fostering* at 33.
8. [1976] Fam 185 at 197 C.

required only in exceptional circumstances[9]. However, no matter on whose initiative the order is made there are circumstances where consent may have to be declined. This may occur where his appointment might involve him in a conflict of duties, as for example, where he already represents an adult party who is under a mental disability or where due to pressure of work he is unable to accept further appointments. This latter situation has yet to arise though it is by no means inconceivable that it will occur as the number of referrals has more than doubled since 1974[10]. At the same time increasing use is being made of Rule 115 of the Matrimonial Causes Rules 1977 by which children may be separately represented in matrimonial proceedings under the 1973 Act[11]. At the very least the increasing use of the Official Solicitor as guardian ad litem will mean that longer delays in the production of the report can be expected.

Although the consent of the Official Solicitor is a prerequisite to his acting as guardian ad litem it by no means follows that merely because he is willing to act the court must appoint him. Hence as *Taylor v Taylor*[12] shows, the court is quite at liberty to refuse to make the appointment even if the Official Solicitor himself is not unwilling to act. Indeed in *Taylor* Baker P (sitting in the Court of Appeal) said that he did not think such a refusal was an appealable matter provided the judge has all the relevant information before him.

C. FORM OF APPOINTMENT

No formal order of appointment is necessary but the common practice when the ward has been joined as a party is for the Official Solicitor to be constituted guardian ad litem by order of the court expressed to be conditional upon his consenting to act[13]. It may happen, however, that the Official Solicitor will already be present at the hearing prior to his

9. N Turner (1977) 2 *Adoption and Fostering* at 33. The question of costs is discussed post p. 188.
10. In 1974 106 wardship cases were referred to the Official Solicitor—Judicial Statistics 1974 Cmnd. 6361 C.18 and in 1976 there were 218 referrals—1976 Cmnd. 6875 Table C14. In 1977, Cmnd. 7254, Table C11, however, there were only 203 referrals but a further increase seems likely in 1978.
11. Referrals under r.115 were 116 in 1974, 111 in 1975, 150 in 1976 and 137 in 1977.
12. (1975) 5 Fam Law 151.
13. See N Turner (1977) 2 *Adoption and Fostering* at 32, 33.

appointment as a result of informal approaches by a party or the court. On such occasions he may then indicate his willingness to act.

Upon appointment he will not normally receive any instructions in writing or otherwise. Where his duty is to represent a party the record of his appointment is enough[14]. Notice of the appointment will be sent to the minor defendant by the court by post[15].

D. WHO CAN APPOINT

Both a judge and a registrar have powers to appoint a guardian ad litem; both can act either on their own motion or upon application. It is perhaps a moot point whether a registrar has the power to appoint the Official Solicitor to act as guardian ad litem if his appointment is opposed by one of the parties. In any event it is suggested that where the appointment is opposed the dissenting party would be well advised to seek a hearing before a judge on the matter[16].

E. THE TIMING OF THE APPOINTMENT

The Official Solicitor should always be appointed as early in the proceedings as possible. In any event in cases to which Order 90, rule 3(2) applies he is or should be brought in at the very beginning but in other cases he should be appointed as soon as the court concludes that the representation of the ward is necessary in the light of Order 15, rule 6. There is, however, no rigid rule on the timing of the appointment and of course it may only be during the course of proceedings that the need for representation becomes apparent. In practice, therefore, the Official Solicitor may be brought into a wardship case as guardian ad litem either on an application by a party or by a registrar or judge of his own motion at virtually

14. If, however, the duty is of an official nature (such as that imposed in *Harbin v Masterman* [1896] 1 Ch 351) it should be specified in writing, normally in the form of a note from a judge sufficiently defining the scope of what he is to undertake.
15. See *Rayden on Divorce* (13th Edn. 1979), p. 1118.
16. Particularly in view of *Taylor v Taylor* (1975) 5 Fam Law 151 which shows that appeals might be difficult. For circumstances when the appointment should be opposed see post p. 179.

any stage in the proceedings: Hence appointments may be made on the issue of the Originating Summons if Order 90, rule 3(2) applies and on any interlocutory hearing before a registrar or judge or in the course of a substantive hearing before a judge who may, for example, adjourn after the case has opened and the written evidence read, and appoint the Official Solicitor before oral evidence is taken. He may be appointed by a judge after judgment has been given as for example where help may be required to supervise the order. It is even possible that the appointment might be made by the Court of Appeal after the appeal has been opened and adjourned for the purpose[17]. In other words whenever the court considers his appointment would be beneficial it is free to invite him to act.

One word of warning may be given to parties seeking the Official Solicitor's appointment. The present Official Solicitor, Mr. Turner, is on record as saying that he does not like being brought into cases as a last resort gesture[18]. He instanced the case of a child being obdurate in refusing to see a parent entitled to access notwithstanding the skill of the judge and welfare officer concerned. A case of this type is *Taylor v Taylor*[19] (which case Mr. Turner thought ought to be more widely known) where for some years after her divorce, the mother who was entitled to access had been unsuccessful in seeing her children because of their refusal to see her. As a last resort she sought the appointment of the Official Solicitor in the hope that something could be done but this applicaton was refused which decision was upheld on appeal. Baker P (sitting in the Court of Appeal) commented that as a trial judge he had in recent years asked the Official Solicitor to act in cases where access would not work but that he could not remember any case where such intervention had been successful. Mr. Turner has commented[20]:

> 'Hopes that if I am brought in my staff may be able to do something are likely to be disappointed and my intervention may do more harm than good.'

17. This was done in *Re B* Court of Appeal (Civil Division) Transcript No. 237 of 1976.
18. (1977) 2 *Adoption and Fostering* at 34.
19. (1975) 5 Fam Law 151.
20. (1977) 2 *Adoption and Fostering* at 34.

F. CIRCUMSTANCES IN WHICH THE OFFICIAL SOLICITOR MAY BE INVOLVED AS GUARDIAN AD LITEM.

It will have become evident that the Official Solicitor is by no means involved in all wardship cases[1]. In so far as local authorities are concerned, for example, there should be no need for the Official Solicitor's involvement unless the court considers that the ward's interests are not being adequately represented. Again if all that is required is a 'report on the ward's background' then the appointment of a court welfare officer rather than the Official Solicitor will be sufficient.

The decision of whether to appoint the Official Solicitor, however, is not always easy and must inevitably depend upon the facts of each case and upon judicial discretion. In principle where the appointment is made pursuant to Order 15, rule 6 the court should believe that representation of the ward is necessary to ensure that all matters in dispute in the case may be effectively disposed of. A good guide as to the necessity of such representation is to consider whether it is possible that the interests of the minor may take second place to the evidence and arguments of the adult adversaries[2].

Although there are no hard and fast rules for determining the type of case in which a minor might advantageously be represented there are a number of situations where the Official Solicitor will in practice be appointed or where he will commonly be appointed[3]. One class of case where representation is regarded as essential is in the so-called 'teenage wardship' cases, that is, where the parents are in dispute with their child rather than with themselves over their child. This will occur where the parents wish to restrain the continuation of what in their view is an undesirable associaton between their child and a third party. Discussion of the Official Solicitor's role in such cases will be deferred to Chapter 10 but suffice to say at this stage that it is important to realise that the Official Solicitor is the *child's* representative

---

1. He is involved in about two out of every seven cases. The figures are the same both in London and the Provinces.
2. See Heilbron J in *Re D* (*a minor*) (*wardship: sterilisation*) [1976] Fam 185 at 197B.
3. The following discussion is based on the circumstances outlined by N Turner in (1977) 2 *Adoption and Fostering* at 33, 34.

and that the appointment is by no means to be regarded as a device for endorsing the parents' view.

Again in general where both parties request the Official Solicitor's appointment or where one asks and the other does not oppose, the court, though not bound to do so, is more than likely to make the appointment. The court is also likely to appoint the Official Solicitor in cases where it is dissatisfied with the way the interlocutory processes are being dealt with or where the parties are not complying with directions within the time allowed. Appointment might also be made where during the interlocutory stages it seems that the parties might be helped to an agreed order.

Discussion of other situations where the Official Solicitor might usefully be brought in may best be divided between cases where the parents are in dispute with themselves over their child and cases where the dispute is between parents and third parties.

i) *Inter-parental disputes*

There are a number of situations where the Official Solicitor's appointment may be thought desirable in cases involving separated and 'warring' parents.

Where the child has wishes of his own an independent assessment may be required and this becomes even more urgent where there are allegations of 'brain-washing'. It is true that the judge could see the child in private in order to ascertain his views but such a course of action does not commonly find favour among the judiciary partly because not every judge will be confident of his ability to conduct such interviews and partly because the interview might not produce the desired results since the child even with the most deft handling might feel ill at ease in such unusual surroundings. The court is more likely to regard the better course in such circumstances as being to ask the Official Solicitor, whose experience in such matters is perhaps unrivalled[4], to report as to the child's wishes if it is possible to ascertain them.

Of course the child is more likely to have views of his own the older he is and the situation just outlined is most likely to

4. See Cross J's comment in *Re S (an infant)* [1967] 1 All ER 202 at 208D.

arise in cases where the child is in or approaching adolescence. However, the desirability of independent representation is not confined to such age groups, for as Mr. Turner has said in his experience 'quite young children can have very strong ideas of their own, which it would be foolhardy to try to ignore, but the very existence of which parents cannot bring themselves to admit'[5].

Even if the child is very young there may still be cases where the Official Solicitor's appointment is desirable. This will arise where one party challenges the fitness of the other to have care and control or access on medical grounds or because of their alleged depraved or criminal conduct. In these cases independent medical opinion might well be of assistance to the court and indeed, as will be seen[6], it is in exceptional cases open to the Official Solicitor to file a confidential report to the court which is not available to the parties.

The need for independent representation will also arise in cases where the ward is alleged to be mentally or emotionally unstable. Indeed it has been repeatedly emphasised that the parties should not take it upon themselves to have the ward psychiatrically examined without the court's or the Official Solicitor's knowledge and should in any event seek the court's prior sanction. As Cross J said in *Re S (an infant)*[7]:

> 'If both sides agree that an examination is necessary and agree on the person or persons to conduct it then normally no doubt there would be no reason for the court to refuse to follow their wishes. If they disagree, however, then it would seem right that the Official Solicitor should be appointed guardian ad litem of the ward . . . and that he should decide, subject to the views of the judge whether or not an examination is needed. Further if he decides that it is needed then, as it seems to me, he should instruct the psychiatrist or psychiatrists in question so as to ensure that he or they have all the relevant material and can see both parents.'

Although these comments were made obiter they have subsequently been endorsed by the Court of Appeal[8] and the profession has recently been reminded to abide by the prac-

5. (1977) 2 *Adoption and Fostering* at 33.
6. Post p. 185.
7. [1967] 1 All ER 202 at 209.
8. See *B (M) v B (R)* [1968] 3 All ER 170 at 174 per Willmer LJ. See also Goff J in *Re RP(M) (an infant)* [1968] 1 All ER 691n at 692.

tice[9]. The rationale of the practice is to save the minor undergoing unnecessary examinations but where such examination is necessary to ensure that psychiatrists who give evidence in wardship cases receive unbiased instructions. While these reasons may seem sound it does mean that a party will find it difficult to challenge the evidence adduced[10].

The appointment of the Official Solicitor is common in cases involving an international element, that is, where for one reason or another a child has been brought to England from a foreign jurisdiction. The appointment is desirable particularly where the co-operation of foreign courts or welfare agencies, or the help of British Consular officials overseas might have to be sought or where it is thought necessary to have a person visit another country in order to make a report.

Cases involving an international element often involve kidnapping in the sense that one parent has unilaterally brought the child to England but kidnapping does not have to involve another jurisdiction. The Official Solicitor's appointment is desirable in kidnapping cases generally because the future welfare of the child will still be in jeopardy and may require particularly careful handling. As Mr. Turner has commented[11]:

'In such cases the problems may only really begin after the child has been traced and this is not always appreciated by the plaintiff, or his or her advisers.'

Another situation where the Official Solicitor's involvement may be thought necessary is where proprietary rights are in issue, that is, either where the ward is wealthy in his own right or where the parties, though nominally disputing care and control are in reality fighting about the matrimonial home etc. In these cases there is an obvious danger that the ward's interests will take second place to the arguments of the parents.

ii) *Parents' disputes with third parties*

As in the case of inter-parental disputes the appointment of the Official Solicitor in cases of dispute between parents and

9. *Re A-W (minors)* (1975) 5 Fam Law 95 per Dunn J.
10. For further discussion on this point see ante p. 65.
11. (1977) 2 *Adoption and Fostering* at 34.

third parties will be desirable where the child is old enough to have and does have strong views of his own or where there is a conflict about medical evidence. Again his involvement is desirable where the dispute is between the natural parents and foster parents for there is an obvious danger of the child's interests taking second place.

Perhaps more difficult is the involvement of the Official Solicitor in cases involving local authorities. As Mr. Turner has pointed out[12] there is in any event, as evidenced by the Children Act 1975[13], a growing realisation of the desirability of separate representation of children in care proceedings. However, the appointment of the Official Solicitor is by no means automatic in wardship cases involving local authorities. The view can legitimately be taken that the local authority will in most cases have the child's best interests at heart and will have the expertise to ascertain and protect those interests. In many cases therefore the Official Solicitor's appointment will be regarded as unnecessary[14]. Equally there will be other cases where the Official Solicitor's appointment will be desirable if not essential. One example is where the parents and the local authority are implacably opposed to each other so that a fresh unbiased view would be a decided advantage. Another obvious example is where the local authority's bona fides are being challenged. The Official Solicitor's appointment might also be ordered, if, for example, the local authority has filed conflicting evidence or where, in any event, there is conflict as to medical evidence.

Occasionally local authorities might find themselves in agreement with the parents but in dispute with foster parents. Again in such cases the Official Solicitor's appointment is by no means automatic but would certainly be desirable where the relationship between the foster parents and the local authority has broken down so that there is animosity between them and would seem to be essential where the local authority's bona fides were challenged.

Hitherto consideration has been given to the necessity of independent representation during proceedings but it is

12. (1977) 2 *Adoption and Fostering* at 34.
13. Which by ss.58 and 64 provides for separate representation in care proceedings both under the Children Act 1948 and the Children and Young Persons Act 1969 respectively.
14. See for example *Re B* (*a minor*) (*wardship: child in care*) [1975] Fam 36, [1974] 3 All ER 915.

worth adding that it is occasionally advantageous in cases involving local authorities that the Official Solicitor be appointed after the decision. This could arise, for example, where the decision goes against the local authority thereby placing them in an invidious position for future applications should the need arise. As an example one might cite *Re Cullimore*[15]. In that case the issue was whether the child suffered from brittle bones thereby rendering the child's injuries accidental, or whether the parents had wrongfully inflicted the injuries. In the event the child was found to be suffering from brittle bones but though the parents were granted care and control the wardship order was continued and the Official Solicitor was appointed guardian ad litem. In this way the court was able to keep the case under review and in so doing released the local authority from what might otherwise have been a difficult task in view of the obvious suspicion the parents would have had of the authority.

G. OPPOSING THE OFFICIAL SOLICITOR'S APPOINTMENT

Just as it is open to any party to request the Official Solicitor's appointment so it is open to them to oppose his appointment.

There are not many occasions where it is desirable or indeed prudent to oppose his appointment, but there is one occasion where it is now apparently essential. This is where the local authority wish to take the preliminary point of law that the court should decline jurisdiction to interfere in the case[16]. It is established that if the Official Solicitor is appointed and having made his investigation takes a view contrary to that of the local authority, it is not open to that authority to take the point of jurisdiction. This is the conclusion of Balcombe J in *Re D (a minor)*[17]. As he said:

'If the Official Solicitor rendered a report indicating that he took the view that the child's welfare required a course of action different from that which the local authority was taking, the court would be failing in its duty if it

---

15. *Re Cullimore (a minor)* (1976) Times, March 24. Discussed post p. 303.
16. Following such cases as *Re M (an infant)* [1961] Ch 328, [1961] 1 All ER 788 and *Re T (AJJ) (an infant)* [1970] Ch 688, [1970] discussed in detail in Chap. 11.
17. (1978) 122 Sol Jo 193, Times, February 14.

declined to exercise the wardship jurisdiction so as to
resolve the conflict.'

It is difficult to disagree with the learned judge's conclusion
for it would certainly seem both a waste of time and money
and contrary to the child's interests to allow a case to be
adjourned for reports only to have the preliminary point as
to jurisdiction pleaded at the later date. The consequence of
Re D is that local authorities must oppose the Official Solicitor's appointment and pursue immediately the jurisdiction
point. Furthermore they would be well advised to argue the
point before a judge and accordingly if the other party seeks
the Official Solicitor's appointment (which might seem a
good tactic to overcome the jurisdiction argument) before a
registrar the local authority shoud oppose the appointment
and ask for the matter to be heard by the judge.

To what extent the reasoning of Balcombe J as to the
appointment of the Official Solicitor will apply to other cases
where issue as to the exercise of jurisdiction is to be raised is a
matter of debate. At first sight, for example, there seems to be
an analogy with cases involving a foreign element where one
of the parties wishes to seek a peremptory order for the child's
return to the jurisdiction whence he came[18]. However, while
it might certainly be in that individual's interests to oppose
the Official Solicitor's appointment if only to avoid delaying
proceedings, it is unlikely that his appointment would preclude the argument as to the jurisdiction since evidence as to
the ward's well-being will be material to the decision of
whether to make the order sought or whether to investigate
the case on its merits[19]. On the other hand where it is sought
to argue that the court has no jurisdiction at all (as opposed to
a discretion to exercise it) as, for example, where diplomatic
immunity is pleaded or, arguably, where an alien minor's
entry into the country has been refused by the immigration
authorities[20] then it would seem to follow from *Re D* that the
court is bound to refuse at the outset a request to appoint the
Official Solicitor.

Another reason (though less compelling) for opposing the
Official Solicitor's appointment is to avoid the delay inevitably caused while the necessary investigations are conducted.

18. For a discussion of such applications see Chap. 12.
19. In *Re H (infants)* [1965] 3 All ER 906 the court made a summary order for
    the child's return even though the Official Solicitor had been appointed.
20. Discussed in Chap. 2.

Such an objection might carry weight if made by a local authority provided there are no compelling reasons for separate representation and provided there is enough information available to the court[1].

A third possible reason for opposing the Official Solicitor's appointment is because there is some other suitable person willing to act as guardian ad litem, but this point is rarely pleaded and, as has been previously pointed out)[2] is not likely to succeed at least where the court is acting of its motion.

IV The role of guardian ad litem

A. NATURE OF FUNCTION

When appointed to act as guardian ad litem the Official Solicitor is in the words of Goff J[3]:

> 'not only an officer of the court and the ward's guardian but he is a solicitor and the ward is his client.'

Since he is a practising solicitor the Official Solicitor normally acts not only as guardian ad litem but also as his own solicitor[4]. Other persons acting as guardian ad litem must act by a solicitor[5]. The advantage of the Official Solicitor acting in both capacities is, as Mr. Turner has pointed out[6], that it 'at least eliminates the possible risk of

1. It would seem pointless, however, as happened in a case known to the authors, to oppose the Official Solicitor's appointment in favour of the appointment of a court welfare officer, since in either event there will be delay in obtaining reports and there is little evidence to suggest that welfare officers are any quicker than the Official Solicitor in conducting their inquiries. There might, however, be good reason to oppose the Official Solicitor's appointment in favour of a welfare officer where what is really required is a welfare report.
2. Ante at p. 169.
3. In *Re R (P.M.) (an infant)* [1968] 1 All ER 691n at 692n.
4. N. Turner (1977) 2 *Adoption and Fostering* at p. 32. Solicitors are, however, occasionally instructed to act for the ward in which case they look to the ward for information but to the Official Solicitor for formal instructions.
5. RSC Ord. 80, r.2(3).
6. (1977) 2 *Adoption and Fostering* at 32. As Mr Turner says such conflicts are likely to arise in connection with appointments made under the Children Act 1975, where guardians ad litem are drawn from a panel. The hybrid role of the Official Solicitor also avoids the difficulties referred to by Brightman J in *Re Whittall, Whittall v Faulkner* [1973] 3 All ER 35, [1973] 1 WLR 1027 and by Megarry J in *Re Barbour's Settlement, National Westminster Bank v Barbour* [1974] 1 All ER 1188 at 1191. See the references in the Supreme Court Practice 1979 Vol. 1 at 1249, 80/2/14.

disagreement on the line to be taken and the manner of presentation of the case on behalf of the child.'

The essential function of a guardian ad litem is according to RSC Order 80, rule 2(2) to do on behalf of the party under the disability anything which in the ordinary conduct of the proceedings is required to be done by the party concerned if he were not under disability. Authority[7] does exist for saying that if the guardian ad litem does anything in the proceedings beyond the mere conduct of it, whatever is done must be for the benefit of the person under disability or must be done with the court's sanction or approval otherwise it will be invalid and ineffective or may be set aside. However, the Official Solicitors acting as guardian ad litem of minors in wardship cases over the years have accepted responsibilities beyond the mere conduct of proceedings[8]. The present Official Solicitor sees his primary role as giving the child either through him or counsel instructed by him, a voice in the proceedings[9]. Nevertheless it is still true that major decisions must be approved by the court. Lord Denning MR has pointed out[10] that as guardian ad litem the Official Solicitor does not have custody of the ward nor does he stand in loco parentis nor, one might add, is he a welfare officer. Instead all he does is to represent the ward in the conduct of the suit. One consequence of this is that his decisions do not rest on his unfettered discretion so that on occasions, as for example, to order a blood test[11], to have the ward examined by a psychiatrist[12] or to compromise an action on the ward's behalf[13], he must seek the prior consent of the court. In each of these instances, however, the court whilst not being bound will have the greatest respect for the Official Solicitor's views[14].

7. *Rhodes v Swithenbank* (1889) 22 QBD 577. See Supreme Court Practice 1979 at 1249.
8. This is explained partly because as an officer of the court he is available to carry out a variety of duties see *Harbin v Masterman* [1896] Ch 351, and because historically he has become closely involved with the welfare of his wards.
9. (1977) 2 *Adoption and Fostering* at 32 and 34.
10. *Re L (an infant)* [1968] P 119.
11. *Re L (an infant)* [1968] P 119.
12. Re S (an infant) [1967] 1 All ER 202 at 209.
13. *Re L (an infant)* [1968] P 119.
14. As is evidenced by *Re D (a minor)* (1978) 122 Sol Jo 193. See also Cross J's comments in *Re S (an infant)* [1967] 1 All ER at 208 E-F.

B. THE REPORT

Upon his appointment the Official Solicitor will receive the court files on the case which should highlight the area or problems that need to be investigated. His principal task is to place before the court, usually in the form of a report, evidence which he considers to be material on the ward's behalf. There is, however, no mandatory duty to file a report and in emergencies for instance oral evidence may be given instead[15].

To obtain the necessary information the fullest enquiries are made. All the parties including, where appropriate, the ward will be interviewed, as will friends and relations. Help and advice of such persons as school teachers, welfare workers, doctors, priests, local authorities and any others who have knowledge of the case will also be sought. In short all avenues are explored in order to obtain an overall picture of the ward's current situation, so as to enable the Official Solicitor to form an objective and independent assessment of the ward's interests.

It may be that the Official Solicitor considers that the ward should undergo medical or psychiatric examination (indeed the question of such an examination might have been specifically referred to him) in which case provided the court sanctions the decision, he will be empowered to make the necessary arrangements. In other words it will be the Official Solicitor who instructs the practitioner and not the parties[16]. However, the Official Solicitor himself is in no way committed to accepting the view of the practitioner and is not precluded from obtaining a second and possibly contrary opinion[17].

The task of obtaining the information for the report is normally delegated to one of the Official Solicitor's officers. That officer[18] will be responsible for the drafting of the report but, if the officer is of a junior grade, it will first have to be approved by a senior officer and then sent to the Official Solicitor or his Deputy for final consideration and signature.

15. N Turner (1977) 2 *Adoption and Fostering* at 35.
16. If the parties are agreed on an expert it is unlikely that the Official Solicitor will seek a different expert at least initially.
17. Per Cross J in *Re S (an infant)* [1967] 1 all ER at 209G.
18. This account of the officer's responsibilities is taken from the account by N Turner (1977) 2 *Adoption and Fostering* at 35.

In difficult cases there will be discussion between the officer concerned and the Official Solicitor and in exceptional cases counsel's views may be sought. The report is to be regarded as that of the Official Solicitor in his quasi corporate capacity rather than of any individual officer though in case of factual queries the court will normally allow questions to be directed to the officer who conducted the enquiries. The officer responsible for the case will also prepare instructions and briefs to counsel (though again these have to be approved either by the Litigation Principal or by the Official Solicitor or his Deputy) attend hearings before the registrar (with or without counsel as is appropriate) and with counsel attend hearings before the judge.

It will be appreciated that as it will take some time to conduct the necessary inquiries and file the report, there must inevitably be a lengthy adjournment. Of course the time needed to prepare the report will vary according to the circumstances but the likely minimum period is six weeks with an average of some two to three months but it can be longer than that.

i) *Form of Report*[19]

The report takes the following form. Normally there is an introduction in which is set out, the steps taken in the proceedings, the issues which are believed to be at stake and the documentary evidence which has been perused and the names and identities of the persons interviewed or otherwise communicated with. Following the introduction there is a detailed and mainly chronological account of the enquiries made which is based on the attendance notes made by the officer conducting the enquiry. All relevant correspondence and reports are annexed and identified as though exhibited to an affidavit. Following this account there is an analysis of the relevant issues and of the possible options open to the court. The report concludes where practicable, with submissions made to the court on the ward's behalf. It is, however, not always possible to make such submissions as, for example, where there is substantial conflicting evidence resolution of which must await judicial determination.

19. This account follows that given by N Turner ibid., at 35.

In such cases the report will indicate that counsel will make submissions for the ward at the hearing.

It has recently been argued[20] that the report should be confined to giving an unbiased view of the facts and should not contain any specific recommendation. Baker P emphatically rejected the argument saying:

> 'It would be a great disservice to the interests of children and in respect of information available to the court, if it were thought that the Official Solicitor was in any way inhibited in making a recommendation to this court . . . either in a report or when he has heard the evidence and the cross examination of the parties.'

We would endorse this view since the Official Solicitor may be in a position to provide the court with another perspective having, unlike the court, probably seen the child and the parents in their home environment.

ii) *Submission of the Report*

When completed the report is sent to the court and a copy is usually sent to the parties[1]. However, it was held by the House of Lords in *Re K*[2] that parties do not have an absolute right to see the report and the judge is entitled to act upon it without disclosing its contents. Hence when in the Official Solicitor's opinion disclosure of the report would be harmful to the ward the report can be submitted confidentially to the court leaving it to the judge's discretion whether to withhold its contents. Prior to *Re K*[3] it was not uncommon for the Official Solicitor to submit, as he did in this case, both an open Statement of Facts and a confidential Report but the House of Lords made it clear that confidential submission was not to be adopted as a matter of routine but only in exceptional circumstances[4] and according to Lord Evershed[5] on such occasions the Official Solicitor should explain to the judge the reasons which have persuaded him to adopt such a course.

---

20. In *Re W and W (minors)* (1975) 5 Fam Law 157.
 1. As was done for example in *Re F (otherwise A) (a minor) (publication of information)* [1977] Fam 58, [1976] 3 All ER 274.
 2. [1965] AC 201, [1963] 3 All ER 191.
 3. See N Turner (1977) 2 *Adoption and Fostering* at 35.
 4. Per Lord Devlin at 242.
 5. [1965] AC 201 at p. 222.

It is to be emphasised that confidential submission still leaves the judge with a discretion whether to disclose the contents and a common practice and one which was recommended in *Re K* itself is for the judge to disclose the report to the parties' counsel only.

Re K was specifically concerned with the Official Solicitor's report and it must be pointed out that the practice of confidential submissions does not apparently extend to reports of other persons acting as guardian ad litem[6]. The case was also concerned with wardship but as the principle that the child's welfare is paramount is applicable to all proceedings concerning the legal custody and upbringing of children[7], it is submitted that the principles outlined in the case are not confined to wardship. It is accepted[8], for instance, that the High Court judge has the power in matrimonial proceedings to interview children privately and there seems no reason why the judge should not also have the power not to disclose the contents of the Official Solicitor's report. It should be added that in cases where the report is disclosed to the parties, care should be taken not to publish its contents since that can amount to contempt of court[9].

C. THE HEARING AND AFTER

At the hearing before the judge and where issues of importance are expected to arise before the registrar, the ward will be represented by counsel who may examine witnesses, address the court on the ward's behalf and lead evidence. In particular he may file evidence on the medical and welfare aspects. Any witness called by him can be cross examined. The question also arises as to whether the officer responsible

---

6. See Lord Evershed at 217. Parties have no *right* to see local authority case records made under the Boarding Out of Children Regulations 1955, reg.
   10. See *Re D (infants)* [1970] 1 All ER 1088, [1907] 1 WLR 599, though in certain circumstances the *court* may override the privilege. The guardian ad litem's report in adoption proceedings are always confidential. Hence where there are concurrent wardship and adoption proceedings the parties will be advised to seek the report under the wardship proceedings since it will normally be disclosed to them.
7. Pursuant to s.1 of the Guardianship of Minors Act 1971 (as amended by s.36 of the Domestic Proceedings and Magistrates' Courts Act 1978).
8. *H v H* [1973] Fam 62, [1973] 1 All ER 801.
9. S.12 of the Administration of Justice Act 1960 but see *Re F (otherwise A) (a minor)* [1977] Fam 58, [1977] 1 All ER 114 which is discussed in Chap. 7.

for the report can himself be cross examined on it. We take the view that there should be power to do so unless the report has been held confidential[10]. Although this may be thought to be contrary to the general rule that a party's representative cannot be cross examined our submission can be justified in view of the additional role of the guardian ad litem as a reporting officer.

The Official Solicitor's duties may not necessarily end with the conclusion of the main hearing. His staff may be called upon to assist in working out the order. For example, he can offer advice on access, schooling or other problems. He can provide a channel of communication between parties who cannot communicate direct. He can take the initiative in bringing back the case before the court. In this regard it might be added that in appropriate cases the Official Solicitor can bring contempt proceedings in relation to the wardship hearing. This was done for example in *Re F (otherwise A) (minor)*[11] where certain newspapers had published references to previous wardship proceedings. A detailed account of this case and other contempt issues connected with wardship was dealt with in chapter 7.

Examples of some of these roles can be found in the following cases. In *Re Cullimore (a minor)*[12] the Official Solicitor was appointed at the conclusion of the hearing in which it was found that the ward's injuries were due to brittle bones, presumably to maintain a watching brief over the child and to bring the matter back before the court should circumstances warrant it. In *Re R (PM) (an infant)*[13] the court during interim proceedings directed that 'the parents shall have access either jointly or separately at such times as they agree, or in default of agreement as the Official Solicitor directs, but that there shall be no access, save in emergency, during the first three weeks'. The court also observed that if the Official Solicitor felt that either parent was abusing access or that their access was harmful, then he could bring the matter back to the court.

Although circumscribed, the effect of the order in *Re R (PM) (an infant)* was to vest control of the interim access order

10. See ante at p. 61.
11. [1977] Fam 58, [1976] 3 All ER 274.
12. (1976) Times, March 24.
13. [1968] 1 All ER 691n. at 693.

in the Official Solicitor. It should be said, however, that such an order is unusual. There is no question, for example, that the Official Solicitor should provide staff to supervise access on a regular basis[14]. Occasionally his officers will be present on occasions of interim access but not so much to supervise (as in *Re R (PM) (an infant)*) as to observe with a view to giving the court an impartial account as to the child's relationship with those to whom access has been granted. Such presence might also assist the officer in deciding what submission to make on the question of long term access. There may be occasions where the officer has gained the ward's confidence and where it is proposed to reintroduce the child to a parent who has not had access for some time when it may be convenient for the officer to be present as supervisor to give the ward some sense of support.

As well as not being able to supervise access the officer cannot offer direct welfare service or accommodation for homeless children or disburse money unless it can properly be included in a bill of costs. He may apply for help from local authorities or other welfare agencies.

V   Costs

Although the Official Solicitor's Department is maintained as an Office of the Supreme Court out of money voted for the purpose by Parliament it is expected so far as possible to pay its way.

Formerly the Official Solicitor would only consent to act on behalf of a minor if his costs were guaranteed and indeed a solicitor's undertaking was required. This practice was essentially a legacy of the ad hoc development of the mid nineteenth century when 'official' duties such as visitation of contempt prisoners were regarded as being covered by his salary while he could hope to recover costs in relation to representation inter alia of infants. The current position is that a solicitor's undertaking is not called for though a party seeking his appointment might occasionally be asked for a personal undertaking to meet any costs ordered by the court. Even then as Mr. Turner has commented[15] 'this is normally

14. See N Turner (1977) 2 *Adoption and Fostering* at 34.
15. Ibid. at 36.

no more than a formal warning that he may be required to pay the costs whatever the outcome of the proceedings'. Where the court has acted of its own motion in appointing the Official Solicitor then normally no undertaking at all is sought.

So far as liability to pay costs is concerned it is established by *Re PC (an infant)*[16] that the Official Solicitor is entitled to costs on a party and party basis as though he were the successful party. This rule applied equally where the Official Solicitor is appointed upon request of the parties or by the court on its own motion. In *Re P C (an infant)* a father issued a summons asking that his daughter be made a ward of court in order to restrain a certain man from marrying her, and an ex parte injunction was granted restraining the man and the child from intermarrying, associating or communicating with one another. Subsequently, the father applied for an order committing the man for contempt for breaking the order and by another motion he also sought an injunction restraining the man and the child from intermarrying. At the adjourned hearing of the two motions it was decided by the court that the daughter should be represented by the Official Solicitor[17]. There were a number of further hearings. It was held that the Official Solicitor was entitled to costs from the parents incurred in the performance of his duties as guardian ad litem in respect of all motions where the child was a party but not in relation to the motion which was solely against the man in question.

Re PC was specifically concerned with a case where there was no suitable defendant other than the ward. In other cases where there are two opposing parties but where the ward is joined as a party, the costs[18] of the Official Solicitor will fall at the court's discretion on one party or another or upon them jointly and severally in such proportions as may be deemed reasonable in the circumstances, their respective means being a relevant consideration.

16. [1961] Ch 312 (not [1962] Ch as cited in (1977) *Adoption and Fostering* at 36). See also *Re C (CA) (an infant)* [1964] 2 All ER 478, [1964] 1 WLR 857.
17. NB the naming of the ward as a party at this stage is illustrative of the old and somewhat clumsy procedure. The practice now is for the court to name the child as defendant at the outset—see RSC Ord. 90, r.3(2). Discussed ante at p. 39.
18. Normally no order is made as to costs between the parties.

Mr. Turner has pointed out in deciding what order as to costs should be made[19]:

> 'the Court will take into account the paramountcy of the welfare of the ward, and will not make an order which might put in peril a parent's ability to make proper financial provision for the ward.'

Where a party is legally aided then his liability for costs including that of the Official Solicitor acting for the ward is limited by section 8(1)(*e*) of the Legal Aid Act 1974. This section provides that:

> 'liability by virtue of an order for costs made against him with respect to the proceedings shall not exceed the amount (if any) which is a reasonable one for him to pay having regard to all the circumstances, including the means of all the parties and their conduct in connection with the dispute.'

VI Conclusions

It would be hard to overestimate the value of the Official Solicitor's services. The office has acquired considerable and unique experience of interviewing parties and as the Latey Committee commented[20] the Official Solicitor and his staff execute their often difficult and delicate tasks with humanity and expertise. The court is not bound by the Official Solicitor's views or recommendation but his report is treated with respect and ensures that the ward's interests are specifically brought to the court's notice. The office itself seems a strong but flexible one which works well under a largely unwritten constitution. The fact that the holder is a senior ranking solicitor adds to the efficiency of the office since his views and authority are more respected. The point should be made, however, that it is doubtful whether as presently constituted the office could handle a vast increase in cases and an expansion of his office might detract from its efficiency and humanity. This may be one argument against the setting up of branch offices in the provinces. Another is

19. (1977) 2 *Adoption and Fostering* at 36.
20. (1967) Cmnd. 3342, para. 218.

that the current referrals[1] simply do not justify such expansion even though the travelling time involved in dealing with such cases is substantial. To a certain extent the work is cut down by dealing with non-controversial interlocutory applications by post and with some more difficult ones by agents. Nevertheless as one commentator has said[2]:

'It is possible that increasing awareness of the jurisdiction will lead to a significant rise in the number of cases referred to the Official Solicitor throughout the country. At some point the advantages of a small, coherent group of people centred in London will be outweighed by the expense and delay caused by dealing with cases arising throughout the country.'

1. The current referrals from the District Registries are estimated to be between 60 and 70 (100 to 120 if MCR 1977, r.115 cases are included). The unknown factor, of course, is whether these figures would increase if there were branch offices.
2. John Eekelaar: *Family Law and Social Policy* (1978, Weidenfeld and Nicholson), p. 114.

Chapter 9

The Court Welfare Service

I Use of service in wardship

Although the use of the Official Solicitor's services in wardship is well known it is perhaps less well known that in wardship proceedings the court can also draw upon the services of a court welfare officer. The court welfare service is more immediately associated with divorce proceedings[1] and indeed no specific reference is made in the rules[2] with regard to calling for welfare reports on wards. In fact, in London something in the order of 200 wardship cases were referred to the court welfare service in 1976 representing over ten per cent of the total work load[3].

1. It is in this context that discussion will be found in other textbooks—see e.g. *Rayden on Divorce* (13th Edn. 1979), pp. 589, 590 and 1037. For a discussion on the future role of the welfare service in divorce see Jean Graham Hall: 'The Future of the Divorce Welfare Service' (1977) 7 Fam Law 101 and Susan Maidment: 'The future of the Divorce Court Welfare Service—an Alternative View' (1977) 7 Fam Law 246.
2. There is reference to wardship cases in the commentary to the Supreme Court Rules. See Rules of the Supreme Court Practice 1979 Vol. 1, p. 1344, para. 90/3/5. Rule 95 of the MCR 1977 specifically refers to matrimonial proceedings which by Rule 2(2) is defined by reference to s.50 of the Matrimonial Causes Act 1973. The definition does not include wardship, but there is no reason to suppose that the practice is any different in wardship cases.
3. The following figures were kindly supplied by Mr R Tolson, Senior Court Welfare Officer: In 1975, 2134 cases were referred to the court welfare service in London, of which 136 were wardship cases. In 1976 there were 201 wardship cases out of a total of 1910 referrals and up to July 1977 there were 143 wardship cases out of a total of 1044 referrals. It can be seen from these figures that increasing use is being made of welfare officers in wardship cases.

The court welfare service itself is relatively new[4] and extensive use of its officers in wardship cases really dates from the transfer in 1971 of the jurisdiction from the Chancery to the Family Division, though it was by no means unknown for Chancery judges to call for a welfare report in the years immediately preceding the transfer[5].

A welfare officer is a qualified probation officer. In London there is a permanent staff of 9 attached to the Supreme Court whereas in the provinces the Principal Probation Officer combines his services as Divorce Court welfare officer with his other duties. A welfare officer cannot act without a court direction but a report can be called for, either by a judge or a registrar at any stage of proceedings[6]. As in the case of the Official Solicitor, appointment of a court welfare officer can be made either by the court acting on its own motion or upon application. By analogy with rule 95(2) of the Matrimonial Causes Rules 1977 any party can request a registrar to call for a welfare report before the application is heard. Provided the registrar is satisfied that the other parties consent and that sufficient information is available to enable the officer to carry out the investigation, the matter may be referred to a court welfare officer for investigation and report before the hearing. Local authorities might sometimes find it advantageous to seek a welfare report so as to relieve their own social workers having to make a report and thereby preserving the confidence and co-operation of their clients[7]. Normally

4. The service was set up in response to the recommendations of the Denning Committee on Procedures in Matrimonial Causes—Final Report 1947 Cmnd. 7024. The first scheme, which was experimental, was set up in London pursuant to a *Practice Direction* dated 25 May 1950, signed by Lord Merriman P—see *Rayden on Divorce* (8th Edn. 1960), p. 1426. The scheme became permanent and applicable in the provinces following the recommendation of the Morton Commission on Marriage and Divorce (1956) Cmnd. 9678.
5. But see the comments of Buckley J in *Re A-H (infants)* [1962] 3 All ER 853 at 855.
6. Cf. MCR 1977, r.95(1).
7. In any event some social workers may be unfamiliar with the High Court jurisdiction and a report of a welfare officer may give greater assistance to the court. NB *President's Direction* 1962, August 14 (No. 27) referred to by *Rayden on Divorce* (13th Edn. 1979), pp. 1037, 1038, 3701 whereby if in divorce proceedings it comes to the registrar's notice on examination of the papers prior to giving directions for trial that a child of the family is in care of a local authority and no report by the court welfare officer has been filed or called for, the registrar will call for a report which should be filed in time to be available for the Judge at the hearing. Presumably a similar standpoint would be taken in wardship proceedings.

reports will be called for before the full hearing but it can be required at any stage of the proceedings even after the hearing as for example to indicate how a particular order is working out[8] or to supervise access arrangements[9].

II Welfare officers' functions and their relationship with the official solicitor

Whether or not a report will be called for will obviously depend upon the circumstances of the case but it will also very much depend upon the individual registrar or judge. One difficulty is whether to call for a welfare report rather than to appoint the Official Solicitor. In this regard it is important to differentiate the functions of a welfare officer from those of the Official Solicitor. Unlike the Official Solicitor *welfare officers do not represent the ward's interests*. Instead their function is to provide the court with an objective report[10] on the child's situation. Their expertise relates to the welfare of children and essentially their role is a supportive and advisory one. They may also be called upon to provide a counselling and conciliatory service. The Official Solicitor on the other hand will be actually representing the child but whilst he is obviously concerned with the child's welfare it has to be remembered nevertheless that his report will be that of a lawyer and not a social worker. There can never be a definitive answer as to who should be appointed but the following examples may provide a basis for making the appropriate choice. The appointment of the Official Solicitor as the ward's legal representative will be desirable, where it appears that the interest of the child may diverge from that of the parties. This may occur where the dispute is between parent and child as with the prevention of 'undesirable' associations or where the child has suffered at the hands of the parents or where he is being used as a pawn. The Official Solicitor's appointment will be most desirable whenever the

---

8. See *Re L* (*minor*), Court of appeal, (Civil Division) Transcript No. 425 B, of 1976.
9. *Re K* (*infants*), Court of Appeal (Civil Division) Transcript, No. 84 of 1976.
10. Correctly referred to as a 'welfare report' and not a 'social inquiry report' per Baker P in *Pilcher v Pilcher* (1976) Times, February 7.

determination of a point of law which impinges on the ward's future is an issue.

The welfare officer's appointment on the other hand may be preferred where the court only requires a report on the child's background and present home circumstances, and where the issue before the court does not indicate that the child's best interests will be conflicting in any way with that of the parties to the action. The need for a report alone may arise where one party is unconcerned about the welfare of the child, where the children may be separated from each other or where there is a third party seeking care and control.

There will be a clear need for a report where there are doubts about the suitability of the parties' proposals for the child's future or where the child is or has recently been involved with a welfare agency[11]. Whether this should be provided by the Official Solicitor or the welfare officer must depend on the general considerations already outlined.

Although the court is not at the outset likely to employ both their services, the appointment of one does not preclude the appointment of the other[12]. The Official Solicitor may well be called in, for instance, after the welfare report has been made in order to provide the child with an advocate at the hearing[13]. In such cases the role of the Official Solicitor will be virtually confined to providing the ward with an advocate to assist in reaching, if possible, a consent order or if there is a contested hearing to ask questions and make submissions on material provided by the welfare report. Alternatively the welfare officer may be appointed after the hearing, in which the Official Solicitor has been involved as the ward's guardian ad litem, in order to supervise a transfer of care or to control or arrange or supervise access.

Although there is no formal link between the Court Welfare Service and the Official Solicitor's office, where both are involved in the same case there is close co-operation between the two and in particular care will be taken to avoid duplication of work.

11. In such a case an additional report may frequently be sought from that agency.
12. See, for example, *Re B*, Court of Appeal (Civil Division) Transcript No. 237 of 1976.
13. It may be, however, that following the Official Solicitor's appointment the welfare officer will drop out from the case.

III The report

Once he has been directed to make a report the welfare officer will receive from the court all the relevant papers[14]. He will then visit and interview the various parties, including the child, at their respective homes. He can, at his discretion, extend his enquiries to the family doctor, school teacher or any other appropriate person whose observations would appear to be helpful[15]. It will be appreciated that seeing the parties in their various homes may involve extensive travel; nevertheless it has been said that it is undesirable to have two reports from different welfare officers so that as far as possible there should only be one[16].

Theoretically, the obtaining of information is easier in wardship cases since all the parties are compellable witnesses and directions may be sought from the registrar in cases of difficulty. In matrimonial proceedings, on the other hand, there can be difficulty in seeing the parties since the officer has no legal mandate to enter a home. However, in practice in both cases these difficulties are virtually non-existent as most people are only too anxious to discuss their children and other troubles.

It obviously takes time to prepare the report and this is often a contributory factor in the delay in bringing a wardship case to a final hearing. The minimum time in which a report can be expected to be completed is likely to be six weeks but the average time is two to three months and in some cases it can be considerably longer than that. To avoid further delay, it is provided by a *Practice Direction*[17] that a solicitor should consult the welfare officer to obtain an estimate of the approximate date when the report is likely to be available and in the light of this fix a date for the hearing.

The welfare report should contain a statement of the facts as found by the officer and while his views are clearly likely to

---

14. Cf. MCR 1977, r.95(3)(a) 'the court welfare officer may inspect the court file'.
15. See Gerald Sanctuary and Constance Whitehead: *Divorce—and After* (1970 Gollancz) 136.
16. Per Baker P (1973) 117 Sol Jo 88, *Practice Note (welfare reports) C v C* (1972) Times, November 7th not 9th as cited in the Supreme Court Practice 1979 Vol. 1, para. 90/3/5).
17. [1972] 2 All ER 352, [1972] 1 WLR 506.

be reflected by his report, it need not contain any specific recommendations[18].

Formerly when the report was completed it was submitted to the registrar who had a discretion whether to release the report immediately to the parties or to withhold it until the court hearing. Now[19], however, reports in wardship matters are treated like any other report in custody and other ancillary matters and upon notification by the registrar the report can be bespoken in the usual way by the solicitors or by the parties, if in person[20]. The only occasion when a report would be scrutinised is when the officer specially draws the attention of the registrar to the contents of the report. What is not clearly established is whether there are circumstances in wardship when the report can be withheld from the parties altogether. By analogy with *Fowler v Fowler and Sines*[1] where the Court of Appeal held that it was improper for a judge to interview a welfare officer in private during matrimonial proceedings, it would seem that the report should always be disclosed to the parties. Moreover, this view might be thought to be endorsed by *Re B (minors)*[2] where Baker P commented that copies of the report should be made available to the parties in custody cases especially if an appeal is contemplated. Baker P, however, does not state that disclosure of the report is mandatory, while *Fowler* must be considered in the light of the House of Lords decision in *Official Solicitor v K*[3] which, as we have seen, established that the Official Solicitor's report could be kept confidential if the interests of the ward dictated. Since the House of Lords in

---

18. Cf. *Re W and W (minors)* (1975) 5 Fam Law 157 where Baker P pointed out that a recommendation adverse to one of the parents would make subsequent working or co-operating with that parent difficult and sometimes impossible. This reasoning perhaps has less impact in wardship cases since a welfare officer, at any rate one based in London, is not necessarily going to have further contact with the parties after the hearing. It might be added that a report can be adverse without specific recommendations simply by indicating the problems of a particular course of action.
19. Pursuant to the Registrar's Circular of 15 December 1977.
20. Cf. MCR 1977, r. 95(3)(*b*) which states: 'after completing his investigation, the officer shall file his report and the registrar shall thereupon notify the parties that they may inspect it and may bespeak copies on payment of the prescribed fee'.
1. [1963] P 311, [1963] 1 All ER 119.
2. (1977) Times, July 23.
3. [1965] AC 201, [1963] 3 All ER 191. Discussed ante at p. 185.

Official Solicitor v K reversed the Court of Appeal[4], whose decision had been relied upon in *Fowler*, it would seem that a welfare report ought in principle to be similarly treated. As non-disclosure can only be justified where the child's interests would otherwise be harmed the circumstances in which a welfare report could be withheld must be extremely limited.

IV The hearing

Although it is possible for the welfare officer to be cross-examined on his report the more normal practice, if further elucidation is required, is for the judge to ask questions in both parties' presence directed to an explanation or expansion of the report[5]. As we have mentioned *Fowler v Fowler and Sine* stands as authority for saying that a judge cannot discuss the case with the welfare officer privately during a hearing but in view of *Official Solicitor v K* it is now probably better to say that exceptionally this can be done where harm to the ward would otherwise ensue[6].

If it is sought to cross-examine the welfare officer it would seem prudent to seek his attendance prior to the hearing. As Stamp LJ has said[7]: 'I should be sorry if it was the duty of a welfare officer who had made a report in infant proceedings to attend the court at the hearing in absence of any request made for that purpose unless the welfare officer himself thought that his presence would be useful'.

The report is intended to aid the court and of course it is not binding[8]. Nevertheless, it has been held[9], though not in wardship, that where the court differs from the welfare officer's views it is essential to give the reasons. This statement underlines the regard with which welfare reports are held by the court.

Although the preparation and submission of the report is the welfare officer's major task his duties may not end with

4. [1963] Ch 381, 390.
5. See Davies LJ in *Re K (infants)* [1963] Ch 381 at 412.
6. For a similar view see *Rayden on Divorce* (13th Edn. 1979), p. 1037 based on the reasoning of Lord Evershed in *Official Solicitor v K* [1965] AC at 219.
7. *Re DA (infants)*, Court of Appeal, (Civil Division) Transcript No. 171 of 1976.
8. His recommendations were not followed, for example, in *Re L (minor)*, Court of Appeal (Civil Division) Transcript No. 425B of 1976.
9. Per Ormrod J in *Clark v Clark* (1970) 114 Sol Jo 318.

the hearing. He can be called upon to make a report at some later point indicating how the order is working out[10]. He may be called upon to supervise the transfer of care and control and he may be asked to assist in the arrangements over access[11]. Such assistance may be particularly useful in cases where communication between the parents is impossible, and to have a go-between in such cases can be a tremendous help. Indeed, it is open to either or both parties to ask the court to authorise the court welfare officer to act between them on behalf of the children[12].

10. *Re L (minor)*, Court of Appeal (Civil Division) Transcript No. 425 B of 1976.
11. See *Re K (infants)*, Court of Appeal (Civil Division) Transcript No. 84 of 1976.
12. See Gerald Sanctuary and Constance Whitehead: *Divorce—and After* op. cit at p. 147.

Chapter 10

The Role of Wardship and its Interaction with Related Jurisdictions

I Introduction

Wardship has an enormous range of uses. The concern of this and succeeding chapters is to discuss and compare the role of wardship in the context of the other jurisdictions concerned with children. In fact the relationship between wardship and other related jurisdictions is extremely complex. This is because while the number of jurisdictions concerned with children are themselves legion wardship is unusual if not unique in that it can be used in different capacities. First it can be used as an original jurisdiction. There are occasions when wardship is the only remedy open to a party, while in other situations the prerogative jurisdiction exists merely as one of the options open to a party. Wardship can also be used either as a supplementary or a supervisory jurisdiction, so that even if a court or some other body has already made a decision, wardship may provide a means of having that decision supplemented or reviewed.

In this chapter we shall discuss the role of wardship mainly in the context of the jurisdictions dealing with custody, guardianship, adoption and (when in force) custodianship. The relationship between wardship and the powers of local authorities over children is considered in Chapter 11, while the use of wardship in connection with 'kidnapping' is discussed in Chapter 12.

Consideration will first be given to the use of wardship by parents, then to the use by non parents, and thirdly to the possibilities of the use by or on behalf of the child. The initial division is not intended to be rigid so that, for example, the use of wardship to non parents who are also qualified to apply for a custody order will be dealt with under the first heading while use of wardship to parents in connection with adoption will be considered under the second.

II Parental applications

A. 'TEENAGE WARDSHIPS'

For the most part parental applications to make their children wards of court are made in the course of a matrimonial dispute between themselves. These applications will be discussed shortly when consideration is given to the relationship between wardship and the various custody jurisdictions. It may be, however, that the parents are united but are in dispute with their child or alternatively with a third party. In such cases unless the dispute concerns the custody of the child then the only course open to the parties to bring the issue before the court is via wardship[1].

The classic instance of the exclusive use of wardship in this context is where the parents are united in their desire to prevent their child continuing with what in their view is an undesirable association. Such applications, however, are not the only examples of the use of wardship by united parents. If the parents wish to restrain the activities of third parties on the grounds that their child may thereby be harmed then wardship is the only means of doing so. It is true that the likelihood of such applications being successful are not very great in view of the decision in *Re X* (*a minor*)[2] where the court refused an application to restrain the publication of a book on the grounds that it was psychologically harmful to

1. If the parents are contesting custody against a third party then they can apply under the Guardianship of Minors Act 1971, s.9. In such circumstances, however, it might be quicker and more efficacious to institute wardship proceedings particularly if that party is threatening to take the child out of the jurisdiction. It is true that the courts now have the power under s.13A (substituted by the Domestic Proceedings and Magistrates' Courts Act 1978) to restrain the child's removal from the jurisdiction but this power only arises after a custody order has been made—see post p. 210. Apart from s.9 of the 1971 Act the next widest provision is the Guardianship Act 1973 s.1(3) under which a mother or father may apply for the court's directions on any question affecting the child's welfare and *on which they disagree*. In such circumstances the court's sole function is to give directions on the specific point in dispute. It has no power to make a custody or access order—s.1(4).
2. [1975] Fam 47, [1975] 1 All ER 697.

the ward. However, as was discussed earlier[3], the decision does not rule out the possibility of success in other more appropriate circumstances.

Applications to prevent the continuation of an undesirable association are often referred to as 'teenage wardships' for obvious reasons. As Lord Cross once wrote[4]: 'In these cases the ward is nearly always a girl or young woman ... who is having, or is plainly about to have, sexual intercourse with some man of whom her parents disapprove.' However, while such applications most commonly involve a female ward they need not do so nor do they necessarily have to relate to the prevention of a personal relationship with or the marriage to a particular person. Applications could certainly be made to prevent the child associating with 'undesirable' groups such as drug addicts, hippies or religious sects.

The motivation for such applications may of course vary. In the past[5], particularly in the nineteenth century property considerations were behind the bulk of applications, wardship being used to prevent the marriage of the ward to a person of inferior rank and fortune and, especially in the case of female wards, to prevent the ward's property passing on marriage to the 'undesirable man'. Given this background it is perhaps not surprising that the contempt in marrying a ward without the court's consent was regarded as a strict offence in that no mens rea was required[6]. Today the motivation is less likely to be to protect property interests than to protect what in the parents' view is the ward's moral and social welfare, but obviously the objections which the parents entertain to the person in question are varied. As Lord Cross wrote[7]:

'Sometimes he is himself married—with or without the hope of getting a divorce. Sometimes he has a criminal record of greater or less seriousness. Sometimes he has a record of seduction of young women. Sometimes he has

3. See Chapter 5 and Chapter 6.
4. See Cross: 'Wards of Court' (1967) 83 LQR 200, 209.
5. For an account of the old cases concerning marriage of a ward see e.g. Eversley on *Domestic Relations* (6th Edn. 1951) 602–10 and Seton's *Judgments and Orders* (7th edn. 1912), Vol. II 1004–19. See also *Rayden on Divorce* (13th Edn. 1979), pp. 1129–30.
6. It is still regarded as a strict offence but some doubt has been cast on this by Lord Denning MR in *Re F (otherwise A) (a minor) (publication of information)* [1977] Fam 58 at 88G. Discussed ante p. 141.
7. (1967) 83 LQR at 210.

no apparent means of support and appears to be battening on the ward. Sometimes again the chief objection is social class or colour. It must, of course, often happen that parents disapprove of the associates male or female of their sons; but it is in fact rare for a 'teenage' boy to be made a ward. This is because even nowadays girls are generally considered less able to fend for themselves than boys. In particular, of course, boys do not have babies.'

To these examples one might add that applications can and are made to prevent what are feared to be a lesbian or homosexual relationship or to curtail what seems to be an excessive interest by an older person in the child in question.

In past decades a number of teenage wardship cases hit the national headlines[8] but with the reduction of the age of majority to 18[9] the number of cases have declined although disputes are apparently still not infrequent[10].

As we have seen[11] the invariable practice in such cases is to name the ward as a party and to appoint the Official Solicitor to represent the ward's interests. To ascertain the facts the Official Solicitor[12] ordinarily sees the ward first and hears the ward's side of the story. He will then see the parents, and in the words of the Latey Committee's report[13] he 'probes their evidence and finds out as much as he can of the family background, seeing others where useful'. Finally he will see the third party concerned. At the end of his investigation the Official Solicitor will make a written report including his submissions which in due course will be sent to the judge. It will take some time to complete the investigation so that in cases where immediate action is required, for example, to stop the ward from eloping, the parents should apply immediately to the judge for an interim injunction. In these cases the court will act on the parents' affidavits without the benefit of the Official Solicitor's report. However, as Lord

8. Particularly *Re Elwes* (1958) Times, 30 July. See also *Re Crump* (*an infant*) (1963) 107 Sol Jo 682.
9. Under s.1 of the Family Law Reform Act 1969.
10. See the comments of Mr Norman Turner (the present Official Solicitor) in (1977) 2 *Adoption and Fostering* at 33.
11. See Chapter 8. See RSC Ord. 90, r.3(2). The person against whom an order is sought is *not* made a party to the wardship proceedings.
12. For an account of his role in such cases see the Latey Committee Report (1967) Cmnd. 3342 paras. 208–11 and Cross (1967) 83 LQR at 210.
13. Ibid., at para. 210.

Cross has said it is 'by no means unusual for the report of the Official Solicitor to put a different complexion on the case and for the interim order to be subsequently discharged or modified'[14]. The Official Solicitor's task is not to 'rubber stamp' the parents' view but to discover what is best for the ward. It may be that the companion in question is not the ogre the parents have presumed or represented him to be.

At the best of times the Official Solicitor's task is a delicate and difficult one[15]. For those wards amenable to persuasion his intervention can be successful as, for example, where a teenager has got out of his or her depth in pursuing an undesirable association and has a conscious or subconscious desire to be extricated from it. As Mr Norman Turner (the present Official Solicitor) has said[16]:

'Orders and injunctions in wardship might achieve this without loss of face to the ward and without destroying the last vestiges of the relationship between ward and parents, but only if very carefully handled not only by the guardian ad litem but by the parents and advisers.'

At worst the Official Solicitor's intervention allows the parties time to think about their position but at the end of the day if the ward remains recalcitrant there is little that can be done about it. As Lord Cross said[17] the court may in the end either have to throw in its hand either by 'dewarding' her or by giving its consent to the marriage assuming that the pair wish to get married and can legally do so.

Even if the court does make the order for which the parents have asked there is no guarantee that it will be obeyed. In the recent case of *Re F (otherwise A) (a minor)*[18], for example, the parents tried to prevent their daughter from seeing a man who was much older than herself and who took drugs. During an argument about this relationship the daughter left home and the parents instituted wardship proceedings. The court ordered that the ward should return home and the man in question not to harbour her, but in fact the daughter never returned home and was eventually placed in a hostel specialising in the care of adolescent girls.

14. (1967) 83 LQR at 210.
15. Particularly if the ward is already pregnant. See the Latey Report at para. 211.
16. (1977) 2 *Adoption and Fostering* at 30, 33.
17. (1967) 83 LQR at 211.
18. *Re F (otherwise A) (a minor) (publication of information)* [1977] Fam 58, [1977] 1 All ER 114.

The court does have the power to punish even a ward for contempt for not obeying a court order[19], but to imprison the ward seems to defeat the very object of the action. The practice now is for the court not to put itself in a conflicting position, so that the order is not made against the ward but only against the third party[20].

Parents should think carefully before warding their child in such circumstances. It must always be regarded as a remedy of the last resort and it should be remembered that the court's task is to consider dispassionately what is best for the ward, not what is best for the parents. If the ward is really intransigent then the wardship proceedings are unlikely to produce useful results. In these circumstances as Mr Turner has said[1]: 'The parents may feel let down by the Law and disgruntled about the cost of it all'. He concluded that in any event the cases usually involve a difficult exercise in judgment by the guardian ad litem and sensitive counselling of the parents by their adviser.

B. WARDSHIP AND CUSTODY

i) *Introduction*

Determining which of the parents should have the right to look after and bring up their children often falls to be decided by the courts acting under their custody jurisdiction. Precisely which of the custody jurisdictions will be involved depends upon the context in which the issue is raised. If, for example, the parties are also seeking a divorce, nullity or judicial separation, then provided the child is a 'child of the family' for the purposes of the 1973 Act[2] custody will be decided as an ancillary matter under the Matrimonial Causes

---

19. *Re Leigh* (1888) 40 Ch D 290 at 294 *Re H's Settlement, H v H* [1909] 2 Ch 260. For modern examples see *Re Elwes* (1958) Times, July 30 and *Re Crump (an infant)* (1963) 107 Sol Jo 682. For a critical comment see (1963) 113 LJ 585. Discussed in Chapter 7.

20. Even so the ward could be guilty of contempt if she aids and abets a breach of a court order. See Chapter 7.

1. (1977) 2 *Adoption and Fostering* at 33.

2. 'Child of the Family' is defined by s.52 of the Matrimonial Causes Act 1973 as: '(a) any child of both parties to the marriage; and (b) any other child, not being a child who has been boarded out with those parties by a local authority or voluntary organisation, who has been treated by both of those parties as a child of their family'. For an interpretation of the phrase 'treating the child as a child of the family' see *W(RJ) v W(SJ)* [1972] Fam 152, [1971] 3 All ER 303 and *A v A* [1974] Fam 6, [1974] 1 All ER 755.

Act 1973[3]. Custody can also be determined under the 1973 Act if application is made for maintenance under section 27[4]. If instead of a divorce one spouse wishes to seek a matrimonial order against the other (i.e. a maintenance order) then provided the child is a 'child of the family' for the purposes of the 1978 Act[5] any custody issue can be decided by a magistrates' court under the Domestic Proceedings and Magistrates' Courts Act 1978[6]. If the parents' sole dispute concerns the child then the most appropriate custody jurisdiction is that of the Guardianship of Minors Acts 1971 and 1973[7] under which applications may be made to a magistrates' court, a county court or the High Court. In addition and as an alternative to these custody jurisdictions parents may also seek care and control via wardship proceedings.

ii) *Wardship and custody orders compared*

The effect of the custody order granted under the 1973 Act is to vest in the person granted custody all the parental rights and duties over the child.

In this context the expression 'parental rights and duties' is a comprehensive term[8] comprising not only the right to the de facto care and control of the child (including the right to discipline the child and to consent to medical matters concerning the child) but also, as one judge put it[9] a 'bundle of powers' including:

'the power to control education, the choice of religion and the administration of the infant's property... entitlement to veto the issue of a passport and to with-

---

3. S.42. If the proceedings are undefended they will be heard by the Divorce County Court otherwise they will be heard by a judge of the Family Division of the High Court.
4. S.42(2). Under s.27 (as amended by the Domestic Proceedings and Magistrates' Courts Act 1978) application may be made during the subsistance on the grounds that the applicant has failed to provide reasonable maintenance either for the applicant or any 'child of the family'.
5. 'Child of the Family' is now defined in the same way as under the 1973 Act. See s.88(1) of the Domestic Proceedings and Magistrates' Courts Act 1978.
6. Under s.8.
7. Applications may be made by the mother and father of the child including the putative father—Ss.9, 14 of the 1971 Act.
8. For a review and analysis of parental rights and duties see Eekelaar: 'What are Parental Rights?' (1973) 89 LQR 210.
9. Per Sachs LJ in *Hewer v Bryant* [1970] 1 QB 357 at 373.

hold consent to marriage [and] the power physically to control the infant until the years of discretion.'

Under the Domestic Proceedings and Magistrates' Courts 1978 and the Guardianship of Minors Act 1971 the court may only grant 'legal' custody to one person which vests all parental rights and duties as relate to the *person* of the child[10]. Such orders do not therefore vest rights or duties over the child's property and in this respect only are therefore narrower than under the 1973 Act. Where a putative father is granted custody under the 1971 Act not only will he be vested with the rights and duties outlined above, but he will also be considered the child's guardian for the purposes of adoption and his agreement to the adoption will therefore be required[11].

Occasionally instead of granting custody to one person the court may 'split' the order. Under the 1973 Act the appropriate method of doing this is to grant joint custody to the parties with care and control to one of them[12], the effect of which will be that the person having care and control will be entitled to take the day-to-day decisions concerning the child's upbringing but the more long term legal powers, for example, to control the child's education will be vested in the parties jointly. Under the 1971[13] and 1978 Acts[14] the court can order that the parent not given legal custody shall retain 'all or such as the court may specify of the parental rights and duties comprised in legal custody (other than the right to actual custody of the minor) and shall have those rights and duties jointly with the person who is given the legal custody of the minor'. Under these new provisions the court will be empowered to make more precise split orders if it is thought desirable.

10. Pursuant to the definition under s.86 of the Children Act 1975.
11. Adoption Act 1958, s.57(1) as amended by the Children Act 1975 Sch. 3 paras 39(a)(b).
12. Formerly the split order commonly took the form of granting custody to one but care and control to the other parent, but the provision under s.1(1) of the Guardianship Act 1973 by which mothers and fathers of legitimate children have equal and separately exercisable rights is thought to have removed its rationale. See *Justice: Parental Rights and Duties and Custody Suits,* 1975 para. 19 and Harris (1973) 137 JPN 774. See also Lowe (1977) 127 NLJ 184. For a review of the courts' powers to make 'split' orders see *Jussa v Jussa* [1972] 2 All ER 600, [1972] 1 WLR 881.
13. Guardianship of Minors Act 1971 s.11A(1) (as substituted by the Domestic Proceedings and Magistrates' Courts Act s.37).
14. Domestic Proceedings and Magistrates' Courts Act 1978, s.8(4).

Even if one parent is awarded sole custody that does not mean that the other parent ceases to have any rights. The other parent may still be granted access and can be ordered to pay maintenance. It has also been established[15] that the person granted custody cannot unilaterally change the child's surname at least by any formal steps[16]. He must first either obtain the other parent's consent or the court's permission. In any event a custody order is not final so that either parent may seek a variation of the original order in the light of changed circumstances.

For the most part the parent awarded custody under any of the jurisdictions will be able to bring up his child free from interference from the other parent and free from interference by the court. A wardship order on the other hand is more analogous to a joint custody order with care and control to one party with the important difference that custody is vested in the court. A person granted care and control of a ward will have the de facto care and control of the child with the consequential power to take day-to-day decisions such as disciplining the child or consenting to medical matters but he will remain subject to the court's control in other matters. Indeed, as we have seen, it has been said[17] that 'no important step in a ward's life may be taken without the court's consent'. In practical terms this means that the child cannot be taken out of the jurisdiction, including therefore a visit to Scotland without the court's prior consent[18]. Consent to the ward's marriage will have to be given by the court[19] and changing the child's surname will not be possible other than with the court's consent[20]. How far the court would wish to exercise control in other matters is perhaps debatable, but in principle at least the court should be informed of any proposed changes which would affect the court order[1].

15. *Y v Y* (*child: surname*) [1973] Fam 147, [1973] 2 All ER 574. Under MCR 1977, r.92(8) parental assent must be in writing. See also *Practice Direction* [1977] 3 All ER 451 sub nom *Rice v Rice* [1977] 1 WLR 1256 and *D v B* (*otherwise D*) (*child: surname*) [1979] 1 All ER 92, [1978] 3 WLR 573 and *L v F* (1978) Times, August 1.
16. Cf. *R(BM) v R(DN)* (*child: surname*) [1978] 2 All ER 33.
17. Per Cross J in *Re S* (*infants*) [1977] 1 All ER 202, 207. Discussed ante at p.
18. As emphasised by the *Practice Direction* [1977] 3 All ER 122 [1977] 1 WLR 1067.
19. As emphasised by the Marriage Act 1949, s.3(6).
20. Cf. a custody order where a child's surname can be changed with the other parent's written consent.
1. See the discussion ante in Chapter 5.

It is the continued control by the court which distinguishes a wardship order from a custody order, though perhaps one should be wary of making too much of this point since in practice the court's powers will remain dormant save in cases of difficulty. Like a custody order, a wardship order is not permanent nor does it sever the other parent's links with the child. Access can be granted and maintenance ordered in the same way as in custody and again the parties may seek a fresh order in the light of changed circumstances. In both jurisdictions in deciding who should look after the child the court is statutorily enjoined[2] to regard the child's welfare as the first and paramount consideration.

iii) *Choice of jurisdictions*

a) **Factors in favour of custody**

Although for the practical purposes of bringing up the child there is probably little to choose between the two orders, parents would normally be advised to seek a custody order. There are a number of reasons for saying this. First, wardship is solely concerned with the child so that if the parties are seeking matrimonial orders in addition to custody they will in any event have to invoke the appropriate jurisdiction (i.e. the divorce jurisdiction under the 1973 Act or the matrimonial jurisdiction under the 1978 Act) to gain that relief and it would seem prudent and desirable that the same court should also resolve the custody issue[3]. Second, even where the dispute solely concerns the child it may be preferable to apply for custody under the Guardianship of Minors Acts 1971 and 1973 since such applications can be made in the lower courts and will be considerably cheaper, quicker and more convenient than a wardship application. On this basis an applicant is more likely to obtain legal aid for custody. The third advantage of custody is, as we have seen, that the person awarded custody can in so far as he is empowered to act at all, act without the court's interference whereas a parent granted care and control of a ward will remain subject to the court's direction.

2. Under the Guardianship of Minors Act 1971, s.1.
3. In divorce proceedings the court has to be satisfied with the arrangements for the child before a decree absolute can be granted—Matrimonial Causes Act 1973, s.41.

b) Factors in Favour of Wardship

i) Preventing child's removal from the jurisdiction. Despite the above mentioned factors which weigh heavily in favour of seeking a custody order, wardship does have advantages which may on occasions prove useful to a parent. One advantage is the immediacy of the effects of wardship which is particularly useful where a parent is faced with a threat by the other parent (or indeed by someone else) to remove the child from the jurisdiction. It will be recalled[4] that one of the automatic consequences of warding a child is that he cannot be lawfully removed from the jurisdiction. This embargo applies as soon as the originating summons under the Law Reform (Miscellaneous Provisions) Act 1949 is filed[5]. In other words no specific court order need be obtained, though to take advantage of the administrative procedure[6] to prevent unauthorised removal a notice, signed by a registrar or district registrar (commonly referred to as the 'Home Office letter'), certifying that the child is a ward of court should be obtained at the same time as filing the application.

It is this immediate and automatic effect which distinguishes wardship from the custody jurisdictions. Under the Domestic Proceedings and Magistrates' Courts Act 1978[7] and the newly amended Guardianship of Minors Act 1971[8] the relevant court can direct that no person shall take the child out of England or Wales except with the Court's leave but this order can only be made on or after making a custody order[9]. Hence the power will be ineffective to prevent the child's removal unless custody proceedings are already on foot or where a custody order has already been made[10]. Under the Matrimonial Causes Act 1973, however, either party can

---

4. The automatic effect of wardship is discussed in Chap. 5.
5. As is made clear by the *Practice Direction* [1977] 3 All ER 121. In cases of extreme urgency an order preventing the child's removal can be obtained from a High Court judge before the originating summons has been issued on terms that such a summons will be issued as soon as possible. See *Re N (infants)* [1967] Ch 512, [1967] 1 All ER 161 discussed ante at p. 57.
6. For details of which see Chap. 12.
7. S.34.
8. S.13A as substituted by the Domestic Proceedings and Magistrates' Court Act 1978, s.39.
9. It will be noted that the power to make the prohibitory order is only exercisable upon a party's application. A custody order made under the 1973 Matrimonial Causes Act, however, normally includes a prohibitory order. See the Matrimonial Causes Rules 1977, r.94(2).
10. Even then a wardship application may be quicker and possibly more effective since the court can draw on the services of the Tipstaff—see below.

apply at any time after filing a petition in matrimonial proceedings[11] for an order preventing the removal of any child of the family under 18 out of England and Wales without leave of the Court[12]. Under the 1973 Act therefore an order restraining removal can be obtained before any other order. It has even been held that in extreme emergencies the court can make such an order prior to the filing of a petition on terms that the petition will be filed as soon as possible[13]. Like wardship once a prohibitory order has been made advantage can be taken of the administrative arrangements designed to prevent unlawful removal[14].

It will be seen, therefore, that the procedure under the 1973 Act does provide an alternative means of countering a threat to remove a child even when no other proceedings are pending. It will be noted, however, that a specific court order is required under the 1973 Act and though no doubt such an order can be obtained quickly in cases of urgency, nevertheless the applicant must prove his case. There is no such requirement in wardship and for this reason the required relief may be obtained more quickly. A more practical limitation of the 1973 Act is that the procedure can only be invoked where other matrimonial relief is sought. If the threat of removal is made as it were 'out of the blue', the immediate concern is likely to be for the child rather than for personal relief, and for this reason wardship may be thought more appropriate since it provides a remedy where no other relief is sought.

Quite apart from the above considerations it is to be noted that the wardship jurisdiction is wider than the 1973 Act. First the embargo against removing the ward lies against anyone whether or not they have notice of the wardship[15], whereas an order under the 1973 Act will only be enforceable against those who have notice of it[16]. Secondly, whereas wardship can be invoked in respect of any child who owes

11. For the meaning of 'filing a petition in matrimonial proceedings' see *Rayden on Divorce* (13th Edn., 1979) pp 1052, 1053.
12. Matrimonial Causes Rules 1977, r. 94(1).
13. *L v L* [1969] P. 25 at 27.
14. *Practice Direction* [1973] 3 All ER 194, [1973] 1. WLR 1014. See also the *Supreme Court Practice* 1979, Vol. 1 at p. 1343 for details of which see Chap. 7.
15. See Chaps. 5 and 6.
16. Following the normal rule in the case of injunctions see e.g. Borrie and Lowe: *The Law of Contempt* (1973), pp. 317, 318 it is to be noted that notice alone is sufficient i.e. there is no necessity to serve a copy of the order—see RSC Ord. 45, r.7(6).

allegiance to the Crown[17] petitions can only be made under the 1973 Act if one of the parties to the marriage is domiciled or habitually resident for one year in England and Wales immediately preceding the filing of the petition[18]. Moreover, the child must be a 'child of the family' for the purposes of the 1973 Act[19].

ii) Powers of enforcement. Another advantage of wardship is that the court has an effective means of enforcing its orders.

As we have seen[20], it can not only impose the sanctions available for contempt for disobedience of a court order but it can also direct the Tipstaff[1] to take the child into his custody and to deliver him to the person named in the order. This power is certainly wider than the enforcement powers of either the magistrates' court or the county court. It is arguably wider than the High Court's powers of enforcement under its custody jurisdiction, for while the latter can punish disobedience of a mandatory order by committal, sequestration or a fine, it is not clear whether it can direct the Tipstaff to take possession of the child[2]. Wardship is also more efficacious in cases where attempts are made to conceal the child, since the court can summarily order any person who may be in a position to give information as to the ward's whereabouts to attend the hearing[3]. In custody proceedings the High Court has no such powers although once committal proceedings have been brought, it can act on its own motion to order witnesses to attend[4].

---

17. It can be made in respect of any minor who is of British nationality or even an alien minor who is physically present or ordinarily resident in England and Wales. See Chap. 2.
18. Under s.5 of the Domicile and Matrimonial Proceedings Act 1973.
19. For the purposes of the 1973 Matrimonial Causes Act, s.52(1) to be a child of the family the child must either be legitimate or treated as a child of the family. For the meaning of 'treated' see e.g. *W(RJ) v W(SJ)* [1972] Fam 152, [1971] 3 All ER 303 and *A v A* [1974] Fam 6, [1974] 1 All ER 755.
20. Ante at p. 161.
 1. RSC Ord. 90, r.3A.
 2. See the comments of the Law Commission Working Paper No. 68 (1977) para. 6.23.
 3. Including a solicitor *Ramsbotham v Senior* (1869) LR 8 Eq 575 and a banker *Mustafa v Mustafa* (1967) Times, September 11 & 13. Discussed ante at p. 50.
 4. *Yianni v Yianni* [1966] 1 All ER 231, [1966] 1 WLR 120, *N v N* (1969) 113 Sol Jo 999.

It may be, therefore, that where a parent wishes to recover possession of the child he may be better advised to bring wardship proceedings especially if there is reason to believe that a court order will not be obeyed, or that the other parent or third party has gone into hiding with the child.

iii) Continued supervision by the court. The fact that a ward remains subject to the court's control may on occasion be seen as an advantage over custody. A parent granted care and control of the ward may feel secure in the knowledge that he has the powers of the court behind him and ease of access to the court in cases of difficulty. This may be useful where some future problem is likely to occur as, for example, where interference by the other spouse seems possible.

As a rider to this it might be pointed out that in divorce, nullity or judicial separation proceedings, the court has the power[5] to direct that proper proceedings be taken for making a child a ward, and such a course of action might be thought appropriate where there is a danger of problems such as mentioned above occurring in the future.

iv) One circumstance where wardship must be used

Not everyone entitled to bring matrimonial proceedings against the other spouse will be able to bring proceedings in respect of the child. This is because the child must be a 'child of the family' before a custody or access order can be made either under the Matrimonial Causes Act 1973 or the Domestic Proceedings and Magistrates' Courts Act 1978[6]. No such problem will occur where the child is the legitimate child of both parties to the marriage, but it may occur where one of the spouses is not the parent of the child in question. In such cases it will have to be shown that the child has been *treated*[7] as a child of the family. Failure to show this will be fatal to the application and the only remedy then open to the non-parent[8] even to apply for access is to ward the child.

---

5. By Matrimonial Causes Act 1973, s.42(1).
6. The definition is now the same under both Acts. See s.52 of the 1973 Act and s.88(1) of the 1978 Act.
7. For the meaning of 'treated' see *W(RJ) v W(SJ)* [1972] Fam 152, and *A v A* [1974] Fam. 6, [1974] 1 All ER 705.
8. The parent can apply under the Guardianship of Minors Act 1971.

v) *Conflict of jurisdictions*

a) **Divorce proceedings**

i) *Former position.* By way of introduction to the issue of clash of jurisdictions it is instructive to examine how the conflict between the divorce jurisdiction of the old Divorce Division and the wardship jurisdiction of the Chancery Division was resolved since in many ways the solution established a basis for solving the current conflicts.

Where a child had been warded during divorce proceedings, but before any custody order had been made by the Divorce Division, it was held at first by Wrangham J in *Andrews v Andrews and Sullivan and Sullivan*[9] that a divorce judge had no power to make an order since once wardship had been invoked that jurisdiction superseded the divorce jurisdiction over the child. This view seemed to be endorsed by the leading judgment of Upjohn J in *Re Andrews (infants)*, *Sullivan v Andrews* where he said[10]:

> 'Where an infant is made a ward of court before any order of a judge of the Divorce Division, it is, I think, universally accepted, probably as a matter of law, but certainly as a matter of comity between judges, that no order will be made by a judge of the Divorce Division, but it will be left with the judge dealing with the wardship proceedings, for the reason that, unlike judges of the Divorce Division, a judge of this division nearly always retains each infancy matter that comes before him under his own particular and personal control'.

Subsequently, however, the Court of Appeal in *Hall v Hall*[11] disapproved of Wrangham J's decision inasmuch as he intended to say that as a *matter of law* the Divorce Division had no jurisdiction once wardship was invoked. It was held that once the Divorce Division had begun to exercise its jurisdiction it was not ousted by the institution of wardship proceedings and it certainly could make an order, if as in the case before them, no order had been made in the Chancery Division. The court, however, unanimously approved Upjohn J's statement in *Re Andrews* that the[12]:

9. [1958] P 217, [1958] 2 All ER 305.
10. [1958] Ch 665 at 668.
11. [1963] P 378, [1963] 2 All ER 140.
12. [1958] 1 Ch 665 at 669.

'exercise by the judges of the Divorce Division of their statutory powers cannot in any way fetter the powers of the Chancery Division exercising the jurisdiction of the Crown as *parens patriae* over wards of court'.

On this basis it was not doubted that in the event of conflicting orders the Chancery Order would prevail, though Russell LJ preferred to say[13] that the divorce judges' jurisdiction to make orders in the first place was limited to the extent that they were not empowered to make an order which conflicted with a Chancery order.

Despite the overriding jurisdiction Upjohn J[14] commented, that where an infant had been made a ward after a judge of the Divorce Division had made a custody order, the Chancery Division would as a matter of comity normally refuse to consider an application on its merits. Instead the matter would be left to the divorce judge and to avoid any difficulty the child would normally be dewarded. However, Upjohn J said that the Chancery Division would undertake an investigation into the merits where the previous custody order was a consent order or where, as in an undefended divorce, there had been little or no investigation into the merits of the case. There were also exceptional cases where despite an earlier investigation of the merits of the case the Chancery Division would undertake a fresh review. This would occur where, for example, some wholly new question arose as in *Re Andrews* itself where the mother discovered that her ex husband, who had been awarded custody, planned to take the children out of the jurisdiction. Other examples where a Chancery judge might intervene were said to be where property matters were in issue or where the court's continuing supervision, for example, as to education, might be an advantage.

Upjohn J also mentioned that a change of circumstances might justify a review, though precisely what change the learned judge had in mind was not entirely clear. In the latter case of *Re A–H (infants)*[15] Buckley J refused to interfere with a prior decision of a divorce judge, holding that where the relief sought could just as easily be obtained in the Divorce Division the proper course was to go back to that Division. In

---

13. [1963] P 378 at 389.
14. In *Re Andrews (infants)*, *Sullivan v Andrews* ibid., at 668.
15. [1963] Ch 232, [1962] 3 All ER 853.

other words a mere change of circumstances would not be sufficient to justify the exercise of the wardship jurisdiction. On the other hand where the relief sought fell outside the Divorce Judge's powers then a wardship application would be appropriate.

It would seem, therefore, that while it was established that wardship was the overriding jurisdiction, in practice the Chancery Division would not exercise that jurisdiction without paying regard to any prior decision of the Divorce Division, and indeed in that event, the Chancery judge would not normally investigate the merits of the case unless there were special reasons for doing do. It is interesting to note that a similar approach has been adopted in connecton with the powers of a judge of the Family Division under wardship to review a custody order of the magistrates' court.

ii) *Present position.* There can no longer be a conflict of juris-dictions between the different Divisions of the High Court, since both divorce and wardship are now heard by the Family Division[16]. However, the fact that a child is a ward does have an impact on subsequent divorce proceedings inasmuch as the proceedings must be transferred to the High Court even if undefended[17]. In practical terms this may not make much difference to the parties since they will complete and file their divorce petition in the usual way, though the subsequent pronouncement of the decree and the arrangements concern-ing the children must be dealt with by a judge of the Family Division, and consequently the costs will be higher. No doubt in such cases regard will be paid to the terms of the existing wardship order though obviously a change of circumstances may cause a judge to look at the matter afresh.

It is quite possible that wardship proceedings may be brought in respect of a child who is the subject of a custody order in previous divorce proceedings. If the object of such an application is to have the original decision reviewed then it is unlikely to succeed. The normal course will be either to

16. By the Administration of Justice Act 1970, s.1 and Sch. I though as has already been noted (see p. 44) wardship cases can in rare circumstances still come before the Chancery Division.
17. Matrimonial Causes Rules 1977, r.97(2).

appeal or to seek a variation, for while it is theoretically possible in a truly exceptional case for a judge to deem it appropriate to exercise his wardship jurisdiction and hear the case afresh on its merits, it is difficult to conceive of an example where this might be necessary. It is true that unlike custody the court continues to exercise control over the ward, but it is to be remembered that where such supervision is thought necessary the court in divorce proceedings can direct that the child be made a ward[18].

On the other hand wardship proceedings may be brought in respect of a matter totally unconnected with the original custody order, as, for example, where the mother fears that her second husband is about to take the child out of the jurisdiction. In such cases there is no conflict with the previous order and the court will be free to exercise its wardship jurisdiction upon the usual considerations.

b) Custody proceedings under the Guardianship of Minors Acts 1971 and 1973 or the Domestic Proceedings and Magistrates' Courts Act 1978

i) Concurrent applications. It is quite possible that wardship proceedings may be instituted concurrently with custody proceedings either under the Guardianship of Minors Acts 1971 and 1973 under which applications may be brought in the High Court, county court or magistrates' court or the Domestic Proceedings and Magistrates' Courts Act 1978 under which applications are brought in the magistrates court. In the event of the two proceedings being brought in the Family Division[19] there would seem to be no problem inasmuch as the proceedings can be merged and heard together. Indeed wardship applications are often coupled with an application under the 1971 Act. Whether the judge in custody proceedings would grant an adjournment on the basis that one of the parties intended to issue wardship proceedings is a matter for conjecture, but presumably an adjournment would only be granted, if at all, where *a)* the relief which was genuinely sought was outside the power of the court to grant and *b)* such proceedings would be brought quickly.

18. Under s.42(1) of the Matrimonial Causes Act 1973.
19. I.e. a wardship application and a custody suit under the Guardianship of Minors Act 1971.

Where a child is the subject of pending wardship proceedings, then the magistrates' court and the county court
will normally adjourn any custody proceedings[20]. This is
also the practice where magistrates are faced with concurrent
divorce proceedings[1]. It is not that magistrates do not have
jurisdiction in such cases, but that as a matter of comity and
common sense it is appropriate that the lower court should
defer to the higher court. As Simon P said in *Kaye v Kaye*[2]:

> 'It is not a question of jurisdiction at all, it is a question
> of the exercise of discretion to proceed or adjourn'.

Though it might be possible to argue that the institution of
wardship proceedings ousts the magistrates' jurisdiction, it is
submitted that it does not do so. Indeed if the wardship
proceedings have become stagnated[3], then it might be
appropriate for the magistrates (or county court judge) to
make at least an interim order.

If during proceedings either before magistrates or a county
court judge one party seeks an adjournment on the basis that
he intends to bring wardship proceedings, it is submitted that
careful thought should be given to the request. In *Jones (EG) v
Jones (EF)*[4] the Court of Appeal warned justices to consider
very carefully before adjourning custody proceedings where
one of the parties proposes to bring a divorce suit, since the
result may be that the children's future may be left in
suspense for a considerable period. A similar argument could
be put forward in relation to wardship, since it may certainly
take some time for a hearing to be fixed especially if one party
is merely procrastinating. Accordingly, it is submitted that
before granting an adjournment justices should at least be
satisfied that the party seeking it genuinely intends[5] to bring
wardship proceedings, and it may be that they should be
satisfied that the relief sought is outside their powers to grant.
In any event it might be thought prudent to grant a short-
term adjournment rather than to adjourn sine die.

20. This was done, for example, in *Re K (minors) (children: care and control)*
[1977] Fam 179, [1977] 1 All ER 647.
1. See e.g. *Rayden on Divorce* (13th Edn., 1979), pp. 1277, 1278, 1279 and the
cases there cited.
2. [1965] P 100 at 105.
3. As happened e.g. in *Hall v Hall* [1963] P 378 at 382.
4. [1974] 3 All ER 702, [1974] 1 WLR 1471.
5. In *Re P (AJ) (an infant)* [1968] 1 WLR 1976 Cooke J suggested that the court
would not exercise its wardship jurisdiction if it was not satisfied that the
proceedings were genuine. See post p. 221–2.

ii) The use of wardship after a custody order has been made. The more usual conflict of jurisdiction problem arises where wardship proceedings are instituted during the subsistence of a custody order, that is, after the initial proceedings have been concluded. The problem so far encountered has been concerned with the High Court's inherent jurisdiction to interfere with an existing magistrates' court order though the conflict could just as easily involve a county court order[6], and the powers of intervention ought to be the same. Accordingly the following discussion must be taken to apply to county court orders as well.

It is well established that the existence of a custody order made by justices does not destroy the High Court's prerogative powers under its wardship jurisdiction. As Stamp J said in *Re H (GJ) (an infant)*[7]

> 'the prerogative powers of the Queen as parens patriae in relation to infants are not destroyed but at the most limited, as a result of the exercise of the powers in relation to infants in magistrates' courts'.

The problem then is not whether the High Court retains its power to act during the subsistence of a custody order but as to when the court will exercise that power.

c) Supplementing magistrates' orders

In general the court will be prepared to exercise its wardship jurisdiction during the subsistence of a magistrates' custody order where the relief prayed for falls outside the powers of magistrates to grant. In other words the High Court is prepared to *supplement* a magistrates' court order. In such cases there is of course no *conflict* of jurisdictions.

This was first established by *Re H (GJ) (an infant)*[8]. A mother had previously been granted custody with access being granted to the father. Subsequently the father tried to take the child out of the jurisdiction and the mother instituted wardship proceedings with a view to obtaining an

6. Made under the Guardianship of Minors Act 1971.
7. [1966] 1 All ER 952 at 953. In *Re P (infants)* [1967] 2 All ER 229 at 234. Stamp J commented: 'The exercise of a limited statutory jurisdiction over children does not, in the absence of express words in the statute, fetter the powers of the Chancery Division [now the Family Division] in exercising the jurisdiction of the Crown as parens patriae over wards of court.'
8. [1966] 1 All ER 952 [1966] 1 WLR 706.

injunction to restrain the father from taking the child out of the jurisdiction. As magistrates then had no such powers[9] the relief prayed for was granted, and in addition it was specifically directed that the child should reside with her mother at her address and continue with her present education. Stamp J commented that the magistrates' order:

> 'in no way precludes this court from making orders in the exercise of the prerogative powers of the Queen in relation to infants not inconsistent with orders made by the magistrates' court. What I am asked to do today is merely to make an order which will supplement the order which has already been made in relation to the infant by the magistrates' court and this I will do'.

In view of the Domestic Proceedings and Magistrates' Courts Act 1978 under which both magistrates[10] and county court judges[11] have the power to prohibit the child's removal, it is interesting to speculate whether *Re H (GJ) (infant)* will now be followed. It is submitted that it should be, because the wardship application in no way challenges the validity of the original custody order. In any event, in view of the speed and the greater enforcement powers, wardship may still be a more effective way of preventing the child's removal.

Wardship may also be used to supplement the enforcement powers of the magistrates. The only power available to magistrates to enforce both a custody and an access[12] order is by the Magistrates' Courts Act 1952, section 54(3) (as amended)[13], which provides that a person disobeying the order can be fined £50 for every day the default continues to a maximum of £1000 or committed to prison until the defaulter remedies his default up to a maximum of two months. There is no direct power to ensure that the child is physically returned[13a]. Under wardship the High Court has more effective means of enforcing its orders, in particular by drawing upon

---

9. See *T v T* [1968] 3 All ER 321, [1968] 1 WLR 1887. The court now has such powers. See below.
10. Under ss.34, 39.
11. Under s.13A the Guardianship of Minors Act 1971 as substituted by s.39 of the 1978 Act.
12. S.54(3) has been held applicable to breach of access orders see *Re K (a minor) (access order: breach)* [1977] 2 All ER 737, [1977] 1 WLR 533.
13. By s.78 of the Domestic Proceedings and Magistrates' Courts Act 1978.
13a. But see section 33 of the Domestic Proceedings and Magistrates' Courts Act 1978.

the services of the Tipstaff to secure compliance with any direction relating to a ward[14]. Illustrative of the use of these enforcement powers is *Re P (AJ) (an infant)*[15].

A mother had been granted custody by magistrates, but the father neither appealed nor complied with the order and the child continued to live with him. The mother took out habeas corpus proceedings to enforce the magistrates' order, but these proceedings were adjourned sine die when the father announced that he intended to commence wardship proceedings. The originating summons was issued on the same day. In the subsequent wardship proceedings, although Cooke J refused to interfere with the magistrates' decision, he ordered that the child should not be dewarded unless and until the father complied with the High Court order to return the child, and in the meantime the mother was given liberty to apply to the court if the father remained obdurate. It was held that such an order could be made as it supplemented the order of the justices and saved the mother the expense of having to revive the habeas corpus proceedings.

It would seem that following this decision, where an aggrieved party wishes to invoke the aid of the High Court to enforce a magistrates' court order, the better course might be to institute wardship proceedings rather than habeas corpus proceedings, since unlike the latter the former are not liable to be superseded. Indeed it has recently been said[16] that the writ of habeas corpus has no place in the Family Division especially in proceedings concerning children. The issue is better dealt with under wardship.

Another circumstance where a wardship order could usefully supplement a magistrates' court order would be where the applicant wishes to restrain the child from marrying or continuing an 'undesirable relationship'[17]. Wardship could also be invoked if it was sought to establish that the child had an interest in a property fund. In both these cases the remedies sought would be outside the powers of magistrates to grant. However, even if the relief sought is outside the powers of

14. RSC Order 90, r.3A. Furthermore in wardship the court can exact and enforce undertakings unlike magistrates who have no such powers. See Bagnall J in *Re D (minors) (wardship: jurisdiction)* [1973] Fam 179 at 194B.
15. [1968] 1 WLR 1976.
16. Per Bush J in *Re K (a minor)* [1978] LS Gaz. R 711 relying on a statement of Ormrod LJ in an unreported decision.
17. Discussed ante p. 201 et seq.

magistrates the High Court must be satisfied that the applicant is genuinely seeking the court's assistance. In *Re P (AJ)* (*an infant*), for example, counsel stated he might wish to raise the question whether the child had an interest in a trust fund prima facie belonging to the mother. There was no evidence that the issue was seriously raised and accordingly Cooke J rejected the submission[18].

d) Reviewing custody orders
A leading decision on the powers of the High Court to *review* a magistrates' decision is *Re D (minors)*[19]. In that case a man left his wife and returned to Scotland. She followed him to Scotland, but the attempted reconciliation failed and she returned to England with the two children. She brought custody proceedings in England which first came before a stipendiary and a lay magistrate. Custody was granted to the father, and because no stay of execution was granted, the children went to Scotland with their father. The mother wanted to appeal but was unable to do so because inexplicably legal aid was at first refused. When aid was granted the mother instead made the children wards of court.

Bagnall J made it clear[20] that, although he was prepared to exercise his wardship jurisdiction, it was only because of the wholly exceptional circumstances that existed in the case namely:

(1) As the children were in Scotland there were difficulties of enforcing any order and of giving and seeking any undertakings all of which were matters which the magistrates could not effectively deal with.

(2) The mother was for all practical purposes precluded from appealing by the refusal to grant legal aid.

(3) There was an irregularity in the procedure by which the order was made, in that there was a change in the court's composition which in itself would have justified an appeal by which the case would have been sent back to be decided before a freshly constituted court.

Having decided that the exercise of the wardship jurisdiction

18. [1968] 1 WLR at 1981.
19. [1973] Fam 179.
20. Ibid., at 193.

was justified, Bagnall J heard the case on its merits including events that happened after the original hearing and made a different order to that of the magistrates, namely, a joint custody[1] order with care and control to the mother and reasonable access to the father.

While *Re D* certainly illustrates the possible use of wardship in special circumstances, it cannot be taken as establishing anything more than that. Indeed Bagnall J specifically rejected the argument that he had an *unfettered* discretion under wardship to deal with questions of custody on its merits despite the existence of an order of a magistrates' court. Counsel had sought to argue that the previous decisions were wrongly decided and in any event were not binding upon him, but Bagnall J specifically endorsed what he considered to be[2]:

'a formidable body of authority which propounds as a principle that the court in wardship proceedings will not make a determination on the merits where there is a subsisting and effective order of the magistrates' court, unless either some relief is sought which cannot be obtained in that court, or there are some other wholly exceptional circumstances; and that neither changes in the relevant facts, nor mere complexity in the issues involved, constitute exceptional circumstances.'

Among the decisions endorsed were *Re K (KJS) (an infant)*[3] and *Re P (AJ) (an infant)*[4], both of which clearly established that parties who are dissatisfied with a magistrates' court order should either appeal or seek a variation if circumstances have changed and not use wardship. In *Re K (KJS)* justices had granted custody of a child to the mother with reasonable access to the father. Subsequently, as a result of dissatisfaction with the amount of access he was actually obtaining, the father instituted wardship proceedings with the sole view of obtaining a fresh access order. His application was rejected; the child was dewarded and the father was ordered to pay

1. To enable the joint custody order to be made Bagnall J (ibid., at 197) ordered that the proceedings be amended so that they were also entitled under the Guardianship of Minors Act 1971. Presumably to accommodate the joint custody order the wardship order would have to be discontinued.
2. [1973] Fam 179 at 192.
3. [1966] 3 All ER 154, [1966] 1 WLR 1241.
4. [1968] 1 WLR 1976.

costs. As Buckley J said[5]:

> 'This is a matter which could perfectly well have been raised in proceedings before the justices who are already seized of the matter. The magistrates had already made an order as to access and if the father considered that he was not getting reasonable access, the proper course was to go back to the magistrates and ask for a more specific order'.

In Re P (AJ)[6] where, it will be recalled, in the face of habeas corpus proceedings to enforce a magistrates' order, the father instituted wardship proceedings, it was sought to argue that there were nevertheless special circumstances justifying the exercise of the wardship jurisdiction. First it was contended that a material fact, namely, the mother's pregnancy, was not brought to the magistrates' notice, and secondly that there had been a change of circumstances since the decision, in that the father had now obtained a more permanent arrangement for looking after the child. Neither of these arguments impressed the court. As Cooke J said these were matters which either could have been taken care of on appeal or in an application to vary the order. Cooke J also rejected the contention that because the case was complex it was better dealt with by the High Court in wardship. He said that the complexities of the case were certainly not exceptional, and it was not enough to show that a decision was one which might involve difficult questions.

Following these cases therefore the normal course for parties to adopt in the face of a valid and subsisting custody order made by magistrates is either to appeal against the order or to seek a variation.

If an application is made to invoke wardship, it was established by *Re P (infants)*[7] that in deciding whether or not to exercise the jurisdiction the court is not obliged to hear all the evidence since to do so, as Stamp J said, would proliferate litigation. Instead the court should inquire into the facts as far as necessary to determine whether relief is genuinely sought which justices are not empowered to give, or whether there is some very special reason for invoking wardship[8].

---

5. [1966] 3 All ER 154 at 155.
6. [1968] 1 WLR at 1981–3.
7. [1967] 2 All ER 229.
8. Ibid., at pp. 236, 237.

These cases seem clearly to have established that it is only in exceptional circumstances that the court would under its wardship jurisdiction actually review a magistrates' custody order. Indeed the only reported[9] case where the court did intervene was in *Re D* where the facts were admittedly extreme in that through no fault of her own the mother had effectively lost her right of appeal, and that in any event there was an irregularity in the making of the order. There are, however, some indications that the court might be prepared to intervene in rather less extreme cases. In *Re P (infants)*, for example, Stamp J[10] stated that had not the parties settled, he would have been prepared to have exercised his wardship jurisdiction. In that case it appeared that there had already been some thirteen prior court hearings, and that for the wardship hearing, as the judge put it, 'the forces were deployed with horse, foot and artillery, and witnesses had been brought up from the country'. Stamp J also bore in mind that if he dismissed the case on the preliminary point of law he would be condemning the father to a further journey to the Court of Appeal followed perhaps by a further trial in the High Court. On the other hand the learned judge made it clear that he did not approve of the wardship application being made in the first place.

Evidence that the court might be prepared to review more often may be found in *Re D (a minor)*[11]. Dunn J accepted that the previous cases had established that the High Court did not as a matter of principle exercise its wardship jurisdiction so as to review facts determined by the justices save in exceptional circumstances, but felt that were the point to fall for his direct decision he would be unable to follow that principle. As he said[12]:

9. In one unreported decision known to the authors wardship was successful in the following circumstances: Magistrates had made an order granting custody to the mother but this was not carried out because the children refused to leave the father. The father applied for a variation on the grounds of the children's refusal to leave, but the same bench confirmed the original order and refused to grant a stay of execution even though the father announced his intention of appealing. Pending that appeal he instituted wardship proceedings and it was held that the court should hear the case inter alia because it had wider powers of enforcement and because it was a matter of urgency that the case should be heard. In these proceedings the father was granted care and control.

10. [1967] 2 All ER 229 at p. 237.

11. [1977] Fam 158.

12. Ibid., at 163.

'In wardship proceedings . . . the welfare. of the child is the first and paramount consideration. That is so as well in matters of procedure as in matters of substance: *In Re K (infants).*[13] I can conceive of many cases in which it is in the interests of the child that a decision of justices should be reviewed in wardship proceedings.

This is particularly so because there is no appeal from justices by way of rehearing[14] in custody proceedings'.

Dunn J then referred to the practice[15], for justices' custody decisions to be reviewed and very often altered in subsequent divorce proceedings, commenting:

'That is done in the interests of the child. I see no reason why, *if the interests of the child require it*, it should not equally be done in wardship proceedings, even though no divorce petition has been filed'[16]. (Emphasis added.)

These statements can only be regarded as obiter since the case was concerned with whether wardship could be invoked following the discharge of a care order under the 1969 Children and Young Persons Act from which there is no

---

13. [1965] AC 201, [1963] 3 All ER 191.
14. Query what Dunn J considered to be a rehearing see n.8 below.
15. This practice is itself a little uncertain. The case usually relied upon as authority for it is *Vigon v Vigon and Kuttner* [1929] P 157, where Bateson J held that a justices' custody decision did not oust the Divorce Court's overriding jurisdiction. Upon appeal ([1929] P 245) the case was sent back for re-consideration on its facts but the Court of Appeal preferred not to decide the jurisdiction issue. At the further hearing ((1929) 141 LT 610) Bateson J, while changing his mind upon the facts upholding in effect the original custody decision of the magistrates, affirmed his view on the jurisdiction. As Stamp J said in *Re P(infants)* [1967] 2 All ER at 235 *Vigon* is not at all a satisfactory authority. Despite this uncertainty it would seem that the court's jurisdiction over children in divorce proceedings is not ousted by a previous custody decision of magistrates though the court would no doubt normally prefer to follow it. See the comments of Bevan: *The Law Relating to Children* (1973 Butterworths), p. 291.
16. This analogy was rejected by Bagnall J in *Re D(minors)* [1973] Fam at 193 on the basis that in matrimonial suits there is always an actual or projected dissolution of marriage and a change of status of the persons principally involved. Under its matrimonial jurisdiction the High Court is concerned with other ancillary matters separate from, but often closely concerned with, the welfare of children of the family which may make it desirable for that court to deal at the same time with all those questions. This is an exceptional circumstance, absent where there are only wardship proceedings. To this one might add that as the judge is statutorily enjoined under s.41 of the Matrimonial Causes Act 1973 to be satisfied with the arrangements for the welfare of the children before granting the decree absolute he has both the authority and the duty to review the custody decision.

appeal. Nevertheless the standpoint of such an experienced judge deserves close attention[17].

Clearly whatever interpretation is to be placed on Dunn J's dictum potentially it represents a significant widening of the wardship jurisdiction and in any event casts doubt on the existing practice of the last decade. It is submitted that the court should be wary of extending wardship, for while there is obviously some merit in having a more flexible approach based on the child's interests, there are also strong arguments for maintaining the traditionally cautious position.

Dunn J thought that it may well be in the interests of the child that the justices' decision be reviewed in wardship particularly as there is no appeal by way of rehearing[18] from that decision. That may be so in exceptional cases but would it generally be for the benefit of the child to be the subject of two complete hearings with the possibility of an appeal after the wardship hearing? The general availability of wardship would surely introduce uncertainty by allowing multiplicity of proceedings and cast doubt on the efficacy and usefulness of the magistrates and so be to the detriment of children generally. As Bagnall J most convincingly said in *Re D (minors)*[19]:

'though it is true that the welfare of infants is paramount, even in relation to procedural matters, in my judgment it is open to the court to determine that in the absence of special circumstances that welfare is achieved by avoiding a multiplicity of proceedings in different courts. . . . In particular, I should regard it as lamentable to cast any doubt on the efficacy and usefulness of the jurisdiction of magistrates' courts

17. Especially because it can be said to be supported by the approach of the Court of Appeal in other areas of wardship. See particularly *Re O (a minor) (wardship: adopted child)* [1978] Fam 196, [1978] 2 All ER 27. Discussed post p. 253. See also *Re L (minors) (wardship: jurisdiction)* [1974] 1 All ER 913, [1974] 1 WLR 250 and *Re C (minors) (wardship: jurisdiction)* [1978] Fam 105, [1978] 2 All ER 230.

18. [1977] Fam at 163. Cf. Cooke J in *Re P(AJ) (an infant)* [1968] 1 WLR at p. 1982 who said an appeal from a custody hearing was by way of rehearing. One explanation of this apparent conflict is that, whereas Dunn J was thinking of a complete rehearing with both parties and witnesses being present, as will be the case in wardship, Cooke J was referring to the fact that the facts of a case are open to review on appeal and that the appellate court is not confined to considering points of law.

19. [1973] Fam at 193, 194.

throughout the country in securing the welfare of children'.

Further it may be doubted whether, apart from a complete re-hearing, where the facts would have to be re-established in the presence of the parties and witnesses, the advantage of which has already been questioned, wardship can offer a litigant any better remedy than an appeal. As Cooke J said in *Re P (AJ) (an infant)*[20] the appellate court has ample powers to make any order which the case may require even to the extent of hearing fresh evidence, and it can of course remit the matter to magistrates for further determination. It is submitted that it is only in exceptional circumstances that the scheme of appeal laid down by statute need be interfered with by way of wardship.

Nevertheless despite these arguments Dunn J's dictum is in line with recent Court of Appeal decisions emphasising that questions of jurisdiction should be resolved entirely on the basis of where the best interests of the child lies[1]. This is said to be justified by the fact that the welfare of the ward is the first and paramount concern. However, as we have argued elsewhere[2], even in wardship the child's welfare is only first and paramount if section 1 of the Guardianship of Minors Act 1971 applies, that is, inter alia[3], when the child's legal custody or upbringing is in issue. It is arguable that as the question of jurisdiction does not in itself *directly* concern the child's legal[4] custody or upbringing, section 1 does not apply. If that were so then the court would not be bound to treat the ward's welfare as its first and paramount concern and could instead take into account other considerations such as, in this case, the importance of allowing magistrates to exercise their discretion. Although this is admittedly a fine construction of section 1[5] nevertheless we favour this view

20. [1968] 1 WLR at 1982.
  1. Particularly that of *Re O (a minor)* per Ormrod LJ, [1978] 2 All ER at 30–1 and *Re H (a minor) (wardship: jurisdiction)*, [1978] Fam 65, [1978] 2 All ER 903.
  2. Ante in Chap. 6.
  3. S.1 also applies where the administration of the child's property is in issue.
  4. The word 'legal' was inserted as a result of the amendment by s.36(1) of the Domestic Proceedings and Magistrates' Courts Act 1978. For the meaning of 'legal custody' see pt. IV of the Children Act 1975 and the discussion thereon ante in Chap. 6.
  5. Though the House of Lords decision in *S v McC* [1972] A.C. 24 supports it. See also *Re X (a minor)* [1975] Fam 47 per Sir John Pennycuick at 62.

because it enables the court to take the more realistic approach of making a general policy decision without it being necessarily dictated by the individual child's interests. Given that Parliament has vested magistrates with a discretion to decide custody issues, one would have thought that policy dictated that intervention should be limited especially as there is a right of appeal.

This limited application of section 1 would be one way of justifying the existing practice of only reviewing magistrates' custody decisions in exceptional circumstances. However, even if this construction of section 1 is rejected and Dunn J's dictum upheld as the correct test, there must surely be some limits to the power to review. On the face of it Dunn J would seem prepared to see wardship being used as an alternative to appealing against a custody decision[6]. Whether the learned judge intended to go that far is a matter of debate but surely the court could not countenance wardship applications being made by litigants who are merely dissatisfied with the custody decision. It is submitted that there should be no intervention where an appeal, or variation application, would provide a satisfactory remedy and that the test of reviewing 'if the interests of the child require it' should be construed accordingly. On this basis the court would not in practice intervene in many more instances than previously. Even so such an approach might still mean that more wardship applications would be made if only to argue that it is in the interests of the child for the merits to be re-heard. Presumably, however, some kind of screening procedure would have to be adopted so as to avoid undue proliferation of litigation[7]. A possible solution would be to limit the initial inquiry into the case to the extent of determining whether it is in the interests of the child for there to be a full investigation[8].

6. Which would directly conflict with *Re K (KJS) (an infant)* [1966] 3 All ER 154, [1966] 1 WLR 1241 and *Re P (AJ) (an infant)* [1968] 1 WLR 1976. See also Ormrod J, *Re H (a minor)* [1978] Fam 65 at 74, [1978] 2 All ER at 907.
7. As feared by Stamp J in *Re P (infants)* [1967] 2 All ER 229 [1967] 1 WLR 818.
8. This approach would be similar to that adopted by the Court of Appeal in *Re O (a minor) (wardship: adopted child)* [1978] Fam 196, [1978] 2 All ER 27.

e) Challenging a decision of the immigration authorities

In *Re Mohamed Arif (an infant)* and *Re Nirbhai Singh (an infant)*[9], two fathers tried to challenge the decision of the immigration authorities to refuse entry to their (alleged) sons by making them wards of court. It will be recalled[10] that one of the issues raised by the applications was whether the court had jurisdiction at all, but in fact the Court of Appeal chose to decide the case on the second issue, namely, assuming that there was jurisdiction, should the court exercise it. The unanimous decision was that the court should not exercise its jurisdiction since there was no suggestion that the officers had acted unfairly. The view taken was that since Parliament had laid down a code for the control of immigrants and entrusted its administration to the immigration authorities the court should not normally use its wardship jurisdiction to clog the statutory machinery or to hold up the implementation of a properly made order for the removal of an infant from the jurisdiction. As Lord Denning MR said[11], provided the officers exercise their jurisdiction honestly and fairly the courts cannot and should not interfere. Intervention could only be justified in the most exceptional cases, namely, where some impropriety or abuse of the statutory power can be shown[12].

Following this decision therefore, even if there is jurisdiction, it will only be in the exceptional circumstances that the court would be prepared to exercise its jurisdiction. Presumably were the court to countenance such an application the allegation of impropriety will have to be stated with particularity and the issue tried as a preliminary point[13].

---

9. The two appeals were heard together—see [1968] 1 Ch 650.
10. See the discussion in Chap. 2.
11. Ibid., at 661.
12. It might be argued that if there is jurisdiction to act at all the court should do so on the basis of what is best for the child and that therefore the statement of Lord Denning MR that the court should act only in 'exceptional circumstances' is wrong. However, one would support his view on the basis that a decision of whether to allow entry into the country falls outside the scope of section 1 of the Guardianship of Minors Act 1971, so that the court is not bound to act in the child's best interests.
13. This is the line taken with regard to reviewing a local authority decision on the grounds of impropriety following the decision of Russell LJ in *Re T (AJJ) (an infant)* [1970] Ch 688 at 694. Discussed post p. 295.

III Non parental applications

A. INTRODUCTION

The fact that wardship can be invoked by any interested party distinguishes it from other child jurisdictions which in the main provide an avenue only for the natural or adoptive parents[14]. For most non parents wardship is the only means or the only practical means by which they can *apply* to the court even for the care and control of a child they have been looking after for some time. It is true that those parties looking after the child can in certain circumstances apply for adoption, but that is a more drastic order which the parties themselves may not desire or which the court may not grant. The parents may well refuse to agree to adoption. Indeed another use of wardship is by would-be adopters who wish to retain care and control of the child after their adoption application has failed[15]. Again it is true that once custody proceedings have been brought non parents can intervene and, in the court's discretion, may be awarded custody[16]. However, intervention of this kind depends upon proceedings being initiated by one of the parents, whereas in wardship non parents can themselves initiate the proceedings.

Short of adoption, therefore, if foster parents, relatives or friends wish to apply for care and control then, at least at the moment, wardship is the only means open to them where both parents of the child are alive. If, however, one or both parents are dead then it may be possible for a non parent to apply to become a guardian and when Part II of the Children Act 1975 comes into force non parents will be able to apply for a custodianship order. The intention of this section is to

14. The exception being where the non-parent can show that the child in question is a 'child of the family' either under the Matrimonial Causes Act 1973 or the Domestic Proceedings and Magistrates' Courts Act 1978.

15. See e.g. *Re E (an infant)* [1963] 3 All ER 874, [1964] 1 WLR 51. Discussed post p. 258.

16. See e.g. *Cahill v Cahill* (1975) 5 Fam Law 16 under the Matrimonial Causes Act 1973 and *Re RA (a minor)* (1974) 4 Fam Law 51 under the Guardianship of Minors Act 1971. N.B. when the custodianship provisions are brought into force then by virtue of the Children Act 1975 Sch. 3 para. 75 (1)(d) there will be no power under the 1971 Act to award custody to a non-parent, but the court will be able to treat the application as one for custodianship. The position is similar under the Domestic Proceedings and Magistrates' Courts Act 1978, s. 8(3).

examine the use of wardship in relation to these alternative actions and finally to consider the relationship of wardship to adoption. It might be said at the outset that if a third party does not seek care and control himself but merely wishes to bring to the court's notice a particular issue concerning the child as, for example, in *Re D (a minor)*[17] where application was made by an educational psychologist to prevent the sterilisation of a child, then wardship is and will remain the only means of doing so.

B. WARDSHIP AND GUARDIANSHIP

The purpose of this section is to consider the extent to which non parents can use guardianship as a means of gaining custody of a child and to consider how this device compares with wardship[18].

i) *Appointments by parents*

To become a guardian a non parent must either be appointed by a parent or by the court[19]. A parental appointment may be by deed or will and takes effect after the death of the appointing parent[20]. Any guardian so appointed acts jointly with the surviving parent unless that parent objects[1]. In the event of an objection or if the guardian considers that the surviving parent is unfit to have custody, the guardian may apply to the court[2], and the court may either refuse to make any order in which case the surviving parent remains the sole guardian or it can direct that the guardian act jointly with the parent or that he shall become the minor's sole guardian[3]. In the latter event the court may make such order regarding the custody of the minor and the right of access to the minor of the surviv-

---

17. *Re D (a minor) (wardship: sterilisation)* [1976] Fam 185, [1976] 1 All ER 326. Discussed ante p. 76.
18. For a further exposition on the law relating to guardianship see e.g. Bevan: *The Law Relating to Children* (1973 Butterworths) Ch 16. Bromley *Family Law* (5th Edn. 1976 Butterworths) 383–95. *Rayden on Divorce* (13th Edn. 1979), Ch. 25.
19. Authority does exist for saying that a child may appoint a guardian for himself. See *Re Brown's Will* (1881) 18 Ch D 61 at pp. 65, 67, 72.
20. Guardianship of Minors Act 1971, ss.4(1), (2).
1. S.4(3).
2. The court can be the High Court, county court or magistrates' court.
3. S.4(4).

ing parent as it thinks fit having regard to the minor's welfare[4].

Where guardians are appointed by both parents, then after the death of the surviving parent the appointees act jointly[5]. In any event where there is a dispute between joint guardians on any matter concerning the child's welfare then either of them may apply to the court for directions[6]. Provided one of the guardians is a parent the court has the power to make such order concerning custody and the right of access to the minor of that parent as it thinks fit having regard to the minor's welfare[7].

Relevance of Wardship

Provided a non parent has been appointed a guardian and he is to act jointly with the surviving parent, there is no need to have recourse to wardship to gain care and control of the minor, since in the event of a dispute the court has adequate powers to deal with custody under the 1971 Act. Presumably, however, if wardship proceedings are issued concurrently with guardianship proceedings under the 1971 Act they will take precedence. It is also possible that wardship proceedings may be brought after a court has made its decision under the 1971 Act. In such cases one would expect the court to exercise its discretion in the same way as it does in relation to custody decisions generally[8]. On this basis recourse may usefully be had to wardship to supplement the order but only in exceptional cases could it be used to have the whole decision reviewed[9].

If the appointed guardian becomes the sole guardian (i.e. in

---

4. S.10(1)(a). Under s.10(1)(b) as substituted by the Domestic Proceedings and Magistrates' Courts Act 1978 s.41(3) the court can order the surviving parent to pay to the guardian a sum of money towards the maintenance of the minor. Any order made under s.10(1) may be varied—s.10(2).
5. S.4(5).
6. S.7.
7. S.11(1)(a). Under s.11(1)(b) as substituted by the Domestic Proceedings and Magistrates' Court Act 1978, s.41(4) the court can order the surviving parent to pay to the guardian a sum of money towards the minor's maintenance. Any order made under s.11(1) can subsequently be varied—s.11(1)(c).
8. Discussed ante at p. 219 et seq.
9. Though, the powers of intervention might be wider if Dunn J's decision in *Re D (a minor) (justices' decision: review)* [1977] Fam 158, [1977] 3 All ER 481 is followed. Discussed ante at p. 225 et seq.

the event of there being no surviving parent)[10], then prima facie[11] he will have the right to the care and control of the minor. Unfortunately, there is no provision in the 1971 Act by which the guardian can enforce his right to care and control against a stranger. Instead recourse must be had either to habeas corpus proceedings or wardship proceedings. However, since it has been said that habeas corpus proceedings are inappropriate to proceedings in the Family Division especially those involving children[12], it will be preferable in cases of dispute to invoke wardship proceedings to gain care and control, although of course in exercising that jurisdiction the court is bound to consider what is best for the child.

ii) *Appointments by the court*

The court's power to appoint guardians principally derives from the Guardianship of Minors Act 1971[13] although the High Court retains its inherent jurisdiction to appoint guardians[14].

The court's statutory power (which in practice is normally invoked) arises in two circumstances. First, under section 3 of the 1971 Act the court can on the death of one parent appoint a guardian either where that parent did not appoint a guardian or where the appointed guardian refuses to act. Second, under section 5 where a minor has no parent, no guardian of the person and no other person having parental rights with respect to him[15], the court may on the application of any person, appoint the applicant to be the minor's guardian.

10. For this purpose the putative father is not a parent. See e.g. *Re N (minors) (Parental Rights)* [1974] Fam 40, [1974] 1 All ER 126, discussed post p. 237.
11. The testator can direct that some other person has care and control.
12. See *Re K (a minor)* [1978] LS Gaz. R 711.
13. Under the 1971 Act the High Court, County Court and Magistrates' Court have powers to appoint guardians.
14. See s.17(1) of the Guardianship of Minors Act 1971 and *Re McGrath (infants)* [1893] 1 Ch 143. The Court retains its inherent jurisdiction to appoint a guardian even though the child is not a ward of court in spite of the Law Reform (Miscellaneous Provisions) Act 1949, s.9, per Stamp J in *Re N (infants)* [1967] Ch 512, [1967] 1 All ER 161—see ante p. 57. Query the extent of the High Court's inherent powers other than to appoint or remove a guardian?
15. It does not matter for these purposes that the child is in care under a s.2 resolution, though once an appointment is made the resolution ceases to have effect—s.5(2).

Although section 5 states that *any* person can apply, it is presumably necessary to show a bona fide interest in the minor before an application can be entertained[16]. Section 3, on the other hand, does not expressly state who can apply but it would seem that applications by any interested person will be entertained[17].

To what extent will these two sections avail a non parent who wishes to gain custody of the child? With regard to section 3 it will be worthwhile to discuss this question in relation to the recent decision of *Re F (a minor)*[18]. The mother left her husband and together with her daughter went to live with the maternal grandmother. Subsequently she obtained a flat for herself and the daughter, but the grandmother maintained contact with the girl and looked after her during the periods when the mother had to stay in hospital to have treatment for cancer from which she eventually died. Almost immediately after the mother's death the father took the child from the grandmother's home to live with himself and the stepmother. The grandmother made the child a ward of court with a view to gaining care and control. She failed partly because of a deplorable delay of over one year before the case was finally heard. It has been argued[19], that wardship was not the only action available since use could have been made of the guardianship provisions under the 1971 Act. It was argued that since the mother had died without appointing a guardian the grandmother could have applied under section 3(2) to become a guardian and asked the court to grant her custody pursuant to sections 7 and 11. Since such an application could have been made to the magistrates' court, it may have been heard much quicker and that might have been to the grandmother's benefit.

At first sight this argument seems attractive, particularly as the action might not only be quicker but also cheaper.

16. By analogy with *Re Dunhill* (1967) 111 Sol Jo. 113. If the applicant has no such interest the application will be struck out as an abuse of process and the applicant will be liable not only to costs but also possibly to a contempt action. See Borrie and Lowe: *The Law of Contempt* (1973, Butterworths), p. 248 et seq.
17. See *Re H (an infant)* [1959] 3 All ER 746 (discussed post at p. 236) where the court heard an application under s.4(2) of the Guardianship of Infants Act 1925 (now replaced by s.3(2) of the 1971 Act) by the dead mother's elder sister, with whom the child was living.
18. *Re F (a minor) (wardship: appeal)* [1976] Fam 238; [1976] 1 All ER 417.
19. By Brenda Hoggett: 'The Orphaned Child, the Judge and the Court of Appeal' (1976) 120 Sol Jo 411.

Unfortunately it overlooks the earlier decision in *Re H* (*an infant*)[20], where Roxburgh J held that where an application is made under what is now section 3(2), the court had to consider 'not whether the appointment of a joint guardian may be some convenient step towards some result which cannot be otherwise obtained, but whether it is desirable to appoint a joint guardian'. He continued: 'If it is not desirable to appoint a joint guardian, it cannot be right to appoint a guardian for some collateral purpose'[1]. In *Re H* (*infant*) itself the guardianship application was made by the dead mother's elder sister with whom the mother (prior to her death) and the child had been living. The father opposed the application. It was common ground that the applicant and the father were not on speaking terms, but in granting the application the magistrates had in mind that their order would enable the applicant to proceed with an application for custody[2]. On appeal Roxburgh J reversed the decision, pointing out that it was hardly likely to be for the child's benefit to have joint guardians who were on the worst of terms. Indeed, the judge described the application as ingenious but novel and irregular and not to be encouraged. He specifically made the point that wardship was available to the sister.

Assuming *Re H* will be followed, and there seems no reason to doubt that it will, since it is a very sensible standpoint to say that the appointment of a joint guardian must be for the benefit of the child, the grandmother in *Re F* would have been unlikely to succeed. Accordingly, at least in cases where there is a dispute between the applicant and the surviving parent the only viable action to obtain care and control is via wardship proceedings.

In so far as section 5 is concerned an application to be appointed a guardian will be perfectly adequate provided there is no one to contest the appplication. Once the applicant is appointed a guardian he will be entitled to care and control though, as we have seen[3], the 1971 Act itself provides no means of enforcing that right against a stranger and instead the guardian will have to rely on wardship proceedings.

20. [1959] 3 All ER 746.
 1. Ibid., at 747.
 2. Which they mistakenly (in view of wardship) thought was the only possible action open to the applicant. See p. 748.
 3. Ante at p. 234.

If, however, two people are contesting the right to become a guardian then as *Re N* (*minors*)[4] shows, an application under section 5 is not ideal. In that case a mother remarried after the death of her first husband who was the father of the two children in question. Four years after her remarriage the mother also died. Shortly before her death the maternal grandmother moved in with the family and both she and the stepfather continued to look after the children after the mother's death. Following a disagreement both applied to be a guardian. The real issue in the case was whether the stepfather was a person who could be considered as having 'parental rights' within the meaning of section 5. On appeal it was held that he was not and that therefore there being no one having parental rights the court had jurisdiction to entertain the guardianship application. The court commented, however, that the wiser course of action in these circumstances would have been to invoke wardship, since the guardianship order would not have been of much use for as Ormrod J said, there are 'no rights under this Act to apply to enforce any of the powers or rights of a guardian'. As Professor Bevan has commented[5] if either the stepfather or the grandmother had been appointed a guardian there would have been nothing to prevent the other from making the children wards of court and asking for care and control. Unless, therefore, the apparent defect in being unable to enforce the rights of a guardian against strangers under the 1971 Act is remedied, contesting parties should use wardship to gain care and control.

C. WARDSHIP AND CUSTODIANSHIP[6]

When Part II of the Children Act 1975 is implemented non parents will be able to apply for what is confusingly to be known as a 'custodianship order'. Since such orders will vest in the applicants almost full custodial rights over children, there can be little doubt that the jurisdiction will significantly overlap with wardship. Indeed it may be said at

4. [1974] Fam 40, [1974] 1 All ER 126.
5. [1974] CLJ 74, 76. Query whether the High Court can under its inherent jurisdiction grant care and control to the guardian. Cf. Bevan *The Law Relating to Children*, p. 403.
6. See also Freeman: 'Custodianship and Wardship' (1977) 7 Fam Law 116.

the outset that the Houghton Committee[7], on whose recommendations Part II is based, apparently overlooked the existence of wardship. This oversight seems clear from their opening comment[8]:

> 'There are many children who are not being brought up by their natural parents but are in the long term care of foster parents or relatives. These people normally have no status in relation to the child, *and the law provides no means by which they can obtain it without cutting his links with his natural family by adoption*'. (Emphasis added)

It is not sought to deny the need for a new action to be available to non parents in the lower courts since wardship being a High Court action is both expensive and time consuming, but consideration ought, at the very least, to have been given to the existing role of wardship which does provide a means by which non parents can acquire a legally protected interest over children. It might be questioned, for instance, whether in view of wardship it is necessary to allow a custodianship application to be made in the High Court. Even apart from this arguably unnecessary duplication of jurisdiction there remains the important question as to how the two jurisdictions will generally inter-relate.

Before considering the likely impact of custodianship upon wardship it will be worthwhile especially since the concept of custodianship is new to examine the provisions of Part II.

1) *The effects of a custodianship order*[9]

The effect of a custodianship order will be to vest 'legal custody' of the child in the applicant or applicants[10] and to suspend the right of any other person to legal custody of the child[11]. By virtue of section 86 'legal custody':

> 'means, as respects a child, so much of the parental rights and duties as relate to the *person* of the child (including

---

7. Report of the Departmental Committee on the Adoption of Children (1972) Cmnd. 5107, Ch. 16.
8. Para. 116.
9. See also Freeman: *The Children Act 1975* (1976, Sweet and Maxwell), 'Custodianship—New Concept New Problems' (1976) 6 Fam Law 57 and Bevan and Parry: *The Children Act 1975* (1978, Butterworths).
10. Children Act 1975, s.37(1).
11. S.44(1). If the applicant is the spouse of the child's parent the effect of the order is to vest joint legal custody in the spouses—s.44(2).

the place and manner in which his time is spent); but a person shall not by virtue of having legal custody of a child be entitled to effect or arrange for his emigration from the United Kingdom unless he is a parent or guardian of the child'. (Emphasis added.)

Since the parental rights and duties are expressed to relate to the *person* of the child it is clear that custodians will have no responsibilities relating to the child's *property*[12]. Other limitations of custodians' powers are that they will have no right to agree or withhold agreement to adoption[12a], nor, it is thought[13], by analogy with custody orders, will they have the power unilaterally to change the child's surname at least by taking any formal steps[14]. On the other hand, the custodian's consent to the child's marriage will be required[15] and custodians will be empowered to apply to rescind a section 2 resolution[16] and obtain an affiliation order[17]. The custodian will of course have de facto care and control of the child and will be able to discipline the child, to agree to medical matters, to decide where the child goes to school and to give permission for a passport application[18].

Like custody a custodianship order will not destroy the legal ties between the child and his natural parents. The court can[19], upon an application by the mother, father or grandparent of the child make such provision as it thinks fit requiring *access* to the child to be given to the applicant, and upon the *custodian's* application the child's mother or father

12. See also Lord Wells-Pestell HL Vol. 356 Cols. 92–3: 'whereas a guardian replaces a parent and has responsibilities relating to both the person and property of the child, a custodian takes over only his responsibility relating to the person of the child, usually in a parent's lifetime and has no responsibilities relating to the child's property'.

12a. This is a necessary inference since the custodian could otherwise agree to adoption by himself. See also *Evans v Parry* op. cit. para. 233.

13. See Freeman (1976) 6 Fam Law 57.

14. It may be possible to change it informally at least provided the real parents' identity is not concealed. See *R(BM) v R(DN)* (*child: surname*) [1978] 1 All ER 33, sub nom. *Rice v Rice* [1977] 1 WLR 1256 and *D v B* (*otherwise D*) (*child: surname*) [1979] 1 All ER 92, [1978] 3 WLR 573. Cf. *L v F* (1978) Times, August 1.

15. Sch. 3 para 7.

16. Sch. 3 para. 5.

17. S.45 and Sch. 3 para. 14—a power which guardians do not have.

18. These last three powers were mentioned by Dr Owen, in his reply to Mrs J. Knight—(Parl. Debs., Commons 1974-5 Vol. 1. S.C. col. 503).

19. By s.34(1)(*a*) as substituted by s.64 of the Domestic Proceedings and Magistrates' Courts Act 1978.

(or both) can be required to pay such periodical payments towards the maintenance of the child as may be specified in the order[20]. Moreover upon the application by the custodian, mother, father or guardian, or by any local authority the court may revoke the custodianship order[1]. Upon revocation legal custody reverts to the person or persons who had legal custody before the custodianship order was made. However, before revoking the custodianship order the court is bound to ascertain who would have legal custody if upon revocation no other order was made[2]. If no-one would have legal custody then the court must commit the child to the care of a local authority[3]. Even if there is someone who would have legal custody the court can in exceptional cases commit the child to the care of a local authority or make a supervision order[4].

ii) *Who can apply?*

There are detailed provisions governing who can apply for a custodianship order. So far as direct[5] applications are concerned the basic scheme is as follows:

> (1) A relative[6] or step-parent[7] may apply if:
>> (a) they have the consent of a person having legal custody of the child *and*

20. S.34(1)(*b*) as substituted by the 1978 Act. By s.34(1)(*c*) the court can order a lump sum to be paid. In either case in deciding how much should be paid, regard should be had to the considerations set out by s.34A (added by s.65 of the 1978 Act). N.B. the limitation under s.34(3) against ordering a putative father to pay maintenance. It has been commented (see Bromley: *Family Law* (5th Edn.) at p. 406) that there are likely to be few cases where a maintenance order would be appropriate. Sed quaere?
 1. S.35. To prevent repeated applications for revocation s.35(2) provides that once an application for revocation has been refused further applications by the same person will not be heard without the court's leave.
 2. S.36(1).
 3. S.36(2).
 4. S.36(3).
 5. There are occasions when an application may be *treated* as a custodianship application—see below.
 6. Defined to include grandparents, siblings, uncles and aunts and the putative father—Children Act 1975, s.107 and Adoption Act 1958, s.57. Query whether the putative father can apply in view of s.33(4) which excludes applications by the mother and father. See n.14 below.
 7. In practice the only step-parents who will be entitled to apply are those who marry the single or surviving parent since s.33(5) prohibits step-parents from applying if in proceedings for divorce or nullity the child was named in an order under s.41(a) of the Matrimonial Causes Act 1973.

    (b) the child has had his home with the applicant for three months preceding the making of the application[8].

(2) Any other person (excluding the mother and father)[9] may apply if:

    (a) they have the consent of a person having legal custody of the child *and*

    (b) the child has had his home with the applicant for periods which amount to twelve months, three of which must precede the making of the application[10].

(3) Any person (excluding the mother and father) not having the consent of a person having legal custody may apply where the child has had his home with the applicant for periods which amount to three years, three months of which, must precede the making of the application[11].

(4) If there are no persons having legal custody (i.e. where the natural parents are dead and no guardians have been appointed)[12] or the applicant himself has legal custody or if the person with legal custody cannot be found then the time limits under (1) and (2) are the *sole* requirements[13].

It is to be noted that by reason of section 33(4) a mother and father cannot apply for a custodianship order. Whether this provision prevents the putative father from applying is uncertain, since the term 'father' is undefined[14]. It is also to be noted that only the consent of one person having legal custody of the child is required though in making the order

---

8. S.33(3)(*a*).
9. S.33(4) Query the meaning of 'father'. See s.95, p. n.14 below post.
10. S.33(3)(*b*). This provision applies to foster parents, neighbours or friends who have been looking after the child.
11. S.33(3)(*c*).
12. Cf. *Re N* (*minors*) (*parental rights*) [1974] Fam 40, [1974] 1 All ER 126.
13. S.33(6).
14. In adoption proceedings the term 'parent' has received a restricted interpretation to exclude the putative father one of the reasons being that the putative father was included in the definition of 'relative'. See *Re M* [1955] 2 QB 479, [1955] 2 All ER 911. The same definition section (s.57 of the Adoption Act 1958) applies to custodianship applications by virtue of the Children Act 1975, s.107 so that it would seem that could apply. However, since he can apply for custody it would seem pointless to allow him to apply for custodianship.

the wishes of both the mother and the father will be relevant[15].

In the case of all applications the child must have had his 'home' with the applicant for the requisite period and in any event for three months preceding the application, but where the child has had his home with the applicants for periods amounting to three years, then once a custodianship application is pending no-one[16], including the local authority[17], if the child is in care, may remove the child from the applicants' custody against the applicants' will without leave of the court. The penalty for unlawful removal will be a fine of up to £400 and/or imprisonment of no more than three months[18].

Apart from the direct applications noted above there are occasions when the court can *treat* an application as being for a custodianship order, namely:

(1) where the application is for an adoption order, but the court feels that the child's interests would be better safeguarded by treating the application as one for custodianship[19].

(2) where upon an application being made by the mother or father under section 9 of the Guardianship of Minors Act 1971, the court is of the opinion that legal custody should be given to a person other than the mother or father[20].

(3) where upon application being made by a party to the marriage for an order under section 2, 6 or 7 of the Domestic Proceedings Act 1978, the court is of the opinion that legal custody should be given to a person who is not a party to the marriage or a parent of the child[1].

15. By regulations issued pursuant to s.40(3) the local authority's report should include the wishes of the mother and father (including presumably the putative father).
16. S.41(1).
17. S.41(2).
18. S.41(3).
19. S.37(1), (2) but it is conditional upon all the requirements for adoption being satisfied.
20. S.37(3). When this provision comes into force it will no longer be possible to award custody to third parties under the 1971 Act. Note the additional power under s.37(4A) (as substituted by s.69 of the Domestic Proceedings and Magistrates' Courts Act 1978) to make a conditional order.
1. S.8(3) of the Domestic Proceedings and Magistrates' Courts Act 1978.

In each of these cases the applicant will be treated as if he were qualified[2] to apply for a custodianship order though it will still be necessary to notify the local authority and to obtain a report[3].

iii) *Procedure and powers*

Applications may be made to the High Court, county court or a magistrates' court[4]. Within seven days of making the application written notice must be given to the local authority in whose area the child resides[5], an officer of which must then make a report for the court[6]. In addition, the court may independently request the local authority or probation officer to make a report on any specified matter[7].

In deciding whether to grant the custodianship order the court is enjoined to regard the child's interest as the first and paramount consideration[8]. The court can in exceptional circumstances instead of granting or refusing to grant a custodianship order, commit the child to the care of a local authority or make a supervision order[9].

iv) *Custodianship and wardship compared*

For the practical purpose of bringing up a child the custodianship order is the equivalent of a custody order save only that the custodian has no responsibilities in connection with the child's property. So far as wardship is concerned, the major difference would seem to be that custody of the child remains in the court whereas a custodianship order vests legal custody in the custodian[10]. This means that a custodian in so

---

2. I.e. there will be no need to prove that the child has had his 'home' with the applicant. This will be more significant for applications under the Guardianship of Minors Act 1971 and the Domestic Proceedings and Magistrates' Courts Act 1978 since to qualify for an adoption order the applicant must have actual custody of the child for at least three months prior to the hearing.
3. Pursuant to s.40 of the Children Act 1975.
4. Ss.33(1), 107, 100.
5. Ss.40(1), 107.
6. S.40(2). For the matters which must be referred to in the report see s.40(3).
7. S.39.
8. S.33(9) states that s.1 of the Guardianship of Minors Act 1971 is applicable.
9. S.34(5) as substituted by s.64 of the Domestic Proceedings and Magistrates' Courts Act 1978.
10. See also Freeman: 'Custodianship and Wardship' (1977) 7 Fam Law 116.

far as he is empowered to act at all may act without the court's intervention, whereas applicants granted care and control of a ward remain subject to the court's control and at least in respect of important matters relating to the ward must seek court directions before acting. This continued control can be seen as an advantage in that it gives the applicants greater security in having the powers of the court behind them and ease of access to the court in cases of difficulty. On the other hand some will see the court's continued control as a disadvantage being a restriction on their powers. In many cases, however, the court's continued control of its ward will remain dormant and is only likely to be activated in cases of difficulty.

Apart from the court's continued control the other important difference between the two orders is that whereas it is specifically provided[11] that a local authority may make contributions towards the cost of the accommodation and maintenance of the child, (except where the custodian is the spouse of a parent of the child), there would appear to be no power to contribute where the child is subject to a wardship order[12].

a) Applicants' choice of jurisdictions

Custodianship will clearly overlap with wardship, so that non parents qualified to apply for custodianship may be faced with a choice of either seeking a custodianship order or a wardship order, it being clear that the latter will *always* be available as an alternative to the former.

As far as High Court applications are concerned it is always possible to couple a wardship application with one under the Children Act 1975, Part II. Indeed as we have suggested elsewhere[13], it may become common practice for those qualified to apply for both to couple their applications in much the same way as wardship applications are presently coupled with applications under the Guardianship of Minors Act 1971. Such a coupling would enable the court, if it thought it appropriate, to discharge the wardship order and grant the applicants custodianship instead.

---

11. By 34(6)—as substituted by s.64 of the Domestic Proceedings and Magistrates' Courts Act 1978.
12. Save the more limited power conferred by s.1(1) of the Children and Young Persons Act 1963.
13. In Chap. 4.

The possibility of coupling applications does not preclude an applicant choosing one jurisdiction rather than another even in the High Court, but there seems little advantage in doing so. The problem of choice, however, is normally more realistically between applying for custodianship in the lower courts and applying for wardship. What factors will be relevant in making that choice?

Applications to the lower courts will generally have the advantage of speed[14], cost and convenience, and so applicants wishing to seek a legally protected right to bring up a child would normally be better advised to apply in the lower courts for custodianship. It is doubtful, however, whether custodianship orders will provide a panacea for all non parental applications and there may still be occasions where faced with a choice it will be worth while invoking wardship. It is worth remembering that a wardship order can be more comprehensive and that its orders are more readily enforceable. If, for example, there is any question of the child being removed from the jurisdiction, then it would seem advisable to invoke wardship[15]. If some future problem is likely to occur, as for example, interference by the parents, then the continued control of the court and ease of access in the event of a dispute might well be an advantage. The court has greater freedom under its wardship jurisdiction. For example, whereas in custodianship access orders are conditional on the main order being made[16], in wardship it is possible for the court to refuse to grant the applicants care and control but to grant them access[17]. Factors such as these might influence applicants with a choice to invoke wardship, but for the most

14. Though in an emergency wardship might well be quicker.
15. Admittedly the court has the power under s.43A (as substituted by s.70 of the Domestic Proceedings and Magistrates' Courts Act 1978) to direct that no person shall take the child out of the jurisdiction but this power only arises after a custodianship or interim order has been made. In wardship, as we have seen (ante p. 72) the embargo is immediate.
16. S.34(1) (as substituted by s.64 of the Domestic Proceedings and Magistrates' Courts Act 1978) states that an 'authorised court may, *on making a custodianship order or while a custodianship order is in force*' [emphasis added] make, inter alia, provisions for access.
17. This point could arise where the court decides to commit the child to the care of a local authority. The court has the power to do this by virtue of s.34(5) of the Children Act 1975 (as substituted by s.64 of the 1978 Act) which provides that the relevant provisions of the Guardianship Act apply. The result of such an order would be to leave access to be decided at the discretion of a local authority. Cf. wardship where the court itself can make directions. See *Re Y (a minor) (child in care: access)* [1976] Fam 125 discussed in Chaps. 5 and 11.

part custodianship will be more than adequate and there seems little reason to doubt that wardship applications by non parents will be significantly reduced.

b) Continued use of wardship where custodianship is unavailable

Although the availability of custodianship will undoubtedly reduce the need to invoke wardship, there will be circumstances where because of the restrictions placed upon custodianship applications, the non parent will have to invoke wardship. Furthermore it seems likely that there will be occasions where it will be preferable to invoke wardship if only to avoid doubts raised by the wording of the statute. In other words wardship will undoubtedly remain useful in filling gaps in Part II and in avoiding technicalities based on statutory interpretation.

It is an essential requirement for custodianship that the child must have had his 'home' with the applicants in any event for a period of three months prior to the application. Any applicant not fulfilling this requirement but who wishes to apply for a legally protected interest over the child will have to invoke wardship where there is no such requirement. The grandmother, for example, in *Re F (a minor)*[18] would not have been able to bring custodianship proceedings since the father had taken the child away from the grandmother to live with him and the stepmother.

Apart from overcoming non-qualification wardship will also relieve applicants from the inevitable doubts raised by the definition of 'home'. Section 87(3) provides that:

> 'unless the context otherwise requires, references to the person with whom a child has his home refer to the person, who disregarding absence of the child at a hospital or boarding school and any other temporary absence, has actual custody[19] of of the child'.

No doubt problems will be raised by the phrase 'any other temporary absence'. Would it for example include possession by the parents?[20] Suppose the applicant allowed the parent to look after the child for what was intended to be a short

18. [1976] Fam 238. Discussed ante p. 235.
19. 'Actual custody' is defined by s.87(1) in terms of actual possession 'whether or not that possession is shared with one or more other persons'.
20. Cf. the position in adoption under previous definitions. See *Re CSC (an infant)* [1960] 1 All ER 711 [1960] 1 WLR 304.

holiday but the parent then refused to return the child. With whom does the child have his 'home'? What would be the position where the parent snatched the child from the applicant? Problems such as these would be but factors in deciding where a ward's best interests lie, but in custodianship they could prove fatal to the application.

Even if the applicant can show that he has provided a 'home' for the child he must still fulfill the time provisions and again wardship is likely to prove useful in avoiding problems created by these time requirements. Indeed anyone wishing to avoid these time provisions will have to use wardship. A problem which seems likely to occur is where a person having the legal custody of the child initially consents to the custodianship application but subsequently, perhaps at the last moment, withdraws his consent. There is no provision in Part II to dispense with that consent, and quite apart from the emotional upheaval, the consequence of withdrawal will be that relatives or step-parents instead of having to provide a home for the child for three *months* will have to do so for three *years*, and in the case of other applicants the period will be extended from one to three years. The most effective response to withdrawal of consent will be to make the child a ward of court where, of course, there is no requirement of having to provide a home for the child, though obviously the longer the applicants have looked after the child the stronger are their chances of being granted care and control. Wardship provides the most immediate means by which non parents can then apply for a legally protected right to look after the child.

c) Use of wardship by those opposed to the custodianship application

Hitherto consideration has been given to the use of wardship from the applicants' point of view, but the jurisdiction might also prove useful to those who are opposed to the custodianship application.

Of course a most effective way for parents to oppose the custodianship application is not to consent to the application in the first place. However, the mere withholding of consent may not be sufficient. This is because the Act requires[1] the consent of only one person having legal custody of the child.

1. S.33(3).

One parent could thus be in the position of opposing the custodianship application while the other parent agrees to it. Indeed it is possible for a custodianship order to be made even though both parents oppose it, since if the child is in the care of a local authority under a section 2 resolution, the local authority can consent to the application[2].

In each of these cases the non consenting parent may find it advantageous to invoke wardship rather than opposing the custodianship application. One advantage of wardship is that the non consenting parent will clearly be a party to these proceedings whereas although the mother's and father's views must be included in the local authority's or probation officer's report[3], in the absence of regulations it is not clear precisely what status such persons will have in the custodianship proceedings themselves. The issue may well be important in deciding whether such persons would be entitled to legal aid. In any event, arguably at least, by bringing wardship proceedings they will be better able to bring their views to the court's notice.

Parents may not be the only persons wishing to oppose custodianship since it is quite conceivable that non parents may wish to do so. For these purposes the putative father will normally rank as a non parent. Again by invoking wardship such non parents will be clearly parties to these proceedings, whereas it is not certain whether such people would be able to oppose the custodianship application at all.

d) Resolving the conflict of jurisdiction

The institution of wardship proceedings as a means of countering the custodianship application is likely to create a conflict of jurisdiction, but it is submitted that the net effect would be to stifle the custodianship application. If the child is made a ward before the custodianship application has been made, then following the position in adoption proceedings no application could be made without the court's leave[4]. Where the applications are concurrent then the usual position

2. This is because the passing of a s.2 resolution vests in the local authority the parental rights and duties which by law the mother and father have in relation to a legitimate child. See the Children Act 1948, ss.2(1) and (11) as substituted by the Children Act 1975, s.57. These rights are wider than those under ss.86 and 85(1) of the Children Act 1975.
3. See s.40(3)(a).
4. *F v S (adoption: ward)* [1973] Fam 203, [1973] 1 All ER 722. Discussed post p. 252.

would be to adjourn the custodianship application in favour of the wardship proceedings[5]. Indeed it might even be possible to seek an adjournment on precisely these grounds[6].

Apart from the conflict just noted there will be other problems relating to the interaction of the two jurisdictions. There seems no doubt that by analogy with custody orders[7], a child who is the subject of a custodianship order can subsequently be made a ward. Wardship could thus be used to supplement a previous court order[8]. To what extent wardship can be used as a means of having the custodianship decision *reviewed* raises the same problems as those discussed in relation to custody orders. The orthodox position is that the court would only be prepared to review a decision in exceptional circumstances, but, as we have seen, doubts about this narrow position have been raised by Dunn J in *Re D (a minor)*,[9] and it may be that the court will intervene whenever it is in the interests of the child to do so.

Apart from these points wardship may be used in connection with problems unconnected with the original order. For example, custodians could make the child a ward to prevent him or her continuing an undesirable association. Third parties could make the child a ward, for example, to prevent a sterilisation being carried out even with the custodian's consent.

D. WARDSHIP AND ACCESS FOR GRANDPARENTS

Although it seems clear that in principle grandparents can invoke wardship simply to gain access to a grandchild,

---

5. At least in the lower courts by analogy with the practice in the face of a divorce petition. Discussed ante p. 214.
6. But see the warning given in *Jones (E.G.) v Jones (E.F.)* [1974] 3 All ER 702, [1974] 1 WLR 1471. Discussed ante p. 218.
7. Discussed ante. Cf. adoption in particular *Re O (a minor) (wardship: adopted child)* [1978] 2 All ER 27, [1977] 3 WLR 732 discussed below.
8. I.e. it can be used in the same way as it can in relation to custody orders. See ante at p. 219. It is to be noted that in line with other amendments the Domestic Proceedings and Magistrates' Courts Act 1978, s.70 inserting s.43A of the Children Act 1975 has given the court the power upon making or during the currency of a custodianship order, to provide that the child should not be removed out of England and Wales. However, as discussed in other contexts, despite this power, wardship might still be used in preference to applying for the order because it might be quicker and more efficacious. See ante at p. 210.
9. [1977] Fam 158, [1977] 3 All ER 481. Discussed ante p. 225 cf. the position in adoption and in particular *Re O* ibid, discussed post p. 253.

concern had been expressed that apart from the undeniably expensive procedure there was no other way such persons could *initiate* proceedings. Agitation for reform[10] eventually culminated in access provisions for grandparents being added to the Domestic Proceedings and Magistrates' Courts Act 1978. However, as will be seen, complex though the provisions are, they are by no means comprehensive and in some cases wardship will remain the only remedy.

The scheme of the 1978 Act is as follows. First, application can be made to a magistrates' court upon the making or during the currency of a custody order under section 8(2) of the 1978 Act [11]. Secondly, application can be made to a magistrates' court, county court or High Court upon the making or during the currency of a custody order under section 9(1) of the Guardianship of Minors Act 1971[12]. Thirdly, application may also be made under the 1971 Act where one or both of the minor's parents are dead though such applications are restricted to the parent of the deceased parent[13]. Fourthly, when in force, application can be made under the Children Act 1975 (again to the three family courts) upon the making or during the currency of a custodianship order[14]. In each of these cases it is made clear[15] that applications can be made notwithstanding that the child is illegitimate.

It will be seen that with the exception of the death of one of the parents, access applications are restricted to cases where a custody order is being made or is currently in force. In other words if the parents themselves are not disputing custody, whether or not they are living together, grandparents cannot apply for access under the 1978 Act provisions. No doubt the problem of lack of access to the grandchild commonly[16] arises following the split up of the family due to marital breakdown or the death of one of the parents, but access may also be denied where there is friction between a united family

10. The prime mover for legislative reform was Robert Rhodes James MP. For an account of his concern and of the earlier Parliamentary history see 'Access rights for grandparents' (1978) 1 *Adoption and Fostering* 37.
11. S.14(1).
12. S.14A(1) of the Guardianship of Minors Act 1971 as inserted by s.40 of the 1978 Act.
13. S.14A(2) of the Guardianship of Minors Act 1971.
14. S.34(1)(*a*) of the Children Act 1975 as substituted by s.64 of the 1978 Act.
15. S.14(6) of the 1978 Act; s.14A(9) of the Guardianship of Minors Act 1971 and s.34(4) of the Children Act 1975.
16. See James: 'Access rights for grandparents' 1978 1 *Adoption and Fostering* 37.

and the grandparents. In such cases, wardship will provide the only course of action to the grandparent[17].

Even where the family has split up the grandparent will not always be able to apply for access under the 1978 Act provisions. In the case of death of one of the parents application can only be made by the parent of the deceased parent[18] and not by the parent of the surviving parent. In such cases resort must be had to wardship. No provision is made in the 1978 Act where custody orders are made under the Matrimonial Causes Act 1973[19]. This may mean that wardship apart no application can be made for access once a custody order has been granted following a divorce, nullity or judicial separation or where application is made for maintenance under section 27[20].

To what extent a wardship application would be successful in cases where the 1978 Act is inapplicable is a moot point. This is particularly so where the dispute is between the grandparent and a united family. If the child is living in an otherwise happy and stable environment it would seem questionable whether it is in the *child's* interest (whose interest and not the grandparents' the court is bound to consider) that possible friction may be caused between the applicants and the parents by granting access. Of course if there is evidence that the child has previously had close contact with the grandparents that might be sufficient to justify the exercise of the jurisdiction. In any event it is suggested that as with parental applications to counter the effect of an adoption order[1], grandparents should have to establish a strong prima facie case before the court will embark upon investigating the merits.

17. But see below.
18. See s.14(A)(2) of the Guardianship of Minors Act 1971.
19. S.42 which is not amended.
20. But query whether grandparents could intervene during the currency of the proceedings and seek access. They can certainly do so for custody. See *Cahill v Cahill* (1975) 5 Fam Law 16. Although s.42 specifically states that the court can make such order as it thinks fit for the *custody* and education of the child of the family, no one doubts the court's power to make access orders to the parties of the marriage. But in any event since the application would be made in the High Court the wisest course of action is to institute wardship proceedings.
1. Following *Re O (a minor) (wardship: adopted child)* [1978] Fam 196, [1978] 2 All ER 27, [1978] 3 WLR 732, i.e. the court should be satisfied that it is in the child's interests for the merits to be investigated.

E. WARDSHIP AND ADOPTION

i) *Introduction*

An adoption order completely and irrevocably extinguishes the legal ties between the natural parents and the child and creates in its place an entirely new legal relationship between the adoptive parents and the child[2]. In wardship, on the other hand, the order is never final since it can be varied; custody of the ward remains vested in the court, and the person granted care and control remains subject to the court's directions and even if care and control is granted to a third party there is no question of severing the natural parents' legal ties with their child. It is clear therefore that wardship cannot be regarded as an alternative means of obtaining a court order equivalent to that in adoption. However, despite their obviously differing roles problems do occur as to how the two jurisdictions interrelate and, as will be seen shortly, wardship may still be usefully resorted to by both sides in adoption proceedings.

ii) *The interaction of wardship with adoption*

a) **Adopting a ward**

There is no doubt that a ward can be adopted, but it was established by the Court of Appeal in *F v S*[3] that before adoption proceedings can be commenced[4] leave of the court is required. In giving leave it was held that the judge only had to consider whether the adoption application is one which is likely to succeed and not whether adoption is in the best interests of the child, since according to Orr LJ that was the very issue that would have to be decided in the adoption application.

With respect to his Lordship this reasoning is surely questionable. It is understandable that the court would not wish to dictate a decision to another court, but in this instance there does appear to be a special case for saying the court must be satisfied that an application for adoption is in the ward's best interests. The court is bound to regard its ward's interests as

---

2. See the Children Act 1975, ss.8(1), 8(3) and Sch. 1 Part II.
3. [1973] Fam 203, [1973] 1 All ER 722.
4. Cf. New Zealand where it was held by Cooke J in *Re N (an infant)* [1975] 1 NZLR 454 that the court's consent before *or after* the adoption application is filed is sufficient. *F v S* refers to the commencement of proceedings. Query whether leave is necessary to *place* a ward for adoption.

the first and paramount consideration[5], and it is surely a dereliction of its duty to allow another court in adoption proceedings to decide where the ward's interests lie. The dereliction is even greater because if section 3 of the Children Act 1975 is applicable[6], the need to safeguard and promote child's welfare is expressed to be the first consideration whereas in wardship the ward's interests are the first and *paramount* consideration. It would also seem to be in the ward's interests for the court to prevent wherever possible multiplicity of proceedings. For these reasons it is submitted that the court in deciding whether to grant leave to start adoption proceedings should consider whether it is in the ward's best interests that an adoption application should be made.

If leave is granted it would be in the ward's interest that the adoption proceedings should be heard as quickly as possible and it would therefore seem appropriate that the court should direct that the adoption hearing be expedited[7].

b) Warding an adopted child

An adoption order does not oust the wardship jurisdiction, so that an adopted child can be subsequently warded. In this respect the adoptive parents stand in no different position to any natural parent. In the recent decision of *Re O (a minor)*[8] it has been held that a *natural* parent can invoke wardship even though the child had previously been adopted.

Obviously the court will not readily allow a natural parent to counter the effect of an adoption order by invoking wardship but there was a difference of opinion as to how the restraint should be operated. At first instance, Latey J whilst

5. By s.1 of the Guardianship of Minors Act 1971.
6. There is some debate as to whether s.3 is applicable at all when considering whether to dispense with parental agreement under s.12. Cf. the views of the Court of Appeal in e.g. *Re P (an infant) (adoption: parental consent)* [1977] Fam 25, [1977] 1 All ER 182 with those of Lord Simon (admittedly obiter) in *Re D (an infant) (parent's consent)* [1977] 1 All ER 145, at 163.
7. It might also be thought appropriate that the subsequent adoption proceedings should be heard in the High Court. Such a recommendation was made in *Re F (an infant)* [1970] 1 All ER 344 at 347 per Harman LJ. Query whether the High Court judge giving leave should hear the adoption case himself.
8. *Re O (a minor) (wardship: adopted child)* [1978] Fam 196, [1978] 1 All ER 145. (First Instance); [1978] 2 All ER 27, [1977] 3 WLR 725, CA.

affirming that the adoption order does not oust the wardship jurisdiction, held[9] it to be incumbent upon a natural parent to show a strong prima facie case justifying the court taking the 'exceptional' course of embarking on a full inquiry into the merits of the case. On appeal, however, it was held[10] that the more appropriate test was whether it was in the best interests of the child that the wardship should be carried through to its conclusion after a full investigation, or whether on the facts as they were put before the court on both sides and by the guardian ad litem, the court could see that it was not in the interests of the ward to pursue the wardship proceedings further. The Court of Appeal agreed that in a normal adoption case where the natural parents had parted with the child, and the adoptive parents had assumed the parental role, a natural parent would have to make a strong prima facie case to justify the matter proceeding further. The case before them, however, was not normal, since it had been shown that the intention of the adoptive father and the mother was that the mother should remain caring for the boy after the adoption. Accordingly, it was held, reversing Latey J's decision, that there was an overwhelming case for hearing the mother's allegations in full. The wardship was therefore continued with the direction that the matter be heard as soon as possible by another judge of the Family Division.

The Court of Appeal's decision to continue the wardship can hardly be faulted since the extraordinary facts clearly warranted the exercise of the jurisdiction. The divergence of opinion as to the test of where the jurisdiction should be exercised does, however, warrant further comment, since it raises the general problem of what limits ought to be put on wardship. In holding that the jurisdiction should only be exercised in exceptional circumstances Latey J's approach was traditionally cautious[11]. The Court of Appeal's decision on the other hand is in line with more recent decisions holding that the test of whether to exercise its jurisdiction to intervene in cases where orders have been made by another

---

9. [1978] Fam at 203, [1978] 1 All ER at 151.
10. Per Ormrod LJ [1978] Fam at 208, [1978] 2 All ER at 30, 31 and per Stamp LJ at 32 p. 210–11 respectively.
11. In line with such decisions as *Re D (minors) (wardship: jurisdiction)* [1973] Fam 179 [1973] 2 All ER 993 (see ante at p. 222); *Re M (an infant)* [1961] Ch 328 [1961] 1 All ER 788, and *Re T(AJJ) (an infant)* [1970] Ch 688 [1970] 2 All ER 865 (see post Chap. 11).

court or body should be based squarely on the interests of the ward[12].

At the heart of the dispute lies the application of section 1 of the Guardianship of Minors Act 1971[13]. If it applies then the 'best interests of the child' test is indisputably correct, since the ward's welfare is of paramount concern. If it does not, then the more limited test may be justifiable because the individual child's interests are not necessarily paramount.

Latey J thought that in this instance section 1 did not apply. As he said[14]:

'It is true that on the face of it the language of section 1 of the Guardianship of Minors Act 1971 has total application to cases concerning the upbringing of children. But it must surely be read in conjunction with the Adoption Acts and the Children Acts enacted both before and since. Otherwise the purpose of the Adoption Acts is or might be nullified. The purpose of the Adoption Acts is to divest the natural parents of all parental rights and to vest all those rights in the adoptive parent or parents, the rationale being that it is in the interest of all concerned, but especially in the interest of the children that this should be so. That being so, Parliament cannot have intended in the same, or a different, breath to have said 'Nevertheless, though a parent has been divested of all rights, he or she can have a change of mind after the adoption order and come to the courts and argue that the child would not be better off with him'.

The learned judge concluded:

'Parliament has said that the adoption order is final with the sole reservation that wardship is available for use in the exceptional case where there are compelling reasons for its use. In simple terms, people must recognise that an adoption order, once made, is in the vast majority of cases the end of the matter and it is in the interests of children that it should be. But there will be some rare cases where the courts should still be able to intervene.'

---

12. Ormrod LJ ibid., at p. 30 expressly followed *Re L (minors) (wardship: jurisdiction)* [1974] 1 All ER 913, [1974] 1 WLR 250 recently reaffirmed in *Re C (minors) (wardship: jurisdiction)* [1978] Fam 105, [1978] 2 All ER 230.
13. For a more general discussion on the application s.1 see ante Chap. 6.
14. [1978] 1 All ER at 149. [1978] Fam at 200.

Although the Court of Appeal may be taken to have rejected Latey J's more limited application of section 1, the court did not expressly address itself to this question. Ormrod LJ[15] merely indicated a personal preference for the 'best interests of the child' test because he considered that 'exceptional circumstances' was unsatisfactory because 'exceptional' is one of those words which means what people want it to mean and it does not help very much. It is submitted therefore that the interpretation of section 1 has yet to be finally settled. As it happens, as Ormrod LJ recognised[16], the application of either test would have justified the exercise of jurisdiction in *Re O* since the facts were clearly exceptional, and in the circumstances it was certainly in the ward's interests to have the merits investigated. We would have preferred, however, to have seen the Court of Appeal deal with the application of section 1 more fully. Either view on section 1 is tenable, but since we are concerned about the general extension of the powers to review decisions of other courts or bodies, we favour the view that the section should be limited in its application. In this respect it seems to us that Latey J's views are to be preferred.

Whatever test is applied it seems clear that in the normal case of an adoption order severing both the natural parent's legal and de facto ties with the child, it will be extremely difficult for that parent to challenge that order via wardship. As Ormrod LJ said in such cases the natural parent would have to make out an 'extremely strong prima facie case to justify the matter proceeding further'. However, there would seem to be a material distinction between a parent trying to use wardship merely to counter the effect of an adoption order and in no way purporting to impugn the success of that order, and an application where it can be shown that the adoption order has for some reason been unsuccessful. In the latter situation it would surely not be difficult to establish an acceptable prima facie case for investigating the merits of the case. Indeed, Latey J gave examples of where intervention might be justified, namely, where the child is being ill-treated by the adoptive parent, or whether the adoptive parent has been sentenced to a long term of imprisonment or has

15. [1978] Fam at 208, [1978] 2 All ER at 30.
16. Ibid., at 209 and 31.

become incapacitated by chronic illness or has died. It is submitted that prima facie evidence of any of the above facts would be sufficient to justify a full investigation into the merits of the case.

On the other hand where a parent wishes to invoke wardship merely to recover care and control without impugning the success of the adoption order, it will normally be exceptionally difficult, short of showing some impropriety, to establish an acceptable prima facie case for intervention[17]. However, as *Re O* shows, there will always be extraordinary cases where intervention may be justified.

c) Another limitation on wardship

Another limitation on the use of wardship in relation to adoption proceedings is illustrated by *Re M (an infant)*[18]. A married couple resident and domiciled in Denmark wanted to adopt an illegitimate girl resident and domiciled in England. They made the child a ward of court seeking an order to allow them to take her to Denmark so they could have the requisite care and possession there. At the end of the period they intended to return to England with the child and apply for a provisional adoption order. It was held that the court had no jurisdiction, even in wardship, to allow the child to be removed since section 52 of the Adoption Act 1958[19] was held to impose an absolute prohibition upon the removal of an infant who is a British subject from the British Isles by a person who was not a parent, guardian or relative with a view to adoption, except under the authority of a provisional adoption order. It was held that the phrase 'with a view to adoption' covered cases not only where the child's removal is for the immediate purpose of adoption but also where, although immediate adoption is not intended, the removal constitutes one step in a larger process the ultimate purpose of which is adoption.

17. The normal course of action for a parent dissatisfied with the making of an adoption order is to appeal. In a case known to the authors a wardship application by a putative father who alleged that he had not been given notice of the adoption proceedings was dismissed, it being held that the appropriate course was to seek leave to appeal out of time.
18. *Re M (an infant) (adoption: child's removal from jurisdiction)* [1973] Fam 66, [1973] 1 All ER 852.
19. S.52 has since been slightly amended by the Children Act 1975. Sch. 4 Part I but the amendment does not affect the decision in *Re M*.

d) Use of wardship in relation to adoption proceedings
Having considered the general relationship between the
two jurisdictions it remains to consider how wardship
might usefully be invoked in relation to adoption proceedings.

It may be said at the outset that potential adoption applicants may choose to invoke wardship instead of applying for
adoption because it is a less drastic order and one which does
not entail obtaining or dispensing with parental agreement.
In *Re R(M) (an infant)*[20], for example, a child was placed with
foster parents with a view to adoption. Subsequently it
became clear that the mother was not going to agree to the
adoption and the foster parents realizing that they were
unlikely to succeed in having the mother's consent dispensed
with, instituted wardship proceedings instead. The case was
then treated like any other wardship case the first and
paramount consideration being that of the child's welfare. In
the event the court held the wardship should be continued
with care and control being given to the mother.

*i) Use of wardship as a means of enabling applicants to retain care and
control.* Wardship may be used by applicants as a means of
retaining care and control of a child in respect of whom their
adoption application has failed. This tactic was successful in
Re E (an infant)[1]. There the adoption application failed
because it was held that the mother had not been unreasonable
in withholding her consent to adoption. Leave to appeal was
refused and the applicants eventually instituted wardship
proceedings by which they sought care and control. The
mother argued first that as the adoption application had failed
she had an absolute right to have the child given up and
secondly that it was abusing the court's process to use wardship for the purpose of obtaining practically the same result
as in the failed adoption proceedings. Wilberforce J rejected
the mother's arguments on the basis that the court was
charged with considering the child's welfare as the first and

20. [1966] 3 All ER 58, [1966] 1 WLR 1527. See also *Re PGP (an infant)* (1977) 4
    Adoption and Fostering 51, CA.
 1. [1963] 3 All ER 874, [1964] 1 WLR 51. Cf. *Re S (a minor)* (1978) 122 Sol. Jo.
    759, where the wardship application was dismissed without hearing the
    merits. In that case the adoption applicants had made no attempt to
    appeal.

paramount consideration in wardship proceedings. On the facts it was held that it was for the child's best interests that care and control be granted to the applicants.

It remains to be seen to what extent *Re E* will avail applicants who have failed in their adoption application. It is true that if the adoption application has been refused wardship is the only means currently available[2] by which the applicants can preserve their legal position over the child[3]. Indeed in one case, *Re C (MA) (an infant)*[4] a High Court judge in an adoption case directed that a child be made a ward of court for the sole purpose of preserving the status quo pending the hearing of the appeal so as to relieve the adoption applicants from having to hand over the child forthwith[5]. Wardship may also be advantageous to the applicants by prolonging the time in which they have care and possession of the child and so strengthening their case for retaining care and control.

Wardship may also be thought to fill a gap in the court's powers in adoption proceedings. As the law now stands, under section 17 of the Children Act 1975, in the event of a refusal to make an adoption order, the court can in exceptional circumstances either make a supervision order[6] or commit the child into the care of a local authority[7]. It cannot, however, grant custody or care and control to the applicants unless it does so by means of an interim order which can be by way of a probationary period of up to two years[8]. An interim order cannot, however, be made unless, for example,

2. Cf. the position when the custodianship provisions come into force. See below.
3. Upon the refusal to grant the adoption order the applicant must return the child to the adoption society or local authority which arranged for the adoption within 7 days of the refusal, but by s.35 (5A) (inserted by s.31 of the Children Act 1975) the court can extend this period up to a maximum of six weeks. In the case of other placements there is no statutory obligation to return the child, but the applicants have no *right* to retain possession of the child and are also therefore liable to habeas corpus proceedings. See e.g. Wilberforce J in *Re E* ibid., at 876 H. However, habeas corpus proceedings are superseded by wardship proceedings see e.g. *Re P (AJ) (an infant)* [1968] 1 WLR 1976.
4. [1966] 1 All ER 838, [1966] 1 WLR 646.
5. See Willmer LJ ibid., at 849. There is no power to authorise the applicants to retain the child pending the appeal. See *Re CSC (an infant)* [1960] 1 All ER 711, [1960] 1 WLR 304.
6. S.17(1)(*a*).
7. S.17(1)(*b*).
8. Under the Adoption Act 1958, s.8.

parental agreement has been obtained or dispensed with[9]. In any event an interim order has the disadvantage of creating uncertainty. In wardship proceedings the court can, of course, grant care and control to the applicants with none of the attendant uncertainty of an interim order and without the statutory constraints such as those referred to above in adoption proceedings.

It is clear therefore that once the adoption application has failed wardship can offer a remedy that the applicants could not otherwise obtain. The question remains, however, whether wardship can be resorted to by *any* applicant who has failed in the adoption application. In *Re E* itself Wilberforce J gave no indication as to the possible limits of wardship. Nevertheless it is worth noting that in *Re E* the adoption application failed because it was held that the mother had not been unreasonable in withholding her consent. There would certainly seem to be a material difference between an adoption application having failed because parental agreement was not dispensed with and an application being refused because it was held not to be for the child's welfare to be adopted by the applicants or to be adopted at all. In the former case it can certainly be envisaged that it might nevertheless be for the child's welfare that the applicants retain care and control[10]. In the latter case it would seem to be an unwarranted duplication of proceedings to allow wardship proceedings to be instituted and would surely be contrary to the child's best interests. It is submitted that where the adoption proceedings fail because the court does not think that it is for the child's interest to be adopted by the applicants, the proper

9. S.8(2). It was unclear whether the consent had to be in respect of the adoption or interim order, but s.19(1) of the Children Act 1975 (which is not yet in force) now makes it clear that the issue of agreement relates to the adoption. Hence under this provision it is clear for example that in *Re E* ibid. the court would have had no power to grant an interim order since the mother's agreement to the adoption had not been dispensed with. In any event the court should formally record that agreement has been dispensed with, where that is the case. *S v Huddersfield Borough Council* [1975] Fam 113, [1974] 3 All ER 296.

10. This may be particularly so where the court has refused to dispense with parental agreement under one of the more technical grounds under s.12 as for example 'abandoning' the child. But following *Re S (a minor)* (1978) 122 Sol Jo 759 applicants should normally, unless there are 'special or convincing reasons', appeal against the refusal to grant adoption. Cf. n.11.

action is for the applicant to appeal, and that recourse to wardship would be rarely justified[11].

The justification for resorting to wardship will be further reduced when Section 37 of the Children Act 1975 comes into force. Under this provision the court will be able to direct that an adoption application be treated as if it were an application for custodianship. This will enable the courts to grant the less drastic order of custodianship and so preserve some of the links between the child and his natural parents. It should mean therefore that the need to dismiss the adoption application altogether will be reduced. However section 37 is conditional upon all the requirements *for adoption*[12] being satisfied including the need for parental agreement or its dispensation[13]. Cases may still arise therefore where despite the failure of the adoption application (i.e. because of parental refusal to agree) it could nevertheless be thought that it is for the child's welfare that the applicants retain care and control.

ii) Using wardship to oppose adoption applications. There is no doubt that wardship can be used as a means of opposing an adoption application. One possible way of doing this is to make the child a ward of court *before* any adoption proceedings have been commenced. Since leave of the court would then be required to start adoption proceedings[14] the onus of going to court would be thrown on the applicant. According to Lane J in *Re B (a minor)*[15] this may well be an

11. I.e. the wardship application should be dismissed in limine. Following the reasoning of the Court of Appeal in *Re O (a minor)* [1978] 2 All ER 27, [1977] 3 WLR 732 the decision whether or not to investigate the merits would depend upon the ward's welfare though a strong prima facie case would still have to be made out. We therefore dissent from the decision in *Re S (a minor)* (1978) 122 Sol Jo 759.

12. Hence it would seem that the parent cannot agree to the application, on the basis of it being treated as a custodianship application. One way round this construction may be to couple the adoption application with a custodianship application under s.33. It should be noted, however, that the time limits under s.33 must be complied with.

13. I.e. in *Re E (an infant)* [1963] 3 All ER 874, [1964] 1 WLR 51 for instance the court would still have been unable to treat the application as one for custodianship.

14. Following *F v S (adoption: ward)* [1973] Fam 203, [1973] 1 All ER 722. Discussed ante at p. 252.

15. [1975] Fam 36 at 44.

advantage to local authorities in respect of a child in their care. Although at first sight this advice appears to have some validity, on closer analysis it is open to doubt. Normally when a child is boarded out to foster parents the local authority has the right to serve written notice to demand the child's return even if he has been placed with a view to adoption[16]. However, once an application has been made to adopt the child, notice for the child's return can only be served by leave of the court. Furthermore[17] the same restriction applies as soon as written notice of the intention to apply for adoption is served, even if the child was not originally placed with a view to adoption. In other words once adoption proceedings have been set in motion, the local authority will be unable to demand the return of even a 'section 2 child' without the court's leave[18]. This latter position, it is true, would be avoided had the child been warded, since the onus would have fallen on the foster parents to seek the court's leave to adopt. However, it is hardly practicable for the local authority to ward every child in their care merely to thwart the possibility of an adoption application. The more realistic course of action is to oppose the adoption application by seeking the court's leave to serve notice for the child's return.

Wardship may be invoked during the pendency of adoption proceedings in which case they will take precedence over the latter thereby preventing or at least delaying the adoption, depending upon the outcome of the wardship application. This is strikingly illustrated by *Re F (an infant)*[19]. There a husband strangled his wife and as a result was detained in a secure hospital, and their daughter went to live with the mother's distant cousin and her husband. Subsequently they commenced adoption proceedings, but shortly after, the mother and sister in law of the father warded the child and sought her care and control. It was clear that the father was the moving spirit behind the application, and that the intention of the wardship proceedings was to stifle the

16. Adoption Act 1958, s.35.
17. Adoption Act 1958, ss. 36(1), (2).
18. See the comments of Buckley LJ in *S v Huddersfield Borough Council* [1975] Fam 113 at 121–2.
19. [1970] 1 All ER 344, [1970] 1 WLR 192 CA. See also *Re A (an infant)* [1955] 2 All ER 202.

adoption application[20]. In the event the application was unsuccessful and care and control was granted to the appellants, Harman LJ expressing the hope[1] that the adoption proceedings might be ordered to be removed to the High Court where the Official Solicitor would be available. The fact that the two proceedings were not heard together is questionable since it is certainly the practice to do so where the putative father opposes the adoption by seeking custody[2] and this should be the proper practice in wardship[3]. Where the two proceedings are merged in the High Court, the child is usually named as a party to the wardship proceedings and the Official Solicitor is normally appointed to act as guardian ad litem in both. Prudent practitioners should, however, seek to ensure that the Official Solicitor's report is submitted in the wardship and not the adoption proceedings since its contents will then normally be disclosed to the parties[4].

Clearly there was little merit in the father's case, but *Re F* does illustrate the effectiveness of bringing wardship proceedings, for whatever procedure is followed, it will initially stop the adoption application from proceeding and if successful, defeat it entirely. It remains to consider who might benefit from using wardship in this way.

Parents of a legitimate child would normally be better advised to oppose the adoption application simply by withholding their agreement. Before the adoption can proceed the parental agreement must be dispensed with by the court, and in considering this the court is bound by the terms of section 12 of the Children Act 1975 which sets out the grounds for dispensation. It is an unresolved issue[5] as to whether in considering section 12, the court is also bound by section 3, which states that in seeking any decision relating to the

20. See Sachs LJ at 347 h.
1. Ibid., at 347 d.
2. See *Re O (an infant)* [1965] Ch 23 and *Re Adoption Application No. 41, 61 (No. 2)* [1964] Ch 48, [1963] 2 All ER 1082.
3. This was done, for example, in *Re R (MJ) (a minor) (publication of transcript)* [1975] Fam 89.
4. Unless it would be harmful to the ward to do so. See *Official Solicitor v K* [1975] AC 201, [1963] 2 All ER 191. Discussed in Chaps. 4 and 8. In adoption the guardian ad litem's report is confidential and can only be disclosed to the parties with the court's leave.
5. Cf. e.g. *Re P (an infant) (adoption: parental consent)* [1977] Fam 25, [1977] 1 All ER 182, CA with *Re D (an infant) (parent's consent)* [1977] 1 All ER 145, 163, per Lord Simon.

adoption, *first* consideration should be given to the need to promote the welfare of the child throughout his childhood. In any event, however, it is clear that unlike wardship, the child's welfare is not the first *and paramount* consideration[6], and it may be therefore the reduced weight of the child's interests will work to the advantage of the parents.

Wardship may however be useful in those residue of cases where its wider powers can be brought to bear with advantage. It might be useful, for example, where the child is in care especially where the parents initially want to have access with a view to recovering the care of the child subsequently.

Although the agreement of a putative father to the adoption is not required[7], he can effectively oppose the adoption without the need to resort to wardship. He can, for instance, apply for custody or possibly just access under the Guardianship of Minors 1971[8], which application will be heard before any final decision is made in the adoption[9]. If he does not seek an order but still opposes the adoption, he can be heard in the adoption proceedings. For the most part these alternative actions are perfectly adequate though as with parents of a legitimate child there may be circumstances where the wider powers of wardship could be used to advantage.

Non parents have no locus standi in the adoption proceedings and therefore their only means of opposing the application is via wardship.

IV Application by the child

The final enquiry in this chapter is to consider the extent to which the child himself may use the wardship jurisdiction. Although it is clear the child can make himself a ward, the difficulty is that he can only do so via a next friend[10]. In the normal course of events the child's parents will be his next friends but, of course, if he wishes to bring proceedings

6. Though query exactly what the difference is.
7. Because he is not a 'parent' for these purposes. See *Re M (an infant)* [1955] 2 QB 479, [1955] 2 All ER 911. If he has previously been awarded custody under the Guardianship of Minors Act 1971 his agreement will be required. Children Act 1975, s.107(1) and Sch. 3, para. 39(*d*).
8. Ss. 9, 14.
9. Both proceedings should be heard together see n.2 above.
10. RSC Ord. 80, r.2.

against his parents then someone else must be found to act as a next friend.

This side of wardship has yet to be developed, so there is no established practice as to who can bring proceedings on behalf of the child. It is perhaps open to doubt, for example, whether the Official Solicitor could, even assuming he consented, bring wardship proceedings as the child's next friend. The pragmatic solution, and the one which has apparently been adopted in the rare case encountered, is to find some relative who is prepared to act on the child's behalf.

One situation where a child may find wardship useful is where he wishes to prevent his parents sending him to another country. It is apparently not unknown for a minor actually to go to Somerset House with this object in mind. This might happen either where the parents wish to return to their country of origin with their child or simply wish to send the child back to the country of origin. Alternatively it may arise because the parents wish to emigrate. Wardship would certainly be an effective counter to such a move for as we have seen[11] as soon as the child becomes a ward he may not be taken from the jurisdiction without the court's prior consent. In such cases provided a relative can be found who will act on the child's behalf, wardship proceedings can be instituted against the parents. Of course, as with all cases, it will then be left to the court to decide the issue on its merits. Presumably the age of ward and length of time spent in England will be important factors.

Theoretically wardship proceedings may be instituted on the child's behalf to settle a dispute over any aspect of the ward's upbringing. It could be used, for example, to resolve a dispute about education, medical treatment, at least if it is non therapeutic[12], or to overcome parental objection to the ward's associates. Whether a minor could use wardship as a means of obtaining maintenance from the parents is more difficult. It will be recalled that the power to order parents to pay a sum of money towards the ward's maintenance is conferred by the Family Law Reform Act 1969, section 6(2)[13]. By this provision the sum ordered cannot be paid to the ward personally, but only to the person having care and control of

11. E.g. in Chap. 5.
12. Following *Re D (a minor) (wardship: sterilisation)* [1976] Fam 185, [1976] 1 All ER 326.
13. See Chap. 5.

the ward, and it would seem unlikely that care and control would be granted to someone who is merely acting as the minor's next friend for the purpose of bringing the proceedings. A minor who has set up a separate home cannot normally look to wardship as a means of obtaining maintenance from his parents. It is true that were he to be committed to the care of a local authority under section 7(2) of the Family Law Reform Act 1969, his parents could then be ordered to pay maintenance under section 6(2)(*b*), but it seems doubtful whether wardship could be used in this way simply to obtain maintenance. Wardship, however, may be of use to a former ward once he becomes of age. Under section 6(4) of the 1969 Act provided a minor has at some point been the subject of an order making him a ward, then upon attaining the age of 18 he can, until he is 21, bring an action for maintenance against his parents and any sum ordered to be paid can be paid directly to the former ward. However, there are problems with the application of the provision. It seems probable that the child must have been the subject of an actual order making him a ward, and in any event the sums are only payable provided the parents are not residing together[14].

It is to be noted section 6(4) had its parallel in section 12 of the Guardianship of Minors Act 1971, in that a person aged between 18 and 21 in respect of whom a guardianship order has been in force, was able to apply for maintenance against either of his parents, but again no liability accrued where the parents were residing together[15]. The powers under the 1971 Act have now been extended as a result of amendments under the Domestic Proceedings and Magistrates' Courts Act 1978[16], by which applications can now be made by minors aged 16 or over, and the provision by which no liability could accrue if parents are residing together has been dropped. Applications, however, remain conditional on orders having been previously made under the 1971 Act[17].

---

14. By virtue of the Family Reform Act 1969, s.6(5), to which it seems s.6(4) is subject. This provision should, it is submitted, be amended in the light of the amendments to the Guardianship of Minors Act 1971—see below.
15. See ss.12(2), (3).
16. S.43, inserting s.12C into the 1971 Act—see ss.12C(4), (5).
17. See also *Downing v Downing (Downing Intervening)* [1976] Fam 288, [1976] 3 All ER 474 where financial provision was obtained by a 20 year old girl under the Matrimonial Causes Act 1973.

Chapter 11

Wardship and Local Authorities

I Introduction

A. DEVELOPMENT OF LOCAL AUTHORITY POWERS

The powers and duties of a local authority to protect and care for children derive largely from the Children Act 1948, the Children and Young Persons Act 1963, the Children and Young Persons Act 1969 and the Children Act 1975[1]. Despite repeated amendments there has been no consolidating legislation nor any overall review of the adequacy of child legislation.

Within this period there have, however, been many changes in social and economic conditions. Attitudes to family life and definitions of the best interests of a child have altered. Different aspects of children's welfare have been the focus of attention at different times. Each of the statutes was the outcome of a government report or white paper which reflected the contemporary public, professional and political concern for specific issues[2], and inevitably, therefore, the legislation has developed in a piecemeal manner.

The Children Act 1948 was the result of the report of the Curtis Committee[3]. This was set up following the death of a foster child, to inquire into existing methods of providing

---

1. There are also the Children and Young Persons Act 1933, the Children Act, 1958 and the Nurseries and Child-Minders Regulation Act 1948. Social services functions are delegated to local authorities by ss.1, 2 and 6 of the Local Authority Social Services Act 1970, as amended by s.195 of the Local Government Act 1972.
2. See the Report of the Care of Children Committee (1946) Cmnd. 6922 (The Curtis Committee); the Report of the Committee on Children and Young Persons (1960) Cmnd. 1191 (The Ingleby Committee); Children in Trouble (1968) Cmnd. 3601; the Report of the Departmental Committee on the Adoption of Children (1972) Cmnd. 5107 (The Houghton Committee).
3. Cmnd. 6922.

for children deprived of a normal home life and to consider what further steps should be taken to ensure that they were brought up under conditions best calculated to compensate for their lack of parental care. In evidence to the committee emphasis was placed on the need to maintain the child in his family wherever and whenever possible and particularly in his early years. There was concern at the low standard of residential care and of supervision of foster children, but the report indicated a preference for a substitute family.

The Act reflects the concerns of the committee. It imposes on the local authority a duty to receive a deprived child into care in certain circumstances and then bring him up according to his best interests[4]. Wherever possible the authority has to secure the discharge from care to parents, relatives or friends as soon as may be. There is little attempt to define the circumstances in which a childhood in care may be a lesser evil than being brought up within the natural family, and the local authority cannot prevent removal from care unless it assumes parental rights[5]. This can only be done where there are no parents or in a specific category of cases where they have by their behaviour rendered themselves unfit to care for the child.

During the 1950s there was an increasing awareness of the need to prevent families breaking up and children being received into care. Social and economic factors were seen as important in family difficulties. Juvenile delinquency began to be attributed in many instances to 'deprivation' rather than 'depravation'. It was thought that intensive preventive work with families could help to solve the problems of offenders and non-offenders.

The Ingleby Committee[6], set up in 1956, investigated these matters and subsequently the Children and Young Persons Act 1963 was enacted. Section 1 made it the duty of every local authority:

> 'to make available such advice, guidance and assistance (including financial assistance) as may promote the welfare of children by diminishing the need to receive children into or keep them in care ... or to bring children before a juvenile court'.

4. S.12 as substituted by s.59 of the Children Act 1975.
5. S.2 as substituted by s.57 of the Children Act 1975.
6. Cmnd. 1191.

Although the Children and Young Persons Act 1933 gave local authorities powers to remove children from their parents when they were in undesirable surroundings, the underlying philosophy was guided by the 1948 and 1963 Acts. Prevention and rehabilitation became the keynote of much of the subsequent work of local authorities, and it was anticipated that this would lead to an improvement in the prevention of delinquency.

These principles were further emphasised in the Children and Young Persons Act 1969. Both offenders and non-offenders were to be dealt with in the same system, and the provisions were designed to discourage either coming before the courts. For both, the powers of the court were directed towards treatment. In fact the aim to reduce the criminal element by raising the age of criminal responsibility was never implemented. The Act does make specific provisions for civil care proceedings[7], but they are heard in a jurisdiction largely designed for juvenile crime.

In the 1970s questions were again raised about the nature and efficiency of child care services. Difficulties were experienced as a result of changes in the structure of local authorities[8]. Children's departments, previously responsible for services to children and their families, were replaced by larger social services departments with responsibilities for the old, handicapped and mentally ill, as well as for children. The creation of a profession to manage all these inevitably lowered the level of child care expertise and raised the pressure of work loads. All this in a bureaucratic structure made it impossible in many instances for local authorities to provide the personalised services for children envisaged in the 1948 Act.

Lack of constructive long-term planning caused increasing concern. In spite of the apparent emphasis on returning children to their parents, it was considered that substantial numbers of children in care were unlikely ever to go back to their families and could not benefit from waiting in vain hope[9].

There was a rising body of opinion that it was not necessarily in a child's interest to return to his natural parents. The

7. S.1.
8. Under the Local Authority Social Services Act 1970.
9. See Rowe and Lambert: *Children Who Wait* (1973).

legal foundation was laid in *J v C*[10] when the House of Lords decided that in a dispute as to custody and upbringing between parents and third parties the interests of the child were first and paramount. This was given philosophical expression in the book *Beyond the Best Interests of the Child*[11], where the importance of 'psychological' parents was emphasised. The issue came into the public eye, however, in 1973 when Maria Colwell was killed by her stepfather after she had been removed from foster parents[12]. Subsequently there were a number of well-publicised deaths of children at the hands of parents to whom they had been returned[13]. Inevitably, there was a demand for a curtailment of parental rights, so that children could be better protected from parental rejection and ambivalence, and plans could be made for their long-term welfare. However, there were contrary arguments, that it was often bad social work practice rather than parental failure which led to children languishing in care or being returned to parents who could not cope. Strengthening the powers of local authorities and third parties might serve to reinforce bad practice and lack of planning, and encourage foster parents, for example, to sabotage a parent's efforts to recover a child.

The trend towards greater recognition of the rights of a child as an individual could not be ignored. The resulting legislation, the Children Act 1975, is an attempt to balance his rights with those of his parents recognising that while most frequently they should coincide, they will at times conflict. This is reflected in section 59 which requires a local authority to give first consideration to the need to safeguard and promote the welfare of the child throughout his childhood. Plans have to be made to take account of the statutory duty, and since initially this will most frequently mean ensuring a good parent–child relationship it is essential to keep the parent involved. The child's rights are also recognised by the power given to local authorities to assume

---

10. [1970] AC 668, [1969] 1 All ER 788.
11. Goldstein, Freud and Solnit (1973 Free Press).
12. See the Report of the Committee of Inquiry into the Care and Supervision provided in relation to Maria Colwell (1974) HMSO.
13. See e.g. the Wayne Brewer Report, Somerset County Council, the Stephen Meurs Report, Norfolk County Council, and the Karen Spencer Report, Derbyshire County Council.

parental rights where a child has been in care under section 1 of the Children Act 1948 for three years.

In more cases than were perhaps previously identified it may be necessary to protect a child against parental rejection and ambivalence and provide for his well-being. While working with parents on a voluntary basis may in many cases be appropriate, not infrequently some controlling power is needed.

One of the consequences of having unconsolidated legislation, drafted at different times to meet special needs, is that it does not always provide solutions for all problems. Since the existing legislation requires specific grounds to be proved before a local authority can obtain powers against the parent's wishes, it is not surprising that some local authorities conscious of their general responsibilities towards children and in particular their statutory duty to children in care[14], are increasingly seeking powers outside the statutory scheme. It is to the wardship jurisdiction that they have turned for assistance.

B. RELEVANCE OF WARDSHIP

It is well established that the wardship jurisdiction is not ousted by the statutory scheme from which local authorities derive their powers. This was first established in cases in which it was sought to challenge the exercise of powers by local authorities in relation to children in their care[15]. More recently it has been realised that wardship can prove advantageous to local authorities. Hence it has been held that authorities might properly ward a child already in their care in order to supplement their statutory powers[16]. The most recent development, however, is the use of wardship by local authorities as an alternative to the statutory scheme so that they can avoid its shortcomings[17].

---

14. S.12.
15. See e.g. *Re M (an infant)* [1961] Ch 328, [1961] 1 All ER 788, and *Re T(AJJ) (an infant)* [1970] Ch 688, [1970] 2 All ER 865.
16. See e.g. *Re B (a minor) (wardship: child in care)* [1975] Fam 36, [1974] 3 All ER 915, and *Re Y (a minor) (child in care: access)* [1976] Fam 125, [1975] 3 All ER 348.
17. See e.g. *Re D (a minor) (justices' decision: review)* [1977] Fam 158, [1977] 3 All ER 481.

There can now be seen three distinct and expanding roles of the wardship jurisdiction:

(1) As an original jurisdiction enabling local authorities to apply to have a child committed to their care in circumstances where this may not be possible under existing legislation.

(2) As a supplementary jurisdiction enabling local authorities to expand or supplement existing powers.

(3) As a supervisory jurisdiction under which local authority powers and decisions may be challenged.

We shall consider these roles under the following headings: use of wardship by local authorities, and use of wardship against local authorities by parents, putative fathers and third parties.

II The use of wardship by local authorities

A. INTRODUCTION

We have already said that wardship can be used to overcome the deficiencies of child care legislation. We shall therefore examine the various provisions with a view to showing the problems for which wardship may provide a remedy. First we shall consider the provisions of the Children Act 1948 and then those of the Children and Young Persons Act 1969.

B. CHILDREN ACT 1948

i) *Reception into care*

The 1948 Act imposes on the local authority a duty to receive a child into care in certain circumstances, but with a view to discharging the child from care as soon as possible. Section 1(1) of the Act states:

'Where it appears to a local authority with respect to a child in their area appearing to them to be under the age of seventeen

(a) that he has neither parent nor guardian or has been and remains abandoned by his parents or guardian or is lost; or

(b) that his parents or guardian are, for the time being or permanently, prevented by reason of mental or bodily disease or infirmity or other incapacity or any other circumstances from providing for his proper accommodation, maintenance and upbringing; and

(c) in either case, that the intervention of the local authority is necessary in the interests of the welfare of the child,

it shall be the duty of the local authority to receive the child into their care under this section.'

By section 1(2) the child can then stay in care until eighteen but this remains subject to section 1(3) by which a parent may request the child's return.

ii) *Assumption of parental rights*[18]

If the local authority consider that it is appropriate to assume the rights and duties of a parent, they may do so by resolution of the appropriate committee, and while the resolution is in force, section 1(3) shall not apply in relation to the person whose rights and duties have been assumed. Section 2(1) sets out the grounds on which the resolution may be passed[19]:

'Subject to the provisions of this Part of this Act, if it appears to the local authority in relation to any child who is in their care under the foregoing section—

(a) that his parents are dead and he has no guardian or custodian; or

(b) that a parent of his—

(i) has abandoned him, or

(ii) suffers from some permanent disability rendering him incapable of caring for the child, or

(iii) while not falling within sub-paragraph (ii) of this paragraph, suffers from a mental disorder (within the meaning of the Mental Health Act 1959), which renders him unfit to have the care of the child, or

(iv) is of such habits or mode of life as to be unfit to have the care of the child, or

18. For a fuller discussion of the working and effect of s.2 see Adcock and White *The Assumption of Parental Rights: A Practice Guide to s.2 of the Children Act 1948* (1977), Association of British Adoption and Fostering Agencies.

19. As substituted by s.57 of the Children Act 1975.

   (v) has so consistently failed without reasonable
    cause to discharge the obligations of a parent as
    to be unfit to have the care of the child, or
  (c) that a resolution under paragraph (b) of this subsection is in force in relation to one parent of the
   child who is, or is likely to become a member of a
   household comprising the child and his other
   parent; or
  (d) that throughout the three years preceding the passing
   of the resolution the child has been in the care of the
   local authority under the foregoing section, or
   partly in the care of a local authority and partly in
   the care of a voluntary organisation,
the local authority may resolve that there shall vest in
them the parental rights and duties with respect to that
child, and, if the rights and duties were vested in the
parent on whose account the resolution was passed
jointly with another person they shall also be vested in
the local authority jointly with that other person.'

The parent has a right of objection to the resolution within
one month of being served with notice of it[20], in which case,
if the local authority wishes the resolution to continue, it
must seek confirmation of the resolution in the juvenile
court[1]. At the hearing the court may order that the resolution
shall not lapse, but shall not do so unless satisfied:

  '(a) That the grounds mentioned in subsection (1) of
   this section on which the local authority purported
   to pass the resolution were made out, and
  (b) that at the time of the hearing there continued to be
   grounds on which a resolution under subsection (1)
   of this section could be founded, and
  (c) that it is in the interests of the child to do so.'[2]

  The usual method of providing security for a child in care
under section 1 is to pass a resolution under section 2 by
which a local authority assumes the rights and duties of a
parent. Difficulties arise where proof is required that the
parent is unfit to care for the child, since most parents are
reluctant to admit this. We have seen that if the parent objects
to the resolution, the local authority must seek confirmation

20. S.2(4).
 1. S.2(5).
 2. Ibid.

from the juvenile court and prove that grounds for a resolution existed both at the time it was passed and at the time of the hearing, and that the resolution is in the interests of the child.

Rules of evidence apply so that the admissibility of hearsay is limited[3]. Specific grounds must also be proved so that it is not open to the court to reach a decision purely on the basis of the welfare of the child. There may be sufficient evidence to support the passing of a resolution by the local authority but insufficient to satisfy a court because of the difficulty of proof in accordance with rules of evidence. Grounds may exist at the time the resolution was passed, but may be incapable of proof by the time of a hearing some time later. It is quite possible that a parent could suffer from a mental disorder at one time, which is impossible subsequently to prove because he refuses medical examination. Equally he may have a mode of life which he is prepared to stop pending the hearing. In both cases the child may have been in care a year or more, and it may be quite inappropriate for him to go back to his parents, and yet there is no statutory procedure for preventing it. Furthermore, the court's sole function is to decide whether or not to uphold the resolution. It cannot, for example, make a supervision order. In all of these cases local authorities may consider it appropriate to use wardship.

iii) *Effect of the resolution*

Parental rights and duties are defined in section 2(11) as 'all rights and duties which by law the mother and father have in relation to a legitimate child and his property except the right to consent or refuse to consent to the making of an application under section 14 of the Children Act 1975 [freeing order] and the right to agree or refuse to agree to the making of an adoption order or an order under section 25 of that Act [adoption of children abroad]'.

Even though the aim of the resolution may simply be to prevent the removal of a child in care under section 1, under the statutory scheme the authority has to assume all the rights and duties[4] of the parent, save those relating to an adoption

3. For the position in care proceedings, cf. *Humberside County Council v D P R (an infant)* [1977] 3 All ER 964, [1977] 1 WLR 1251.
4. See generally J M Eekelaar, 'What are Parental Rights?' (1973) 89 LQR 210.

order or a freeing order. Thus the right to consent to marriage[5] and the right to change the child's name[6] appear to pass to the authority, although the authority may not cause the child to be brought up in a different religious creed[7]. The authority may not desire such drastic consequences, and wardship could provide a satisfactory alternative, which is less threatening to the parent.

iv) *Problems created by section 1(3)*

The apparent simplicity of the scheme is complicated by section 1(3) which states:

> 'Nothing in this section shall authorise a local authority to keep a child in their care under this section if any parent or guardian desires to take over the care of the child, and the local authority shall, in all cases where it appears to them consistent with the welfare of the child to do so, endeavour to secure that the care of the child is taken over either
>
> (a) by a parent or guardian of his, or
> (b) by a relative or friend of his, being, where possible, a person of the same religious persuasion as the child or who gives an undertaking that the child will be brought up in that religious practice.'

This subsection has caused much difficulty in interpretation[8]. Clearly although the scheme of the legislation is to encourage the return of children to their parents, there are cases where this would not be in a child's interests. Reception into care

---

5. The Marriage Act 1949 does not specify whose consent is required to the marriage of a child under 18 who is in care, but in practice registrars require the consent of the local authority if a child is in care under the 1948 Act and parental rights have been assumed under s.2, or if he is in care under the 1969 Act. See further post p. 307.

6. The local authority has a power to make a declaration on behalf of a child so that his name can be changed, if they have assumed parental rights under s.2. See Enrolment of Deeds (Change of Name) (Amendment) Regulations 1969.

7. This applies to any child in care under the 1948 Act (s.3(7)), and to a child in care under the 1969 Act (s.24(3) of that Act). In placing the child for adoption, however, the agency is only required to have regard as far as is practicable to the wishes of the child's parents and guardians as to religious upbringing (Children Act 1975, s.13).

8. See M D A Freeman: 'Children in Care: The Impact of the Children Act 1975' (1976) 6 Fam Law 136; R A H White: 'The Case for Retaining a Child in Voluntary Care' (1976) 6 Fam Law 141, and J M Eekelaar: 'Children in Care and the Children Act 1975' (1977) 40 MLR 121.

may have occurred where the child had actually been harmed by his parents or where this was a grave risk. The local authority may not have wished to take care proceedings under the 1969 Act either to avoid a confrontation in court or because for technical reasons the proceedings would be unlikely to succeed. Alternatively the child may have been received into care from a separated spouse where there was no effective custody order, but the other spouse was unsuitable to have the care of the child. In some cases a child may have languished in care for a long period without any contact with the parents. Pearson LJ expressed the problem thus in *Re S (an infant)*[9]:

> 'One can envisage a case in which the parent is wholly unsuitable to have charge of the child or is for some reason unable to provide for the child's proper accommodation, maintenance and upbringing, and on one day the local authority takes a child into their care, and on the following day the same parent expresses the view that he or she has the desire to take over the care of the child and then the power of the local authority to keep the child in their care apparently ceases.'

Section 1(3) creates two specific problems. The first is whether the local authority has the right to keep the child if the parent expresses a desire to take over his care and whether they can prevent removal or must return the child to the parent. The other is whether if the parent expresses a desire to take over the care of the child he remains in care pending his physical removal.

In relation to the first problem Pennycuick J commented in *Re K R (an infant)*[10] that:

> 'Section 1(3) imposes no mandatory obligation to *return* the infant to the infant's parents. The first limb merely puts an end to the right of the local authority to *keep* the child and the second limb is only applicable where it appears to the local authority consistent with the welfare of the child to secure that the child's care is taken over by others.' [Emphasis added.]

Re K R was approved in *Krishnan v London Borough of Sutton*[11], where a habeas corpus application was made by a father

9. [1965] 1 All ER 865 at 871, [1965] 1 WLR 483.
10. [1964] Ch 455. sub nom. *Re R(K) (an infant)* [1963] 3 All ER 337.
11. [1970] Ch 181, [1969] 3 All ER 1367.

against the local authority for the return of his child placed with foster parents. The Court of Appeal held that in the particular circumstances of the case section 1(3) imposed no mandatory duty to return the child, since the authority might otherwise be subjected to an order which it would find impossible to carry out. Some weight was placed on the fact that the child was nearly eighteen and did not wish to return to her father.

In *Halvorsen v Hertfordshire County Council*[12] Lord Widgery CJ went even further by holding that section 1(3) could not be invoked at all by a parent who was unfit to take over the care of his child. He commented:

'It would be quite astonishing if notwithstanding that the child had been taken into the care of the local authority the parent could immediately demand its return. Indeed there is authority to show that such a right could not exist. There would be no security of action if the parent, having surrendered the child under section 1(1) could immediately claim it back under section 1(3).'

Although the judgment emphasised the practical difficulties, the Court of Appeal in *Bawden v Bawden*[13] considered it to have been wrongly decided and overruled it. Stamp LJ said[14]:

'Once the first limb of subsection (3) is brought into play, the local authority simply has no right to keep the child, if the child is not handed over to the parent . . . as it seems to me that the parent may go and fetch it.'

The Court of Appeal again accepted this interpretation in *Johns v Jones*[15]. Orr LJ said that once a parent has made a request for his child to be returned, the local authority were not allowed to keep the child in care under section 1.

These cases appear to establish that once the parent has expressed a desire to take over the care of his child the local authority cannot prevent him removing the child from care. This is surely a correct interpretation since it is only when a resolution under section 2 is in force that section 1(3) does not apply[16]. An important rider to this, however, is that

---

12. (1975) 5 Fam Law 79. The quotation is from a transcript of the judgment.
13. [1978] 3 All ER 1216, [1978] 3 WLR 798.
14. Ibid., at 1221 and 803 respectively.
15. [1978] 3 All ER 1222, [1978] 3 WLR 792.
16. S.2(6) specifically provides that s.1(3) 'shall not apply in relation to the person who, but for the resolution, would have the parental rights and duties in relation to the child'.

wardship can still be used by the local authority in the interests of the child if they wish to obtain an order to retain the child in care.

Indeed wardship may now be required more frequently in the light of the decision in *Johns v Jones*. In that case a girl aged 3 months was voluntarily placed in care. Almost 7 months later the mother requested by telephone that the child be returned to her. Five weeks afterwards the local authority purported to assume parental rights under section 2. The mother objected, but the juvenile court confirmed the resolution. She appealed to the Divisional Court, arguing that in view of her telephone request to the local authority the child was no longer in care under section 1 and therefore a resolution could not validly be passed. The argument was rejected by the Divisional Court, but found favour with the Court of Appeal. The view clearly expressed in *Johns v Jones* is that, if the parent informs the local authority of his desire to take over the care of the child, the child is not thereafter in the care of the local authority under section 1. Although *Bawden* was cited to support this, it is submitted with respect, that that case did not establish that the child was not in care under section 1, merely that the local authority has no right to *keep* the child if the parent desires to take over his care. Whether that means that the local authority are not permitted to care for the child surely depends on the interpretation of 'keep'. If it means that they have no power to care for him under that section, they cannot care for him at all since there is no other statutory power available. In that case it may be argued that they must positively return the child to the parent, but this is contrary to previous decisions[17] and, it is submitted, cannot be correct[18]. In the alternative, 'keep' could be interpreted as 'prevent removal' and pending removal the child would still be in care under section 1.

If the decision in *Johns v Jones* is correct and the child is no longer in care on the expression of the desire to remove him there are a number of undesirable practical consequences.

First, in many cases the status of the child would be uncertain. A parent could say that he wanted his child back

17. E.g. *Re K R (an infant)* [1964] Ch 455, [1963] 3 All ER 337.
18. At the time of going to press the issues raised by *Johns v Jones* are pending before the House of Lords in *Lewisham London Borough Council v Lewisham Juvenile Court Justices* (1978) Times, November 1.

without any intention of taking over the care, but the authority might be obliged to seek out the parent and return the child. Pending return the child would be in limbo, unless the parent specifically agreed that he could return to care under section 1[19].

Secondly, it would seem that the provisions of the Children Act 1948 will not apply[20]. Therefore the local authority will owe the child no statutory duty of care and will have no power to place or care for him. It would thus appear that any payment of foster allowances would be ultra vires.

A third consequence would be that the local authority has no power to pass a resolution even if there are grounds and the resolution is in the interest of the child. It is established practice to discuss a proposal to pass a resolution with a parent, since he may consent to it. The effect of *Johns v Jones* will be to deter this. Parents may therefore have their rights removed without any opportunity to participate in the decision, for fear that if they do not agree, they may say the words which will operate to terminate the care. It is also clear that there are a number of resolutions thought to exist which are in fact invalid and the child not even in care. A resolution on the ground that the child has been in care for three years[1] will now have to be examined to see whether the parent at any time said that he wanted the child back.

It must be said that the decision serves to increase the instability of children in care under section 1. It may be that local authorities will be obliged to resolve this by instituting wardship proceedings to retain a child in care. Whereas previously such a step might have been necessary in the interests of the child if there was a serious request to remove him, it may now be necessary even where the request is casual. It would be most unfortunate, however, if local authorities felt that they should ward a child every time a parent said he wanted him back, since he may merely be acting on a temporary whim. It is to be hoped therefore that the expres-

---

19. It may be argued that the local authority could take care proceedings under s.1 of the Children and Young Persons Act 1969. The remarks of Stamp LJ in *Johns v Jones* ibid. and by Lord Denning MR in *R v Local Commissioner for the North and East Area of England, ex parte Bradford City Metropolitan Council* [1979] 2 WLR 1 suggest that they both thought so. There would not, however, appear to be sufficient evidence to satisfy the grounds, if the child had only just been discharged from care. See discussion post p. 248 et seq.
20. I.e. Part II, ss.12–17.
1. Under s.2(1)(d), Children Act 1948.

sion of the desire to take over care of the child will be interpreted much more strictly than *Johns v Jones* suggests.

v) *The effect of section 1(3A)*[2]

It is also necessary to consider the effect of section 1(3A) which states:

'Except in relation to an act done—
(a) with the consent of the local authority, or
(b) by a parent or guardian of the child who has given the local authority not less than 28 days' notice of his intention to do it,

subsection (8)(penalty for taking away a child in care) of section 3 of this Act shall apply to a child in the care of a local authority under this section (notwithstanding that no resolution is in force under section 2 of the Act with respect to the child) if he has been in the care of that local authority throughout the preceding six months; and ... in such a case a parent or guardian of the child shall not be taken to have lawful authority to take him away'.

The Houghton Committee[3] referred only to this period of 28 days being used for the purposes of rehabilitation with the parent, although it was widely thought that it could also be used as a period in which to decide what action should be taken in the interests of the child[4].

On the face of it, *Johns v Jones*[5] will prevent a local authority from passing a section 2 resolution even during this 28 day period, since the child will no longer be in care under section 1. If that is so, if the local authority wishes to prevent the child returning to the parent after the expiration of the period it would seem wardship is their only option. It is possible to argue, however, that *Johns v Jones* does not apply to a case where the child remains in care pursuant to section 1(3A), in which case the option of passing a section 2 resolution would seem to still be available. The parent can always avoid the effects of section 1(3A) by requesting return before six months in care have elapsed, and even if section 1(3A) is

---

2. As inserted by s.56, Children Act 1975.
3. Cmnd. 5107.
4. The Government took this view. See Parl. Debs., Commons, Standing Committee A, 29 July 1975, Col. 536.
5. [1978] 3 All ER 1222, [1978] 3 WLR 792.

operative, the parent may defeat its object if he actually removes the child from care, since under the statute there is only a criminal sanction against the parent. Wardship would provide a remedy for recovering the child or ensuring that he is not removed.

vi) *Appeals*

There is now an appeal from a juvenile court decision concerning a resolution to the Family Division[6], but this may not be sufficient to prevent a child moving temporarily out of care, which may not be in his interests. If a local authority fails to have the resolution confirmed, there is no provision for the court to stay execution of its decision. In some cases this may not matter as the parent will not actually remove the child. It will frequently be the case, however, that the parent intends to remove the child immediately, before the appeal can be heard. In such a case the local authority could institute wardship proceedings as a temporary measure to prevent any change in the situation pending the appeal[7]. In this way, a local authority could hope to have the resolution upheld and the wardship subsequently discharged.

Authorities might consider using wardship as an alternative to appealing. At first sight such a use may seem suspect because it appears to be using the jurisdiction as an alternative form of appeal. On closer examination, however, wardship does not operate as an appeal because the issue is different. The question before the appellate court is simply whether grounds exist for the passing of a section 2 resolution, whereas in wardship the court is concerned with the wider issue of what course is best in the child's interests.

C. CHILDREN AND YOUNG PERSONS ACT 1969

i) *Grounds for proceedings*

The procedure laid down in section 1 empowers any local authority, constable or authorised person who reasonably

---

6. S.4A, Children Act 1948, as inserted by s.58, Children Act 1975.
7. The position would appear to be analogous to the circumstances in *Re D (a minor)* (*justices' decision: review*) [1977] Fam 158, [1977] 3 All ER 481. For discussion of this case see post p. 286.

believes that there are grounds for making an order, to bring a child or young person[8] before the court.

The grounds on which a child or young person may be brought before the court, and on which a court may, if of the opinion that any of them is satisfied, make an order, are set out in section 1(2) as follows:

'(a) his proper development is being avoidably prevented or neglected or his health is being avoidably impaired or neglected or he is being ill-treated; or

(b) it is probable that the condition set out in the preceding paragraph will be satisfied in his case, having regard to the fact that the court or another court has found that the condition is or was satisfied in the case of another child or young person who is or was a member of the household to which he belongs; or

(bb) It is probable that the conditions set out in paragraph (a) of this subsection will be satisfied in his case, having regard to the fact that a person who has been convicted of an offence mentioned in Schedule I of the Act of 1933 is or may become, a member of the same household as the child[9]. [or]

(c) he is exposed to moral danger; or

(d) he is beyond the control of his parent or guardian; or

(e) he is of compulsory school age within the meaning of the Education Act 1944 and is not receiving efficient full-time education suitable to his age, ability, and aptitude[10]; or

(f) he is guilty of an offence, including homicide

---

8. In this section all references are to the Children and Young Persons Act 1969, unless otherwise stated. A child is a person under 14 and a 'young person' is a person aged 14 and under 17 (Children and Young Persons Act 1969, s.70(1)) unless the context otherwise requires. In general we have used 'child' to mean a person under 18. For a discussion of the Act see also Graham Hall and Mitchell: *Child Abuse—Procedure and Evidence in Juvenile Courts* (1978 Barry Rose) and Feldman: Care Proceedings (1978 Oyez).

9. This sub-section is added by s.108 and Sch. 3 para. 67 of the Children Act 1975. It should be noted that it refers only to 'child' and not to 'young person', so that proceedings on this ground may only be taken in respect of a person under 14. The Act of 1933 is the Children and Young Persons Act 1933, the first schedule of which lists certain offences against children.

10. Proceedings under this sub-section may only be commenced by a local education authority. (S.2(8)).

and[11] also that he is in need of care or control which he is unlikely to receive unless the court makes an order under this section in respect of him . . .'[12]

The court may also make an interim order for up to 28 days if it is not in a position finally to dispose of the proceedings[13].

If a care order is made in care proceedings it shall be the duty of the local authority to receive the child into their care, and notwithstanding any claim by his parent or guardian, to keep him in their care while the order is in force[14].

The authority shall have the same powers and duties with respect to a person in their care by virtue of a care order as his parent or guardian would have apart from the order[15].

A single magistrate may also make what is known as a place of safety or removal order, which authorises the detention of a child or young person in a place of safety, on the application of a person for authority to do so. The magistrate must be satisfied that the applicant has reasonable cause to believe that any of the conditions set out in section 1(2)(a) to (e) is satisfied. Such detention may be authorised for up to 28 days[16]. An application to the juvenile court or a single magistrate for an interim order may be made during this period, and if the order is refused the court or magistrate may direct that the child or young person be released[17].

ii) *Difficulties created by the grounds*

It cannot be too frequently emphasised that the jurisdiction of the juvenile court is limited. First the court is not looking

11. I.e. there is a double test.
12. The court may then make the following orders under s.1(3) of the Act:
    (a) an order requiring his parent or guardian to enter into a recognisance to take proper care of him and exercise proper control over him (provided the parent or guardian consents, s.1(5)(a))
    (b) a supervision order
    (c) a care order
    (d) a hospital order within the meaning of Part V of the Mental Health Act 1959
    (e) a guardianship order within the meaning of that Act.
    No order may be made if the young person has attained the age of sixteen and is or has been married. (S.1(5)(c).)
13. S.2(10) and s.28(6).
14. S.24(1).
15. S.24(3).
16. S.28(1).
17. S.28(6). Such an application could be made by a parent. See *R v Lincoln (Kesteven) Juvenile Court, ex parte Lincolnshire County Council* [1976] QB 957, [1976] 1 All ER 490.

at the overall welfare of the child with a view to making the best possible arrangements for him, but must consider whether certain specific grounds are satisfied to enable them to make an order for care or supervision. Secondly, the proceedings are inflexible in that the court simply tries an issue and decides whether an order should be made.

The need to satisfy specific conditions raises a number of problems. Section 1(2)(a), the most commonly used section, is drafted in the present tense, so that evidence must be recent at the commencement of the proceedings. If the child is already in care under section 1 of the 1948 Act it is difficult to argue that 'the proper development *is being* avoidably prevented or neglected'[18]. Another problem can arise with the new-born child or inadequate mother. If he has been born in hospital, it may not be possible to give evidence that development is being avoidably prevented or neglected, purely because hospital standards have ensured that he is developing properly. While some of these cases do allow a degree of contact between mother and child, with others it may be quite unsafe to allow sufficient opportunity to test out the relationship and obtain evidence that the child's development is being avoidably prevented or neglected. An example of this type of case is the psychotic mother who may have delusions, sometimes specifically about the child. In cases such as these wardships may provide the only method of making proper arrangements for the child.

iii) *Form of proceedings*

A further problem with proceedings under the 1969 Act is that the form of the proceedings requires the child to be brought before the court[19]. Although it is possible for an order to be made deeming a child under five to have been brought before the court[20], the older child must at least be brought before the court at some stage during each hearing. In some courts it is considered necessary to have sight even of a child under five. There are some cases which require a series of interim orders and on each occasion the child will have to be brought before the court. This is particularly so where a parent is charged with an offence and criminal proceedings

18. But see p. 280, n.19.
19. S.1.
20. S.2(9).

have to be completed before the care proceedings are heard. If the children were wards of court the proceedings could go ahead without any need for the attendance of the child, nor would they be delayed by the criminal proceedings.

The fact that it is the child brought before the court, means that the parents have a limited role[1]. If legal aid is sought, it will be granted to the child, and it is his interest that a solicitor should represent[2]. Indeed in an unopposed application for discharge of an order the juvenile court may order that the parent shall not represent the child[3]. Legal aid may then be granted to the parents[4], but they can in any event only call or give evidence in respect of allegations made against them, and make representations at the end of the evidence[5].

Were wardship proceedings to be brought instead, parents would not be confined to such a limited role. This might be thought in the better interests of the child and for this reason such an application might appeal to local authorities who are reluctant to prevent a parent participating fully in the proceedings.

iv) *Appeal*

Probably the most serious deficiency in the 1969 Act is the lack of right of appeal where magistrates refuse to make an order or discharge an order contrary to the arguments of the local authority[6]. It seems established that wardship can fill this gap. In *Re D* (*a minor*) (*justices' decision: review*)[7] it was held that, notwithstanding the discharge of a care order by the juvenile court, the local authority was entitled to invoke wardship. Dunn J commented[8]:

1. Although they may act on his behalf (S.70(2)). See *R v Welwyn JJ, ex parte s* (1978) Times, November 30.
2. Though in practice instructions are often taken from parents.
3. See s.32A, Children and Young Persons Act 1969, as inserted by s.64 of the Children Act 1975, and Children and Young Persons Act 1969, Commencement Order (No. 1). By s.32B a guardian ad litem may then be appointed to act on behalf of the child.
4. Children Act, s.65(b) inserting s.28(6A) into the Legal Aid Act 1974.
5. Magistrates' Courts (Children and Young Persons) Rules 1970, r.15, as amended by Magistrates' Courts (Children and Young Persons) (Amendment) Rules 1976.
6. They may only appeal against being the authority named in the order (s.21(5)). A child has a right of appeal under s.2(12). This is often exercised by a parent. Query whether this is right since s.70(2) does not refer to s.2(12).
7. [1977] Fam 158.
8. Ibid., at 164.

'Far from local authorities being discouraged from applying to the court in wardship, in my judgment they should be encouraged to do so, because in very many of these cases it is the only way in which orders can be made in the interests of the child, untrammelled by the statutory provisions of the Children and Young Persons Act 1969'.

Although *Re D* was concerned with the discharge of a care order, the position would seem to be the same if an application for a care order was refused.

D. OTHER USES OF WARDSHIP

We have considered a number of reasons why local authorities may wish to use wardship because of the shortcomings of the procedures. To what extent wardship can be used simply as an alternative to the statutory scheme is debatable. There is judicial support for the proposition that an authority should not invoke wardship before exhausting their powers under statute[9]. The more recent trend, however, suggests that the proposition is no longer tenable, though of course questions of cost and convenience will mean that the statutory scheme will normally be used. There are, however, a number of more general reasons for considering wardship as an alternative. As Ormrod LJ said in *Re Y (a minor)*[10]:

'I feel bound to say that I think local authorities might find if they look into it . . . situations in which it would be positively to their advantage to invoke the wardship jurisdiction themselves. It would sometimes avoid their having to take unpleasant awkward decisions themselves which cause great pain and anguish'.

Lane J said in *Re B (a minor)*[11]:

'As a matter of general application it seems to me that there may be various circumstances in which a local authority would be grateful for the Court exercising wardship jurisdiction; local authorities are sometimes faced with difficult and onerous decisions concerning children in their charge; responsible officers of their Welfare Department may be subject to various pressures from within or outside the authority itself. I consider

9. See *Re B (infants)* [1962] Ch 201, [1961] 3 All ER 276, CA.
10. *Re Y (a minor) (child in care: access)* [1976] Fam 125 at 138.
11. *Re B (a minor) (wardship: child in care)* [1975] Fam 36 at 44.

that there would be no abandonment of, or derogation from, their statutory powers and duties were they to seek the guidance and assistance of the High Court in matters of difficulty, as distinct from the day to day arrangements with which as the authorities show, the Court will not interfere.'

This seems to give judicial approval to applications from local authorities where they may want to avoid having to take a decision themselves. This can arise where the child is already in the care of the authority. Normally there is no reason why the authority should not exercise its responsibilities, but these dicta suggest that it would be quite proper to enlist the assistance of the high Court in extreme cases.

Circumstances do occur where the authority will wish to take proceedings, but may consider that the High Court provides a more appropriate forum than the juvenile court. If a case is likely to be long and complex it may not be heard satisfactorily in the juvenile court. Magistrates are frequently not experienced in hearing lengthy and detailed evidence, sometimes from technical or expert witnesses. Judges of the Family Division do have that experience and are used to intricate arguments. It is also likely that evidence will be more exhaustively examined in the High Court, not least because it will have been filed on affidavit in advance in most cases. The points at issue between the parties should be more clearly defined. The judge may also be familiar with the case in advance if he has read the evidence, although this is not invariably done. The permanent nature of the affidavits and the availability of a transcript of the proceedings also present considerable advantages when dealing with evidence, especially in a protracted case. In a juvenile court it is unlikely that there will be a detailed record of the proceedings. There are also administrative problems in many juvenile courts because it is frequently difficult to find sufficient time for a continuous hearing where magistrates have other jobs and where court facilities and court staff are in short supply. It is obviously desirable for a hearing of this nature to be heard continuously if at all possible, and this can usually be done in the High Court.

Another important consideration is that in wardship all persons interested in the child can be made parties to the case[12]. In addition to the parents, the child and the local

12. See Chap. 3.

authority, there may be other relatives or foster parents who are concerned about the welfare of the child. In no proceedings other than wardship is it possible for all these interests to be fully and fairly represented.

The evidence which may be put before the court can be wider in wardship proceedings. Since the proceedings are in the High Court the Civil Evidence Act 1968 applies and the rules of hearsay are relaxed[13]. As the court has a paternal role towards its ward it is argued that it is not bound by the ordinary rules of evidence and procedure and is able virtually to interview parties. The judge has a wide discretion as to what he is prepared to admit. The rules of hearsay do apply in the juvenile court and can restrict the evidence which the court will be allowed to hear[14].

The mental and physical state of one or both of the parents may be relevant to the question of the proper care of the child, but in the juvenile court it will generally not be possible to put such matters in evidence because the parent can simply refuse to be examined[15]. Although the High Court may be reluctant to force a parent to be medically examined, it will be easier for the court to draw an inference if the parent refuses. The court would feel a natural reluctance to vest the care and control of its ward in a person who did refuse, whereas in the juvenile court the local authority has to prove the specific ground.

Situations do also arise where professionals involved with a child disagree as to the appropriate method of handling a case and there may be limited opportunity for these different views to be expressed in the juvenile court. With the broader view of wardship it would be possible to explore and take account of the differences.

One of the problems in the lower courts is the right of the party to apply for discharge[16] or rescission[17] and appeal against the juvenile court decision regularly, so that the case

---

13. But see Chap. 4.
14. The provisions of the Civil Evidence Act 1968 have never been extended to magistrates' courts. See also *Humberside County Council v D P R (an infant)* [1977] 3 All ER 964.
15. This may be relevant to the 'care and control' test in s.1(2), but may be equally important for proving mental disorder on the part of the parent making him unfit to have the care of the child under s.2(1)(b)(iii).
16. S.21(2), (3), but not within three months of the date of dismissal of a previous application.
17. In the case of a resolution under s.2 of the Children Act 1948, by s.4 thereof.

is almost continuously in court. This can have most adverse effects on the ability of the local authority to plan for the long term welfare of a child or work constructively with a parent who is preoccupied with fighting battles in court. The High Court could prevent this by making an order that no further applications could be made without the consent of the court or within a certain period.

Finally a most important reason for consideration of wardship is where the powers given to the local authority by statute are not sufficient to deal with a particular case. For example, application may be made for an injunction to restrain a party from molesting a child in care, or in some instances local authority workers.

Such a case was *Re B*[18], in which the court decided to continue wardship because the stepfather of the child was of a violent nature and might return and create difficulties. The other situation in which it can be important to expand the powers of the local authority is where there is a threat to remove the child from the country, and of course by the simple act of making the child a ward of court, the child is legally prevented from removal.

In conclusion it may be said that there are circumstances in which a local authority should examine whether it is right to ward a child in addition or in preference to other action. Most importantly the welfare of the child is then the first and paramount consideration.

E. DRAWBACKS OF WARDSHIP FOR LOCAL AUTHORITIES

i) *Time*

Inevitably cases in the High Court do take longer. Although in one respect the speed and simplicity with which a child can become a ward and protected by injunction are attractive features, it remains true that it can at the time of writing take five months to obtain a date for a full hearing in London[19]. In spite of indications of the urgency of children's cases, it is still not always remembered that for a child a decision concerning his future must always be urgent. If he is in limbo, insecure and uncertain about who his future

---

18. *Re B (a minor) (child in care)* [1975] Fam 36, [1974] 3 All ER 915.
19. Even in the provinces the delay could be significant.

caretakers will be, who should have access to him and when, and what future plans for him are, it is inevitable that his development will not progress as well as that of a child not subject to such strain.

The time involved in the case also depends on the speed at which parties and their solicitors are prepared to file evidence and undertake the necessary procedures. If a number of parties are involved this will naturally extend the time for the filing of evidence.

A local authority unfettered by the court should be able to exercise its statutory powers quickly, but when the child is also a ward confusion may arise in reaching decisions about his welfare.

ii) *Loss of control*

Once a child in care is warded[20] or a child is placed in care by the court after a wardship application, the local authority is subject to the directions of the court[1]. There may, of course, be cases in which a court in spite of continuing wardship will not interfere with the local authority's discretion over day to day matters. However, it is inevitable that the local authority powers are to some extent fettered and this is an unfamiliar role for them. It is an aspect which they must bear in mind if they propose to make an application in wardship. Even though day to day and uncontentious matters will continue to be dealt with by the authority, any party can apply to the court for directions on the handling of specific matters. This does have the effect that the authority is more answerable, at least in theory, and is also subject to the criticism of the court.

In some cases it is no bad thing that the court can oversee the handling of the case, but it should also be said that if the authority's work with a child is good, it can be a disadvantage that there is a loss of control because the role of the authority may not be so clear cut. If good unfettered decisions are taken, action will be decisive and the child and his parents will know where they stand.

Once a lengthy court case is commenced there may be a tendency between the parties to compromise, which may not be entirely in the child's interest. This can happen with the

---

20. Unless the local authority is simply asking the court to supplement its powers as in *Re B*.
1. See *Re Y (a minor)* [1976] Fam 125, [1975] 3 All ER 348.

best of motives, purely to avoid lengthy uncertainty. Unless one party or the other has a strong case, there may also be an inevitable tendency on the part of the court to find a compromise solution, again, not necessarily in the best interests of the child. These situations are less likely to arise if the child is solely in the care of an authority, which carries out well-prepared plans. In general with good practice and goodwill these problems can be overcome, but it is important for all concerned to be aware of the dangers so that they can be met and resolved.

iii) *Costs*

Legal aid is available for these proceedings[2], but if parties are not legally aided the expense can be prohibitive. It may be quite unfair on parents to take them out of the juvenile court which they could afford into the High Court which they could not. Certainly for local authorities it is much cheaper in visible outgoings to apply in the juvenile court. It may be wise to consider whether the expenditure is worthwhile, balancing cost against the fact that unless a suitable solution for the child is found the expenditure on the child may subsequently be increased through the need to deal with far more serious problems at a later stage.

iv) *Familiarity*

At the present time for most matters where children are concerned with the local authority, applications are made to the juvenile court, and this is a court with which many families in difficulty are familiar. The High Court may present an imposing spectre for them and one with which they are quite unfamiliar. This could put them at a considerable disadvantage in circumstances where they are already at a disadvantage by virtue of having less knowledge at their disposal and fewer facilities than the local authority can call upon. Furthermore, since the juvenile court is the local court it may be felt that it should deal with cases arising in its own area.

In some cases the authority will have no suitable alternative to wardship and there may be others where the decis-

2. See Chap. 4.

ion is in the balance. In those cases careful consideration will need to be given to the advantages and disadvantages.

III Applications against local authorities

A. INTRODUCTION

In considering the involvement of wardship in cases where a child is in the care of a local authority, the circumstances in which the court will entertain an application require close attention. It is open to the authority to waive the point of jurisdiction[3], but there will be cases where the local authority will not wish to surrender their supremacy, and argument will ensue as the court's power to exercise the wardship jurisdiction.

As a matter of principle it is clear that the child may be made a ward of court, and it is the question whether the court will exercise its powers that is important. This is laid down in *Re M (an infant)*[4], a Court of Appeal case in which Lord Evershed MR said:

'(1) The prerogative right of the Queen, as parens patriae in relation to infants within the Realm, is not for all purposes ousted or abrogated as a result of the exercise of duties and powers by local authorities under the Children Act 1948: in particular the power to make an infant a ward of court by invocation of Section 9 of the Act on 1949 is unaffected.

(2) But even where a child is made a ward of court by virtue of the Act of 1949, the judge in whom prerogative powers are vested will, acting on familiar principles, not exercise control in relation to duties or discretions clearly vested by statute in the local authority, and may therefore, and in a case such as the present normally will, order that the child cease to be a ward of court. This result will occasion no surprise to those familiar with wardship proceedings, for in many cases where infants are made wards of court, the directions of the Court are

3. See ante p. 287 et seq.
4. [1961] Ch 328 at 345. Although Lord Evershed MR said that the prerogative jurisdiction was not for all purposes abrogated, thereby suggesting that for some purposes it was ousted, the better view is that the jurisdiction continues to exist even though the court will not exercise it. See e.g. *H v H (child in care)* [1973] Fam 62 at 65 per Wrangham J and *Re B (a minor)* [1975] Fam 36, [1974] 3 All ER 915 per Lane J.

sought only on particular matters, such, for example, as the place of education or to control the activities of the infant in relation to marriage or undesirable associations where a united parental control has failed; in such cases the Court makes no order as to the custody, care, or maintenance for that remains in the hands of unimpeachable parents and the Court does not interfere in relation to such matters.'

Equally important in *Re B* (*infants*)[5] Pearson LJ said:

'the effect of such an Act (conferring on local authorities powers and duties in respect of children) may be, *not . . . to restrict the jurisdiction, but to restrict the scope of the proper exercise of the jurisdiction*'. [Emphasis added.]

Ormerod LJ agreed that it would be open to the authority to make the children wards, but the order would be an empty one. He said[6]:

'No court in the proper exercise of its discretion would make or continue a wardship order for the reason that there is nothing left for the court to do'.

The general rule may, therefore, be stated that the courts will be reluctant to interfere with the exercise of the duties and discretions of a local authority which are clearly vested in them by Parliament. If the court finds something left to do it may exercise its discretion. We shall proceed to examine circumstances which will encourage the court to exercise that discretion.

B. IMPROPRIETY[7]

Lord Evershed MR also said in *Re M*[8]:

'There remains the right (and duty) of the judge in whom the prerogative power is vested to control the

5. [1962] Ch 201 at 223.
6. Ibid., at 216.
7. A possible alternative to wardship is for the parent to claim that he has suffered injustice as a result of improper administration by the local authority pursuant to the Local Government Act 1974 so that the matter can be investigated by a local commissioner. See *R v Local Commissioner for Administration for the North and North East Area of England, ex parte Bradford City Metropolitan Council* [1979] 2 WLR 1. It may be questioned, however, whether a complaint to the commissioner is the appropriate method of having the matter reviewed. The commissioner's powers are limited so that, for example, he cannot force the local authority to take any specific action whereas, in wardship, the High Court can.
8. [1961] Ch 328 at 345.

activities of a local authority in cases where a local authority is shown to be acting in some way in breach or disregard of its statutory duties'.

The court will always be prepared to examine allegations of what may broadly be termed impropriety. If allegations can be substantiated it will then very frequently exercise its wardship powers, because of course the basis of trust by any other party is destroyed.

Allegations of impropriety will normally be difficult to substantiate and the courts have discouraged such allegations being made simply to support a wardship application. As Russell LJ said in *Re T(AJJ) (an infant)*[9]:

'In our view it is important that the person seeking the intervention of the (court) . . . should be required at the outset on affidavit to state with particularity the precise grounds asserted and the facts alleged that are said to constitute these grounds. If possible the evidence should initially be confined to the question whether those grounds exist. Unless some such system is followed there is a danger that much time and expense will be wasted with a full enquiry into the whole case . . . when it may turn out . . . that no special ground existed and that therefore it is not one in which the court will assert jurisdiction.'

An allegation of impropriety on which it is thought to base the exercise of the wardship jurisdiction should therefore be specifically stated in an affidavit and tried as a preliminary matter, before the court proceeds to investigate the merits.

A case in which this procedure was followed was *Re L(AC) (an infant)*[10]. A section 2 resolution was passed on the grounds that the mother had a permanent disability rendering her incapable of looking after her child. The authority served the mother with written notice of the resolution and she served a written counter-notice objecting to it. The authority then complained to the juvenile court. Subsequently a doubt was raised about the competence of the sub-committee to pass the resolution and accordingly a second resolution was passed by a different committee. The authority led the mother's solicitor to believe that it was not necessary to serve another counter-notice to the notice of the second resolution, so that

9. [1970] Ch 688 at 694.
10. [1971] 3 All ER 743.

none was lodged within the required twenty-eight days. A counter-notice was served later, but the authority said that this was out of time. The mother was therefore forced to rely on section 4(3) of the 1948 Act which placed the onus on her to complain to the court and prove that the authority had no grounds for passing the resolution. If the counter-notice had been served in time the authority would have been obliged to complain to the court to establish that there were grounds for the resolution. After her case failed in the juvenile court the mother applied to have the child made a ward of court. It was held that the court should exercise its wardship jurisdiction and investigate the merits of the case. It was held first that the authority had not followed the correct statutory procedure and had thereby deprived the mother of real protection under the Act, secondly that there was a degree of uncertainty and confusion about the source of the authority's statutory power of control over the child, and thirdly there was confusion in the minds of both committees about a material fact, namely, that in spite of her infirmity the mother was capable of looking after at least one of her children.

Cumming-Bruce J ordered that the child should not be dewarded before consideration of the case on its merits. The case illustrates both the usefulness of having allegations of impropriety tried as a preliminary issue, and the kind of circumstances which are likely to give grounds on which such allegations can be based.

Another case in which the jurisdiction was exercised was in *Re D (a minor)*[11]. A child who had been abandoned by his mother shortly after birth lived with his putative father until he was six. He was then received into care when the father committed suicide. The father's sister and her husband wished to take over the care of the child, who had been fostered by the local authority to a woman engaged to the putative father. The authority, however, assumed the rights of the mother to the exclusion of the father's relatives.

Balcombe J decided that he should exercise the wardship jurisdiction, partly because the local authority had not objected to the appointment of the Official Solicitor who had by then produced a report with recommendations contrary to

11. (1978) 122 Sol Jo 193, Times, February 14.

those of the local authority. The other reason was that the local authority committee which passed the resolution did not have sufficient information before it for a proper exercise of its discretion. The local authority was bound to give first consideration to the need to safeguard and promote the child's welfare[12]. That discretion could not properly be exercised without some idea of the practical consequences of the decision, and the committee should have been able to consider whether there was any alternative to an assumption of parental rights. As it had not been able to do so on the information before it, the resolution had not been a proper exercise of its discretion, so that the court would investigate the merits of the case.

The wide discretion of the judge should always be remembered and it must not be imagined that the procedure in *Re T (A JJ)*[13] will always be followed, especially if it can be shown that the child is in urgent need of protection. In a recent unreported case Sir George Baker P said[14]:

> 'The difference seems to me to be that here, . . . there is a crisis and a matter of great urgency. The child was going to be taken out of the jurisdiction by a father who, on the face of it, has a very unsatisfactory history and something has to be done immediately, if anything is to be done, and I am not satisfied that this is a case in which it was possible, or, indeed desirable, to attempt to follow the course suggested by the Court of Appeal.'

In addition to procedural irregularities there may be failures to carry out the duties laid down in section 12(1) of the 1948 Act, which as Balcombe J pointed out in *Re D (a minor)*[15], could be said to show that the local authority is acting in some way in breach or disregard of their statutory duties. There is a general duty for a local authority in reaching any decision relating to a child in their care to 'give first consideration to the need to safeguard and promote the welfare of the child throughout his childhood'; and so far as is practicable to 'ascertain the wishes and feelings of the child regarding the decision and give due consideration to them, having regard to his age and understanding.'

12. Children Act 1948, s.12.
13. [1970] Ch 688, [1970] 2 All ER 865.
14. This is in a case known to the authors.
15. (1978) 122 Sol Jo 193, Times, February 14.

If the authority fail to consider the welfare of the child or fail to make it their first consideration, they would clearly be disregarding their statutory duty. Difficulty might arise in substantiating an allegation of that nature, since such consideration inevitably involves the exercise of discretion. Nonetheless there are circumstances in which an application may be advisable. First there are children in care who are allowed to keep undesirable associations and behave unreasonably with little degree of control. While in some cases this may be inevitable, there are others where an independent observer would have dealt with the child differently. Wardship might provide that extra necessary control. Secondly proceedings may ensure that the local authority have made adequate plans for the long term welfare of the child. The authority may also be forced to reveal information about which it would otherwise be secretive.

Under section 27(4) of the Children and Young Persons Act 1969 a local authority is obliged to review the position of a child in care every six months. Proceedings may reveal that the authority have not complied with their statutory duty. There is provision in the Children Act 1975 for regulations concerning reviews for children in care[16]. If these are breached the High Court may decide to exercise their wardship jurisdiction.

It may be appropriate to challenge the care of the local authority by way of wardship in cases where the authority have exercised their power by restricting the movements of a child in their care. There are cases where an application for discharge of a care order under section 21(2) of the 1969 Act could not be successful, perhaps because nobody but the authority could care for the child. If the authority acted unfairly towards such a child, wardship proceedings might be the only means of forcing the authority to implement their statutory duties to the full. Such an action could be founded on impropriety, and it would appear proceedings could be instituted either by the child (by a next friend) or by his parents.

In few cases can it be said that the local authority have clearly acted with impropriety or in disregard of their statutory duty. In many cases though it can be said that the

16. No regulations have yet been made, but powers exist in s.27(5) as inserted
    by s.108 and Sch. 3 para. 71 of the Children Act 1975.

local authority have not acted with complete precision throughout. They may have failed to take information into account or they may simply have been confused in reaching decisions. Practitioners would do well to bear in mind that an investigation may reveal matters, which would persuade a judge that he ought to review the local authority's handling of a case. Local authorities must equally realise how their work can come under scrutiny.

C. APPLICATION BY PARENTS

i) *Voluntary care*

Where a child is in care under section 1 of the Children Act 1948 and the local authority have not assumed parental rights, the parent is entitled to ask for the return of the child. In such cases there should be no difficulty as the local authority will normally comply with the request. It may be, however, that the authority either cannot or will not return the child, and in such cases the parent may be obliged to seek a court order requiring his return[17].

At first sight it would seem that the appropriate course of action ought to be to issue habeas corpus proceedings, but the cases now establish that such an action is unsuitable. In *Krishnan v London Borough of Sutton*[18], for example, the court refused a habeas corpus application by a father for the return of his child from care under section 1, because it would have required the local authority to enforce removal of the child from foster parents. More recently in *Re K (a minor)*[19] Bush J referred to an unreported decision in which Ormrod LJ said that the writ of habeas corpus had no place in the Family Division especially in proceedings concerning children.

As Bush J said it would be better to deal with such issues under the wardship jurisdiction. It should be said that even if wardship proceedings are instituted, the parent may not necessarily succeed since the ward's interests are first and paramount. In *Krishnan*, for example, wardship proceedings were brought, but after the evidence had been heard, the application was dismissed.

17. If the local authority do not seek an order first.
18. [1970] Ch 181, [1969] 3 All ER 1367.
19. [1978] L S Gaz R 711.

It might be thought that in view of these decisions the local authority need take no action, since the parent will be obliged to institute wardship proceedings to recover the child. However, at least where a serious request has been made, it would surely be bad practice not to take some action to enable plans for the child to be made, and failure to act may be a breach of statutory duty under section 12 of the Children Act 1948.

Wardship may occasionally be helpful to a parent who does not wish to take over the care of a child. In *Re G (infants)*[20], for example, two children were placed in care when their parents separated. The mother subsequently warded them when she was informed that the father wished to remove them from the jurisdiction, and later in the proceedings she sought access. Ungoed-Thomas J stated[1]:

> 'What I am concerned to achieve is that the Council should continue to have the statutory care of the children with the discretions which the statute confers unimpaired, but that the limitation to which that care and those discretions are subjected do not operate to the prejudice of the children; in other words the Council should continue to exercise their statutory care for such time as the statute provides, but that if that care is terminated or is in danger of termination in accordance with the statute, then the powers and discretion of this Court should immediately be brought to bear on the situation'.

He therefore made an order reciting that the children were in the care of the local authority under section 1, that the mother undertook not to remove them from care and the father was restrained from so doing, and provided for access to the parents at the discretion of the authority. The authority undertook to apply for directions before any change was made in care.

ii) *Compulsory care*

Where a resolution under section 2 of the Children Act 1948 has been passed vesting parental rights and duties in the local

20. [1963] 3 All ER 370.
 1. Ibid., at 374.

authority, or where a care order has been made under the Children and Young Persons Act 1969 the powers of the local authority are not transient. They continue until the child is eighteen, unless terminated by the procedure set out in those Acts.

The traditional approach has been that the exercise of the wardship jurisdiction is limited. This was established for section 2 cases in *Re M (an infant)*[2]. A child had been received into care under section 1 and boarded out with foster parents. Subsequently the local authority passed a resolution assuming parental rights. Three years later the authority asked for the child to be handed over to them, which request was refused. In response to habeas corpus proceedings by the authority the foster mother warded the child. The court refused to exercise its wardship jurisdiction on the basis that it would not interfere with the proper exercise by the authority of powers vested in them by Parliament.

Re M was followed in *Re T (AJJ) (an infant)*[3] where a child was the subject of a fit person order[4]. There the local authority decided to return the child to his natural mother after he had been placed with foster parents, who then refused to comply and made the child a ward of court. Dismissing the appeal from the refusal of the Chancery Court to exercise jurisdiction, the Court of Appeal compared the local authority powers under the 1948 Act and the 1933 Act and said[5]:

> 'It would indeed be anomalous if the Chancery Court were to decline jurisdiction in the one case but assert it in the other, when in each case the local authority is firmly in the saddle, merely because a different mounting block has been used.'

Both these cases were applications by foster parents wishing to prevent the removal of a child from their care, but it has always been thought that the same principles applied to applications by parents. These decisions, however, now have to be seen in the light of the leading decision in *Re H (a minor)*[6].

2. [1961] Ch 328.
3. [1970] Ch 688.
4. The statutory predecessor of a care order.
5. [1970] Ch 688 at 694.
6. *Re H (a minor) (wardship: jurisdiction)* [1978] Fam 65, [1978] 2 All ER 903.

a) Re H (a minor)

A care order under the Children and Young Persons Act 1969 had been made in respect of a girl in August 1976, after she had received a non-accidental injury. The parents wished to return to their home country with her and their other children, but instead of seeking discharge of the care order under section 21(2) of the 1969 Act, they instituted wardship proceedings seeking care and control of the child and leave to remove her from the jurisdiction. At first instance Balcombe J held, notwithstanding *Re M* and *Re T(AJJ)*, that he was entitled to exercise the wardship jurisdiction because of the special circumstances of the case. Accordingly he gave leave for the ward to be taken permanently out of the country, but stipulated that until she left the jurisdiction she was to remain a ward and in the care of the local authority under section 7 of the Family Law Reform Act 1969[7].

The decision to exercise jurisdiction was upheld by the Court of Appeal but on a different basis. A distinction was drawn between challenging the exercise of a discretionary power and challenging the source of that power. In the latter case it was held that *Re M* and *Re T(AJJ)* did not apply, but instead as Ormrod LJ said[8]:

'the dominant consideration is the welfare of this particular child, but it must be shown that the circumstances are sufficiently unusual to justify the intervention of the High Court.'

In reaching this decision Ormrod LJ made two observations about the decisions in *Re M* and *Re T(AJJ)*. First, although the applicants were foster parents in those cases, the effect had been to leave the natural parents without any means of challenging a local authority decision to make various arrangements for the child. Secondly, no mention of the welfare of the child as the paramount consideration was made in the decisions. While not intending to cast doubt on the binding effect of those decisions, 'at the present time', Orm-

---

7. It is notable that Balcombe J actually made an order committing the child to the care of the local authority under s.7, thereby superseding the care order under the Children and Young Persons Act 1969. It is not clear whether such action would automatically discharge the order, or whether in the event of the child returning to this country after termination of the wardship, she would still be subject to the care order.
8. [1978] Fam at 76, [1978] 2 All ER at 909.

rod LJ considered that these observations were sufficient to discourage extension of the reasoning of those cases to challenging the source of the power.

The High Court would not necessarily allow the source of power to be challenged in wardship. Ormrod LJ referred to the type of considerations which might be relevant in deciding whether to exercise the jurisdiction, such as:

(1) Whether the powers of the juvenile court (and presumably he might have added the powers of the local authority) are adequate to protect the interests of the child or whether the wider powers of the High Court are necessary, e.g. to grant injunctions[9].

(2) Whether the interests of the child would be better served by the more flexible type of care order possible under section 7 of the Family Law Reform Act 1969.

(3) Whether wardship would provide a better forum considering procedural matters such as facilities for trial and the rules governing appeals.

(4) Whether the High Court may be a more suitable venue for cases involving a large body of evidence or conflicting views of evidence[10].

The approach laid down by *Re H* would seem to justify the earlier decision in *Re Cullimore (a minor)*[11]. That case concerned a 15 month old girl who early in life had had diagnosed a condition known as brittle bones. After further injuries care proceedings were taken in the juvenile court and a supervision order made. When more injuries were discovered a place of safety order was taken, but the father then made the child a ward of court to have the matter reviewed. The issue before the court was whether the several fractures suffered by the ward were the result of non-accidental injury caused by the parents or by reason of the fact that the child suffered from brittle bones. It was held, after a five day hearing, that on the balance of probabilities the child was

---

9. As in *Re B (a minor)* [1975] Fam 36, [1974] 3 All ER 915.
10. Ibid., at 76 and 909 respectively. (3) and (4) had hitherto only been used as factors in influencing local authority decisions to use wardship. Ormrod LJ seems to be prepared to develop these arguments more widely.
11. (1976) Times, 24 March.

suffering from brittle bones and accordingly the place of safety order was discharged. However, whilst care and control was granted to the parents, the wardship order was continued to enable the Official Solicitor to act as the child's guardian ad litem.

It appears that no issue was taken on the point of jurisdiction, but the exercise of it may be justified on the basis that like *Re H*, the father in *Re Cullimore* was challenging the source of power given by the place of safety order. The case could also be regarded as 'unusual'[12], justifying the exercise of the jurisdiction, in view of its complexity and probable length of hearing.

b) Commentary

Re H is the first case in which the court has allowed wardship to be used to supersede the statutory scheme. It may be considered a logical extension of *Re D (a minor)*[13] which established that a local authority could ward a child after the discharge of a care order. Indeed, one of the arguments which persuaded the court to exercise jurisdiction was that the local authority might in any event have warded the child, if the juvenile court had discharged the order. Therefore, the decision in *Re H* puts the parent in the same position as the local authority in being able to have recourse to the prerogative jurisdiction.

Logical and apparently justifiable as this step may be, it is nevertheless a very significant extension of the use of the jurisdiction. The immediate consequence may be that parents will use wardship as a means of having a care order discharged rather than use the statutory scheme[14]. Such applications may be additionally attractive in that, unlike an application to discharge under section 21(2) of the 1969 Act, a parent will be able to have his own interests fully represented[15].

The implications of *Re H* go beyond the danger that wardship will be used instead of the statutory scheme. Indeed,

---

12. Ormrod LJ in *Re H* suggested that unusual circumstances were a prerequisite to exercising jurisdiction.
13. *Re D (a minor) (justices' decision: review)* [1977] Fam 158, [1977] 3 All ER 481.
14. S.21(2) Children and Young Persons Act 1969.
15. See discussion ante p. 286.

the basis of the decision gives rise to serious cause for concern, since it may provide an opportunity for far wider development. Much will depend on how liberally the courts interpret 'the unusual circumstances' which would justify their intervention. Certainly the circumstances considered sufficiently unusual by Ormrod LJ would seem to pave the way for a wide variety of applications. In particular, the suggestion that a sufficiently unusual consideration to justify the intervention of the High Court could be the opportunity of making a more flexible type of order is bound to encourage more wardship applications.

A parent wishing to challenge a decision by the local authority over access might be advised to apply to have the care order set aside (so challenging the source of power) and argue that the child would benefit from the more flexible committal to care by the High Court under section 7 of the Family Law Reform Act 1969. Before reaching a decision on this the court might have to conduct a fairly thorough investigation. If reason was found for the use of wardship the court would then have to continue to exercise its jurisdiction, but even if it did not, it would have heard all the evidence, and the object of limiting the exercise of the jurisdiction would have been defeated. It can be seen that there could be a cumulative effect, so that the more the court became involved in the case, the more likely it is to exercise the jurisdiction.

A further implication of the decision is to throw doubt on the decisions in *Re M* and *Re T (AJJ)*, so that it may even be possible for a parent openly to challenge the exercise of local authority discretion. This possibility may be implied from Ormrod LJ's observation that the natural parents would otherwise be left without any means of challenging a local authority's decision. It is interesting, though, that the examples he gives all concern extreme circumstances such as denial of access, and it is submitted that such a conflict would be better resolved by requiring the local authority to show that it had acted in accordance with its statutory duty in making the welfare of the child its first consideration.

Whether the court will be prepared to expand the exercise of the jurisdiction remains to be seen, but it should be pointed out that the facts of *Re H* were particularly unusual. The court took the view that the juvenile court would have been unable to discharge the care order since they could not be satisfied that the child would receive proper care and control[16], whereas in wardship the judge could balance the risks and make the best possible order. This was especially important in view of the family's desire to return to Pakistan[17].

In the light of the facts in *Re H* it should not be assumed that the court will be readily disposed to extend its jurisdiction[18]. It would be all too easy to argue that a more flexible type of order would be advantageous to the child. It is certainly questionable whether on that basis all such cases should be transferred to the High Court. This would not only overburden the wardship jurisdiction, but could also have distinct disadvantages for the planning by local authorities for children in their care[19]. In our submission, therefore, the point has now been reached at which the court must consider carefully how far it wishes to open up the activities of local authorities to review and the basis on which this should be done. This is the subject of further discussion in the final part of this chapter[20].

16. S.21(2A) of the Children and Young Persons Act 1969, as inserted by s.108 and Sch. 3 para. 69 of the Children Act 1975, provides: 'A juvenile court shall not make an *order* under subsection (2) of this section in the case of a person who has not attained the age of 18 and appears to the court to be in need of care and control unless the court is satisfied that, whether through the making of a supervision order or otherwise, he will receive that care or control.' [Emphasis added.] It is not clear whether '*order*' refers to a supervision order or an order to discharge a care order. Dunn J in *Re D (a minor)* assumed that it was an order discharging a care order, and the Court of Appeal in *Re H* took the same view. However, it is by no means certain that s.21(2) requires a juvenile court to make any order, unless it is making a supervision order. It could be that the intention of the subsection was to prevent a juvenile court making a supervision order where the local authority could not adequately supervise a child, and the section as a whole is at least open to that interpretation.
17. The local authority could have arranged for the emigration of the child with the consent of the Secretary of State under s.17 of the Children Act 1948.
18. Where, for example, an application is made because the family wishes to leave the country, the court will wish to be certain that their desire is genuine.
19. It will be essential for local authorities, if they so wish, to make an objection to the exercise of the jurisdiction as soon as possible after issue of the proceedings. Any delay will mean that the court is more likely to investigate the merits of the case, especially if the Official Solicitor has been asked to represent the child and prepare a report. See *Re D (a minor)* (1978) Times, February 14.
20. See post p. 320.

iii) *Use of wardship in relation to parental rights*

We have seen that in principle a parent may still not use wardship to challenge the lawful exercise of a discretion vested in the local authority by virtue of the Children Act 1948 or the Children and Young Persons Act 1969. This principle is limited to matters which are within the exclusive discretion of the authority, so that wardship can be used to challenge any action which falls outside the scope of their powers. The precise scope of local authority powers[1] is uncertain, and we shall be concerned to comment on five particular issues.

It must be pointed out that even if a parent is successful in invoking the wardship jurisdiction that would not necessarily mean that his so-called 'right' would be upheld, since the court would be concerned with the welfare of the child.

a) **The right to consent to marriage**

While the Registrar of Marriages requires the consent of the local authority if the child is subject to a care order or a resolution, it is not clear that the parents are in all circumstances excluded. Although on the wording of section 3 and Schedule 2 of the Marriage Act 1949 and section 2(11) of the Children Act 1948, it would seem to be the better view that the right to consent passes to the authority rather than accrues to the authority in addition to the parent, the point is untested[2]. On this approach it would not be possible to use wardship. It is submitted, however, that it would be bad local

---

1. The only clear distinction that can be drawn is that in respect of a child in care the local authority always has the powers in ss.12–17 of the Children Act 1948, but that if the parental rights have been assumed under s.2 or there is a care order under the 1969 Act, the powers are more extensive. It must be doubted whether Ormrod LJ's comment in *Re H*, that the local authority has the right to control the child after a resolution has been passed, implying that they have no right before, is correct, since they do have the powers in ss.12, 13 to take decisions for the child, subject to the right of the parent to remove the child from care. See generally
J M Eekelaar, 'What are Parental Rights?' (1973) 89 LQR 210 and
J M Thomson: 'Local Authorities and Parental Rights' (1974) 90 LQR 310 and (1975) 91 LQR 14.
2. Lord Evershed MR in *Re M (an infant)* [1961] Ch 328, [1961] 1 All ER 788 thought that marriage might come outside the local authority powers, but this would appear to be incorrect, at least since s.2(11) was introduced by s.57 of the Children Act 1975.

authority practice not to consult the parent, unless the welfare of the child required otherwise.

b) The right to change the child's name

A local authority has a limited power to execute a statutory declaration on behalf of a child applying for a change of name, where a resolution under section 2 of the 1948 Act is in force[3]. There is, however, no authority for changing the name without the consent of the parents if they are alive, except through adoption or other court order. This may apply even to a change of name by repute. If no other proceedings were appropriate it would appear that a parent could apply in wardship if, for example, a foster parent changed the name of the child[4].

c) The right to make decisions about the child's property

Section 2(11) of the Children Act 1948 now specifically vests the property of a child in the local authority, where they have assumed rights and duties. There are no similar provisions for a care order. It would therefore appear that while the court could not entertain a wardship application in respect of property where the child is subject to a resolution, unless there was impropriety, it could do so if he was subject only to a care order.

d) The right to choose a child's religion

Under section 3(7) of the Children Act 1948 and section 24(3) of the Children and Young Persons Act 1969 a local authority has a duty not to cause the child to be brought up in any religious creed other than that in which he would have been brought up if there had been no resolution or order. If the child's religion is being changed the authority would not be acting in accordance with its statutory duty so that a parent could base an application in wardship on impropriety[5].

3. See Enrolment of Deeds (Change of Name) (Amendment) Regulations 1969.
4. It is not unusual for foster parents, like step parents, to wish to change a child's name to theirs, on the basis that it makes him part of the family and creates less difficulty at school. This may even be done without the local authority being aware of it. It is submitted that the cases on change of name generally are applicable, but these are conflicting. See e.g. *R(BM) v R(DN)* (*child: surname*) [1978] 1 All ER 33 sub nom *Rice v Rice* [1977] 1 WLR 1256, *D v B (otherwise D) (child: surname)* [1979] 1 All ER 92, [1979] 3 WLR 573 and cf. *Re W G* (1976) 6 Fam Law 210 and *L v F* (1978) Times, 1 August.
5. But see ante p. 276 n.7 for position on placing for adoption.

e) The right to access

Access is a controversial subject, in respect of which there is considerable uncertainty. However, although the courts have avoided defining precisely the nature of the powers vested in the local authority the cases do seem to suggest that in the absence of impropriety the court will not interfere with their decision about access.

The clearest pointer to this position is *Re Y (a minor)*[6]. It will be recalled[7] that the issue in that case was whether, in exercising its power in wardship proceedings in committing the ward to a local authority's care, the court was also empowered to make specific directions as to access. It was held that the court was so empowered since it is specifically provided that in such cases the local authority's powers 'shall be subject to any direction by the court'. At first instance Arnold J had held local authorities did not have the power to control access under sections 1, 12–14 of the Children Act 1948 and hence a judge in wardship proceedings was entitled to 'fill the gap'. Ormrod LJ rejected this reasoning holding that the local authority did have power to control access even under section 1, but that where a child had been committed to care by the court[8] such powers were subject to the court's control[9]. In reaching this decision Ormrod LJ commented[10]:

'I have not the slightest difficulty in understanding the anxiety of a local authority in relation to a decision which says in terms that in every case in which a child is in their care under s.1 of the 1948 Act they have no power to control access. I can fully understand their anxiety and their desire to get that decision, if possible, reversed; clearly it would lead to chaos in the administration of their highly responsible duties under the various Children Acts.'

There can surely be little argument with the conclusion that

6. *Re Y (a minor) (child in care: access)* [1976] Fam 125, [1975] 3 All ER 348.
7. See ante p. 90.
8. As in this case under s.7(2) of the Family Law Reform Act 1969, whereby the child is to be treated as if in care under s.1 of the Children Act 1948.
9. By s.7(3) the provisions of s.43(5) of the Matrimonial Causes Act 1973 are specifically applied to committal to care in wardship, and this makes the exercise of local authority powers in respect of a child in care 'subject to any directions given by the court'.
10. [1976] Fam at 140. This view is criticised by Freeman (1976) 6 Fam Law 136 sed quaere?

local authorities' powers under section 13(2) of the 1948 Act include the power to grant access.

If there is a power to grant access there must surely be a power to withhold it. Indeed, from the practical point of view it is essential for the authority to be able to limit access in so far as it is in the long term interests of the child, since the parent could otherwise thwart attempts to provide consistent and proper care for the child. If the local authority has the power to control access as against the parent, it would seem to follow that this is a discretion, with which the court will not interfere.

Unfortunately Ormrod LJ's decision in *Re Y* does not entirely settle the matter, because it is unclear whether local authorities are to be regarded as having *sole* control of access where there is no statutory provision making their powers subject to the directions of the court. The tenor of his judgment suggests that the matter is within their sole control, but it could be argued that this is obiter, since the case was only specifically concerned with the powers the court has for committing a child to care under section 7 of the Family Law Reform Act 1969. Accordingly, reference must be made to other decisions.

The other relevant cases, which concern applications by putative fathers, also support the view that access is a matter within the discretion of the local authority. In *Re O*[11], for example, a putative father warded his two children, who were in care under the 1969 Act, when foster parents with whom they had been placed applied to adopt them. Balcombe J held that he should not make any order as to access as that was within the discretion of the local authority.

A similar decision was reached in *Re K (an infant), Re M (infant), Hertfordshire County Council v H*[12] where a putative father applied under sections 9 and 14 of the Guardianship of Minors Act 1971 for access to his child in respect of whom the rights and duties of the mother had been assumed under section 2 of the 1948 Act. Although it was acknowledged that the putative father had no parental rights for the local authority to assume, and that under the 1971 Act he did have a right to apply for, inter alia, access, it was nevertheless held

11. (1978) 1 *Adoption and Fostering*.
12. [1972] 3 All ER 769.

that the court should not interfere in the absence of any impropriety[13]. As Payne J said[14]:

> 'Bearing in mind the existence of the order under s.2 of the Children Act 1948 it seems to me that the justices in the circumstances of this case had no alternative but to decline the application of the father and to leave the discretion with regard to access to the local authority.'

However, Payne J specifically avoided reaching a decision as to whether the court had *power* to make an order. This question did arise in *R v Oxford City Justices, ex parte H*[15]. The putative father applied for custody of his child under sections 9 and 14 of the Guardianship of Minors Act 1971 in the magistrates' court. The parental rights of the mother had been assumed under section 2 of the 1948 Act. The justices refused to hear his complaint and he sought an order of mandamus. The Divisional Court held that the magistrates should hear the case having in mind as the first and paramount consideration the welfare of the child in the light of all the relevant circumstances including the existence of the section 2 resolution. These two decisions are not easily reconciled, though Bagnall J suggested that there might be a difference between asking for custody and asking for access, since access was 'a matter which must necessarily be under the day to day control and discretion of the local authority'[16]

Despite these cases it has been argued that as access is a basic right of the child rather than the right of the parent, it is not a right taken over by the local authority[17]. The decision in *M v*

---

13. In *S v Huddersfield Borough Council* [1975] Fam 113, [1974] 3 All ER 296, Buckley LJ referred to *Re K*, commenting that it established that the discretion with regard to access lay with the local authority, but did not decide whether that was correct. In that case the court gave a father access to a child in care against the wishes of the local authority, during the period of an interim adoption order, on the basis that in adoption matters the legislation did not give local authorities any preference over the views of parents.

14. Ibid., at 772.

15. [1975] QB 1, [1974] 2 All ER 356.

16. Ibid., at 360. It is an unfortunate side effect of this decision that a putative father could acquire the right to remove his child without the local authority being heard on the matter. It is submitted that there should be a requirement to serve notice of the proceedings on the local authority and an opportunity given for them to be heard. They may, of course, have to resort to wardship to protect the child's interests.

17. See Thomson (1974) 90 LQR 310, 313.

M[18] has been cited as authority for this proposition. That was a case in which custody of a boy was granted to the husband with reasonable access to the wife. After some difficulties the husband prevented access, and the wife applied to the court. The magistrates' court held that it was in the boy's interests that access should at that time be discontinued. Wrangham J upheld this decision, and while accepting that access could be a basic right in the child he said[19]:

> 'That only means this, that no court should deprive a child of access to either parent unless it is wholly satisfied that it is in the interests of that child that access should cease, and that is a conclusion at which a court should be extremely slow to arrive.'

It is submitted that in respect of children in care, it is a conclusion which has to be made, if at all, by the local authority under the powers delegated to them, and the remarks may be taken as guidance for local authorities in the exercise of their discretion.

Although it is true that the statutes refer to parental rights, it must be acknowledged that it has now become inappropriate to think in such terms where the welfare of the child is concerned, so that it would be preferable to avoid basing decisions on such tehnical arguments. The technicalities are, however, avoided if the argument of Ormrod LJ in *Re Y* is accepted, that section 13(2) of the Children Act 1948 vests powers to control access in the local authority. There can be little satisfaction with a law which is so uncertain in such an important respect. Nevertheless, the general position of non-interference with access decisions seems perfectly justifiable. If the courts were able to review any decision about access, considerable uncertainty would result since no local authority decisions could be regarded as final. One of the difficulties in the general approach outlined is that it enables local authorities to deny access entirely, without giving any opportunity of challenging such action. Such a decision necessitates very careful consideration of the needs of the child and should only be taken after comprehensive plans for his future have been made. It must be absolutely clear that it is not in the interests of the child for him to have contact with the parent. If all these steps have been taken, then the local

18. [1973] 2 All ER 81.
19. Ibid., at 85.

authority will be properly exercising its discretion, and it is submitted is in as good a position to decide the matter as the court. If the local authority cannot demonstrate that it has acted properly in this respect, then this would be revealed on a preliminary application in wardship based on breach of statutory duty[20]. The power to intervene in such cases is arguably sufficient to safeguard the interests of aggrieved parents without causing serious inconvenience to local authorities. Hence it is submitted that on policy grounds alone the argument that a parent can have an access decision reviewed by the courts by invoking wardship, should be rejected.

D. APPLICATIONS BY PUTATIVE FATHERS

The position of a putative father requires separate consideration, since he is not within the contemplation of the statutory scheme. He cannot apply on behalf of the child for discharge of a care order under the 1969 Act nor require a child in care under section 1 of the 1948 Act to be handed over to him[1]. Furthermore, he does not have rights which can be assumed under section 2 of the 1948 Act. He does, however, have the right to apply for custody under the Guardianship of Minors Act 1971, which would for all these purposes put him in the same position as a parent.

We have seen that the court will probably not allow wardship to be used to challenge the exercise of local authority discretion over access[2]. Where the putative father seeks custody, however, in view of the decision in *R v Oxford City Justices, ex parte H*[3], he may not need wardship, since he could obtain custody in the lower courts. It is necessary to distinguish between the child in care under the 1948 Act and one in care under the 1969 Act. If the putative father applies for custody in respect of a child in care under the 1948 Act, the court can hear the case, having in mind as the first and paramount consideration, the welfare of the child in the light

20. The parent could then apply, alleging what we have broadly called impropriety. See ante p. 294.
 1. For the purposes of s.1(3) of the Children Act 1948, the putative father is a relative, by virtue of s.59, so that the local authority can, if they think it consistent with the welfare of the child, discharge the child to his care.
 2. See ante p. 311.
 3. [1975] QB 1, [1974] 2 All ER 356.

of all the circumstances[4], including the fact that the child is in care. If the rights and duties of the mother have been assumed under section 2 that is another consideration which the court can bear in mind.

If there is a care order the position is different because, even if the putative father obtained custody, he would not have any right to remove the child, but only to apply for discharge of the order on behalf of the child[5]. It is not clear from *Re H (a minor)*[6] whether the principles of that case would be extended to putative fathers, enabling them to challenge the source of the power. It would have the advantage of ensuring that the whole matter is decided on one application[7].

It may in any event be helpful to consider wardship for a putative father, since if he is making allegations of impropriety, these are best dealt with in the High Court, where if necessary the court can continue to supervise the matter.

Apart from the right to apply for custody and access the position of the putative father would appear to be the same as for third parties.

E. APPLICATIONS BY THIRD PARTIES

The circumstances in which third parties are likely to make a successful wardship application against a local authority are rather more limited. The applicants may be foster parents, relatives, or any other person having an interest in the child. All of these will have difficulties persuading the court to interfere with the local authority decision if the child is in care.

i) *Foster parents*

Foster parent applications require the most careful consideration. There is an increasing emphasis on the role of a

---

4. S.1 of the Guardianship of Minors Act 1971, as amended by s.36(1)(a) of the Domestic Proceedings and Magistrates' Courts Act 1978, will apply in such a case.
5. S.21(2) and s.70(2) of the Children and Young Persons Act 1969.
6. [1978] Fam 65, [1978] 2 All ER 903. See ante p. 302 for discussion of the case.
7. If the domestic court were to take over care proceedings in addition to custody, the case could be heard by magistrates rather than in the High Court. In those areas where the juvenile court comprises the same personnel as the magistrates' court it is not unknown for them to decide both matters at the same hearing.

foster parent and a greater understanding of their role as 'psychological' parent for many children. Through organisations such as the National Foster Care Association, they are becoming more aware that they may have power to influence decisions taken about the future of the child they foster. In particular they do have an interest[8] in that child and can therefore apply to make him a ward. Whether the court will exercise its wardship jurisdiction will depend to a large extent on whether the child is in voluntary care or compulsory care.

a) Voluntary care

An important limitation of the powers of the local authority in respect of a child received into care under section 1 of the Children Act 1948 is that they are transient, as they end immediately the parent requests the return of the child pursuant to section 1(3). At first this limitation did not appear significant. In *Re A B (an infant)*[9], for example, a child was received into care under section 1 and boarded out to foster parents. Subsequently the putative father married another woman; the couple wanted the care of the child and the mother supported them. The foster parents did not wish to return the child, and so the local authority commenced habeas corpus proceedings. Although the authority would have been prepared to leave the child with the foster parents, they took the view that section 1(3) obliged them to recover the child and return him in accordance with the mother's wishes. Lord Goddard CJ decided first that the authority were bound to arrange for the mother to have the child, and secondly that the foster parents had no answer to the local authority's demand for the child to be given up.

In the later case of *Re K R (an infant)*[10], however, the court decided to exercise its wardship jurisdiction. In that case a child was received into care under section 1 and placed immediately with foster parents, but four years later the mother expressed her desire to the local authority to take over the care of the child pursuant to section 1(3). The foster parents and the authority jointly applied to make a child a ward and asked for care and control to be given to the foster parents. The mother contended that in view of her request she

8. See ante p. 37.
9. [1954] 2 QB 385, [1954] 2 All ER 287.
10. [1964] Ch 455, [1963] 3 All ER 337.

had an unchallengeable right to the possession of her child and accordingly sought to have the child dewarded and returned to her. Her request was rejected and Pennycuick J said[11]:

> 'Once the notice had been given, it is I think clear, not only that the common law rights of the mother revive but also that the jurisdiction of this court in relation to the infant becomes fully effective. Accordingly it must be open to any person interested to apply to this court for an order concerning the care and control of the infant'.

He declined to deward the child and ordered that the case should be heard on its merits.

This approach was affirmed by the Court of Appeal in *Re S (an infant)*[12] which again concerned a child received into care under section 1 and boarded out to foster parents. Six years later the mother asked to take over the care of the child and considering themselves bound to comply with the request, the authority proposed to place the child in a residential school with regular access to the mother and her husband. In response to this the foster parents warded the child, but no hearing was sought for another four years, by which time the boy was ten. It was held on appeal that the court did have jurisdiction to hear the case. Lord Denning MR said[13]:

> 'It seems to me to be very important that the jurisdiction of the Court of Chancery over its wards should be maintained, even when a local authority has taken a child into its care under section 1. The reason is because the statute gives to the natural parent the right to demand that the local authority give the child up to him or her, if he or she desires to take over the care of the child. *The imminence of such a demand is a very relevant consideration.* Their care may be terminated at any moment. That puts the welfare of the child at peril. The child must be taken away from a good home with foster parents, and removed to a very undesirable home with the child's natural parents who the child does not know in the least. In order to avoid this peril and to secure the welfare of

11. [1963] 3 All ER at 342.
12. [1965] 1 All ER 865.
13. Ibid., at 868.

the child, the jurisdiction of this Court must be maintained'. [Emphasis added.]

It is to be noted that *Re S* goes further than *Re K R* in that, although it was unclear whether the mother had actually expressed a desire to take over the care of the child, it was nevertheless held that the *imminence* of the demand might be sufficient to allow the court to exercise its jurisdiction. Furthermore, unlike *Re K R*, in *Re S* the foster parents were the sole applicants, though it must be added that there was no evidence to suggest that the local authority thought that it was ever in the child's best interests to be returned to the parents. Rather their suggestions for the child's future were prompted by their belief that they were powerless to do otherwise in view of the mother's request.

The fact that the authority felt bound to act seems to make the case similar to *Re A B*[14]. Nevertheless Lord Denning MR felt able to distinguish that case. As he said[15]:

'That case was within the second part of section 1(3) in that it "appeared to" the local authority to be consistent with the welfare of the child for the child to be taken over by the couple. It was therefore the duty of the local authority to secure this; and it was a proper case for habeas corpus to issue in aid of this duty. That was sufficient for the decision of the case. I cannot regard the case of *Re A B (an infant)* as authority for the proposition that, in cases that fall within section 1 of the Children Act 1948, the prerogative power of the court is ousted'.

While it is questionable on the facts whether Lord Denning MR was correct in his interpretation of *Re A B*, the implication of his distinction is that the court even in wardship proceedings will not interfere where a local authority has sought the return of a child because they feel that it is consistent with his welfare. Such a distinction is in line with the traditional view that the courts should not interfere with the proper exercise of a discretion by the local authority.

It should be noted that the principle established by *Re K R* and *Re S* is limited to either where the parent has made a request for the return of the child or where such a request is

14. [1954] 2 QB 385, [1954] 2 All ER 287.
15. [1965] 1 All ER at 868.

imminent. Where no request is made the position of foster parents as against the local authority would appear to be the same as if the child is in compulsory care.

b) Compulsory care

Where the child is in compulsory care the position is governed by *Re M (an infant)*[16] and *Re T(AJJ) (an infant)*[17] which establish that the court will not interfere with the proper exercise of a local authority discretion. These cases of course put foster parents in an extremely weak position and it is therefore important to establish as early as possible what line the local authority will take. If, for example, they support the foster parent as against the parent, then recourse can be had to wardship, possibly by a joint application. Wardship may still be invoked if the local authority, while not supporting the application, do not actually oppose it[18]. If, however, the authority are opposed to the foster parents, then in the absence of impropriety or other special circumstances a wardship application is unlikely to be successful.

It is possible that the court will be prepared in the light of *Re H (a minor)*[19] to reconsider the position established by *Re M* and *Re T(AJJ)*. It is questionable, however, whether foster parents can expect an extension of the powers of review, since the Court of Appeal seemed to have in mind the position of parents.

Even though *Re M* and *Re T(AJJ)* do apply, foster parents will be able to use wardship if they can prove impropriety[20]. In this respect authorities should be wary of misleading foster parents. For example, leading them to expect that there are good prospects of adopting the child, when in fact there are not, has been held as sufficient grounds for exercising the wardship jurisdiction. Equally if there has been no planning and the foster parents' relationship with the child has been allowed to drift for a long period, it may be alleged that the local authority has not fulfilled its duty to promote and safeguard the welfare of the child throughout his childhood in accordance with section 12 of the Children Act 1948. This

16. [1961] Ch 328, [1961] 1 All ER 788.
17. [1970] Ch 688, [1970] 2 All ER 865.
18. It would seem that they are failing in their statutory duty if they have no view on the matter.
19. [1978] Fam 65, [1978] 2 All ER 903.
20. See ante p. 294.

may be sufficient to show that the local authority has acted in breach of its statutory duty.

ii) *Relatives*

For the most part relatives are in the same position as foster parents, save that the local authority has a duty under section 1(3) of the 1948 Act to consider whether it is in the interests of the child for him to be discharged to relatives. For this purpose 'relatives' includes the putative father[1].

It is to be noted, however, that wardship cannot be used simply to review a decision not to act under the second limb. This is demonstrated by *Re C(A)(an infant)*[2], where a putative father sought to ward a child who had been received into care under section 1 and boarded out to foster parents, so that he could take him out of the jurisdiction. The local authority opposed the application and it was held that as the evidence, that the authority was completely satisfied that the child's welfare was best served by his remaining in care, was unchallenged, the court could not exercise its wardship jurisdiction without conflicting with or encroaching on the local authority's sphere of discretion. Accordingly, the court ordered the child to be dewarded.

If, however, the authority fail to give adequate consideration to their duty under section 1(3), even in passing a section 2 resolution, the court may be disposed to exercise its jurisdiction. In *Re D (a minor)*[3] a child who had been abandoned by his mother after birth lived with his putative father until he was six. When his father died he was received into care and boarded out with a woman who had been engaged to the putative father. The father's sister and her husband wished to take over the care of the child, but the authority refused to give them the care and assumed the rights of the mother. Balcombe J exercised the jurisdiction, partly on the basis that in passing the resolution assuming the rights, the local authority had not considered the possible alternatives, which could presumably have included discharge to relatives.

1. S.59 of the Children Act 1948.
2. [1966] 1 All ER 560, [1966] 1 WLR 415.
3. (1978), Times, February 14, 122 Sol Jo 193.

iii) *Other persons*

There are unlikely to be many circumstances in which other persons wish to dispute the exercise of local authority powers[4]. In so far as they may wish to take over the care of the child, their position is similar to that of foster parents, except of course that their relationship is likely to be much more tenuous. In so far as they wish to influence other decisions in respect of the child, it would seem to depend on whether it is a matter within the discretion of the authority. If it is, the court will be reluctant to exercise jurisdiction unless there is impropriety, but if the matter is outside the control of the local authority, probably wardship could be invoked.

IV A basis for the relationship of wardship and local authorities

We have adverted on a number of occasions to the need to reach a decision on the degree to which the High Court will use wardship to review the activities of other courts or bodies who have powers in the sphere of child welfare. As has been seen from many of the cases in this chapter, it is no less of a problem where the conflict lies between local authorities and wardship. Two major policy problems are central to the discussion. First, since Parliament has by statute delegated certain powers to local authorities and juvenile courts, how far is it proper for the courts to interfere with the exercise of those powers? If they go too far the effect may be to undermine other jurisdictions. Furthermore, the court cannot adequately deal with all the cases that would arise if they undertook wide powers of review. We must therefore ask where should the lines be drawn. *Re M (an infant)*[5] provided quite clear guidelines for the exercise of wardship in relation to local authorities' powers, but, as Ormrod LJ pointed out in *Re H (a minor)*[6], it failed to consider the application of what was then section 1 of the Guardianship of Infants Act 1925.

---

4. There are now, however, a number of organisations concerned to protect the interests of children in care. Their most hopeful use of wardship might be to try to extend the boundaries of impropriety, and thereby improve the standards of local authority care.
5. [1961] Ch 328, [1961] 1 All ER 788.
6. [1978] Fam 65, [1978] 2 All ER 903.

Unfortunately, the Court of Appeal in *Re H* failed in any detail to consider the application of what is now section 1 of the Guardianship of Minors Act 1971, and the extent to which the welfare of the child is the first and paramount consideration in wardship. At first instance in *Re H* Balcombe J took the course of considering the matter in two stages. He said[7]:

> 'It seems to me that the first question I have to consider is whether there are special circumstances to justify the court exercising its jurisdiction in wardship, notwithstanding the jurisdiction of the juvenile court to discharge the care order in respect of the child'.

Having decided that the circumstances did justify the exercise of the wardship jurisdiction he said:

> 'Accordingly I proceed to consider what course will best promote the welfare of the child, which I am directed by statute to regard as the first and paramount consideration'.

The Court of Appeal made no such distinctions and considered that phrases such as 'special circumstances' or 'special reasons' were not very helpful, it being necessary to discern the principles underlying the cases. The important principle in these circumstances is whether section 1 applies to the decision to review other jurisdictions and that has not been answered.

If the argument of Ormrod LJ in *Re H (a minor)*[8] is followed, section 1 would seem to apply, but the court must first be satisfied that there are 'unusual circumstances'. It would still be open to the court to decide not to exercise the jurisdiction on the basis that there were no unusual circumstances. The extent of those unusual circumstances would remain to be decided. This seems a strange method of limiting first and paramount, which of its nature should mean it is the governing factor. Alternatively the courts could decide that section 1 applied, and fulfil the requirement by not reviewing cases except where a clear need for wardship was demonstrated. A preliminary application to prove this need could provide the necessary safeguards against improper use. This approach could be justified on the basis that multiplicity of proceedings is contrary to the interests of

7. [1978] Fam at 69.
8. Ibid.

the child. A third possibility is to place a narrow construction on the meaning of 'legal custody and upbringing', so that it does not include the decision whether or not to exercise the jurisdiction, where there is a conflict with a local authority. It is submitted that this would provide a clearer rationale, which could be applied to the other areas of conflict of jurisdiction. It is also in line with the approach adopted by Balcombe J in *Re H*. By this means the court will be less obliged to intervene, but will retain the discretion to do so, and it will be possible to balance interests and apply the appropriate weight where it is required.

In a jurisdiction like wardship where the central concern is the child, his interests will of course still be of the utmost importance, but the proposed limitation may provide the basis for a modern appraisal of the problems of the relationships between the High Court, the inferior courts and local authorities. This approach is not without precedent since Lord McDermott in *S v McC, W v W*[9] distinguished between the 'custodial' jurisdiction and the 'protective' jurisdiction. In the former, section 1 is clearly applicable, but in the latter the court is, initially at least, concerned to protect the child. Whether the protection should be given depends on an assessment of various interests, and if they conflict they have to be weighed. When deciding how to carry out its functions as a guardian, the issues are clearly questions within the ambit of legal custody and upbringing and therefore require the welfare of the child to be given first and paramount consideration. When the court is deciding whether to *become* a guardian and provide a child with the benefit of wardship, it may properly be said that the court is exercising a protective jurisdiction.

The second issue which causes concern is the extent to which wardship may be used to avoid the limitations imposed by statute. If statute provides a basis for the exercise of powers by one body in certain matters, it may be questioned whether that body should then seek to evade the established scheme by recourse to another system[10]. In our view it is justifiable because of the importance of the welfare of the child, but careful consideration needs to be given to

9. [1972] AC 24. Discussed in Chap. 6.
10. E.g. a local authority using wardship as a simple preference to the Children and Young Persons Act 1969.

whether a child's best interests are served by preferring wardship to the statutory procedures. It will be a matter for the legal advisers of local authorities to weigh all the factors involved in each case. It will also be essential for the technical disadvantages created by statutory procedures to be removed so that cases can be properly heard in the lower courts.

Chapter 12

Kidnapping

I Introduction

In the course of a matrimonial dispute it not infrequently happens that one parent removes the child from the other either against the other's will or without the other's knowledge. The problem is most acute when the child is surreptitiously removed from one jurisdiction to another but the dispute need not involve an international element. To the 'aggrieved' parent the disappearance of his child is equally distressing and a matter of urgency whether the child is believed to be within the jurisdiction or not.

The problem of the unilateral removal of a child by one parent from another is variously referred to as 'child snatching' or 'kidnapping'. For convenience we have entitled the chapter 'Kidnapping' though it should be understood that a parent would not actually be guilty of the crime of kidnapping since he has a prima facie right to the possession of his child[1].

It is proposed to discuss first the problems arising exclusively within the jurisdiction and then to consider the international problem.

II Problems arising exclusively within the jurisdiction

The removal or threatened removal of a child by one parent from another potentially raises two issues. First the aggrieved parent may wish to discover his child's whereabouts and secondly he may wish to take steps to prevent his child's

1. He may, however, be guilty of contempt of court. See Chap. 7.

removal from the jurisdiction. In either event it may be advantageous to invoke the wardship jurisdiction.

A. TRACING A WARD

As in the case of missing children generally, a parent can attempt to trace a 'snatched child' without court intervention both by contacting the police and by seeking the help of government departments, notably the Department of Health and Social Security. In such cases it is discretionary both for the police and DHSS to assist in tracing missing children[2]. In practice, however, difficulty may be encountered in obtaining confidential information from the DHSS[3]. One advantage of invoking wardship is that there are formal arrangements both with government departments and the police for tracing a missing ward. Indeed in so far as they relate to children[4] the formal arrangements with the government departments only apply to tracing wards of court. Wardship has further advantages over other proceedings in that the parties are required[5] to state the whereabouts of the ward if known to them and the court has summary power to order any person who might have information of the ward's whereabouts to attend the hearing and give evidence[6]. Finally as in other High Court proceedings the services of the Tipstaff can be obtained to trace missing wards.

i) *The services of the Tipstaff and assistance by the police*

As has been mentioned elsewhere[7], pursuant to RSC Order 90, rule 3A the court can order the Tipstaff to secure compliance with any direction relating to a ward of court. The Tipstaff's services are commonly used to trace missing wards. In this respect he works closely with the police.

2. See the statement of Dr Shirley Summerskill in the debate on the Mark Allingham case. H. C. Debs, Vol. 946 Col. 1844.
3. This was the experience of Mrs Allingham. See H. C. Debs, Vol. 946, Col. 1843.
4. Cf. tracing missing husbands against whom a maintenance order is made. See below.
5. By RSC Ord. 90, r.3(4)(5) and (6). See Chap. 4.
6. See e.g. *Rosenberg v Lindo* (1883) 48 LT 478 and *Ramsbotham v Senior* (1869) LR 8 Eq 575. Failure to do so amounts to a contempt. See Chap. 7.
7. Chap. 5.

The formal co-operation of the police in this respect is a relatively recent development[8]. Formerly their assistance was not available on an official basis except where the child was thought to be in danger or in need of care or where the order for the return of the child was coupled with a committal order against the absconding parent. Since 1973, however, it has been agreed that whenever the Tipstaff requests the police for assistance in tracing a child, whose return has been ordered by the High Court, a description of the child and brief details of the relevant circumstances should be included in the Police Gazette by the force from whose area the child had been taken and inquiries should be made by the police in the area where the child was thought to be. These arrangements are described in the following terms by a Home Office Circular[9]:

'The circulation should expressly state that the police have no power of detention unless a committal order exists or the [child] is found in conditions where section 1 of the Children and Young Persons Act 1969 apply. If the [child] is traced, the Tipstaff should be informed immediately so that he can enforce the High Court order. . . . The length of time an entry remains in circulation in the Police Gazette is a matter for the Chief Officer of Police concerned, who may like to ensure that the Tipstaff is consulted before any entries are cancelled'.

The usual procedure upon being directed to trace a missing ward is for the Tipstaff to contact A 7 Division (by telephone in cases of emergency) to register the child as a missing person and to circulate the relevant information about the child. The Tipstaff himself will be on 24 hour call to receive any information that the police may have and will personally travel to obtain custody of any child found. Upon discovery of the child the common practice will be to inform the other parent or his solicitor. Where care and control has already been granted the child may be delivered to that person.

8. The following account is largely taken from the English and Scottish Law Commissions' joint working paper: *Custody of Children—Jurisdiction and Enforcement within the United Kingdom* 1976, Law Com. Working Paper No. 68 and Scots Law Com. Memorandum No. 23, paras. 6.29–6.30.
9. Home Office Circular No. 174/1973, paras. 4 and 5.

ii) *Assistance by government departments*

Formal arrangements for enlisting the help of government agencies to trace a missing ward are provided for by a 1973 *Practice Direction*[10]. It is to be noted that though the direction also applies to tracing missing husbands against whom a maintenance order has been made it does not apply to tracing children who are the subject of custody orders. In such cases, however, it may be possible to seek help on an informal basis[11].

The arrangements under the *Practice Direction* are as follows.

Application should be made to the court which may then request the address of a missing person or the person with whom he is said to be, from the records of the Department of Health and Social Security, Passport Office or Ministry of Defence. The request to the department will be made officially by the registrar and should certify that the child is the subject of wardship proceedings and cannot be traced, and, if appropriate, that he is believed to be with the person whose address is sought.

The most likely source of information is the Department of Health and Social Security, as their records are the most comprehensive. The department will not supply an address unless it is satisfied that the person sought has been reliably identified. It is therefore important that the solicitor should give the registrar as much as possible of the following information: national insurance number, surname, full Christian (or fore) names, date of birth (or, if not known, approximate age), last known address, with date when living there, any other known addresses with dates, and if the person sought is a war pensioner, his war pension and service particulars. A search will be made on the basis of a person's full names and date of birth, but the chances of accurate

10. [1973] 1 All ER 61 and see Supreme Court Practice 1979 p. 1345.
11. Even so it is difficult to justify why custody orders are excluded from the arrangements especially as the Law Commissions in their joint working paper on *Custody of Children—Jurisdiction and Enforcement within the United Kingdom*, ibid., at para. 6.40 in custody proceedings as in wardship the welfare of the child is the paramount consideration. The Commissions propose that the facilities be available to trace the whereabouts of a missing child in respect of whom a custody order has been made by a supreme court in the United Kingdom and of the person with whom he is alleged to be.

identification are increased by the provision of more identifying information.

A search may also be made in respect of persons registered for general medical service in the National Health Service. As much as possible of the information above and the National Health Service number if known should be provided. The address at which the person was living when he last registered for medical service should be disclosed.

In both cases it is unlikely that a person can be traced quickly through these procedures, since he may not immediately need to notify a change of address. Second searches may be made after a reasonable interval.

If these and other reasonable inquiries have failed to reveal the correct address, or if there are strong grounds for believing that the person sought may have made a recent application for a passport, inquiries may be made to the Passport Office. The following information should be provided: surname, full Christian (or fore) names, exact date of birth (or, if not known, approximate age), place of birth, occupation, whether known to have travelled abroad, and if so destination and dates, last known address, with date living there, and any other known addresses with dates.

The solicitor must also send a written undertaking that information given in response to the inquiry will be used solely for the purpose of tracing a missing ward, or the person with whom he is thought to be living. Although it is not specified in the *Practice Direction*, presumably this must include purposes in connection with the wardship proceedings, such as service of notice of proceedings or a subpoena on the person sought.

Where the person sought is known to be serving or have recently served in the armed forces, the solicitor may obtain the address for the purposes of wardship proceedings direct from the service department. His request for information should be accompanied by a written undertaking that the address will be used by him solely for the service of process and will not be disclosed to the applicant or any other person except in the normal course of proceedings. If an applicant is acting in person, the service department will disclose the address of the person sought to the registrar on receipt of an assurance that the applicant has given an undertaking that the information will be used solely for the purpose of serving process in the proceedings.

The following information should be provided: surname, full Christian (or fore) names, service number, date of birth (or, if not known, age), rank and, in the case of a soldier, regiment or corps, date of entry into the service, and if no longer serving, date of discharge, any other information such as last known address.

Although other departmental records are less likely to be of use, if the circumstances suggest that they will, application may be made by the registrar. In that case the information will be passed on to the solicitor (or the applicant if acting in person) on an undertaking to use it only for the purpose of the proceedings.

We have already seen that any person may be compelled to attend court and reveal information as to the whereabouts of a ward[12]. Relatives or friends who are likely to keep in contact with the person who is sought will often be useful sources of information. Such clues will obviously be followed up by an inquiry agent who will also investigate last known addresses, employers, schools if the child is of school age, and social contacts. If these inquiries do not lead to the missing persons being traced, then departmental records may provide the answer.

It is not clear in general how directly the person sought must be involved in the proceedings, and whether the arrangements are limited to those cases where the missing ward is thought to be with the person, or that person is a party to the proceedings. It is submitted that it should extend to circumstances where a person is thought to be able to provide information as to the whereabouts of the ward. Since the application is normally made by the registrar, he will no doubt consider the relevance of the request for information and require it to be justified if necessary. He will thereby be in a position to gauge the importance of an application and prevent any abuse of the process.

Without requiring other controls[13] on movement and general reporting of whereabouts of children, which would seem to be an undue restriction of liberty, these procedures

12. See ante at 325.
13. E.g. by introducing an identity card system.

go as far as is possible in providing the means for tracing a person[14]. They are likely to lead to the discovery of most people who endeavour to lead a normal life. Unfortunately, even then they will probably not operate very quickly and as we are constantly aware speed should be of the essence in wardship. It is more likely that a person who is prepared to change name and lifestyle or drop out of society will be able to evade discovery for a substantial period.

It will often be helpful to obtain a court order for return of the child so that publicity may be given to the case. An order can be made in open court, so that a request for help in tracing the child may be made in the press[15]. This may precede or supplement the use of other provisions, or be used where they have failed. A decision as to the appropriate steps will depend on the nature of the case and perhaps an assessment of the reaction of the person sought and the way he is treating the child. For example, if publicity would probably drive him to seek refuge in Southern Ireland it would be preferable to seek information through confidential sources.

B. PREVENTING THE REMOVAL OF THE WARD FROM ENGLAND AND WALES

Where it is desired to prevent a child's removal from the jurisdiction, wardship remains one of the best methods of control that can be effected if only because the restriction on removal applies immediately that the child is warded. Despite the immediate effect, however, where a wardship application is made specifically to prevent removal it might be preferable to seek an injunction specifying that a named person shall not remove the child, since such an order can act as an additional deterrent.

i) *Administrative arrangements for preventing wards from leaving the jurisdiction*

Once a child has been warded advantage can then be taken of arrangements designed to prevent, as far as practicable, such a

14. This is a view endorsed by Dr Shirley Summerskill. See H. C. Debs, Vol. 946 Col. 1845.
15. It is a long standing practice of the courts to enlist the aid of the Press in order to trace a missing ward. See e.g. *Re R(MJ)* (*a minor*) (*publication of transcript*) [1975] Fam 89, [1975] 2 All ER 749.

child leaving the jurisdiction[16]. The court or a properly interested party may give written notice to the Passport Office that a passport should not, without the leave of the court, be issued in respect of the child. Unless such written notice has been received, the Passport Office will not inquire whether the child is a ward.

Even if a current passport exists for the child, the Home Office will be prepared, on request, to try to prevent the unauthorised removal of a child from England and Wales. Practitioners have been further reminded of this recently[17]. Where there are grounds for believing that an unauthorised removal from the jurisdiction is likely to occur, the Home Office will be prepared to place a child on the 'Stop List' and try to prevent removal by alerting the major sea and airports. Solicitors who wish to take advantage of this facility should produce to the Home Office:

(i) Where there is an order making the child a ward of court, a copy of that order, or

(ii) In cases of urgency after the commencement of the proceedings but before any order for wardship is made, a notice (in the form of a letter addressed to the Home Office) signed by the registrar or district registrar of the Family Division of the court in which the proceedings have been instituted.

Application for the issue of a Home Office letter may be made ex parte to the registrar. Application should be made to the Children's Division at the Home Office, or the Aliens Office if the child is not a British subject. Although technically a copy of the order forbidding removal or the Home Office letter should be produced, this should not delay a request for precautions to be taken in an emergency. In such a case if the point of departure is known the immigration officer there should be contacted direct. Precautions are generally maintained for three months.

The assistance of the Home Office should not be invoked merely as a precautionary measure, but only when absolutely

16. First introduced pursuant to a *Practice Note* [1963] 3 All ER 66. See also the Supreme Court Practice 1979 p. 1345. Similar arrangements apply to cases where the child is subject to a custody order (or a care and control order) which provides that the minor may not go or be taken out of the jurisdiction without leave of the court. See *Practice Direction* [1973] 3 All ER 194, [1973] 1 WLR 1014 and r.94(1) of the Matrimonial Causes Rules 1977.

17. See the *Practice Direction* [1977] 3 All ER 122, [1977] 1 WLR 1067.

necessary, and it is known that there is a real risk of the child being removed from the jurisdiction. When a name has been entered on the Home Office list, the measures taken are more likely to prove successful if solicitors communicate with the Home Office as soon as they receive any definite indication as to when, from which port, and for what destination the infant is likely to be removed. It is said that it does not help to notify the Home Office of a general suspicion that a child is likely to be removed, or to request that all major ports should be alerted, but presumably such a precaution is better than none if the point of exit is not known. Recent figures show that the Home Office receive about 400 requests annually, and only in about ten of these is any attempt made to remove the child, of which over half are prevented[18]. While the Home Office does what it can to ensure that the orders of the court are effective, the measures can be evaded and do not guarantee success in preventing removal[19].

Clearly no system will be infallible, especially since the 'Stop List' does not extend to prevent a child leaving any port outside England and Wales. The Law Commissions propose[20] that the procedure should be available to prevent a child from leaving any port in the United Kingdom once a supreme court in any of the jurisdictions has made a prohibitory order. It was not recommended, however, to make any provision to control travel within the United Kingdom[1]. Clearly the efficacy of the precautions would be greatly enhanced if their suggestions were implemented. Apart from these much needed reforms it might also be suggested that the means for checking whether a person is on the 'Stop List' could also be improved. For example, greater use of computers could be considered. A list of prohibited persons could be passed on to the various airlines and fed into their computerised systems. Alternatively there could be a central computer run by the Emigration Department into which a list of prohibited persons could be fed[2].

18. See Law Com. Working Paper No. 68 p. 121 n.13. In fact more than 600 written requests were made in 1977. At any one time between 200 and 300 names are on the 'Stop List'.
19. See the case referred to in a letter to the Law Society Gazette ((1978) 75 Law Soc Gaz at 253) where the precautions failed even though it was known which plane the child was leaving on.
20. Law Com Working Paper No. 68 para. 6.19.
 1. Ibid., at para. 6.18.
 2. We are grateful to Mr S B Klarfeld for these suggestions.

ii) *The powers of the police and Immigration Officers to detain the child*

The arrangements just referred to depend for their efficacy on the services of the Immigration Officers. Although an Immigration Officer has no statutory powers to detain persons seeking to embark, where the act done is in vindication of a High Court order or which prevents the unlawful removal of a ward it is unlikely that a successful action could be brought against him. In practice the Immigration Service works in close co-operation with the police.

The procedure for preventing removal is as follows. Primarily persuasion will be used. The Officer will point out to the adult that he may not leave the country without the court's permission. Unless evidence of consent from the court is produced the intending traveller will be warned that since the child is a ward he must remain within the jurisdiction. If the traveller accepts this, no further action will be required. If, however, the warning has no effect and the traveller persists in trying to embark the matter is then brought to the attention of the police. The police officer should also attempt to dissuade the person attempting to take the ward out of the jurisdiction. If this is unsuccessful then as a final resort force may be used to detain the child. It is to be noted that it is only the child who will be prevented from embarking though it may be possible to arrest the adult either for contempt or for causing a breach of the peace or acting in a manner likely to cause such a breach.

If the ward is detained he will be held according to the Tipstaff's instructions.

III The exercise of jurisdiction over children brought to England from a foreign country

A matter of increasing concern in today's mobile society is the removal of children from one jurisdiction to another. Such transfers may be made for a variety of reasons but undoubtedly of greatest concern are the so-called 'kidnapping' cases, that is, where one party either by force or deception unilaterally takes a child from the jurisdiction in which he has had his home, to another jurisdiction.

As far as the English courts are concerned the problem of who should have the long term right to look after a child in such circumstances usually falls to be decided in wardship proceedings since the invocation of that jurisdiction offers the best safeguard against the child's further removal from England or Wales. Since the basis of the wardship jurisdiction is extremely wide, provided the child is physically present or at least ordinarily resident in England, the issue is not whether the court has jurisdiction to hear the case but how that jurisdiction ought to be exercised. No matter how the problem is raised the court will be faced with the basic issue of whether to send the child back to the jurisdiction whence he was taken or to allow him to remain in England. In making that choice, however, the court may also be faced with a subsidiary and preliminary issue of whether it should investigate the full merits of the case or simply make a summary order for the child's return.

A. GENERAL CONSIDERATIONS

Determining what is best for the ward can never be an easy task but the decision is rendered more difficult where an act of kidnapping is involved. In such cases the court will be faced with one party who is seeking to regain care and control of a child who has been wrongfully taken from him, while the other will be seeking judicial sanction for what may be a deliberate flouting of a foreign court order. Such a contest places the court in a very real dilemma for if the kidnapper is granted care and control that will be seen as giving an advantage to the 'wrongdoer', but while a court can hardly condone such a wrongdoing both in the interests of justice and comity, such an order may be justified in the interests of the child, and it is those interests the courts are statutorily enjoined to serve. The problem then for the courts is how such apparently conflicting interests should be reconciled.

B. RELEVANCE OF A FOREIGN COURT ORDER

The English court's attitude to the force of a valid and subsisting foreign custody order has changed over the years. In the nineteenth century, foreign orders were generally regarded as binding. In *Nugent v Vetzera*[3], for example, the court refused to interfere with the appointments made by an Austrian court with respect to Austrian children who had since been sent to England to be educated. In making this decision Wood VC commented[4]:

> 'It would be fraught with consequences of very serious difficulty and contrary to all principles of right and justice, if this Court were to hold that when a parent or guardian (for a guardian stands in exactly the same position as a parent) in a foreign country avails himself of the opportunity for education afforded by this country, and sends his children over here, he must do it at the risk of never being able to recall them, because this court might be of the opinion that an English course of education is better than that adopted in the country to which they belong. I cannot conceive anything more startling than such a notion, which would involve on the other hand this result, that an English ward could not be sent to France for his holidays without the risk of his being kept there and educated in the Roman Catholic religion, with no power to the father or guardian to recall the child. Surely such a state of jurisprudence would put an end to all interchange of friendship between civilised communities.'

An exception to this approach was where the foreign order concerned a child who was a British subject. In *Dawson v Jay*[5], for example, the court refused to allow a maternal aunt to have custody of an infant who was a British subject so that she could take her back to America where the child was born

---

3. (1866) LR 2 Eq 704. See also *Di Savini v Lousada* (1870) 18 WR 425. See also the comments in Seton's *Judgments and Orders* (7th Edn. 1912), Vol. II at pp. 953, 994 and 1001.
4. Ibid., at 712.
5. (1854) 3 De G, M & G 764. The principal ground for this decision was that it would amount to an abdication of its function if the court sent a ward who was a British subject to another jurisdiction over which it had no control. See Lord Cranworth LC ibid., at 772 respectively. See also the comments of Wood VC in *Nugent v Vetzera* (1866) LR 2 Eq 704 at 713, and of Lord Simonds in *McKee v McKee* [1951] AC 352 at 365. It should be added that the English court did not necessarily regard a Scottish court order binding. See e.g. *Stuart v Marquis of Bute* (1861) 9 HLCas 440, one of the earliest reported cases of 'kidnapping'. In *Nugent v Vetzera* ibid., at 713 Wood VC justified this decision on the basis that the child in question was a subject of the United Kingdom and had large property situated inter alia in England. See also the comments of Lord Simonds in *McKee v McKee* ibid., at 365.

and resided for ten years, even though she had been appointed the child's guardian by a court in New York.

Although foreign orders were generally regarded as binding, even in *Nugent v Vetzera*[6], Wood VC allowed for the possibility of interference by the English court at least in cases where to do otherwise would amount to an abdication of jurisdiction. As Morton J observed in *Re B—'s Settlement, B v B*[7], however, it was uncertain what Wood VC's view would have been had there been evidence that it would be most detrimental to the health and well-being of the children if they were removed from England and sent to Austria. The learned judge pointed out that whatever may have been the position in the nineteenth century the courts were now statutorily enjoined[8] to regard the child's welfare as the first and paramount consideration. The consequence of this provision[9] was that in his view the court was bound in every case to exercise its own independent judgment when dealing with custody of a ward even though that child may be subject to an order of another court of competent jurisdiction. In other words the English court was not bound by the foreign order and was certainly not obliged blindly to follow it, though of course due weight would be given to the views of the tribunal particularly where the child was a national of that country. In *Re B* itself care and control of a child born in Belgium was granted to the mother who was a British national and with whom the child had been living in England for the previous two years, even though a Belgian court had granted custody to the father who was a Belgian national living in Belgium.

That Morton J had laid the foundation for the modern approach was confirmed when it was approved in the leading decision in *McKee v McKee*[10]. In that case the father had deliberately flouted a Californian court order granting custody to the mother by taking the child to Ontario in Canada without either the court's or the mother's consent.

6. (1866) LR 2 Eq 704 at 714. One example cited by Wood VC was where the foreign guardians had abandoned the children.
7. [1940] Ch 54 at 62.
8. In *Re B's Settlement, B v B* the relevant statutory provision was s.1 of the Guardianship of Infants Act 1925. See now s.1 of the Guardianship of Minors Act 1971.
9. Cf. Lord Simonds in *McKee v McKee* [1951] AC 352 at 366 who commented that s.1 had introduced no new principle of law but merely enacted the rule which had long been acted on in the Chancery Division.
10. [1951] AC 352.

The first instance judge, notwithstanding the existence of the Californian order and the father's conduct, decided to hear the case on its merits, and, having done so, concluded that it was in the child's interests that custody be granted to the father. The Privy Council upheld both the decision to hear the case on its merits and the order that the father should have custody. With regard to the status of a foreign court order Lord Simonds said[11]:

> 'the welfare and happiness of the infant is the paramount consideration in questions of custody.... To this paramount consideration all others yield. The order of a foreign court of competent jurisdiction is no exception. Such an order has not the force of a foreign judgment: comity demands not its enforcement, but its grave consideration.... This distinction which has long been recognized in the courts of England and Scotland (see *Johnstone v Beattie*[12] and *Stuart v Marquis of Bute*[13], and in the courts of Ontario (see, e.g. *Re Davis (infant)*[14] and *Re Gay*[15]), rests on the peculiar character of the jurisdiction and on the fact that an order providing for the custody of an infant cannot in its nature be final.'

It is to be emphasised that both *Re B* and *McKee* made it clear that a foreign judgment was not to be ignored but that its weight depended upon the circumstances. Indeed both judgments but particularly that of Lord Simonds left it open that there may be cases where it would be in the child's interests that the court should not look beyond the circumstances in which its jurisdiction was invoked and for that reason give effect to the foreign judgment without further inquiry[16]. In other words it was specifically recognised that there may be circumstances where the court would be justified in making a summary order for the child's return to the jurisdiction whence he was taken. In the event in neither case was a summary order thought justifiable. In both

11. [1951] AC 352 at 365.
12. (1843) 10 CL & F in 42.
13. (1861) 9 HLCas 440, 11 ER 799.
14. (1894) 25 OR 579.
15. (1926) 59 OLR 40.
16. See Lord Simonds [1951] AC at 363 and Morton J in *Re B—'s Settlement, B v B* [1940] Ch at 64. For other cases where the court did investigate the merits see e.g. *Re A (an infant)* (1959) Times, March 25 and *Re Kernot (an infant)* [1965] Ch 217, [1964] 3 All ER 339. In the latter case an important factor was that the Italian court would have applied English law anyway.

cases the relevant court order was two years old since when circumstances had changed making it justifiable not to follow the order but to investigate the facts anew. In any event in *Re B* it was uncertain whether the Belgian order was made upon the footing of what was best for the child or whether it was regarded as a matter of course that the father should be granted custody since he was the guardian under Belgian law, the applicant in divorce proceedings (instituted in Belgium) and the only parent in Belgium.

C. THE USE OF THE SUMMARY ORDER

Although *Re B* and *McKee* were important decisions establishing that an English court was not bound by a foreign judgment, but was instead bound to exercise its own independent judgment in making a decision as to the child's custody and upbringing, they marked but the beginning of the development of the court's approach to kidnapping. The major development over the last two decades has concerned the use of summary orders in kidnapping cases. Although, as we have seen, Lord Simonds in *McKee* specifically allowed for the possibility of such an order being made, nevertheless he endorsed the Ontario judge's decision to investigate the full merits of the case. It was left to the leading decision of *Re H (infants)*[17] to consider further precisely when a summary order should be made.

i) *Re H (infants)*[17]

The father was an American citizen and the mother though born in Scotland had been resident in the USA for 20 years. The two children aged 8 and 7 were born in the USA and had spent all their lives there. The mother entered into a separation agreement with the father by which it was agreed that she should have custody of the children but that she should not without consent remove them outside a 50 mile radius of where she was living. This agreement was later embodied in a New York Supreme Court order. In contravention of this order, and therefore in contempt of the court, the mother, without the consent of the father, brought the children to England with the intention of permanently residing here.

17. [1965] 3 All ER 906 (first instance), [1966] 1 All ER 886 (CA).

Within four months of her arrival in England the mother made the children wards of court (by way of a precaution to prevent their removal from the jurisdiction), but it was the father's motion, launched within seven months of the children's arrival, that came before the court. In that motion the father asked for the children to be delivered into his care with liberty to take them back to New York. The mother contended that the English court should investigate the merits of the case and after hearing all the evidence decide whether in all the circumstances prevailing at the date of the judgment it was in the children's interests to remain in England with the mother. The father contended that the children should be sent back to New York at once, leaving the New York court to decide the issue on its merits.

It was argued on behalf of the mother that once wardship proceedings had been launched, even by someone who had brought the child to England wrongfully and in defiance of the laws of the country where his home is, then unless there were exceptional circumstances (and it was submitted there were no such circumstances) the court was bound to investigate the full merits of the case[18]. This argument was rejected both by Cross J at first instance and by the Court of Appeal, it being held that what was established was that the court had a *discretion* to investigate the full merits of the case.

It was held on the facts that the appropriate order in this case was that the children should be sent back to New York. The court was satisfied that the children would suffer no harm if they were sent back to America with their father, and that since the children were American and since the mother had behaved most reprehensibly, it was right that the court should make a summary order for the children's return.

In reaching this decision Cross J specifically singled out for condemnation the act of kidnapping, commenting that the[19]:

'sudden and unauthorised removal of children from one country to another is far too frequent nowadays, and, as it seems to me, it is the duty of the courts in all countries

18. Reliance for the submission was based on *Re B* supra and *McKee v McKee* supra and in particular on the remark of Lord Simonds in *McKee* ibid., at 365-6. 'There is in fact no *via media* between the abdication of jurisdiction which he [i.e. the judge] rejected, and the consideration of the case on its merits, in which the respect payable to a foreign order must always be in the foreground.'
19. [1965] 3 All ER at 912 I.

to do all they can to ensure that the kidnapper does not gain an advantage by his wrongdoing.'

He pointed out that if the merits were to be investigated by the English court, it would cause grave injustice to the father since in the time it would take to collect the necessary evidence the children would have become more settled in England, making it more unlikely that they would be ordered to return to the USA. In summarising the considerations relevant to a kidnapping case Cross J said the court had to weigh on the one hand the public policy aspect such as the question of comity and forum conveniens and the injustice done to the wronged parent and on the other hand the interest of the child. He held that the interest of the child was sufficiently taken into account if the court was satisfied that to send the child back would cause him no harm. The Court of Appeal upheld both the decision to send the children back and importantly the general approach to kidnapping at least where as in the case before them wardship proceedings had been brought quickly[20].

ii) *Development of the use of a summary order to combat kidnapping*

There seems little doubt that *Re H* established a doctrine to apply in kidnapping cases. An important element of the decision was the emphasis placed on the injustice done to the 'innocent' parent if the other parent were to be allowed to derive an advantage by kidnapping a child from one jurisdiction to another. The case established the following approach: that if one parent kidnaps a child from another jurisdiction where that child has had his home, then in subsequent wardship proceedings, provided it is satisfied that no harm will come to the child, the English court will send the child back to the foreign jurisdiction without further investigating the matter. In other words provided wardship proceedings are brought quickly[1], the court would only

---

20. See e.g. Willmer LJ [1966] 1 All ER at 888, 889 and Russell LJ at 893.
   1. Aliter, if some time has elapsed since the order. See e.g. *Re T (an infant)* [1969] 3 All ER 998, [1969] 1 WLR 1608 where the court order was 12 years old and had since been modified by consent and where the child in question was 16 and who had strong views on where and with whom he wanted to live. See also *Re T A (infants)* (1972) 116 Sol Jo 78.

investigate the merits of a case to the extent it is necessary to determine whether the child would suffer harm. The same approach was again adopted by Cross J and affirmed by the Court of Appeal in *Re E (an infant)*[2] though this time with the opposite result. The case concerned the child of American parents who was born in America. Following divorce, the father, in contested proceedings, was awarded custody of the child. Following the father's death the father's sister, who was resident in England, travelled to the United States and took the child back with her. Subsequently an American court made an order granting custody temporarily to the child's mother. As soon as she could afford to, the mother travelled to England, whereupon the father's sister started proceedings making the child a ward of court. It was held on these facts that the child should not be sent back because there were special circumstances which obliged the court to order that the child remain in England. The most important factor was that, unlike *Re H* where the children had two homes in America, in this case the only home which the ward had in America had been destroyed so that her freshly acquired home in England was her only home. It was held that it would be disastrous for the child to return to America with her mother and an order was made accordingly. Cross J with whom the Court of Appeal agreed made it quite clear that he deprecated the act of kidnapping even though the circumstances in this case dictated that the child remained in England. He said[3]:

'In modern conditions it is often easy and tempting for a parent who has been deprived of custody by the court of country 'A' to remove the child suddenly to country 'B' and to set up home there. The courts in all countries ought, as I see it, to be careful not to do anything to encourage this tendency. The substitution of self help for due process of law in this field can only harm the interests of wards generally, and a judge should, as I see it, pay regard to the orders of the proper foreign court unless he is satisfied beyond all reasonable doubt that to do so would inflict serious harm on the child.'

Such a statement is clearly indicative both of the court's

2. [1967] Ch 287, [1967] 1 All ER 329 [first instance], [1967] 2 All ER 881 (CA).
3. Ibid., at 330 specifically approved by Willmer LJ [1967] 2 All ER at 885 I.

dislike of kidnapping and of an approach to deal with the problem.

iii) *Kidnapping defined*

Until *Re T (infants)*[4] kidnapping cases had always involved the breaking of a foreign court order but the concept was extended to include the unilateral withdrawal of children from their home by the parent without the other's consent. Harman LJ commented[5]:

> 'It seems to me that the removal of children from their home and surroundings by one of the parents who happens to live in or have connections with another country is a thing against which the court should set its face, and that, unless there is good reason to the contrary, it should not countenance proceedings of that kind.'

In that case, unknown to her Canadian husband who was away on a hunting trip, an English born mother brought her two children aged 6 and 5 to England from Canada where hitherto they had spent their lives. At first instance, Penny-cuick J relying on *Re H* held that since the children were Canadian and belonged to a Canadian family, and since no obvious harm to them would be involved in their being returned to Canada, the proper courts to determine their future were the Canadian courts. Accordingly, the father was granted leave to take the children back to Canada.

The decision to return the children was upheld on appeal but it was accepted that the judge had erred in relying on *Re H* since his decision had been made after considering all the evidence which the parties chose to present to the court. In other words the judge had not made a summary order. Nevertheless the tenor of both Harman and Russel, LJJ's judgments was that had a summary order been sought the circumstances were such that it would have been granted.

The meaning of 'kidnapping' was also considered by the Court of Appeal in *Re A (infants)*[6] which concerned the movement of children from Jersey to England. The important point in this case was that the children were moved

4. [1968] Ch 704, [1968] 3 All ER 411.
5. Ibid., at 715. See also his comment at 713: 'This has been described as a "kidnapping" case. And so in my view it is.' See also the same judge's comments in *Re A (infants)* [1970] Ch 665 at 673.
6. [1970] Ch 665, [1970] 3 All ER 184.

to the father's parents in England with the consent of the mother on the understanding that they were to be returned to the mother in Jersey within one month. Subsequently the father changed his mind and the children were not returned. The father made the children wards of court to restrain the mother from taking them out of the jurisdiction and asking that they should be allowed to reside in England with his parents. The mother sought an order giving her care and control with liberty to take the children back to Jersey.

It was argued on the mother's behalf that as this was a kidnapping case the court should make a summary order for the children's return unless satisfied they would come to harm in Jersey. It was held by Harman LJ that the mother's contention amounted to an unwarranted extension of the meaning of kidnapping. He held that the case before him was not a kidnapping case since the children had been brought to England with the agreement of both parties and the father had not been found guilty of a fraud as he had genuinely changed his mind while the children were in England[7]. Harman LJ commented[8]:

'In my judgment, the children not being here as the result of some deceit or wrongdoing, it is quite unheard of that this court should decline jurisdiction and say that it will have no more to do with them.'

D. THE PRESENT POSITION

The four leading cases of *Re H, Re E, Re T* and *Re A* undoubtedly established a principle to be applied in kidnapping cases. Indeed *Re A* provides authority for saying that the summary order can *only* be granted in a kidnapping case. It seems clear, however, that these cases can no longer be regarded as good law at least in so far as they treated kidnapping as a special case though the decisions themselves can no doubt be justified on the individual facts. Lord Salmon (sitting in the Court of Appeal) has said in *Re M–R (a minor)*[9] that a summary order can be made in non kidnapping cases

7. As may be appreciated whether or not a party has genuinely changed his mind can be a fine point. Cf. *Re S(M) (an infant)* [1971] Ch 621, [1971] 1 All ER 459 where fraud was suspected but not proved.
8. Ibid., at 674.
9. (1975) 5 Fam Law 55.

and the leading decision in *Re L (minors)*[10] establishes that because the ward's welfare is the first and paramount consideration, kidnapping is but one of the factors in deciding whether to make a summary order.

i) *Re L (minors)*

The cases prior to *Re L* laid considerable emphasis on the parental interest in kidnapping cases and in particular to the injustice done to the so-called 'innocent' party if care and control is granted to the person who has wrongfully brought the child to England. The interests of the individual child were only taken into account to the extent that the court had to be satisfied that the child would not be harmed if he were returned to the jurisdiction whence he was taken. In other words provided proceedings were brought promptly the summary order would only be *refused* if it could be shown to be *against* the child's interests. In *Re L (minors)*, however, Buckley LJ once again[11] emphasised that in making *any* decision, including that of a summary order, the child's welfare must always be treated as the first and paramount consideration. As he said[12]:

> 'judges have more than once reprobated the acts of 'kidnappers' in cases of this kind. I do not in any way dissent from those strictures, but it would, in my judgment, be wrong to suppose that in making orders in relation to children in this jurisdiction the court is in any way concerned with penalising any adult for his conduct. That conduct may well be a consideration to be taken into account, but, whether the court makes a summary order or an order after investigating the merits, the cardinal rule applies that the welfare of the infant must always be the paramount consideration.'

His lordship explained how the welfare principle applied in 'kidnapping' cases: where the court embarked upon a full-scale investigation of the merits he held there was no distinction between a kidnapping case and any other case—the court is called upon to weigh the various factors of which kidnap-

10. [1974] 1 All ER 913.
11. As Lord Simonds had done in *McKee v McKee* [1951] AC 352, [1951] 1 All ER 942.
12. [1974] 1 All ER 913 at 926.

ping would be one (albeit a possibly important factor) and make a decision upon the basis of what is thought to be in the ward's best interests. Where the court makes a summary order without investigating the merits, such a decision still had to be justified in the ward's best interests though in a different way. As Buckley LJ said[13]:

'To take a child from his native land, to remove him to another country where maybe, his native tongue is not spoken, to divorce him from the social customs and contacts to which he has been accustomed, to interrupt his education in his native land and subject him to a foreign system of education, are all acts (offered here as examples and, of course, not a complete catalogue of possible relevant factors) which are likely to be psychologically disturbing to the child, particularly at a time when his family life is also disrupted. If such a case is promptly brought to the attention of a court in this country, the judge may feel that it is in the best interests of the infant that these disturbing factors should be eliminated from his life as speedily as possible. A full investigation of the merits of the case in an English court may be incompatible with achieving this. . . . An order that the child should be returned forthwith to the country from which he has been removed in the expectation that any dispute about his custody will be satisfactorily resolved in the courts of that country may well be regarded as being in the best interests of the child.'

In reaching his decision Buckley LJ relied on the House of Lords decision of *J v C*[14] since that case had made it plain that the principle that the welfare of the child is the first and paramount consideration was of universal application wherever the custody or upbringing of a child is in question. His lordship also sought to explain the earlier Court of Appeal decisions such as *Re H* as depending upon the principle of what was in the best interests of the children. With all due respect to Buckley LJ while decisions like *Re H can* be so justified the two cases establish fundamentally different approaches. The '*Re H*' approach places the burden on the 'kidnapper' to adduce evidence that it would be harmful to

13. [1974] 1 All ER 913 at 925, 926.
14. [1970] AC 668, [1969] 1 All ER 788.

the child to be returned whereas the '*Re L*' approach places the burden on the 'innocent' party to show that it is in the child's best interests that a summary order be made. Buckley LJ's comments, however, on the principles to be applied when making summary orders were in fact obiter since the order was made after consideration of all the relevant circumstances. Moreover, no question of comity arose since no foreign order had been made. What had happened was that an English born mother had brought her two children aged 11 and 9 to England from Germany, where they were born and had spent all their lives, on the pretext of a holiday with the pre-conceived intention of permanently remaining there. It was held after consideration of all the evidence that as the children had always been brought up in Germany and were German nationals, it was in their long term interests that they should continue to live in Germany, and accordingly it was ordered that the children be returned to Germany, ceasing to be wards on their return and that they remain in their German born father's custody until further order.

ii) *Subsequent decisions*

In view of these facts it might have been possible to argue that Buckley LJ's judgment should not be regarded as authoritative. Although its significance was perhaps not immediately appreciated[15] it is now clear that *Re L* should be regarded as the locus classicus on the subject. In *Re K* (*infants*)[16], for example, Stamp LJ specifically endorsed Buckley LJ's comments that the cardinal rule, even when making summary orders, is that the welfare of the infant is always the paramount consideration. *Re K* was another case where the mother brought the children to England on the pretext of a holiday. At first instance Payne J made a summary order for the children's return to Canada upon the basis that it was a kidnapping case. This decision was, however, reversed on appeal it being held that there was evidence that such an order

15. See for instance *Re M–R* (*a minor*) (1975) 5 Fam Law 55. It is also worthy of note that none of the leading text books have seen any special significance in the decision.
16. (1976) Times, March 9, 6 Fam Law 150 and the editorial comment at 151,2. See also the comments (1976) 6 Fam Law 94. See also *Re C* (*a minor*) (1976) 6 Fam Law 211.

would do positive harm[17] to the children and hence was not for their benefit. Ormrod LJ expressly said[18] that cases like *Re H* might require some reconsideration in view of the decision in *J v C*.

Although *Re K* fully supported the approach laid down in *Re L* references were made to the possible harm that might have resulted had the summary order been made. It was perhaps because of these references that the first instance judge, Judge McLellan, again applied the '*Re H*' approach, in *Re C (minors)*[19]. The judge had commented that kidnapping was but one of the factors to be taken into account but continued:

'I must, as I understand the matter, make a peremptory order for the return of these children unless I am satisfied that there is some obvious moral or physical danger involved in making such an order[20].'

On appeal Ormrod LJ held this statement to be a serious misdirection[1]. He held that following *Re L* the principles to be applied when the court is called upon to consider whether or not to make a summary order, are exactly the same as in all other decisions relating to the welfare of children.

'In other words, using for a moment the American terminology, all decisions relating to the welfare and future of the children have to be decided on the "best interests" of the children principle and no other glosses are to be put on that test. The judge, in thinking that he had to find some obvious moral or physical danger was clearly, in my judgment, putting on the judgment of Buckley LJ a gloss which was unwarranted.'

Re C posed a difficult set of facts for the court. Following divorce proceedings a consensual custody order of the three children in question was made in favour of the American born mother who then returned to California where she

---

17. The children had been in England for about 18 months and were well settled into English schools and had satisfactory accommodation. On the other hand, if they were returned to Canada they would be living in entirely unfamiliar accommodation as the father had sold the matrimonial home. It was also borne in mind that the Canadian court might even have granted custody to the mother.
18. As reported in (1976) 6 Fam Law at 151.
19. [1978] Fam 105, [1977] 3 WLR 561. Sub nom *Re 'NC, JC and AC' Minors* (1977) 7 Fam Law 240.
20. Ibid., at 114 and 568 respectively.
1. Ibid., at 114 and 567 respectively.

married the American born step father. The English born father also remarried and resided in England though he and his wife visited California for a few weeks and saw the children from time to time. Unfortunately, some eighteen months after her remarriage the mother died leaving the children in the step father's care. As soon as he heard of the mother's death the father flew to California but almost immediately upon his arrival, the step father and two of his relatives applied for a custody order. An interim order was granted in favour of the applicants. In subsequent proceedings, but pending the final hearing, the father was granted access and in deliberate breach of the order brought the children to England.

Within two months of the children's arrival in England, wardship proceedings were instituted in England by the step father who sought a summary order for the children's return. The issue was perhaps made more difficult since there was evidence against the step father that he from time to time smoked cannabis, while the father had since become a Jehovah's Witness. Notwithstanding the judge's incorrect approach, his decision not to order the children's return to California was upheld upon the 'welfare' principle. An important feature in the case was that it was thought likely that the Californian court would grant custody to the natural father on account of its preference for the blood tie. There was, therefore, a real risk that even if the children were sent back, they would only be placed again with their father in England. In fact the Court of Appeal went further, holding that in view of the evidence before it, viz both English and American welfare reports, care and control of the children should be granted to the father though under supervision of the relevant local authority.

In the light of these decisions it is clear that the correct approach in every case[2] is to decide the issue of jurisdiction on the basis of what is best for the child's welfare. It should be noted, however, that the court has one of two options: it can either decide to make a summary order for the child's return or investigate the full merits of the case and make any order

2. Hence the suggestion in *Hannagan v Hannagan* Court of Appeal (Civil Division) Transcript No. 151 of 1976 that a summary order could not be made because the children were British subjects (though brought up in France) is surely wrong.

that is appropriate. Once the court has embarked upon a full inquiry, however, it cannot then simply send the child away and leave it to the court of the foreign country concerned to make an order. This was established in the important but unreported Court of Appeal decision in *Re B and S (infants)*[3].

iii) *Procedure*

It should be noted that in seeking a summary order, or even seeking leave to take a child out of the jurisdiction, an application should not be made ex parte at least where the other parent is in the jurisdiction. This was established by *Re C (a minor)*[4]. In that case a German mother signed a paper authorising an English father to take their illegitimate son to England for a limited period. Upon his failure to return within the stipulated time the mother came to England, warded the boy and sought on an ex parte application leave to take the boy back to Germany. At first instance, the application was granted, but the father applied for a stay of execution pending a proper hearing. It was held on appeal that the order giving leave to take the child back to Germany was not one which should have been made on an ex parte application. In the event, however, the judge's order was upheld.

Where an order giving leave to take a child out of jurisdiction is granted, the proper course if the other party wishes to appeal is to seek a stay of execution pending the appeal. Of course, the court may not accede to such a request. It may be satisfied that an undertaking to return the child if called upon to do so, given by the person granted leave, is sufficient[5]. If, however, a stay is granted then, especially if the stay is short, the solicitors should proceed with the appeal with the greatest possible diligence and speed. In *Re A and J P (infants)*[6] a mother was ordered to have her children placed on a flight to Milan. Execution of the order was stayed for 14 days pending the appeal. In fact the appeal was heard some three months later, yet no application had been made for a further stay nor for the appeal to be expedited. Stamp LJ commented that in

3. Court of Appeal (Civil Division) Transcript No. 292 of 1976.
4. (1976) 6 Fam Law 211.
5. As it was in *Re L (minors)* [1974] 1 All ER 913 at 916.
6. (1977) 127 NLJ 1151; Court of Appeal (Civil Division) Transcript No. 23 of 1977.

failing to proceed with the appeal the *solicitors* had failed, as officers of the court, in their duty to the children.

Both these procedural points are further reminders that the principle that the ward's welfare is the first and paramount consideration applies with equal force to procedural as well as substantive matters[7].

E. PROPOSALS FOR REFORM

The global problem of 'kidnapping' admits of no simple solution. Perhaps the best remedy that can be attained is international agreement on recognition and enforcement of orders concerning children. However, before such agreements can be reached there has to be agreement on the criteria on which decisions relating to children should be reached, and in cases where the adults are in different jurisdictions, there must be some means of resolving which court in which jurisdiction should decide the dispute on its merits. Neither of these points is easy to resolve and they have proved considerable stumbling blocks to the international negotiations on the problem.

Currently the United Kingdom is participating in the Council of Europe which in 1976 produced a draft convention. Unfortunately the convention did not command universal support among its 20 members and is in the course of being revised. The problem has also been explored in the Commonwealth and the subject was discussed at the Commonwealth Law Ministers Conference in Winnipeg in 1977. It is understood that the matter is to be followed up by the Commonwealth Secretariat. No early solution can be expected from either source[8].

It was perhaps bearing in mind the difficulty of reaching agreement at international level that the English and Scottish Law Commissions confined their first working paper to resolving conflicts of jurisdiction within the United Kingdom[9].

---

7. Cf. *Official Solicitor v K* [1965] AC 201, [1963] 3 All ER 191.
8. In the Allingham debate Dr Shirley Summerskill promised no speedy solution. See H. C. Debs, Vol. 946 Col. 1850. She did say, however, at Col. 1848 that if no multinational agreement could be reached attempts may be made to arrange bilateral agreements.
9. Custody of Children—Jurisdiction and Enforcement within the United Kingdom 1976. Law Com. Working Paper No. 68 and Scots Law Com. Memorandum No. 23.

One proposal of the Law Commission is that there should be a scheme of recognition and enforcement of custody and wardship orders within the United Kingdom. It is perhaps a sad commentary on the priority accorded to children that no such scheme already exists, and it is to be hoped that the proposals will be implemented as soon as possible.

Perhaps more controversially the Commissions recommend that there should also be specific provision to deal with kidnapping in the new unified jurisdictional rules. It was thought that specific directions were necessary because[10]:

> 'kidnapping is too important a matter to be left at large and the courts [and lay magistrates, in particular], the parties and their advisers should have greater guidance on this point than would be afforded by the rebuttal presumption test without more'.

Hence for the purposes of establishing 'habitual residence' (which it will be recalled[11] was in the Commissions' basic proposal for the new unified jurisdictional rules) the recommendation is[12]:

> (a) there should be a presumption that a child's habitual residence is in the country where he has resided cumulatively for the longest period in the year immediately preceding the commencement of the proceedings. But
>
> (b) where the child's residence has been changed without lawful authority during the year immediately preceding the commencement of the proceedings, no account should be taken of that changed residence in reckoning the periods of the child's residence for the purposes of (a) above.'

The basic philosophy of the proposal seems to be that the best solution for dealing with kidnapping is that the court of the jurisdiction to which the child has been unlawfully brought should have no jurisdiction at all. This is surely a questionable policy since even the narrowest of jurisdictional rules will not eliminate kidnapping and it seems preferable to allow the parties some redress in the courts, if only to seek a summary order for the child's return, rather than to allow matters to drift.

---

10. At para. 3.76.
11. See Chap. 2.
12. Para. 3.78.

Even if it is thought preferable to have some specific rule to deal with kidnapping, it is not at all certain that the Law Commissions' proposal is ideal. Indeed it is not clear exactly how the proposal will operate. Presumably, where a child is kidnapped from the matrimonial home, say in England, then provided the 'innocent' party brings proceedings within twelve months the presumption will be that the child is habitually resident in England since in that year ignoring the changed residence the child will have spent the longest period there. This in itself could produce an odd result in cases where the hearing is delayed. For example, a child may be kidnapped when he was six months old, proceedings being brought nine months later and the hearing six months after that. The presumption will be that a child who at the date of the hearing is 21 months old will be presumed to be habitually resident in a jurisdiction in which he has spent only six months of his life.

Another problem relates to rebutting the presumption as it is unclear whether a 'kidnapper' will be precluded from establishing that a child is habitually resident in a jurisdiction to which he has been taken if he has spent less than a year there. To make sense of the provision it would seem that the parent would be so precluded unless he could establish that the child was habitually resident in that jurisdiction for a period *more* than twelve months prior to the commencement of the proceedings. If this is a correct interpretation then it is submitted that the provision is too rigid and in any event is too long a period to be ignored in a life of a young child[13]. If this interpretation is incorrect and the 'kidnapper' can nevertheless adduce evidence to establish the child's habitual residence it would seem to undermine the proposal altogether.

Another criticism is that the changed residence is only to be ignored where the child's residence has been changed 'without lawful authority'. There is bound to be a problem with the meaning of 'without lawful authority'. It was envisaged that it would apply where the residence was changed in breach of a UK court order or against the will of

13. Lord Denning MR in *Re P(GE)* (*an infant*) [1965] Ch at 586 envisaged a much shorter period to show acquiescence in a change of residence. As he said 'six months delay would, I should have thought, go far to show acquiescence'.

a person, such as a parent or guardian having the legal right to fix the child's residence. Authority already exists[14] that where the parent removes the children to another jurisdiction with the consent of the other, merely for a temporary visit, and subsequently changes his mind and refuses to return the children that does not constitute 'kidnapping'. The question is whether it would constitute 'without lawful authority'. If it did then the period of changed residence would be ignored; if it did not then there would be a presumption in favour of the latter jurisdiction. It seems questionable whether jurisdiction should depend on such fine points. For these reasons it is submitted that careful consideration be given to whether the proposal for dealing with kidnapping should be implemented.

14. *Re A (infants)* [1970] Ch 665, [1970] 3 All ER 184. Discussed ante at p. 342.

Chapter 13

Conclusions

I Introduction

As has been seen wardship is an ancient jurisdiction, but one which until comparatively recently has lain dormant, and largely restricted to the wealthier classes who sought to protect their daughters and their property from fortune hunters. The procedural jungle and the expense of the Chancery Division of the High Court militated against too frequent a use of such an exclusive remedy. The past thirty years have seen the removal of many of the obstructions, though it has not been until the last decade that the opportunities wardship offers have begun to be fully realised.

First the Law Reform (Miscellaneous Provisions) Act 1949 removed the basic procedural obstacles and enabled a child to be made a ward of court for no reason other than to place him under the protection of the court. Secondly the expansion of legal aid under the Legal Aid and Advice Act 1949 substantially broadened the categories of people who were able to take advantage of the jurisdiction. Thirdly the transfer in 1971 from the Chancery Division to the Family Division has given wardship considerable impetus, since it made the procedure available in the district registries[1]. As the hearing can take place locally, the necessity for an expensive and inconvenient outing to the High Court in London can be avoided[2]. Furthermore the Family Division is less concerned

1. I.e. any district registry having a divorce county court within its district. MCR 1977, r.2(2).
2. The statistics show a steep rise in wardship applications in the district registries. In 1974 there were 286 out of a total of 959; in 1975 the respective figures were 411, 1203; in 1976 494, 1369 and in 1977 there were 620 out of a total of 1491.

with procedural rules and technicalities, so that it is better able to concentrate on safeguarding the welfare of the child[3].

During this time there have been social changes. Notably there is public concern about the welfare of children. As a Government Minister said in Parliament: 'A nation's children represent a nation's future. How society treats its own children is a good reflection of the overall health and stability of that society'[4].

While legislation has generally served to provide a poor reflection of our overall health and stability in this respect, wardship has in its own way been endeavouring to ensure that the interests of children are given proper recognition.

II Wardship in context

Such a well established jurisdiction as wardship clearly has an important role to play in the child welfare system. Indeed the great value of the jurisdiction is that it is available as an alternative or supplementary system. However, the recent growth in its use as a jurisdiction for review has put its relationship to other parts of the system into a state of flux. Its further development in this respect needs careful consideration. It is important to view the whole issue in context and guard against a piecemeal approach which could threaten the existence of the whole system. Factors which have led to an increase in the use of wardship could both overburden the jurisdiction and undermine the authority and smooth running of the other component parts of the system.

A. DIFFERING ROLES OF WARDSHIP

The current work of the jurisdiction may be seen as comprising four main, but sometimes overlapping roles, namely, as an original jurisdiction, as a jurisdiction of review, as a supplementary jurisdiction and as a fail-safe or 'long stop' jurisdiction.

3. This ability is also enhanced by the fact that the Family Division is solely concerned with family matters while the old Chancery Division was not.
4. Dr David Owen MP in a debate on the Children Bill H.C. Vol. 893 col. 1821.

i) *As an original jurisdiction*

Wardship is clearly available as a jurisdiction in its own right and in this role it is invoked most frequently to resolve inter-parental disputes particularly when one party is threatening to remove the child from the country. It is also invoked in cases of dispute between parents and their child. Finally it is used by non parents who have no other means of bringing the issue before the court.

Ironically at a time of general expansion in wardship there have been or are likely to be developments which can be expected to reduce the need or opportunity for invoking the jurisdiction in this respect.

First came the reduction in the age of majority from 21 to 18[5], which had the inevitable effect of reducing those applications intended to protect teenage daughters from undesirable associations. Secondly the Children Act 1975[6] introduces the new concept of custodianship, which will, when implemented, enable certain non-parents to acquire rights in respect of children, which hitherto could only have been obtained through wardship or guardianship. Thirdly sections 34, 39 and 70 of the Domestic Proceedings and Magistrates' Courts Act 1978 give magistrates and county courts the power to order that no person shall take a child out of England and Wales while a custody (or custodianship) order made by their court is in force, except with the leave of the court[7]. This may reduce the need to ward the child[8].

Finally it is also possible that new rules will be introduced to make habitual residence the basis for the court to accept jurisdiction[9]. That would reduce the number of applications in respect of children brought into the country from abroad.

ii) *As a jurisdiction of review*

The courts have recently been most active in reviewing the decisions of other bodies. The prevailing trend is to treat the

5. By s.1 of the Family Law Reform Act 1969.
6. Part II.
7. By virtue of amending the Guardianship of Minors Act 1971, which amendment also gives the High Court such powers.
8. I.e. if the threat of removal becomes apparent during the proceedings. However, as we discussed in Chap. 10 wardship will remain the best jurisdiction where the threat is made before *any* proceedings have been made. The new power might reduce the need to use wardship to supplement a custody or custodianship order.
9. I.e. if the Law Commission proposals were ever implemented. See Chaps. 2 and 12.

welfare of the child as the first and paramount consideration as a principle of universal application so that the court will rarely be restrained from review. A number of cases illustrate the point. It was established by *Re L (minors)*[10] that in 'kidnapping' cases, choice of forum and the decision to exercise jurisdiction, is dependent upon the child's best interests. Indeed, Buckley LJ's judgment in *Re L* may well be regarded as a landmark not only in kidnapping cases, but in wardship as a whole. In *Re D (a minor)*[11] Dunn J has said obiter that review of a magistrates' custody order should be justified upon the child's best interests and not merely undertaken in exceptional cases, as was formerly the position. In adoption the Court of Appeal in *Re O (a minor)*[12] over-ruled a traditional first instance judgment, holding that intervention in wardship even at the behest of the natural parent should be based on the child's welfare and not as Latey J had suggested, only in exceptional circumstances. There is a hint in *Re H (a minor)*[13] that the courts will seek to review local authorities' powers over children on the basis of the welfare principle. Although the court stopped short of saying this, traditional decisions like those of *Re M (an infant)*[14] and *Re T (AJJ) (an infant)*[15], which established that the courts will not normally interfere with the exercise of local authorities' powers, may have to be re-appraised.

iii) *As a supplementary jurisdiction*

Wardship may on occasions be profitably used to supplement existing powers. A local authority[16] may wish to increase its powers in respect of a child in care under the Children Act

10. *Re L (minors) (wardship: jurisdiction)* [1974] 1 All ER 913, [1974] 1 WLR 250. See also *Re C (minors) (wardship: jurisdiction)* [1978] Fam 105, [1978] 2 All ER 230. Discussed fully in Chap. 11.
11. *Re D (a minor) (justices' decision: review)* [1977] Fam 158 at 161–3. But cf. Ormrod LJ's comments in *Re H (a minor) (wardship: jurisdiction)* [1978] Fam 65, 76–7, [1978] 2 All ER 903 at 907–9. Discussed in Chap. 11.
12. *Re O (a minor) (wardship: adopted child)* [1978] 2 All ER 27, [1977] 3 WLR 732. Discussed in Chap. 10.
13. [1978] Fam 65, [1978] 2 All ER 903. Discussed in Ch. 11.
14. [1961] Ch 328, [1961] 1 All ER 788.
15. [1970] Ch 688, [1970] 2 All ER 865.
16. In *Re B (a minor) (wardship: child in care)* [1975] Fam 36, [1974] 3 All ER 915 for example, Lane J thought that wardship could profitably be used to prevent a violent father from discovering the whereabouts of his child. For further discussion on this see Chap. 11. For the use of wardship as a supplementary jurisdiction in respect of custody or custodianship orders see Chap. 10.

1948 or the Children and Young Persons Act 1969, as for example, to stop the child leaving the jurisdiction or to obtain an injunction restraining other acts prejudicial to the child[16].

iv) *As a fail safe or 'long stop' jurisdiction*

Wardship is always available as a court of last resort, which is particularly useful for unusual, novel or complex applications. The limits of the jurisdiction in handling novel cases have not yet and may never be fully defined. Recently wardship has been used to prevent sterilisation of a child[17]; to determine the care and control of a child conceived by AID, when the donor was paying the host mother to have his child[18]; and to restrain publication of a book on the grounds that it would adversely affect the interests of the child[19]. This last case may be thought to have defined some limits in that it decided that the welfare of the child would not always outweigh competing interests but even this decision has not closed the door to further expansion. We have yet to see, for example, whether the court would countenance wardship being used to prevent a child having an abortion[20] or to prevent the withdrawal of a life-support system for a child[1].

B. RELATIONSHIP WITH OTHER JURISDICTIONS

The main concern in considering the role of wardship within the system as a whole is to ensure that a balance is maintained notably with the jurisdiction of other courts and with powers delegated to local authorities under child care legislation.

The increasing use of wardship as a means of reviewing previous decisions is in our submission in danger of upsetting the balance. Indeed it is our opinion that a watershed has

17. *Re D (a minor) (wardship: sterilisation)* [1976] Fam 185, [1976] 1 All ER 326.
18. Reported at first instance as *Re C (a minor)* [1978] LS Gaz R 711.
    Subsequently the case went to the Court of Appeal on the issue of access.
    See (1978) Times, July 19.
19. *Re X (a minor) (wardship: jurisdiction)* [1975] Fam 47, [1975] 1 All ER 697.
20. Cf. *Paton v Trustees of British Pregnancy Advisory Service* [1978] 2 All ER
    987, [1978] 3 WLR 687, where a husband failed to obtain an injunction
    to prevent his wife from having an abortion. Query if the unborn child
    could have been warded. See Chap. 2.
1. See Chap. 5 for further discussion.

been reached (and perhaps even passed)[2] beyond which further expansion should not be contemplated without careful consideration of the consequences.

i) *Cause for concern*

There are a number of reasons for concern. First the number of wardship cases are increasing to a level where the strain on the jurisdiction is unacceptable. The delays are already acting against the interests of the child and it is doubtful, for example, whether the Official Solicitor will be able to cope with any further increase. In 1967 the Latey Committee[3] were concerned with the problems of expansion. This fear is more real now than it was then, and we would like to reiterate their fears. Historically wardship has always been a small jurisdiction, but one which has tried to deal exhaustively with the cases before it. If it becomes too big the enormous respect which has attached to wardship may lessen, and if the courts do not themselves impose limitations there is a danger that eventually there will be legislation to control it. This would be a great pity since its non statutory foundation is one of its most attractive features. Once it became a statute based jurisdiction it would inevitably assume a technical nature which may prevent it serving the interests of the children who really require it.

Secondly, the increased expansion tends to undermine the authority and confidence of the lower courts and statutory agencies[4]. Magistrates do have an important role and a degree of expertise and experience in children's cases, which should be increased with the advent of the domestic courts panel[5] required by the Domestic Proceedings and Magistrates' Courts Act 1978. This should be fostered rather than threatened. A further disadvantage of the expanding use of wardship in this respect is that it results in multiplicity of proceedings which in itself may be contrary to the child's interests.

2. In view of *Re H (a minor) (wardship: jurisdiction)* [1978] Fam 65, [1978] 2 All ER 903.
3. Report of the Committee on the Age of Majority Cmnd. 3342, paras. 194–5.
4. See the fears expressed in the Justice of Peace journal. 'Wardship and Care Proceedings' (1978) 142 JPN 37, 38.
5. Though some petty sessions have had successful domestic panels for a number of years.

Similarly local authorities now have social workers with a developing knowledge and experience and the opportunities of frequent consultation with specialists who have worked in child care for many years. They have to work with children from day to day, and their judgment on matters of opinion ought to be given considerable weight. If their decisions become subject to continual review there must be disadvantages. More often no decision will be taken to plan for a child's future for fear that it is the wrong one. If a decision is taken it will be analysed to such a degree that the child will have been in limbo uncertain of his future for far too long. It may also mean that a quite disproportionate part of a social worker's time is spent in court justifying a decision.

ii) *Application of the welfare principle*

Central to the issue of how widely wardship can be used as a jurisdiction to review, lies the application of the welfare principle, namely, that the child's welfare is of first and paramount concern. There is a tendency to treat this principle as being of universal application yet it is axiomatic that this cannot invariably be the case. Moreover, the statutory enjoinder to do so is expressly limited to cases where the child's legal custody or upbringing or the administration of his property is in issue[6]. The traditional inability or reluctance to define the circumstances in which the child's welfare is the first and paramount consideration is bound to lead the jurisdiction into difficulties. For example, if the child's interests are first and paramount should not the courts be able to review the decision of immigration officers not to allow an alien minor into the country?[7] Again, if the child's interests are always first and paramount will not this lead to impossible conflicts with the criminal and military jurisdictions?

Although the court's reluctance to fetter its jurisdiction by rigid rules is understandable the time seems ripe to reappraise the relationship of wardship with other jurisdictions and in particular to consider the application of the welfare principle.

---

6. S.1 of the Guardianship of Minors Act 1971 as amended by s.36 of the Domestic Proceedings and Magistrates' Courts Act 1978.
7. Cf. *Re Mohamed Arif (an infant)*, *Re Nirbhai Singh (an infant)* [1968] Ch 643, [1968] 2 All ER 145. Discussed in Chaps. 2 and 10.

One approach is to recognise that the welfare of the ward cannot always be the first and paramount consideration and that it should only be so where the child's legal custody and upbringing or the administration of his property is *directly* in issue. In other words it should be recognised that section 1 of the Guardianship of Minors Act 1971 has a limited application. Such a position would not mean that the wardship jurisdiction could not be exercised in circumstances falling outside the scope of section 1. On the contrary, the jurisdiction would retain its protective function[8]. In such cases, however, the welfare of the ward would not be the first and paramount concern and although inevitably it would continue to be important nevertheless it would have to be weighed in the balance with other policy considerations.

The virtue of this approach is that it provides some guidance as to the limits of the jurisdiction without interfering unduly with the judge's discretion. It is politically attractive because it must be accepted that there are some factors which have to outweigh the child's welfare. Finally it is less likely to lead to the use of wardship simply as a form of appeal.

It remains to consider what support there is for such an approach. Perhaps the best support is *Re X* (*a minor*)[9] in which the Court of Appeal refused to restrain the publication of a book because of the harm it might have done to the child. Sir John Pennycuick considered[10] the issue to fall outside the scope of section 1 and all three judges were agreed that the interests of freedom of speech outweighed the particular child's interests. There is also support in the House of Lord's decision of *S v McC*[11] where it was held that the issue of whether to order a blood test to establish evidence of paternity did not directly concern the issue of custody and hence fell outside the scope of section 1. In both these cases had the section been interpreted widely its application would have been justified.

The limited application of section 1, it is submitted, helps to explain the apparently conflicting decision of the House of Lords in *Official Solicitor v K*[12] in which it was held that even

8. Discussed further in Chap. 6.
9. [1975] Fam 47.
10. Ibid., at 62.
11. [1972] AC 24. See particularly Lord MacDermott at 50–51.
12. [1965] AC 201, [1963] 3 All ER 191. See also *Re R(MJ)* (*a minor*) [1975] Fam 89, [1975] 2 All ER 749. Discussed in Chaps. 4, 5 and 7.

in procedural matters the ward's welfare is first and paramount. In that case the issue was whether or not evidence should be *disclosed* to the other party and since that disclosure was directly relevant to the ward's upbringing it was correct to apply section 1. Finally it should be said that the limited application does not in any way conflict with the leading House of Lords decision in *J v C*[13] since that case clearly concerned the custody and upbringing of the ward albeit that the dispute was between parents and 'strangers'. Hence, important though the decision is, it is not necessarily relevant in considering matters which fall outside section 1.

On the basis of the above cases it is submitted that there is support for the limited application of section 1. The question remains as to whether it should apply to the issue of review. As a matter of interpretation it is clearly tenable to say that the question of whether to review a local authority or justices' decision concerns the child's custody and upbringing and that therefore section 1 applies. On the basis of *S v McC*, however, it is possible to argue that the issue of jurisdiction does not in itself *directly* concern the question of custody and upbringing and for the policy reasons already outlined we would favour this restricted interpretation. It may be thought, however, that the approach in the so-called 'kidnapping' cases is against this restricted interpretation, since it is clearly established that the decision of whether to exercise the jurisdiction or make a summary order is governed by what is best for the child[14]. In our submission these cases are distinguishable from those in which a decision has already been made by an English court or body. It is a well known principle of private international law that a foreign judgment may not be relied upon for enforcement in a subsequent jurisdiction elsewhere, unless it is final, binding and not subject to variation in the forum pronouncing it[15]. Custody

13. [1970] AC 668, [1969] 1 All ER 788. This case has been regularly cited in subsequent wardship cases as establishing the true basis on which the court acts.

14. See the leading decision of *Re L (minors) (wardship: jurisdiction)* [1974] 1 All ER 913, [1974] 1 WLR 250 followed inter alia by *Re C (minors) (wardship: jurisdiction)* [1978] Fam 105, [1978] 2 All ER 230. Interestingly, in *Re L* ibid., at 924, Buckley LJ did expressly refer to the question of the application of s.1 commenting: '*without deciding that question*' that in his opinion it would apply.

15. See e.g. *McKee v McKee* [1951] AC 352, [1951] 1 All ER 942. Dicey and Moris: *The Conflict of Laws* (9th Edn., 1973), p. 1037.

orders are never final and can be varied by the forum making it and are not therefore binding on the English courts. Moreover, not all 'kidnapping' cases involve a foreign court order[16] and it seems sensible to apply the same principle to what is essentially the same problem. In the case of reviewing a decision of an English court or statutory agency, on the other hand, since Parliament has expressly vested a discretion in such bodies and moreover provided a system of appeal it seems right that there should be a restricted role for wardship.

Although the cases seem to be moving towards accepting that section 1 applies to the question of deciding whether to review[17], there is still agreement that there should be some limitation on the exercise of the wardship jurisdiction. Even in *Re H* (*a minor*)[18] where earlier cases such as *Re M* (*an infant*)[19] and *Re T* (*AJJ*) (*an infant*)[20] were called into question because of their failure to consider the application of section 1[1], Ormrod LJ commented[2] that though the dominant principle is the welfare of this particular child 'it must be shown that the circumstances are sufficiently unusual to justify the intervention of the High Court'. Such a statement as this certainly does not preclude a restricted application of section 1[3]. Indeed such an approach would seem to accommodate Ormrod LJ's views and uphold the restricted approach laid down by the earlier cases.

It is obvious from Ormrod LJ's comments that even if section 1 is held to apply to deciding whether to review, the occasions on which the court will intervene will still be limited. The approach that seems to be favoured is to say that wardship should only be invoked where its wider substantive or procedural powers are of advantage to the child. This is a viable approach. It has the virtue of being flexible and less

16. See e.g. *Re T* (*infants*) [1968] Ch 704, [1968] 3 All ER 411.
17. See e.g. *Re O* (*a minor*) (*wardship: adopted child*) [1978] Fam 196, [1978] 2 All ER 27 and *Re D* (*a minor*) (*justices' decision: review*) [1977] Fam 158, [1977] 3 All ER 481.
18. [1978] Fam 65, 75-6, [1978] 2 All ER 903 at 909a-d.
19. [1961] Ch 328, [1961] 1 All ER 788.
20. [1970] Ch 688, [1970] 2 All ER 865.
 1. Then s.1 of the Guardianship of Infants Act 1925.
 2. [1978] Fam at 76c, [1978] 2 All ER at 909e.
 3. It is certainly consistent with Balcombe J's approach at first instance, (see [1978] Fam 69-70) since he first looked to see whether there were grounds to intervene and only after holding that there were did he apply the principle that the ward's interests were first and paramount.

technical than the alternative view that we have forwarded. Moreover, if it is accepted that it is not generally in the interests of the child to allow multiplicity of proceedings the balance between the jurisdictions may not be widely upset.

Under this approach wardship should not be used simply as a form of appeal, and presumably the applicant would have to justify the exercise of the wardship jurisdiction as a preliminary point before the full merits are investigated.

Despite its attractions there are dangers in this approach. First it would seem to encourage more applications to be made which even if summarily dismissed will still be unsettling to the child. More importantly it would seem to allow in principle the review of the exercise of a discretion outside cases where impropriety or misuse of powers is alleged. While this may be an advantage to the particular child it would in our opinion jeopardise the welfare of children generally for the reasons we have already stated. It is really on this basis that we favour the restricted application of section 1. In this way the court can make a policy decision on the basis of the interests of children generally rather than being dictated by the interests of the particular child.

III Wardship as a procedure

A. ADVANTAGES

Wardship is surely the best jurisdiction for ascertaining the child's interests, though obviously even as the guardian the court cannot provide the day to day supervision of upbringing that the child needs. It is, however, a most flexible and informal jurisdiction which, unencumbered by statutory constraints, provides a wide variety of powers and remedies for different situations. While it remains small it can offer parental protection and continued control over the affairs of the ward. Those concerned with its administration, the judges, registrars and the Official Solicitor, are accessible and competent. Written evidence can be filed so that the issues between the parties are clear, and the court has the ability to handle detailed and complex material. Furthermore the jurisdiction provides an opportunity for a variety of competing interests to be separately represented in the proceedings.

B. DISADVANTAGES

The jurisdiction is not without its problems. Although it may now be used in the provinces, wardship still carries a considerable London bias because the judges and registrars there are generally more experienced, its procedure is generally drafted with the principal registry in mind and the Official Solicitor is centralised there. In common with other jurisdictions there is a continuing reluctance to place much weight on expert child care evidence. This is unfortunate because, although many judges do have considerable experience in dealing with children's cases, there are also members of other professions who have developed expertise through working with children.

However, there are two outstanding problems, both arising by reason of wardship being exclusively a High Court jurisdiction.

i) *Costs and legal aid*

As cases must be brought in the High Court it is inevitable that the cost is higher than in other proceedings, and this is increased because they often raise more difficult issues meriting more detailed preparation and longer hearings. Since wardship enables wider interests to be represented than in a normal custody hearing, there is further danger of greater expenditure. As a result wardship has gained a reputation for expense which suffers by comparison with other children's proceedings. Like any litigation, if a case develops into a protracted battle it will cost money, but by no means all cases need to end in lengthy hearings, since wardship provides opportunities for negotiations to satisfy all parties.

What is most important is that where a child's interest is involved the decision as to whether proceedings are instituted and if so which, should not be governed by the question of cost, but by what is best for the child. It is not intended to suggest that wardship is always the proper forum for a case, but only that money should not be the ruling factor.

Similarly the decision to grant legal aid should be based on which proceedings are most appropriate. It is the experience of many that it is difficult for an applicant to get legal aid to institute wardship proceedings. It appears to be far less difficult as a defendant. It is impossible to know for certain why this is so, but it seems to be the case that an applicant must have exhausted all possible alternative remedies for the relief he is seeking. It is submitted that if this is what is happening it is the wrong approach, and that the applicant should only have to show that wardship is the most appropriate jurisdiction.

Although legal aid is available, a party outside the income and capital limits may be placed at a disadvantage and virtually held to ransom by an opponent who is legally aided or to whom money is no object, and who is prepared to drag the case out at considerable expense to both the legal aid fund and the other party. Even the threat of proceedings could unfairly inhibit a person conscious of financial considerations from pursuing his case. This is of course a complaint common to all proceedings, but it is clearly most important to ensure that the views of all relevant parties are heard before reaching a decision about the welfare of a child. Perhaps the income and particularly capital limits could be raised exceptionally in children's cases[4].

ii) *Delay*

Although emergencies can be dealt with very quickly, obtaining a final hearing at any rate in London will most likely take at least five months. This clearly creates injustice. It can prejudice the welfare of the child and the interests of the parties and can dictate the decision. Although it is appreciated that High Court matters inevitably take time, there have been directions that children's cases should be treated with urgency, but it is impossible to be confident that this has by any means invariably been followed by the courts or the legal profession. Both must become more conscious what an adverse effect delay may have on the interests of the child.

In 1967 the Latey Committee[5] having predicted an increase in the use of wardship, commented:

'We take this opportunity of stressing the urgency, in

---

4. Differentiating the type of proceedings for the purpose of legal aid and advice is not unprecedented. Under the Legal Advice scheme for example matrimonial cases are distinguished from other proceedings in the amount of advice (without authority) that can be dispensed under the scheme. The principle of varying limits for different types of cases is also embodied in the Legal Aid Bill 1979.

5. (1967) Cmnd. 3342 para. 195.

our view, of procedural reforms which will where possible eliminate opportunities for delay, whether these
arise by accident or by deliberate exploitation of the
rules'.

The expansion has occurred as predicted, but reforms to
prevent delay have not.

At present it is all too easy for one party to manipulate the
proceedings to his advantage by failing to file evidence in
time and there seem to be inadequate sanctions available to
the court to deal with this. This is a different kind of problem
from any other type of court proceedings. Usually the court
can make an order and give judgment in default if it is
ignored. With the welfare of a child such an order would
probably in itself be against the child's interests, being made
without full consideration of all the evidence, and most
likely requiring sudden removal of the child from its home,
since it is the party with possession of the child who is likely
to be delaying. In matrimonial matters too there is usually
less of a problem because the dispute is between father and
mother solely. In wardship there may be a number of parties
to file evidence and when that is done the Official Solicitor or
Court Welfare Officer may have to begin his work. Amid all
that there is plenty of room for manoeuvre by a person who
has the child and wants to maintain possession. The fact that
his welfare is the first and paramount consideration in deciding where he is to live, is of scant recompense to a child who
has endured uncertainty and been the victim of a court battle
delayed for a year or more. These difficulties arise because
parties not infrequently ignore the time limits for filing
evidence, and then the responsibility for fixing a hearing lies
with them.

At present the only control that the registrar has is to order
evidence to be filed within a certain time and certify the
matter fit for the judge[6]. If one party is obstructive the
registrar may order that the child is made a party and represented by the Official Solicitor, who will be able to ensure that
the necessary steps are taken to get the matter heard by filing
his own report. By the time it is thought appropriate to have
the Official Solicitor in to speed the case there will already
have been excessive delay.

6. Failing to file evidence can be a contempt. However the likelihood of
   committal proceedings being successfully brought against a solicitor are not
   high, though the threat of committal can be effective.

It is submitted that there is an argument for even greater intervention by registrars. If they were available in sufficient numbers, they could keep a constant watch on cases and order the parties to appear before them to explain their current position, if the case was not progressing sufficiently quickly. Perhaps a better defined procedure might also help to relieve the problem. It is suggested that the following might provide a basic formula:

1. Outline evidence in support of the application should be filed within 14 days of the issue of the originating summons. There is often no need for detailed and lengthy affidavits.

2. The initial evidence of any other party should be filed within 14 days thereafter, specifying what parts of the plaintiff's case are disputed.

3. The first hearing before the registrar should be automatically fixed for the first available day 28 days after the issue of the originating summons. If evidence has not been filed he could investigate why, and make appropriate directions including, if necessary, the appointment of the Official Solicitor as guardian' ad litem for the child. If some evidence has been filed he could examine its adequacy and consider the parties' applications on the need for further evidence or investigation. He could either give further time for this or direct that it may be filed before the final hearing. Alternatively he could direct that the application was an inappropriate use of the jurisdiction and send it straight to the judge to dismiss it. If necessary he could continue the wardship while other arrangements were made to safeguard the child's interests, such as an application to a lower court.

If an immediate injunction was sought on the issue of the proceedings there is frequently no less need for a speedy final hearing. Some of the evidence will have been filed in support of the application for an injunction and so the judge can make directions for the subsequent early disposal of the case, or refer the matter to the registrar.

Where an applicant will be prejudiced by delay because it enables the other party to retain possession of the child, his legal representatives must try to ensure that they get an early hearing. Defendants will then be forced to file their evidence or justify an adjournment. One reason which sometimes causes delay is that the parties feel obliged to file voluminous evidence. Much of it will not be relevant or will be unnecessarily elaborate on undisputed points. If the evidence on affidavit is restricted to its essential elements in respect of each witness, time will be saved and an early hearing can be obtained. The evidence will be analysed then at some length.

An alternative method of reducing delay might be to dispense with the registrar entirely, and have all matters including interlocutory applications dealt with by the judge[7]. A case could be allocated to a judge immediately the originating summons is issued and an initial hearing take place within a few days.

There is now a judge to hear emergency applications, and if these were taken in rotation the case could be reserved to him. One advantage would be that he could give an early indication of the view he might take of the matter. The additional work he would gain might be offset by the increase in cases which did not reach him for a final hearing.

The disadvantages would, however, appear to outweigh the advantages at present. The registrar is such a well-established figure in wardship that it is difficult to foresee what would happen without him. It could certainly be anticipated that there would be less easy and informal access for rulings on minor points. More importantly it would be difficult for the judge to maintain a parental eye on the progress of the ward. Since this proposal would require a considerable increase in the number of judges in the Family Division, it would not seem to be practical for the time being, if at all.

iii) *Other procedural reforms*

The transfer to the Family Division has lessened procedural problems but they do still exist and it would be helpful to practitioners to reduce them. Many practitioners are not experienced in High Court matters, especially those dealing with children's cases, and there is therefore a reluctance to advise that a child should be warded.

Order 90 of the Rules of the Supreme Court could be redrafted to provide a clearer guide to wardship. This should

7. This is the procedure adopted by the Commercial Court.

include cross-reference to other orders where appropriate to remove the existing doubt about which orders apply to wardship. The confused unwritten rules[8] about the powers of a registrar could without difficulty be divided into those matters always within his power, those never within his power and those where he retains a discretion. The procedural maze would then be rather easier to follow. Further the consequences of wardship could be made more clear. At present the only ones specified in the Notice of Wardship[9] are that the ward must not marry or leave the jurisdiction without the consent of the court. As there are other automatic consequences binding on persons other than the ward these should surely be made clear and specified in both the rules and the notice. All these matters could be included in appropriate forms for wardship proceedings, distinct from other High Court forms, and published as such in the 'White Book'.

IV Reforms to other jurisdictions

A. EXTENSION OF WARDSHIP

If wardship is the best jurisdiction for considering a child's interests, it is arguable that it should be extended to other courts. In particular it has been suggested that it should be available in the county court[10]. This would have the advantages of being local and cheaper. Furthermore in the provinces the judges and registrars who sit in the divorce county courts are the same as those who sit in the district registries. In London the county court judges sometimes sit as deputy High Court judges.

It must be admitted that these are strong arguments, but on balance it is submitted that the jurisdiction should remain vested in the High Court. At present the Official Solicitor does not operate in the county court[11], and it would certainly

---

8. Discussed in Chap. 5.
9. Form FD 590 (see Appendix) the wording of which we understand is under review. The consequences are only obliquely referred to in the Supreme Court Practice.
10. A notable supporter of this view is Judge Jean Graham-Hall who has delivered a number of interesting lectures and papers on the subject.
11. He may be appointed in the divorce county courts in divorce proceedings pursuant to MCR 1977, r.115.

require an expansion of his office to do so. Above all though the jurisdiction of wardship benefits by being small and special to the High Court. If it were widely extended it would lose its aura and special nature.

B. EXTENSION OF OTHER POWERS

Restricting the wardship jurisdiction to the High Court does not prevent the extension of some of its powers to the inferior jurisdictions. There are in particular some matters for which wardship is currently used where High Court expertise is not required.

i) *Preventing removal from the country*

The simple act of making a child a ward of court[12], for which application a person has only to show an interest[13], is sufficient to prohibit him leaving the country. We have previously mentioned that by sections 34, 39 and 70 of the Domestic Proceedings and Magistrates' Courts Act 1978 magistrates' courts and county courts[14] can make an order forbidding removal of the child when they have made a custody order in respect of him. It would seem consistent to empower such courts to make an order in anticipation of custody proceedings, since that would at least require some judicial decision where none is now needed in wardship[15].

ii) *Child protection legislation*

We have examined in Chapter 11 the problems which sometimes result in local authorities and parents resorting to wardship to avoid the restrictions of child protection legislation. We would not favour any general expansion of the grounds on which the juvenile court can make orders. It is submitted that a wide power to interfere with parents' rights

---

12. I.e. by the issue of an originating summons under the Law Reform (Miscellaneous Provisions) Act 1949.
13. Under the *Practice Direction* [1967] 1 All ER 828, [1967] 1 WLR 623.
14. The 1978 Act also empowers the High Court to make such orders when acting under the Guardianship of Minors Act.
15. It would also be consistent with the power of the court in divorce proceedings. See MCR 1977, r.94.

such as exists in wardship should be administered in the High Court, where it can be carefully scrutinised. In the lower courts it is appropriate, where the local authority is initiating action, that specific grounds should be proved before a child can be removed or kept from his parents.

On five specific points amendments may be thought appropriate. In each case the party suffering as a result of the provision might now be obliged to apply for relief in wardship, although it is quite clear that the matter could be adequately dealt with in the juvenile court with little alteration to the present arrangements.

1. There ought to be a right of appeal against a decision in care proceedings under the Children and Young Persons Act 1969, for the child, his parents and the local authority. This would be consistent with the provisions in the Children Act 1948[16]. The appeal should be to the Family Division and not to the Crown Court.

2. Notwithstanding the decision in *Johns v Jones*[17] a local authority should be able to pass a resolution under section 2 of the Children Act 1948 if they have actual custody[18] of the child, provided the initial reception into care was voluntary.[19] Although there are objections to this on the basis that reception into care is voluntary, section 2 restricts that concept. If the local authority feels that the parent is not fit to care for the child on specific grounds they should have the opportunity to prove that. If the parent is serious in his desire to remove the child from care he can object to the resolution and the matter will be heard in court. In most cases the child will in any event have been in care for some considerable time.

3. The grounds for care proceedings under section 1(2)(a) of the Children and Young Persons Act 1969 should be amended to read:

'the proper development of the child *has been* or is being avoidably prevented or neglected, or his health *has been*

16. As provided for under s.4A as substituted by the Children Act 1975, s.58.
17. [1978] 3 All ER 1222, [1978] 3 WLR 792. Discussed in detail in Chap. 11.
18. I.e. where the child is in the de facto care and possession of the authority.
19. Even if this suggested amendment is not accepted there should be some clarification of what is meant by requesting the child's return under s.1(3). Casual requests, or 'lapsed' requests (i.e. those not acted upon) should surely be excluded.

or is being avoidably impaired or neglected or he *has been* or is being ill-treated'[20]. [The amended parts are in italics.]

This would enable proceedings to be taken where the child was initially received into care under the 1948 Act but plans for voluntary care had been unsatisfactory. It would have the advantage of encouraging voluntary care and co-operation between parents and local authorities, while enabling steps to be taken to protect the child if necessary. Abuse of the new grounds by simply raking up past history would be prevented by a proper interpretation of the requirement to prove the overriding factor in care proceedings, that the child is in need of care or control which he will not receive unless an order is made.

4. The grounds for discharge of a care order[1] should be amended to indicate that the welfare of the child is the first and paramount consideration. This would clarify the issue for the juvenile court and represent the proper balance of interest after the child has been in care under an order. It would also be clear that the justices could decide on what was most in the child's interest even if they could not be satisfied that he would not still need care or control[2].

5. Parents ought to be made parties to the care proceedings[3]. Unless they have a full right to be heard, there seems to be every justification for them to apply in wardship, since they could argue that through the failure

---

20. Amending the tense to include past events would not unduly widen the scope of the provision since it would still be restricted to provable facts. S.1(2)(a) could also be amended to include the future tense but this would radically alter the present jurisdiction since it would involve magistrates predicting what might happen in the future i.e. it would allow decisions to be taken upon unknown facts. Such an amendment would, it is submitted, vest too great a power in the lower courts. If a local authority wants to have the care of the child on such speculative grounds the most appropriate venue is surely the High Court acting under its wardship jurisdiction.

1. At present governed by the Children and Young Persons Act 1969, Ss.21(2) and 21(2A). (Inserted by the Children Act 1975 Sch. 3 para. 69.)

2. This would enable the court to discharge an order in circumstances like *Re H (a minor) (wardship: jurisdiction)* [1978] Fam 65, [1978] 2 All ER 903. See Chap. 11. However, it might be thought that this would vest too much power in magistrates.

3. The present form of care proceedings makes the child sole person before the court. See Chap. 11.

of the court to give them a full hearing the interests of the child were not best served[4].

iii) *Custody proceedings*

It would be possible to broaden the scope of the Guardianship of Minors Acts 1971 and 1973 by allowing non-parents to *apply* for custody[5]. However, the need for amendments in favour of non-parents is reduced by the custodianship provisions[6]. Although these provisions will not provide a panacea for non-parents[7] it would at least be wise to await their implementation before arguing for further reform.

A further amendment might be to allow local authorities to intervene in custody proceedings in order to seek care. Whether statutory amendment is necessary, however, appears doubtful since there appears to be nothing in the rules to prevent such intervention at present.

iv) *Procedural changes in the lower courts*

Further thought might also be given to the introduction of written material in the magistrates' court. In custody cases where the court requires a welfare report, it can be submitted in writing as evidence and the reporter called to court to give further evidence if necessary. This could be extended to require parties to provide a written statement of their case, so that they would know what was in issue, in both care and custody proceedings. In some cases such as care proceedings, statements could be admitted under section 9 of the Criminal Justice Act 1967 and admissions accepted in respect of them.

The principles of the Civil Evidence Act 1968 could be extended to the magistrates' court. This would relax the rules of hearsay and bring that court into line in practice with other courts. It would avoid the need to resort to wardship purely

4. Such an argument would be but an extension of the principle laid down by *Re H (a minor)* ibid.
5. At the moment non-parents can intervene in such proceedings. See *Re R (an infant)* [1974] 1 All ER, 1033n. But when the Children Act 1975 Sch. 3 para. 75(1)(d) comes into force the court will have no power to grant custody to third parties. Instead the application will be treated as one for custodianship pursuant to s.37(3) of the Children Act 1975.
6. For details of which see Chap. 10. See also Bevan and Parry: *Children Act 1975* (1978 Butterworths).
7. See Chap. 10.

because important evidence was inadmissible in the lower court[8].

V The family court

The establishment of a family court has been attractive to family lawyers for more than a decade, though there is little sign that there is any prospect of realisation in the near future. This reflects uncertainty about how such a court could best operate, and a fear that reorganisation would require an unacceptably high financial commitment. The Finer Report[9] commented that in spite of the enthusiasm for a family court system, there was in this country, unlike North America, a dearth of material setting out the attributes and advantages of such a system[10].

The argument for a family court seems particularly strong. It would provide a unified jurisdiction with one comprehensive code of legal principles rather than the present fragmentary system which has a variety of personnel administering different rules. The emphasis ought to be on welfare with professional help available to the parties.

The structure is more open to argument. The Finer Report suggested[11] a three tier system similar to the Crown Court with business distributed according to its length or complexity and involving lay magistrates, registrars and judges, in some cases sitting together. The Family Division of the High Court would be on the top tier of the family court and the link with the rest of the higher judicial system.

Further problems for any family court lie in delimiting the boundaries of its jurisdiction and establishing the basis on which its decisions will be reached. This is especially relevant in determining how children are to be treated, and the weight to be accorded to their welfare. At present there are three types

---

8. For the rules of evidence in wardship proceedings see Chap. 4.
9. Report of the Committee on One Parent Families (1974) Cmnd. 5629 paras 4.278–4.424.
10. See now Cretney: *Principles of Family Law* (2nd Edn, 1976) pp. 451–8, Eekelaar: *Family Law and Social Policy* (1978) pp. 146, 198, 276; *Proposals for a Family Court* by Judge Jean Graham-Hall referred to by the Finer Report at para. 4.280; *The Case for Family Courts*, a report of the Conservative Lawyers; *The Case for a Local Family Court*, Justices' Clerks' Society; *Justice: Parental Rights and Duties and Custody Suits* (1975) para. 89.
11. Ibid. at paras. 4.351–4.357.

of child jurisdictions: criminal[12], local authority care and custody. They overlap at various points and can be different facets of the same problem of the dysfunctional family, so that it may be a matter of chance that leads a child into one jurisdiction rather than another. Yet the criteria for reaching decisions in different jurisdictions are inconsistent. While there may be some justification for different treatment in the criminal field based on the need for protection of the public, it is difficult to justify this in the civil context. It is undesirable to continue to view care and custody as distinct and separate concepts. Statutory authorities and welfare agencies have become involved in the formerly private disputes over children, and simultaneously they have involved private individuals in their care of children through fostering, custodianship and adoption.

The current difficulties in reconciling the two jurisdictions are caused by the separate evolution of child protection and private custody disputes, and a failure to appreciate that both are equally the products of disturbed family life.

On questions of legal custody and upbringing it has long been established that in disputes between parents the welfare of the child is the first and paramount consideration[13], and since *J v C*[14] it has been clear that this also applied to cases between parents and third parties. At the same time, however, the child protection statutes have required that a specific set of circumstances must be proved before any order can be made, and it is implicit in this that the court cannot necessarily act in the best interests of the child. Furthermore, once the child is in the care of the local authority their duty is to give first consideration to promoting and safeguarding the long term welfare of the child.

Ironically it would thus appear that a child in the care of a local authority is less likely to have his best interests safeguarded than a child who is simply the subject of a dispute

12. It is beyond the scope of this book to consider problems arising from the criminal jurisdiction but there is ample debate elsewhere on the philosophy of the Children and Young Persons Act 1969, see e.g. M. Berlins and G. Wassell: *Caught in the Act* (Pelican 1974) e.g. Allison Morris and M. McIsaac: *Juvenile Justice* (Heinemann 1978). See also *Children and Young Persons Act 1969* Cmnd. 6444.

13. It was first put in statutory form in s.1 of the Guardianship of Infants Act 1925, and is now reenacted by s.1 of the Guardianship of Minors Act 1971 as amended by the Domestic Proceedings and Magistrates' Courts Act 1978.

14. [1970] AC 668, [1969] 1 All ER 788.

between parents, or between parents and a third party who is not the local authority. In such circumstances local authorities who are concerned generally about the welfare of children will not be restricted by technical requirements, but will inevitably be considering whether the interests of the child will be better served by an application in wardship. It is submitted that these difficulties provide evidence that what is required is a child welfare law of universal application, which would be possible as part of the jurisdiction of a family court.

The relationship of this court to the welfare agencies such as the Official Solicitor, the court welfare service and local authority officers acting as guardians ad litem would have to be rationalised. If the Family Court deals with all matters relating to children, it would appear sensible for all the services to be amalgamated and available for the use of the court and parties who are or may be involved in proceedings. The independence of the welfare agencies would have to be secured, and they should provide both the legal expertise of the Official Solicitor and the social work expertise of the court welfare service and local authorities.

VI Wardship and the family court

All too often the existence of wardship is overlooked when reforms are considered but it is important that it should not be forgotten when consideration is given to the establishment of a Family Court. For example, consideration could profitably be given to the extent to which the procedure in wardship could be adopted in the new court. Secondly, consideration ought to be given to the question of whether wardship should continue as a separate jurisdiction. It is our view that it should continue, being administered by the top tier, if Finer's suggestions as to structure are adopted. The need for its wide powers should, however, be met in part by the extended powers of the Family Court, so that the jurisdiction could revert to being the select jurisdiction of former years. We envisage that the jurisdiction would remain useful where children require the continuous protection of the court. This could occur, for example, where there was an abuse of power by the person vested with custody or where there are special unforeseen circumstances. The jurisdiction ought also to be of use where there is an international element involved. In other words the parental jurisdiction would remain useful where what is required is more than a resolution of a dispute as to custody, access, adoption, or local authority care.

Special mention should be made of the future role of wardship in relation to local authority care. It might be envisaged that there should be greater co-operation between local authorities and the Family Court in the sense that the court should be more concerned than at present with the authority's long term plans for the child. One such scheme is to maintain court involvement with decisions concerning the retention of a child in care, but in addition authorities would be required to bring the matter before the court where there was a change in nature of the original powers given. This would occur, for example, if adoption was sought or even if access was denied in such a way that it changed the relationship between the natural parent and his child. As the nature of the care would also inevitably change if a child remained in one place without being legally secure for some time, the authority might also be required to inform the court of their future plans for the child. Failure to make proper plans would be a ground for making the child a ward of court. Similarly, as at present, failure by the authority to carry out their duties or abusing their powers would be grounds for warding the child. Under this scheme, however, there would be no need for a general supervisory power. For the scheme to be workable both the courts and the authorities would have to operate on the same principle and that in general, it is submitted, should be that the child's welfare is the first and paramount consideration.

The suggested scheme would offer many benefits. It would meet the criticism frequently levelled against local authorities that they erode the relationship between parent and child without the parent having an opportunity to prevent this. Social services departments would be able to fulfil their primary function of caring for the child within the powers given to them and they and other individuals would be able to formulate plans and seek the court's approval knowing thereafter that their scheme would be carried through. At the same time the continued existence of wardship would pro-

vide a valuable check against abuse of powers without being a
threat to the authorities' legitimate plans.

Should, as we have submitted, wardship be retained in any
future Family Court, we would like to see it remain essentially non statutory. In this way the jurisdiction will remain
flexible and so enable it to remain as an invaluable 'safety
valve' within the welfare system.

VII What price the child?

It is submitted that a system of family courts with a close
relationship to wardship could provide a suitable solution to
what should be an increasing demand for a rationalised
approach to family law. It has been our concern to examine
wardship in the light of its development and where it stands
within today's complex framework. Its standing has been
such that it must have a lot more to offer in the future.
Ultimately it may change more as a result of political decisions than because of concern for children. Much depends on
the priority accorded to the interests of children, both within
family law itself and as a political issue. Given the resources
we could have the option of a more extensive wardship
jurisdiction, properly staffed and well supported, or a small
wardship jurisdiction with a well-developed system of
family courts, either of them well-run and equally fair to all
children. On balance we favour the retention of wardship as a
small exclusive jurisdiction designed to deal with exceptional problems. However, our views are necessarily tentative. Far more study will have to be done to see which of these
or any other systems will provide the best long-term solution.

Appendix

List of forms

Originating Summons.

Notice of Wardship.

File No. Slip.

Certificate as to other pleadings.

Notice of appointment to hear originating summons.

Memorandum of appearance.

Notice: Ward not to leave Jurisdiction (Home Office letter).

Certificate of permission to remove Ward.

Leave to remove ward from England and Wales.

Notice of Appointment to Hear Representations Before Child is Committed to Care of Local Authority.

Minor no longer Ward.

Originating Summons

IN THE HIGH COURT OF JUSTICE
FAMILY DIVISION, PRINCIPAL REGISTRY

IN THE MATTER OF . . . a minor and in the matter of the Law Reform (Miscellaneous Provisions) Act 1949 and in the matter of the Guardianship of Minors Acts 1971 and 1973. (*where appropriate*)

Between . . . Plaintiff

and . . . Defendant

To
of
in the   of

Let the defendant within 14 days after service of this summons on
him inclusive of the day of service cause an appearance to be entered
to this summons which is issued on behalf of the plaintiff

of

By this summons the plaintiff claims against the defendant

The date of birth of the minor is
The present whereabouts of the minor are

IMPORTANT NOTICE: It is a contempt of Court, which may be
punished by imprisonment, to take any child named in this summons out of England and Wales, even to Scotland, Northern
Ireland, the Republic of Ireland, the Channel Islands or the Isle of
Man, without the leave of the Court.

If the defendant does not enter an appearance such judgment may
be given or order made against or in relation to him as the Court
may think just and expedient.

Dated the . . . day of . . .19 . . .

NOTE. This summons may not be served later than 12 calendar
months beginning with the above date unless renewed by order of
the Court.

This summons was taken out by

of

[solicitor for the said] Plaintiff

TO THE DEFENDANT(S) (Other than the minor)

TAKE NOTICE that, pursuant to Order 90, rule 3(5) and (6) of the
Rules of the Supreme Court—
(1) you must, forthwith after being served with this summons lodge
in the above-mentioned Registry a notice stating your address and

the whereabouts of the minor (or if it be the case that·you are unaware of the minor's whereabouts), and, unless the Court otherwise directs, you must serve a copy of such notice on the plaintiff; and

(2) If you subsequently change your address or become aware of any change in the minor's whereabouts you must, unless the Court otherwise directs, lodge in the above-mentioned Registry notice of your new address or of the new whereabouts of the minor, as the case may be, and serve a copy of such notice on the plaintiff.

Any notice required to be lodged in the above-mentioned Registry should be sent or delivered to the Principal Clerk (CD) Principal Registry of the Family Division, Somerset House, Strand, London WC2R 1LP.

DIRECTIONS FOR ENTERING APPEARANCE
The defendant may enter an appearance in person or by a solicitor either (1) by handing in the appropriate forms, duly completed, at the Principal Registry of the Family Division, Somerset House, Strand, London WC2R 1LP or (2) by sending them to that office by post. The appropriate forms may be obtained from the Principal Clerk (CD) of the Principal Registry.

Notice of Wardship

TO THE APPLICANT AND HIS/HER SOLICITOR. A copy of the appended notice should be served on the defendant (or, where the defendant is a minor, on the person on whom the originating summons is served) with the originating summons, the original being produced at the time of service. A copy may also be served on any other person who should be made aware that the minor is a ward of court.

Whenever the age and situation of the minor are such that he or she may be in need of advice and assistance a copy of this notice should also be served on him or her, whether or not he or she is the defendant.

No. . . . of 19 . . .

PRINCIPAL REGISTRY OF THE FAMILY DIVISION
Somerset House Strand London WC2R 1LP

TAKE NOTICE that

became a Ward of Court on ... 19   pursuant to the provisions of Section 9 (2) of the Law Reform (Miscellaneous Provisions) Act 1949.

A Ward of Court may not marry or go outside England and Wales without the leave of the Court but is under no further restraint until the Court's directions are given.

Where necessary, a guardian (probably the Official Solicitor) will be appointed to present the Ward's views to the Court and give any necessary assistance. If the Ward is in doubt about what to do, he or she may approach the Official Solicitor, 48/49 Chancery Lane, London, WC2A 1JR (Telephone number 01-405 7641 Extension 3088), who will give advice pending the formal appointment of a guardian.

Registrar

FD 590

File Number Slip

PRINCIPAL REGISTRY OF THE FAMILY DIVISION
Somerset House, Strand, London WC2R 1LP

FILE NO. ... OF 19 ...

In the matter of
and in the matter of the Law Reform (Miscellaneous Provisions) Act 1949
and in the matter of the Guardianship of Minors Acts 1971 and 1973. (*where appropriate*)

Between ... Plaintiff

and ... Defendant

This ... originating summons
was lodged on the ... day of ... 19 ... and has been given the number shown above which must be endorsed on all documents filed in the Registry.

Dated the ... day of ... 19 ...

Registrar

Address all communications for the Court to the Principal Registry of the Family Division (CD) Somerset House, Strand, London WC2R 1LP quoting the file number shown on this form. The Registry is open from 10 a.m. till 4.30 p.m. on Mondays to Fridays.

D.265

Certificate as to other pleadings

No. . . . of 19 . . .

IN THE HIGH COURT OF JUSTICE
FAMILY DIVISION, PRINCIPAL REGISTRY

In the matter of . . . a minor and in the matter of the Law Reform (Miscellaneous Provisions) Act 1949 and in the matter of the Guardianship of Minors Acts 1971 and 1973. (*where appropriate*)

Between . . . Plaintiff

and . . . Defendant

I/We hereby certify that

(a) there are/are not* in existence matrimonial proceedings in which the minor is a child of the family, namely*[1]

and

(b) there are/are not* other proceedings in which the minor is involved, namely*[1]

Signed

Solicitor for the Plaintiff

* Delete as appropriate.
[1] Give details of proceedings.

FD 592

Memorandum of appearance to originating summons (wardship)

IN THE HIGH COURT OF JUSTICE
FAMILY DIVISION, THE PRINCIPAL REGISTRY

IN THE MATTER OF . . . .

Between . . . Plaintiff
and . . . Defendant

Please enter an appearance for
in this matter

DATED the . . . day of . . . 19 . . . .

(Signed)

whose address for service is

(1) Copy heading and title from summons.
(2) Give full name of defendant wishing to appear.
(3) To be signed by the defendant or solicitor entering appearance.
(4) A defendant appearing in person must give his residence and if he does not reside in England or Wales some other place in England or Wales to which communications for him should be sent. Where the defendant appears by solicitor, the solicitor's place of business in England or Wales should be given and if he is the agent of another solicitor, the name or firm and place of business of the solicitor for whom he is acting.

NOTE.—Additional notes for the guidance of defendants seeking to enter an appearance are given hereafter.

ADDITIONAL NOTES
1. The defendant must give his or her full name and a female defendant must add her description, such as spinster, married woman, widow or divorced.

2. Where the defendant is a minor or other person under disability, the appearance must be entered by a solicitor.

3. A defendant who wishes to appear in person may obtain help in completing this form from the Principal Registry of the Family Division (Contentious Dept.) Somerset House, Strand, London WC2R 1LP.

4. Where the defendant is unable to give the number of the action or any other information required to identify it, the summons served on the defendant should be produced for the court's inspection when the appearance is entered.

5. Where the appearance is entered by leave of the court a copy of the order granting leave must accompany this form.

6. These notes deal only with the more usual cases. In cases of any difficulty it is advisable to attend at the court office for the purpose of entering an appearance.

Notice: Ward not to leave jurisdiction

PRINCIPAL REGISTRY OF THE FAMILY DIVISION
SOMERSET HOUSE, STRAND, LONDON WC2R 1LP

To: The Under Secretary of State
     Home Office

Dear Sir,
TAKE NOTICE that the undermentioned minor is a Ward of Court and

[TAKE NOTICE that by reason of an Order of Mr. Justice . . . made on the . . . day of . . . 19   the undermentioned minor] . . . should not be allowed to leave the jurisdiction of the High Court of Justice without a specific Order to that effect which Order should be produced to the appropriate immigration officer.

There is no reason to believe that at the date hereof any such Order has been made.

The minor referred to is

                    Yours faithfully

                                        Registrar

Certificate of permission to remove ward

PRINCIPAL REGISTRY OF THE FAMILY DIVISION
SOMERSET HOUSE, STRAND, LONDON WC2R 1LP

IN THE MATTER OF . . . a minor.

Referring to the order in this matter dated . . . whereby . . . , . . . the . . . herein was given leave to remove the minor . . . out of England and Wales subject to the conditions set out in such order.

I certify that these conditions having been complied with the said minor may leave England and Wales for a period of . . . from

DATE

                                        Registrar

This certificate should be carried during the journey for production to the immigration authorities.

Leave to remove ward from England and Wales

IN THE HIGH COURT OF JUSTICE
FAMILY DIVISION, PRINCIPAL REGISTRY

IN THE MATTER OF . . . a minor and in the matter of the Law Reform (Miscellaneous Provisions) Act, 1949 and in the matter of the Guardianship of Minors Acts 1971 and 1973. (*where appropriate*)

Between . . . Plaintiff and . . . Defendant.

Upon hearing . . . for the . . . and upon reading

And the above named minor having become a Ward of Court on the . . . day of . . . 19 and being still a Ward of Court, whereby the said minor is not permitted to leave England and Wales without leave of the Court;

IT IS ORDERED that the . . . do have leave to remove the said minor out of England and Wales from time to time [for periods each not exceeding . . .], on condition that on each occasion the said . . . shall lodge in the Principal Registry of the Family Division at least seven days before the proposed departure:

(a) a written consent in unqualified terms by the . . . to the minor's leaving England and Wales for the proposed period;

(b) a statement in writing giving the date on which it is proposed that the minor shall leave England and Wales, the period of absence and the whereabouts of the minor during such absence; and

(c) a written undertaking by the . . . to return the minor to England and Wales at the end of the proposed period of absence.

Rule 93(1) Form 18

Notice of appointment to hear representations before child is committed to care of local authority

[*Heading as before*]

TO

TAKE NOTICE that if you wish to make representation before an order is made committing . . . to the care of the . . . council, you should attend before . . . at . . . on the . . . day of . . . 19 , and that if you do not attend at the time and place mentioned, such order will be made and proceedings taken as the judge thinks fit.

NOTE: Where a local authority to whose care a child is committed wish to ask for a financial provision order in favour of the child, they must, within seven days after receiving this notice, file an affidavit as to the property and income of the party against whom the order is sought and must at the same time send him a copy of the affidavit. Within four days after receiving the local authority's affidavit the party against whom the order is sought may file an affidavit in reply and, if he does so, he must send a copy of his affidavit to the local authority.

Dated this . . . day of . . . 19   .

Registrar

Minor no longer ward

PRINCIPAL REGISTRY OF THE FAMILY DIVISION
SOMERSET HOUSE, STRAND, LONDON WC2R 1LP,
TELEPHONE 01-405 7641

The Assistant Under-Secretary of State
Children's Department
Home Office
Whitehall
LONDON SW1.

Dear Sir,
  I have to inform you that the undermentioned minor ceased to be a Ward of Court on . . . 19   and may leave the jurisdiction of the High Court without a specific Order to that effect.

NAME:

Yours faithfully

Registrar

Index